Reading Certainty

Studies in Medieval and Reformation Traditions

VOLUME 237

The titles published in this series are listed at *brill.com/smrt*

Reading Certainty

Exegesis and Epistemology on the Threshold of Modernity

Essays Honoring the Scholarship of
Susan E. Schreiner

Edited by

Ralph Keen
Elizabeth Palmer
Daniel Owings

TUTA SUB AEGIDE PALLAS · 1683 ·

BRILL

LEIDEN | BOSTON

Cover illustration: Agostino Ramelli, “Plate 188: Book Wheel.” In *Le Diverse Et Artificiose Machine Del Capitano Agostino Ramelli*. Paris, France, 1588. Public Domain; image courtesy Science History Institute.

LC record available at https://lccn.loc.gov/2022046710

Typeface for the Latin, Greek, and Cyrillic scripts: “Brill”. See and download: brill.com/brill-typeface.

ISSN 1573-4188
ISBN 978-90-04-18651-4 (hardback)
ISBN 978-90-04-52784-3 (e-book)

This book is printed on acid-free paper and produced in a sustainable manner.

Printed by Printforce, United Kingdom

Contents

Preface VII
Notes on Contributors X

PART 1
Forerunners

1 An Exercise in "Thinking Nature": Eriugena's *Periphyseon* against the Background of the History of Exegesis and Patristic Reception 3
Willemien Otten

2 "Blessed Jerome": The Protestants and the Vulgate in the Sixteenth Century 19
Bruce Gordon

3 Waiting for the Miracle: Uncertainty, Superstition, and Trust in Jean Gerson 39
Matthew Vanderpoel

PART 2
The Reformation

4 Early Modern Protestants and the "Hard Knots" of the Epistle to the Hebrews: A Study of Reformation Certainty 57
Ronald K. Rittgers

5 Melanchthon and the Utility of the Liberal Arts 78
Ralph Keen

6 Distinguishing Divine and Human Speech: Idolatry and the Words of Institution in the Eucharistic Debates 112
Daniel Owings

7 The Reformation of Doubt: Incredulity, Faith, the Body, and the Search for Certitude in Early Lutheran Interpretations of John 20:24–31 136
Barbara Pitkin

8 A Clearness Uneasily Observed: Leprosy, Perception, and Certitude in Calvin's *A Harmony of the Gospels Matthew, Mark, and Luke* 175
Mark M. Lambert

9 Not without Scripture: William Perkins, the Light of Nature, and Proofs of the Existence of God 203
Richard A. Muller

10 The Suffering and Death of Christ as Epistemological Framework in Reformation-Era Lutheran Teaching: Martin Luther, Veit Dietrich, and Cyriacus Spangenberg 223
Vincent Evener

PART 3
Into Modernity

11 Visions and Prophets in Seventeenth-Century Lutheran Germany: The Case of Jacob Fabricius 247
Jonathan Strom

12 "Much More for Use in This Present Age": Augustine Baker and Life-Writing at Cambrai Abbey, 1624–1633 265
Karen E. Park

13 Evidence of Things Unseen: John Wesley's Hermeneutics of Conscience 278
William Schweiker

14 The Bible and Evangelical Christianity in Fascist Italy: The Vatican and Polemical and Physical Violence 297
Kevin Madigan

Afterword: Pages on Life's Way 314
Elizabeth Palmer

Index 319

Preface

In an evolution that in some ways resembles the progress of the Reformation itself, conceptions of early-modern religious reform have undergone a transformation from an old order to a new: the former usually depicted as fixed, and the latter as fluid. Any survey of introductory treatments of the Reformation over the course of the last half century will reveal that a Protestant-dominant narrative has gradually given way to one of various definitions and judgments about core notions and pivotal moments. What had once been seen as the recovery of the clear gospel after centuries of medieval obfuscation has been replaced by a historical arc in which religious differences of the sixteenth century serve as background for wars of religion extending into the seventeenth. A central element in this transformation has been a deconfessionalizing of sorts regarding the Reformation itself, whereby the early Luther, once the solitary and heroic figure from whom all else radiated, stands alongside religious thinkers and leaders (and not a few rulers) who collectively represent the age of reformations, plural.

It was Heiko Oberman who, more than any other, articulated the tension between continuity and change as theologians of the late fifteenth century contended with the thought of their predecessors. Largely under his influence, the Renaissance-Reformation paradigm was replaced by a Medieval-Reformation one, with harvest rather than breakthrough the organizing metaphor. A generation of historians emerged to change the way the Reformation was understood, and many would in turn train another generation of interpreters. This volume honors the work of one who placed her own efforts at the conjunction of tradition and originality in articulating the tension in early-modern thought between certainty and doubt.

From her early work in the history of exegesis to the magnum opus on the search for certainty in early modernity, Susan Schreiner has worked closely to appreciate the complexity and difficulty of the search for sure understanding during the Reformation era. With clarity and honesty Schreiner has drawn the attention of her readers and students to the causes of uncertainty and reasons for doubt: the inscrutability of God's ways during the Plague, the elusiveness of clarity and sufficiency in scripture, and the persistence of doubt regarding the matter weighing most heavily on her subjects' minds, personal salvation. Woven throughout this body of close work is a sense of irony that in matters in which certainty is most needed it seems always out of reach. Sure knowledge of divine benevolence, and assurance of salvation, remained out of reach for many during a time of religious discord and political turmoil.

The need for certainty, for comfort in adversity and stability amidst change, was so central among the authors to whom Susan Schreiner devoted her efforts that her research has been invested with singular seriousness. Schreiner's disposition in wrestling with authors who were themselves wrestling with scriptural texts has been one of deep respect for the authors. In her work, Schreiner recognizes and presents the desire for an unshakable faith as the common impetus for thinkers both Catholic and Protestant, in their full variety under those rubrics. Hers is a research project that is not shaped by confessional interests but by the paradox that the knowledge most earnestly sought was (and remains) beyond the reach of limited human reason.

In conceptualizing faith as the quest for unshakable assurance rather than as the confident possession of it, Susan Schreiner has woven the course of Reformation thought into the history of skepticism and explored the ways in which the corpus of scriptural revelation, through the mediation of human (and humanist) interpreters, yielded a fragile confidence for some and rigorous insistence for others during an era in which nearly every central doctrine was subject to strident controversy.

A body of scholarship that has contributed to the history of exegesis, the evolution of Protestant theology, the concept of faith in some of the more influential thinkers of the early-modern era, and epistemology cannot fail to have placed a wide range of scholars in debt to Susan Schreiner. The contributions that follow indicate the extent of that debt and the range of her work. For the history of exegesis we have careful studies of interpreters from Eriugena and Gerson to Spangenberg, Fabricius and Gerhard, and Perkins and Wesley; on the authority of the Bible, there are contributions on the institution of the Eucharist and the function of scriptural warrants in early 20th-century Italian politics; and with comparative approaches to exegesis, there are essays on the interpretive history of the Epistle to the Hebrews and the Sermon on the Mount. The concept, better called the problem, of certainty runs throughout these studies, as does its twin sensation, doubt; consolation and the miraculous are likewise represented.

The range of topics and authors, the tension between ambiguity and knowledge when engaging the canonical texts, and the persistent awareness of the finitude of reason offer a conceptual framework (an architectonic, to use one of Schreiner's favorite words) for the essays here. It is a testimony to her example that each study displays the clarity and rigor for which she is known in both her teaching and writing. It is worth pointing out that these papers were written during a period of discomfort and anxiety, as the modern-day plague of COVID-19 seized the population and changed work habits and closed libraries. In our own way, the authors here have displayed unusual perseverance in carrying out their work under strenuous conditions in order to honor Susan Schreiner.

Notes on Contributors

Willemien Otten
is the Dorothy Grant Maclear Professor of Theology and the History of Christianity at the University of Chicago Divinity School. Her research focuses on the medieval and early Christian intellectual tradition. Otten's latest study, *Thinking Nature and the Nature of Thinking: From Eriugena to Emerson* (Stanford, 2020), approaches ideas of nature and human selfhood across a wide array of thinkers, from Augustine to William James and from Maximus the Confessor to Schleiermacher. She is faculty co-director of the Martin Marty Center for the Public Understanding of Religion and one of the editors of the *Journal of Religion*.

Bruce Gordon
is Titus Street Professor of Ecclesiastical History at Yale Divinity School. In 2021 he published *The Oxford Handbook of Calvin and Calvinism* (Oxford) and *Huldrych Zwingli: God's Armed Prophet* (Yale). His *John Calvin's Institutes of the Christian Religion* (Princeton, 2016) looks at the reception from the sixteenth century to the age of YouTube of one of the defining works of the Reformation. He is the author of *Calvin* (Yale, 2009), a biography of the Genevan reformer, and the *Swiss Reformation* (Manchester, 2002). He is currently writing The *Bible: A Global History* for Basic Books.

Matthew Vanderpoel
is a Teaching Fellow in the Divinity School and the College at the University of Chicago, and a scholar of premodern Christianity. Drawing on methods from cultural and intellectual history, literary studies, and contemporary theory, their work considers medieval theology, poetics, and scholastic thought. Vanderpoel's current research connects fourteenth-century debates over the gendered dynamics of intellectual and religious authority to the period's renewed concern with the material processes underlying sensation, cognition, and epistemology.

Ronald K. Rittgers
is Professor of the History of Christianity at Duke Divinity School, where he holds the Chair in Lutheran Studies. His research centers on the religious, intellectual, social, and cultural history of medieval and early modern Europe. He is author of *The Reformation of Suffering: Pastoral Theology and Lay Piety*

in Late Medieval and Early Modern Germany (Oxford, 2012) and *A Widower's Lament: The Pious Meditations of Johann Christoph Oelhafen* (Fortress, 2021). His next project examines consolation and self-understanding in the Age of Reform. He has served as president of the American Society of Church History.

Ralph Keen
holds the Arthur J. Schmitt Foundation Chair in Catholic Studies at the University of Illinois, Chicago, where he is professor of history and dean of the Honors College. He studies the Protestant Reformation and Early Modern Catholicism, with particular attention to the ways those movements appropriated the classical and patristic traditions. He is an editor of Brill's monograph series *Catholic Christendom 1300–1700*, as well as author of *Divine and Human Authority in Reformation Thought* (Brill, 1997) and *Exile and Restoration in Jewish Thought* (Continuum, 2011). He has served as president of the American Society of Church History.

Daniel Owings
is a graduate of the University of Chicago. His research focuses on the understanding and deployment of the term "idolatry" in Protestant theology, and the ways in which competing understandings of what was at stake in that label correlate to subsequent divisions among Protestant groups. His dissertation is entitled "Idols, Ideals, and Ideology: the Critique of False Religion in the Sixteenth Century." He formerly served as managing editor of *Sightings*.

Barbara Pitkin
is Senior Lecturer in Religious Studies at Stanford University. Her current research focuses on early modern views and uses of the past. She is the author of *Calvin, the Bible, and History: Exegesis and Historical Reflection in the Era of Reform* (Oxford, 2020) and *What Pure Eyes Could See: Calvin's Doctrine of Faith in its Exegetical Context* (Oxford, 1999). She is an editor of the Sixteenth Century Journal, a member of the Praesidium for the International Congress for Calvin Research, and has served as an officer of the Calvin Studies Society.

Mark Lambert
is a Teaching Fellow in the Divinity School and the College at the University of Chicago. His scholarship explores the interdisciplinary entanglement of the history of medicine, historical theology, and medical ethics. Spanning from medieval Europe to the twentieth-century United States, his research on leprosy exhibits a global, transhistorical focus with critical relevance for our

current global context. His current research focuses on the religious milieu of the leprosy settlements on Molokai, Hawaii, with particular attention to the practical theologies of Father Damien de Veuster and Mother Marianne Cope.

Richard A. Muller
is P. J. Zondervan Professor of Historical Theology Emeritus and Senior Fellow of the Junius Institute for Digital Reformation Research at Calvin Theological Seminary. His research has reassessed the development of Protestant thought after the Reformation, with emphasis on the nature of Protestant orthodoxy and Reformed scholasticism in the seventeenth century. He is most recently the author of *Grace and Freedom: William Perkins and the Early Modern Reformed Understanding of Free Choice and Divine Grace.* (Oxford, 2020) and *Divine Will and Human Choice: Freedom, Contingency, and Necessity in Early Modern Reformed Thought.* (Baker Academic, 2017).

Vincent Evener
is Associate Professor of Reformation and Luther Studies at United Lutheran Seminary. His current research examines how traditions of devotion to the passion and associated meditative techniques were transformed and deployed in the sixteenth century by religious leaders seeking to shape Christian selves capable of navigating a divided Christendom, with particular regard to the depiction of human hearts as vulnerable to divine and demonic influences. He is the author of *"Enemies of the Cross": Suffering, Truth, and Mysticism in the Early Reformation* (Oxford, 2021), and serves as director of the seminary's annual Luther Colloquy.

Jonathan Strom
is Professor of Church History and Director of International Initiatives at the Candler School of Theology at Emory University. His research interests include Pietism in continental Europe, the history of the Protestant clergy, and the emergence of modern forms of piety and religious practice. He has written widely on the clergy, lay religion, and reform movements in post-Reformation Germany, and is the author/editor of five books, most recently *German Pietism and the Problem of Conversion* (Penn State, 2018). He is currently writing on the history of the common priesthood.

Karen Park
is Associate Professor of Theology and Religious Studies at St. Norbert College. Her research interests include Marian devotion, shrines, and apparitions as

part of the American religious experience, and the metaphorical use of language in theological and devotional contexts. She also frequently contributes analysis of contemporary American religious life and the religious underpinnings of American political discourse to publications such as *Sojourners*, *Religion Dispatches*, and *Commonweal Magazine*. She is currently working on a book project about American shrines to the Virgin Mary and their historical and social importance.

William Schweiker
is the Edward L. Ryerson Distinguished Service Professor of Theological Ethics at the University of Chicago. His scholarship engages theological and ethical questions attentive to global dynamics, comparative religious ethics, the history of ethics, and hermeneutical philosophy. He is the author of *Religious Ethics: Meaning and Method* (Wiley-Blackwell, 2020, with David Clairmont), and Editor-in-Chief contributor to the three-volume *Encyclopedia of Religious Ethics* (Wiley-Blackwell, 2022). Schweiker is presently writing a book titled *Enhancing Life and the Forms of Freedom*. He is director of the Enhancing Life Project and is an ordained minister in the United Methodist Church.

Kevin Madigan
is the Winn Professor of Ecclesiastical History at Harvard Divinity School, and his research focuses on medieval Christianity. His books include *Olivi and the Interpretation of Matthew in the High Middle Ages* (University of Notre Dame Press, 2003), *The Passions of Christ in High-Medieval Thought: An Essay on Christological Development* (Oxford University Press, 2007), and *Medieval Christianity: A New History* (Yale University Press, 2015). He also has published several articles on the Roman Catholic Church during the Nazi period, and has a book forthcoming on evangelical Christianity and the Vatican in the fascist period.

Elizabeth Palmer
is senior editor at *The Christian Century*. She is the author of *Faith in a Hidden God: Luther, Kierkegaard, and the Binding of Isaac* (Fortress, 2017). She also writes the *Century*'s weekly e-newsletter "Books Worth Reading," and frequently contributes articles on religion in America today and literature. She has served on numerous boards and councils, most recently as governing board member of the "Let's Talk" editorial council. She is an ordained minister in the Evangelical Lutheran Church in America.

PART 1

Forerunners

CHAPTER 1

An Exercise in "Thinking Nature": Eriugena's *Periphyseon* against the Background of the History of Exegesis and Patristic Reception

Willemien Otten

1 Preamble

This article is written in honor of my esteemed colleague Susan Schreiner, whose love for intellectual history I share and to whom I owe many insights that have come to guide my work.[1] A theme we periodically discussed is the history of medieval exegesis, which has in recent decades become sanctioned as an important key to Reformation study. Trained in that tradition, and aware that it can move us beyond a confessional and doctrine-centered approach, Susan Schreiner and I nevertheless concurred in having reservations about the omnivalidity of this exegetical approach. One question we asked is whether it is possible or even preferable to disentangle the history of medieval exegesis from intellectual history more broadly. This question is especially relevant for me as a medievalist since medieval thought betrays a strong biblical character, given that medieval culture interlaced the remains of Roman civilization with Christian themes and motifs.

The following essay explores these questions by means of a concrete medieval case study. My larger methodological question is whether medieval exegesis is always best seen as exegesis, and hence contextualized in terms of biblical reception, or whether we ought to see medieval exegesis as an integral part of a medieval author's thought. There are two related issues at stake here. The first is whether the study of historical exegesis is an equally valuable tool under all circumstances. My sense is that if one approaches medieval exegesis in the context of an interest in historical or thematic biblical reception, it may well be, but if we approach medieval exegetical readings instead as a way to access a thinker's broader intellectual position, the frame of historical exegesis may not be as useful. The second and related issue focuses on whether exegesis is to be considered epiphenomenal or essential to the development of an author's

1 This article draws on the paper I gave for the Medieval Academy on March 27, 2020, entitled "Eriugena's *Periphyseon* as an Exercise in 'Thinking Nature.'"

 | DOI:10.1163/9789004527843_002

intellectual thought. In the first, epiphenomenal, case, one can forge a helpful connection between different authors by focusing on their scriptural readings; in the second, essential, case the exegetical position an author takes is so interwoven with his or her overall thought that any comparisons with other thinkers on the same biblical passage will by default be episodic and partial, and thus have limited validity.

Below I present my medieval case study. In it I invoke the categories of biblical exegesis and, equally relevant for Reformation studies, of patristic reception, which together allow me to make my way into the thought of a particular medieval thinker. Making some comparisons along the way, I use—but in the end will also abandon—the categories of biblical and patristic reception to evoke a richer view of the thought of my author and the text in question, i.e., the *Periphyseon* (or *On Natures*) of the Carolingian Irishman John the Scot Eriugena (810–877 CE).

2 Eriugena as the Last Patristic Cosmologist

Jean Mabillon (1632–1707), the early modern editor of the works of Bernard of Clairvaux (1090–1153), famously called him "the last of the Fathers."[2] For Mabillon, Bernard's virtuoso Latin style raises him to the status of a Church Father with an authority of near-biblical proportions, since Bernard's teaching (*doctrina*) is not marked by philosophical reasons as much as by faithful proximity to scripture and tradition.[3] Not based on style but on the content of his thought regarding nature, creation, and cosmology, I have recently called Eriugena "the last patristic cosmologist."[4] As can be gleaned from the

---

2 See Jean Mabillon, *Praefatio generalis*, § 11, *De Bernardi sanctitate, doctrina et auctoritate in Ecclesia*, PL 182, 25–6: "Antequam ulterius procedamus, juvat expendere duos qui Bernardo tribui solent, titulus, nempe quod sit inter doctores mellifluus, atque ultimus inter Patres, sed primis certe non impar."

3 See Mabillon, *Praefatio generalis*, 25–6: "Patres vocat (sc. Ecclesia) eos, quos sanctitas, doctrina, et antiquitas commendat; doctrina, inquam, Scripturae et traditioni potius, quam rationibus philosophicis inhaerens ... Patres vero nonnisi quos recepta jamdudum auctoritas venerabiles fecit, et modus tractandi res, a philosophia alienus." Translation slightly adapted from Burcht Pranger, "Sic et Non: Patristic Authority Between Refusal and Acceptance: Anselm of Canterbury, Peter Abelard, and Bernard of Clairvaux," in Irena Backus (ed.), *Theological Innovation and the Shaping of Tradition: The Reception of the Church Fathers in the West from the Carolingians to the Maurists* (Leiden: Brill, 1997), 1:169.

4 See my recent article under this title: "Eriugena as the Last Patristic Cosmologist," in Markus Vinzent and I. L. E. Ramelli (eds.), *Studia Patristica CXXII, vol. 19: Eriugena's Christian Neoplatonism and Its Sources in Patristic and Ancient Philosophy* (Leuven-Paris-Bristol:

critical apparatus of the *Periphyseon*'s critical edition,[5] Eriugena harks back occasionally to Origen of Alexandria (fl. ca. 250 CE), and makes extensive use of the thought of Gregory of Nyssa (fl. ca. 380 CE), Dionysius the Areopagite (fl. 530 CE), and, especially, Maximus the Confessor (fl. ca. 600 CE). As has been made clear by Eriugena's modern editor Edouard Jeauneau,[6] furthermore, Eriugena's *Periphyseon* is close to Origen's *Peri Archon* ("On First Principles") both in title and monumental vision.[7]

Eriugena's translation of Gregory of Nyssa's early treatise "On the Making of Man", which he quotes liberally in *Periphyseon* IV as *Sermo de Imagine*, reflects the depth of his patristic interest, as do his translations of Dionysius the Areopagite, especially the *Mystical Theology* and the *Commentary on the Ecclesiastical Hierarchy*, which were to have considerable medieval resonance. Yet Dionysius's relative popularity in the medieval Latin West, thanks to Eriugena's introduction of him, should not make us overlook the importance of Maximus the Confessor for Eriugena, who tells us that Maximus made him truly understand Dionysius.[8] If we oversee the wider patristic cosmological presence in his work—from Origen, through Gregory of Nyssa, to Dionysius and Maximus the Confessor, with frequent references to Ambrose and Augustine as well—, Eriugena appears to display a greater affinity with Eastern than with Western Church Fathers. He finds Greek thinkers more astute, since they engage in allegorical exegesis, and hence often wax more speculatively.[9] By

Peeters, 2021), 127–43. The current essay draws on this article as well as on my recent book *Thinking Nature and the Nature of Thinking: From Eriugena to Emerson* (Stanford: Stanford University Press, 2020).

5 I cite the *Periphyseon*'s five books according to the critical edition by E. Jeauneau in the series Corpus Christanorum Continuatio Mediaeualis [CCCM], vols. 161–65 (Turnhout: Brepols, 1996–2003). The translation I have used is Eriugena, *Periphyseon*, trans. I. P. Sheldon-Williams, rev. J. J. O'Meara (Montreal/Washington: Dumbarton Oaks/Bellarmin, 1987).

6 E. Jeauneau, "From Origen's *Periarchon* to Eriugena's *Periphyseon*," in Michael I. Allen and W. Otten (eds.), *Eriugena and Creation*. Proceedings of the Eleventh International Conference on Eriugenian Studies, held in honor of Edouard Jeauneau, Chicago, 9–12 November 2011 (Turnhout: Brepols, 2014), 139–182.

7 The established Latin title of the *Periphyseon, De diuisione naturae* ("On the Division of Nature"), should be abolished, since it only refers to a part of Book I. The work's full title is *Periphyseon*, "On Natures," which makes for an insightful and intended echo of Origen's *Peri Archon*, "On First Principles."

8 See E. Jeauneau, "Pseudo-Dionysius, Gregory of Nyssa, and Maximus the Confessor in the Works of John Scottus Eriugena," in Uta-Renate Blumenthal (ed.), *Carolingian Essays. Andrew W. Mellon Lectures in Early Christian Studies* (Washington D.C., 1983), 137–49, repr. in E. Jeauneau, *Études Érigéniennes* (Paris: Études Augustiniennes, 1987), 175–187.

9 On Eriugena's choices in assessing Eastern and Western authors, see W. Otten, "Eriugena and the Concept of Eastern versus Western Patristic Influence," *Studia Patristica* XXXVIII (Louvain: Peeters, 1993), 217–224 and, especially, G. d'Onofrio, "The *Concordia* of Augustine

contrast, the cosmologies of Augustine and, before him, Ambrose,[10] are generally more narrowly situated within the biblical-hermeneutical context of their Genesis commentaries. Following the precise order of the *Hexaemeron*, the six days of creation, their texts allow for fewer speculative excursions or cross-connections. Yet it is precisely in his adherence to the *Hexaemeron* format that Eriugena displays a remarkable affinity with the Western Fathers Ambrose and Augustine, even as he also borrows extensively from Basil of Caesarea's *Homilies on the Hexaemeron*.

In light of the above, the question has been asked whether we ought to see Eriugena primarily as a Greek or a Latin thinker.[11] Ever since Frederick Copleston described his philosophical system as "a lofty rock in the midst of a plain",[12] Eriugena has been seen as standing apart from his historical environment. With factors of historical context and intellectual milieu not fully explaining the emergence of his work, interest understandably shifted to tracing its patristic roots, in part to reveal something about his intellectual disposition. Though pertinent, such questions have also been a distraction, as it has taken scholars a long time to see the *Periphyseon*, the cornerstone of Eriugena's oeuvre, for the independent and original work that it is.

Wishing to avoid such distractions, my characterization of Eriugena as the last patristic cosmologist stems at heart from my firm desire to capture his originality, which may seem elusive given the *Periphyseon*'s long and meandering text. And while Eriugena stands indeed apart from his contemporaries in

---

and Dionysius: Toward a Hermeneutic of the Disagreement of Patristic Sources in John the Scot's *Periphyseon*," in Bernard McGinn and W. Otten (eds.), *Eriugena: East and West* (Notre Dame: Notre Dame University Press, 1994), 115–40.

10 The Latin Ambrose is more or less considered a Greek thinker by Eriugena, since he practices allegorical rather than literal exegesis. As such, he is the mirror image of the Greek Basil of Caesarea, Gregory of Nyssa's brother, whom Eriugena considers in his *Homilies on the Hexaemeron* to practice literal exegesis. Still, Augustine is close to Ambrose in adhering to the ordered exegesis of Genesis rather than indulging in freer, more speculative reasoning, as the Greeks tend to do. This brings us back to Mabillon's point that Bernard's teaching is close to scripture and tradition. That Eriugena's is likewise has recently been picked up by Pope Benedict XVI, who gave an address on June 10, 2009 in which he rehabilitated him. The text can be found here: http://w2.vatican.va/content/benedict-xvi/en/audiences/2009/documents/hf_ben-xvi_aud_20090610.html.

11 An interesting approach to Eriugena's handling of patristic sources, with a keen eye for his originality, can be found in John J. O'Meara, "'*Magnorum virorum quendam consensum velimus machinari*' (804D): Eriugena's Use of Augustine's *De Genesi ad litteram* in the *Periphyseon*," in W. Beierwaltes (ed.), *Eriugena: Studien zu seinen Quellen* (Heidelberg, Carl Winter Verlag, 1980), 105–16.

12 F. C. Copleston, S.J., *A History of Philosophy* (Garden City, NY, Image Books, 1962), vol. 2 pt. 1, p. 129.

intellectual command, I still consider it important to see him for the Carolingian thinker that he is.[13] His Carolingian profile is evident from his patchwork style, found also in works by Alcuin of Tours and Theodulf of Orleans, as well as from his predilection for controversy and his preference for dialogue and dialectical argument.[14] Together these Carolingian characteristics shape his thought, even if they do not fully explain the scope and depth of the *Periphyseon*'s project.

3 Eriugena and Augustine as Hexaemeron Commentators

If one were to ask with whom of the Fathers Eriugena stands in closest proximity, which has become the focus of much analysis, my answer would be Augustine. Although this conclusion may seem counterintuitive, since Augustine is a Latin thinker and no champion of allegorical exegesis, it fits with my goal of wanting to capture the *Peryphyseon*'s broader originality. For, this work is in my view best understood as an early-medieval capstone to Augustine's thought on nature and creation. My view has much to do with the hybrid structure of the *Periphyseon*, whose five books are roughly divided into a logical or philosophical/theological first half (through the middle of Book III) and an exegetical second half (until the end of Book V), whose order roughly unfolds according to the Neoplatonic scheme of procession and return that likewise structured the thought of Origen and Thomas Aquinas. As I see it, the connection with Augustine is precisely useful in helping us to understand Eriugena's attraction to the exegetical genre, which defines the *Periphyseon*'s second half but is often underappreciated in scholarship on the work.

The *Periphyseon* is best known for its two divisions of *natura*—its central concept—that dominate the work's first half. A first division of *natura* into being and non-being is followed by a second division into the four forms of nature, ranging from (1) God as creator (*natura creans et non creata*) through (2) the primordial causes (*natura creata et creans*) and (3) spatio-temporal reality (*natura creata et non creans*) back to (4) God as the end goal of creation's return (*natura non creans et non creata*). This more famous fourfold division sets up the work's general structure as adhering to the Neoplatonic

13 See on this W. Otten, "Eriugena's *Periphyseon*: a Carolingian Contribution to the Theological Tradition," in Bernard McGinn and W. Otten (eds.), *Eriugena: East and West* (Notre Dame: University of Notre Dame Press, 1994), 69–93 and W. Otten, "Suspended between Cosmology and Anthropology: *Natura*'s Bond in Eriugena's *Periphyseon*," in *Brill's Companion to Eriugena*, ed. Adrian Guiu (Leiden: Brill, 2020), 189–212.

14 See W. Otten, "Chapter 5: Carolingian Theology," in G. R. Evans (ed.), *The Medieval Theologians* (Oxford: Blackwell, 2001), 65–82.

pattern of procession and return: all things stem from God and are in search of a final state of rest in God. Materially, the book's first half gives us Eriugena's discussion and subsequent rejection of the Aristotelian categories as applicable to God. It thereafter shows him engaged in a lengthy dialectical analysis of affirmative and negative theology, after which he launches his central discussion of creation seen as theophany or divine manifestation. The book's first half culminates in an extensive analysis of God as *nihil* (nothingness) in *Periphyseon* III. At that point Eriugena embarks on the work's second, exegetical part, which is quite different in tone and texture. In it he gives us first a literal exegesis of creation, leaning heavily on Basil of Caesarea's *Homilies on the Hexaemeron* before switching to an allegorical reading of creation and the fall in Books IV and V. Atypically, the *Periphyseon*'s exegetical part does not seem to be animated by an ascetic program, so familiar to us from medieval allegorical thinkers like Gregory the Great or Bernard of Clairvaux.[15] Instead, Eriugena's discussion keeps unfolding according to the Neoplatonic arc of procession and return that he set in motion with the fourfold division of nature.

The unusual circumstance that the *Periphyseon*'s arc of procession and return continues throughout the exegetical second half of the work puts added weight on how we read that part. It is noteworthy that it is at the beginning of Book IV, right in the middle of the exegetical second half of the *Periphyseon*, that Eriugena switches from procession to commence the return. Contrary to the suggestion of the *Periphyseon*'s first editor, I. P. Sheldon-Williams, I do not think the conclusion is justified that we are dealing here with a mere biblical coda to what was initially conceived as a separate dialectical manual.[16] Instead, what we have is a well-composed, even if at times meandering, work of a hybrid dialectical-exegetical nature.

But even if we factor in that procession and return are strands woven through the *Periphyseon*'s meandering text, whose function is to hold the work together and offer the reader a bird's eye view, we should not forget that Eriugena remains consistently focused on *natura*. It is the awareness of this strong focus that allows me to put the spotlight on what I see as a missing link—if we may call it so—in the oeuvre of Augustine. For, if we survey the corpus of Augustine's works, it is easy enough to spot that, whereas he has authored books about selfhood (*Confessions*) and the godhead (*On the*

15 For Gregory the Great, we may think of his *Moralia in Job* as an exegetical monastic text, while for Bernard of Clairvaux, the text that comes to mind is his *Sermons on the Song of Songs*.

16 See on this I.-P. Sheldon-Williams (ed.), *Iohannis Scotti Eriugenae* Periphyseon (*De Diuisione Naturae*) *Liber Primus* (Dublin: Institute of Advanced Studies, 1978), 5–6.

Trinity), he has not authored one about cosmos or creation. Augustine clearly departs from the Eastern, Origenian tradition on this point, which is heavily marked by cosmological speculation. While Augustine stands in the same Christian-Platonic tradition as the Greeks, he engages the topic of cosmos or creation only through the medium of biblical exegesis. Where Origen may have erred on the side of too much speculation, Augustine restricts himself to cosmology through exegesis alone.[17]

What I want to submit here then is that the *Periphyseon*'s second half resembles the scope of Augustine's *De Genesi ad litteram* in its perspective on nature. Augustine's exegetical thought on creation culminates in this work, which is regularly cited by Eriugena. Building off of this insight, I see my label for Eriugena as the last patristic cosmologist boiling ultimately down to the suggestion that we should see the entire *Periphyseon* as the natural theology that Augustine never wrote. By making this suggestion, I do not want to gloss over the fact that Eriugena's *Periphyseon* is at heart a composite work that, in conformity with the Carolingian patchwork-style, has a dialectical first half and an exegetical second half. But seeing the work as composite does not prevent us from seeing it at the same time as a composed whole, one whose overarching arc of procession and return qualifies it best as a theology of nature, a natural theology. As such the *Periphyseon* is a fitting and worthy early-medieval capstone to Augustine's oeuvre, which seems to have been left unfinished precisely on this point.

The next question is how to characterize this natural theology as indeed reflective of Eriugena's, not Augustine's views. For, is Eriugena's preference for dialogue not ultimately also reducible to Augustine, who considered it the mode of discourse that allows one to make the most progress?[18] As I gauge the major differences between them, it is clear that one difference concerns Eriugena's sense of organization as reflected in the *Periphyseon*'s set-up. It is clearly his choice not to stay within the genre of biblical exegesis but to move outside of it, as if he wants to give nature free rein. We see *natura* flex her muscles when we notice that Eriugena does not always move from procession to return in schematic fashion, but can be seen zigzagging between these intellectual goalposts, using a dialectical discourse that has all the traits of a

17 I have made the argument that Augustine writes about nature and creation only through biblical commentary in more detail in W. Otten, *Thinking Nature and the Nature of Thinking: From Eriugena to Emerson* (Stanford: Stanford University Press, 2020), 79–108 ("Creation and the Hexaemeron in Augustine"). My analysis of Augustine here draws on this chapter.

18 On Eriugena's use of dialogue in the *Periphyseon*, see *Periphyseon* I, ed. Jeauneau, CCCM 161, XV–XIX.

Carolingian school dialogue.[19] And yet, he remains steadfastly focused on following *natura*'s trajectory from beginning to end.

4 Eriugena's *Periphyseon* as an Exercise in "Thinking Nature": Three Crucial Passages

In trying to make Eriugena's composite yet composed work understandable to a broader audience of non-specialists—and note that even among medievalists the *Periphyseon* is more often avoided than read—I have recently characterized it as an attempt to "think nature." After explaining why this became my chosen rubric, I will try to offer deeper insight into the *Periphyseon* by highlighting three points, which I have organized around three foundational passages from the *Periphyseon*. Through my discussion of these passages I hope to make clear that, while the history of exegesis and patristic reception can be a useful lens, only a more direct engagement of both the central concept of Eriugena's text, i.e., *natura*, and the particular arguments he puts forth can help us reach a fuller understanding of the *Periphyseon*.

Evaluating the *Periphyseon* as a project of "thinking nature" has the advantage of allowing me to zoom in on Eriugena's natural thought as a dynamically creative construct that finds itself uneasily situated between the two extremes that define the theological discussion of nature in the West to this day, namely pantheism and *creatio-ex-nihilo*. The *Periphyseon*'s ill fit with either category is intimately related to its condemnation by Pope Honorius III in 1225 on the suspicion of pantheism, insofar as that incisive event has retroactively tainted Eriugena's historical profile as that of a heterodox and perhaps gnostic thinker. By seeing him engaged in "thinking nature" I invite readers to reconsider this historical judgment,[20] while simultaneously encouraging them to reconceptualize traditional nature in a more capacious fashion.

What identifying Eriugena as the last patristic cosmologist has allowed me to do is, in a first step, to show that Eriugena's fit with the *Hexaemeron* tradition ought to be taken more seriously than has been done in the past. It has further led me to situate the *Periphyseon* as the cosmology or natural theology that

19 In *Soliloquies* II.7.14 Augustine states, in the context of explaining why his work is a soliloquy and not a monologue, that there is no better way to find the truth than through the question-and-answer method (*cum enim neque melius quaeri veritas possit quam interrogando et respondendo* ...). See Saint Augustine, *Soliloquies and Immortality of the Soul*, with an introduction, transl. and commentary by G. Watson (Warminster: Aris and Phillips, 1990), 88–89.

20 See Otten, *Thinking Nature and the Nature of Thinking*, 1–10, 13–19.

Augustine never wrote. What seeing Eriugena engaged in "thinking nature" allows me to do in a second step is to create more distance between the intimate encounter with nature in thought that marks Eriugena's *Periphyseon* and what we may call "thinking about nature," that is, the process of rational reflection whereby nature is objectified and instrumentalized. Eriugena, for whom *natura* is not only the overarching category that captures all of reality but also the collection of individual creatures that populate it, is keen on the former and not the latter. As I see it then, "thinking nature" is his dialectical way of expressing respect for nature's otherness, that is its character of being authored by the divine and bearing its imprint, even as he attempts to embrace it intimately.

Passage 1:
The first foundational passage takes us to the *Periphyseon*'s opening sentence. Here we see Eriugena not define, but rather evoke or conjure up *natura*, which he divides into being and non-being. Since Eriugena makes clear that nature comprises both being and non-being, whereby non-being is said to be that which transcends human understanding, the inevitable conclusion is that God who defies our understanding is to be categorized as non-being, even if non-being is still an essential part of *natura*. God is therefore to be included in nature.

> *Master*: Often as I ponder and investigate, to the best of my ability, with ever greater care the fact that the first and foremost division of all things that can either be perceived by the mind or transcend its grasp is into things that are and things that are not, a general name for all these things suggests itself, which is *physis* in Greek or *natura* in Latin. Or do you have another opinion?
> *Student*: No. I definitely agree. For when entering upon the path of reasoning, I also find that this is so.
> *Master*: Nature, then, is the general name, as we said, for all things, for those that are and those that are not.
> *Student*: It is. For nothing at all can occur in our thoughts that could fall outside this name.[21]

21 See *Periphyseon* I, 441A, CCCM 161, 3 (transl. Sheldon-Williams, 25): "*Nutritor*: Saepe mihi cogitanti diligentiusque quantum uires suppetunt inquirenti rerum omnium quae uel animo percipi possunt uel intentionem eius superant primam summamque diuisionem esse in ea quae sunt et in ea quae non sunt horum omnium generale uocabulum occurrit quod graece ΦYCIC, latine uero natura uocitatur. An tibi aliter uidetur?

Eriugena's nature is clearly very different from Augustine's creation, which does not include the divine. Rather than venturing into unorthodox terrain, however, Eriugena appears to negotiate two very delicate positions here that he wants to present as reinforcing each other rather than canceling each other out. On the one hand, he considers God as immanent and interior to nature. On the other hand, he respects that God, even as an essential part of nature, cannot be understood and is transcendent. It is as if God is coopted to vouch for *natura*'s all-encompassing character, while lending it at the same time an aura of the unfamiliar and the transcendent.

Passage 2:
The second foundational passage is found at the beginning of book IV and gives us a good foretaste of the final two books of the *Periphyseon*. Having just embarked on the return, Eriugena will devote himself to an allegorical reading of the *Hexaemeron*. Displaying Eriugena's typical brashness, the passage shows his predilection for a stormy sea over calm waters. This image indicates the difficulty of the return, as reason must steer its ship into a safe harbor. The main point I want to highlight, however, is that the biblical Adam serves here as a proxy for Eriugena's medieval reason, that is, the exemplary self that is "thinking nature" as it journeys from process to return.

> S[*tudent*]: Let us spread sail, then, and set out to sea. For reason, not inexperienced in these waters, fearing neither the threats of the waves nor divagations nor the Syrtes nor rocks, shall speed our course: indeed she finds it sweeter to exercise her skill in the hidden straits of the ocean of Divinity than idly to bask in smooth and open waters, where she cannot display her power. For in the sweat of her brow is she to get her bread—so she is commanded—and to till the field of Holy Scripture, prolific as it is of thorns and thistles (that is, a thin crop of interpretations of what is divine), and to follow with the unflagging steps of investigation the study of wisdom, closed to those who spurn it, "until she find the place for the Lord, the tabernacle of the God of Jacob," that is to say until, the grace of God leading and helping and aiding and moving her by frequent and assiduous study of the Holy Scriptures, she may return and reach again

---

Alumnus: Immo consentio. Nam et ego, dum ratiocinandi uiam ingredior, haec ita fieri reperio.
N. Est igitur natura generale nomen, ut diximus, omnium quae sunt et quae non sunt.
A. Est quidem. Nihil enim cogitationibus nostris potest occurrere quod tali uocabulo ualeat carere."

> that which in the Fall of the First Man she had lost, the contemplation of Truth; and reaching it she may love it, and loving it she may abide in it, and abiding in it, she may here find rest.[22]

One of the most difficult points to grapple with in the *Periphyseon* is how far removed we are from the introspection of Augustinian selfhood. While the externalization of the Eriugenian self or reason as biblical Adam may have an alienating effect on the reader, two important aspects should not be overlooked. The first is that the identification of selfhood with Adam has deep roots in Augustine, for whom Adam became truly the founding father of the human race to the point that Augustine's own crises, such as his mindless theft of pears or his crisis of conversion in the garden with the divine command "Pick up and read," seem to have a paradisaical, Adamic quality to them.[23] The second is that Eriugena appears considerably less burdened by original sin than Augustine, perhaps because he lacks Augustinian introspection. At various moments in *Periphyseon* IV Eriugena interprets the occurrence of Adam's sin in such a way that it does not really derail the return (*reditus*), in which he is engaged. Given the unimpeded progress of the *Periphyseon*'s narrative plot, Eriugena's different take on Adam's fall does not point to a diminished selfhood but presents us rather with a different sense of it. For, whereas in Augustine the fall marks the ultimate defeat of humanity, pushing Adam's offspring to a life of shortcomings, for Eriugena the imperfection of life outside paradise appears to be a given that presents him with a unique challenge and even opportunity. Far from paradisiacal leisure, life on the other side of the fall

---

22 See *Periphyseon* IV, 744A–B, CCCM 164, 5 (transl. Sheldon-Williams, 383): "*Alumnus*: Tendenda uela nauigandumque. Accelerat namque ratio perita ponti, nullas ueretur minas, nullos anfractus syrtesue cautesue formidat, cui delectabilius est in abditis diuini oceani fretibus uirtutem suam exercere, quam in planis apertisque otiose quiescere, ubi vim suam non ualet aperire. In sudore enim uultus sui panem suum iussa est uesci, terramque sanctae scripturae, spinas et tribulos (hoc est diuinorum intellectuum exilem densitatem) sibi germinantem studiumque sapientiae spernentibus inuiam assiduis theoriae gressibus lustrare, 'donec inueniat locum domini, tabernaculum dei Iacob,' hoc est, donec ad ueritatis contemplationem, quam lapsu primi hominis perdiderat, frequenti litterarum diuinarum laboriosoque studio, ducente et adiuuante et cooperante et ad hoc mouente diuina gratia, redeundo perueniat, perueniendo deligat, deligendo permaneat, permanendo quiescat."

23 See on this W. Otten, "The Long Shadow of Human Sin: Augustine on Adam, Eve, and the Fall," in: B. E. J. H. Becking and S. A. Hennecke (eds.), *Out of Paradise: Eve and Adam and their Interpreters* (Sheffield: Sheffield Phoenix Press, 2010), 29–49.

acts as an inspiration for reason to do the best it can, as it deftly navigates the ship that is the *Periphyseon* safely ashore.[24]

This crucial difference with Augustine on the understanding of sin and selfhood may shed retroactive light on the *Peripyseon*'s opening passage as well, where we saw nature divided into being and non-being (God), and God as that part of nature that defies human understanding. When Eriugena evokes *natura* as the sum total of reality, we should think of the reality to which he refers as that of life on the other side of the fall. This makes the *Periphyseon*'s journey from procession to return less an idealist exercise than an exhilarating journey that is at once deeply existential and profoundly intellectual.[25]

Passage 3:
My final passage, a pivotal one, is from the beginning of *Periphyseon* V:

> *Master*: Here we are to understand that the Divine Mercy and infinite Goodness, so ready to forgive and pity us, to sigh over the fall of the Divine image, and in His clemency to condescend unto us and to bear in patience the arrogance of man, is saying: ... I behold man driven forth from paradise; formerly blessed, now become wretched; once rich, now needy; once an eternal being, now a temporal; once enjoying everlasting life, now mortal; once wise, now foolish; once a spiritual creature, now an animal; once heavenly, now earthly; once enjoying eternal youth, now growing old; once happy, now sad; once saved, now lost; once the prudent son, now the prodigal; straying from the flock of the heavenly powers I behold him, and I grieve for him. For it was not to this end that he was made: he whom you his neighbors and friends (Job 19:21) now behold driven forth from Paradise into the region of death and misery was formed for the possession of eternal life and blessedness, to consort with the heavenly orders who had adhered to their Creator and remained in everlasting bliss—though a number of them were lost in man's transgression.[26]

---

24 On Augustinian and Eriugenian selfhood, see W. Otten, *Thinking Nature and the Nature of Thinking*, 34–40.

25 Since ontology is linked to intelligibility in Eriugena, there has been considerable scholarship on whether to see him as an idealist. See especially Stephen Gersh and Dermot Moran (eds.), *Eriugena, Berkeley, and the Idealist Tradition* (Notre Dame: Notre Dame University Press, 2006). See further n. 27 below.

26 *Periphyseon* V, 862B–C, CCCM 165, 5 (transl. Sheldon-Williams, 525): "*Nutritor*: Ac si plane diceret diuina clementia infinitaque bonitas, ad indulgendum miserandumque semper facillima, casum diuinae imaginis suspirans misericorditerque condescens hominisque

I have called this passage pivotal because I see it as essential to having the right understanding of Eriugena's project of "thinking nature." While it does not represent any new narratival turn or strenuous rational effort, we can glean valuable new insight from it into nature's deeper character.

From the *Periphyseon*'s very beginning, *natura* can overwhelm its readers with its majestic contours. Intimidated by them, readers like myself have placed much stock in the Neoplatonic categories of procession and return as helpfully guiding Eriugena's path. In consequence, it is easy to overlook what I see as the force of nature's intrinsic character or personality. For, while the structuring principles of procession and return offer us indeed a reliable roadmap through what may otherwise seem uncharted and impassable territory, they are in the end no more than guardrails. In the final analysis, it is *natura* itself that is in control of them, not the other way around.

Precisely this problem, that is, getting a direct handle on *natura* so as to be able to learn from it, is at issue in the above passage. It is relevant to know that just before it, Eriugena has intervened in the story of paradise to salvage the possibility of humanity's return, which Adam's fall threatened to forfeit. Return, it should be made clear, remains his central topic here. He focuses on return by reading Adam's fall not in protological but in eschatological terms, seeing paradise no longer as past history but as an ideal still to be realized at some point in the future. The passage I cited above picks up right after this moment. That is, the possibility of salvation may have been salvaged, but Adam and Eve's reality is that they find themselves locked out of paradise. Rather than presenting us with a dramatic twist, the cited passage offers us respite, a moment to take a deep breath after Eriugena piloted us through a few stormy waves. Absent any narrative thrust, what Eriugena offers us in this passage cannot be neatly squeezed into the schematic unfolding of procession to return. Precisely because Eriugena takes a step back, however, the passage can offer us valuable insight into the deeper role of *natura*. It is as if its true character comes out when Eriugena describes how, despite Adam's fall, empathy and compassion have not entirely disappeared. In fact, quite the opposite is true.

---

arrogantiam patienter sufferens: ... Iam de paradiso expulsum hominem uideo factumque de beato miserum, de copioso egenum, de aeterno temporalem, de uitali mortalem, de sapiente stultum, de spirituali animalem, de caelesti terrenum, de nouo inueteratum, de laeto tristem, de saluo perditum, de prudenti filio prodigum, ex uirtutum caelestium grege errantem, eique condoleo. Non enim ad hoc factus est. Siquidem ad possessionem aeternae uitae ac beatitudinis conditus est ille, quem uos, o uicini eius et amici, in regionem mortis atque miseriae uidetis nunc de paradiso expulsum, caelestes uidelicet ordines alloquens, qui adhaerentes conditori suo in beatitudine perpetua permanserunt, quorum tamen numerus in perditione hominis ademptus est."

For, with compassion and empathy moved inside the bounds of *natura*, they are made an integral and inseparable part of it.

As he does more often in the *Periphyseon*'s exegetical second half, Eriugena starts off his reflective passage by using the device of an exegetical voice-over, adopting the persona of the divine to state authoritatively the consequences of Adam's fall. That Adam has fallen from grace into misery is invariably stressed. But the litany of tragic oppositional pairs with which Eriugena details humanity's fate is interrupted by an unexpected sign of hope condensed in the phrase *ei condoleo* ("I grieve for him"). Spoken by God, it functions as a spark of divine solidarity lodged inside nature, that reality on the other side of the fall, and lights it up. This spark of empathy galvanizes the conversation, elevating it from a school dialogue between a Master and his Student to an existential dialogue conducted directly between God and humanity. Just as Adam walks with God inside paradise, so God and humanity are the central protagonists outside paradise, that is, in the postlapsarian universe. While the partnership of God and humanity is ontologically unequal, on a dialectical level reciprocity of participation, expressed when God says about Adam, "I grieve for him," is essential if *natura* is to continue its course and fully come into its own.

The inextinguishable spark of solidarity that is set ablaze when God laments, "I grieve for him," does not so much actively further the goal of return as it, on a deeper level, colors in *natura*'s inherent values. For instead of a blank cosmos in need of external salvation through the infusion of Augustinian grace, Eriugena portrays *natura* here as having salvation fully ensconced within its bounds. Since God is after all interior to it, the need to go outside itself falls away. At no point, therefore, does Eriugena invite us to climb a pathway out of nature and into mystical union,[27] not even at the work's very end, where humans will see theophanies but not Godself. There is simply no need for such a mystical union, for the *Periphyseon*'s readers, direct but distant offspring of Adam and Eve, are part of the same compromised reality as their ancestors. As we find ourselves in the same broken world, Eriugena's goal is not to sublimate the disappointments of earthly life by overlaying them with an ascetic lifestyle but to exhort us to live through them as best we can in the knowledge that the divine compassion inherent in *natura* will one day lead us into the blessedness of eternal life that is, and always has been, Adam's true home. From the sense of intellectual ownership and consolatory reinvigoration that this knowledge instills in us, it would appear the return flows naturally.

---

27 My project of seeing Eriugena involved in "thinking nature" obviates the need to categorize him as either a mystic or an idealist. See Otten, *Thinking Nature and the Nature of Thinking*, 40–44.

5 Conclusion

Weaving my way back from the above medieval case study, let me make some concluding comments about Eriugena and about the use of biblical exegesis as a model for relevant theological medieval or Reformation study.

In the case of Eriugena, what I have found most striking is that exegesis is not epiphenomenal to the *Periphyseon*'s central argument, since the work's argument continues regardless of the genre of text that is used: dialectical argument, trinitarian speculation, literal exegesis, or allegorical exegesis. Especially the combination of allegorical exegesis and narrative thrust may be specific to Eriugena and is certainly remarkable. Two further points may be worth mentioning. The first is that for Eriugena, as for other Carolingian authors, there seems to be a thin dividing line between the authority of scripture and the authority of the Fathers, which means that Eriugena's exegesis weaves scriptural interpretation together with patristic interpretation in often novel and creative ways. The second point is that we need to take exegesis more seriously not just as a genre but more broadly as an arena where topics may be thought through in unconventional ways. Eriugena's decision to see the story of paradise as one of eschatology rather than protology, for example, has its root in Gen. 3:22 but presents us with a rather daring reading of it with far-reaching theological implications that need to be assessed. Yet when such positions are seen as merely exegetical, their resonance remains confined to the immediate scriptural context. Also, if it is indeed true that exegesis should be taken more seriously as an arena for intellectual exchange, then Henri de Lubac's comment that exegesis and theological science do not diverge until the thirteenth century is not only misguided about the importance of exegesis but reveals his underlying conception of theology to be a scholastic one.[28] Could it be that the implicit privileging of scholastic theology is the real problem in giving exegetical readings short shrift?

If we now turn to biblical exegesis and biblical reception as a non-confessional way to access Reformation texts, I am not sure there is a general statement on this approach that can be embraced. My sense is that we should not think that exegesis will offer us a more unbiased, philological approach. It may or it may not. Insofar as there may be a commonly shared exegetical *Vorlage* for certain diverging exegetical and theological positions in the Reformation era, exegesis or biblical reception could well serve as an interesting tool of comparison to track the shared commonalities alongside any

---

28 See Henri de Lubac, *Medieval Exegesis: The Four Senses of Scripture*, transl. Mark Sebanc (Grand Rapids: Eerdmans, 1998), 1: 27.

emerging differences. But whether the codified exegesis of a biblical text can serve as a touchstone to adjudicate the merits of intellectual or theological choices, I am not sure. Biblical texts have proven to be supple in adopting different guises. If anything, Eriugena pioneered such an approach.

Maybe it is fitting to end this tribute to my colleague and friend Susan Schreiner with an image from Eriugena where he points to the infinite possibilities of exegetical readings, which he links not just with doctrinal positions but, true to his own project, with the variety inherent in nature itself, a variety to be savored and celebrated rather than to be domesticated:

> Far from anything preventing us, reason herself, in my opinion, if we could but listen to her more carefully, insists that we should understand the relation which exists between the Sacred Texts and reality. For there are many ways, indeed an infinite number, of interpreting the Scriptures, just as in one and the same feather of a peacock and even in one and the same point of a tiny portion of the same feather, we see a marvellously beautiful variety of innumerable colours. And the nature of things itself draws us to this understanding.[29]

29 See PP IV 749C, CCCM 164, 13 (transl. Sheldon-Williams, 390): "A. Non solum, ut opinor, nil obstat, uerum etiam ut ita intelligamus ea quae scripta sunt secundum ueritatem rerum factarum, ratio ipsa intentius considerata nos aduocat. Est enim multiplex et infinitus diuinorum eloquiorum intellectus. Siquidem in penna pauonis una eademque mirabilis ac pulchra innumerabilium colorum uarietas conspicitur in uno eodemque loco eiusdem pennae portiunculae. Et quidem natura ipsa rerum ad hunc attrahit intellectum."

CHAPTER 2

"Blessed Jerome": The Protestants and the Vulgate in the Sixteenth Century

Bruce Gordon

The Latin Bible, known from the sixteenth century as the Vulgate, remains the forgotten text of the Protestant Reformation.[1] Yet, in many respects, it formed an essential part of the foundation of an emerging biblical culture. Established narratives of the Reformation privilege the role of the vernacular translation, following Erasmus' call for scripture in the languages of the people. Martin Luther's "exile" at the Wartburg led to the appearance in 1522 of the "September Testament", a translation of the Dutch humanist's Greek New Testament.[2] The clarion cry of "sola scriptura" declared that all men and women not only could, but should, have direct access to the Word of God, liberating them from clerical hegemony. Indeed, Luther saw the Reformation as God's intervention in history to restore the Word, and the printing press was a divinely given tool for the propagation of the Gospel.[3] Change, however, was not linear. At first glance, we find plenty of Protestant hostility to the Latin Bible of the medieval church as the embodiment of false doctrine, oppressive clericalism, and a distortion of the work of Jerome.[4] Yet behind the invective lay a complex

1 This essay is a revision of a plenary lecture given at "The Bible in the Reformation" conference at Baylor University in October 2017. I am indebted to the work of my colleague Matthew McLean of the University of St. Andrews, with whom I am preparing a study of the Protestant Latin Bibles of the sixteenth century. In my treatment of Sebastian Münster, I draw extensively from his work.

2 Euan Cameron, "The Luther Bible," in Euan Cameron (ed.), *The New Cambridge History of the Bible, vol. 4: 1450–1750* (Cambridge: Cambridge University Press, 2016), 217–238; John L. Flood, "Martin Luther's Bible Translation in its German and European Context," in Richard Griffiths (ed.), *The Bible in the Renaissance: Essays on Biblical Commentary and Translation in the Fifteenth and Sixteenth Centuries* (Aldershot: Ashgate, 2001), 45–70.

3 See Andrew Pettegree, *Brand Luther* (New York: Penguin, 2015).

4 There is a large body of work on Jerome and his Latin Bible. A selection of recent scholarship includes, G. Q. A. Meershoek, *Le latin biblique d'après Saint Jérôme: Aspects linguistiques de la rencontre entre la Bible et le monde Classique* (Nijmegen-Utrecht, Dekker & Van de Vegt, 1966); Dennis Brown, *Vir Trilinguis: a Study in the Biblical Exegesis of Saint Jerome* (Kampen: Kok Pharos, 1992); Michael Graves, *Jerome's Hebrew Philology: a Study Based on His Commentary on Jeremiah* (Leiden: Brill, 2007); Adam Kamesar, "Jerome", in James Carleton Paget and Joachim Schaper (eds.), *The New Cambridge History of the Bible: from the Beginnings to 600*

 | DOI:10.1163/9789004527843_003

relationship. The Latin Bible was essential for both Lutheran and Reformed translators and interpreters of the sixteenth century, an indispensable part of their claims to antiquity.

The reformers fully understood that the vernacular was only possible if the church possessed authoritative texts. What that meant, however, would remain contested for generations.[5] Although in the humanist enthusiasm for a return to the original texts meant access to Hebrew and Greek, Latin remained the essential language of translation, biblical interpretation, and doctrinal formulation.[6] The biblical work of the first generation of reformers was a delicate balance of change and tradition. Careful philological study of the Old and New Testaments, they were persuaded, unmasked unbiblical errors, but there was no room for speculative innovation.[7] For Catholics and Protestants alike, the Vulgate, however imperfect, was the essential link to the church's past when Jerome had prepared the best of translations from the original languages. The emergence of Protestant biblical culture in the 1520s was a battle for the inheritance of the great church father, who was lionized in the Renaissance as the model Christian scholar.[8]

(Cambridge: Cambridge University Press, 2013); Matthew A. Kraus, *Jewish, Christian, and Classical Exegetical Traditions in Jerome's Translation of the Book of Exodus: Translation Technique and the Vulgate* (Leiden: Brill, 2017).

5 Bruce Gordon, "The Bible in Transition in the Age of Shakespeare: A European Perspective," in Thomas Fulton and Kristen Poole (eds.), *The Bible on the Shakespearean Stage: Cultures of Interpretation in Reformation England* (Cambridge: Cambridge University Press, 2018), 17–32.

6 Ann Moss, *Renaissance Truth and the Latin Language Turn* (Oxford, New York: Oxford University Press, 2003). On the place of Latin in the Reformed churches, see Peter Stotz, "Heinrich Bullinger (1504–1575) and the Ancient Languages," in Emidio Campi, Simone De Angelis, Anja-Silvia Goeing, and Anthony Grafton (eds.), *Scholarly Knowledge: Textbooks in Early Modern Europe* (Geneva: Droz, 2008), 113–138.

7 Jerry H. Bentley, *Humanists and Holy Writ: New Testament Scholarship in the Renaissance* (Princeton, N.J.: Princeton University Press, 1983); Jaroslav Pelikan, *The Reformation of the Bible, the Bible of the Reformation* (New Haven: Yale University Press, 1996); Henning Graf von Reventlow, *History of Biblical Interpretation*, vol. 4, trans. James O. Duke (Leiden: Brill, 2010). See the essays in Euan Cameron (ed.), *The New Cambridge History of the Bible, vol. 3: From 1450–1750* (Cambridge: 2016).

8 Eugene F. Rice, *St Jerome in the Renaissance* (Baltimore: Johns Hopkins, 1985); John C. Olin, "Erasmus and St. Jerome: The Close Bond and its Significance," *Erasmus of Rotterdam Society Yearbook*, 7 (1987): 33–53; Lisa Jardine, *Erasmus, Man of Letters: the Construction of Charisma in Print* (Princeton: University of Princeton Press, 1993); Mark Vessey, "The Tongue and the Book: Erasmus' Paraphrases on the New Testament and the Arts of Scripture," in Hilmar M. Pabel and Mark Vessey (eds.), *Holy Scripture Speaks: The Production and Reception of Erasmus' Paraphrases on the New Testament* (Toronto: University of Toronto Press, 2002), 29–58; Hilmar M. Pabel, *Herculean Labours: Erasmus and the Editing of St. Jerome's Letters in the Renaissance* (Leiden: Brill, 2008); Robert D. Sider, *The New Testament Scholarship of*

Erasmus very much set the tone with his acknowledgement in his 1516 *Novum Instrumentum* that the Vulgate was the Bible of the Western Church.[9] Against his critics, he was adamant that the Greek text alongside his Latin translation did not form an attack on the venerable Latin translation. Although Jerome's translation did not have the status of the Septuagint as an inspired text, for centuries it had been the foundation of Western Christianity.[10] The Vulgate, however, was not an unproblematic text: by the end of the Middle Ages it existed in an extraordinary range of variants arising from different textual traditions. Significant attempts had been made in the twelfth and thirteenth centuries to make corrections to the Vulgate text.[11] Johann Gutenberg had printed the so-called Paris Vulgate, giving it an authoritative place in the church,[12] but every scholar knew that there were enormous difficulties with corruptions of Jerome's translation.[13] The Complutensian Polyglot was the first major effort of the sixteenth century to revise the text of the Vulgate, but the end result was something different.[14] Nevertheless, the printing revolution only enhanced the Vulgate's status, and by the end of the fifteenth century there were approximately ninety-five editions of the Latin Bible.

The Vulgate was the life-blood of the medieval theological education that produced the Protestant reformers of the first generation, including Martin Luther, Huldrych Zwingli, and Martin Bucer, all of whom received traditional

---

Erasmus: An Introduction, with Erasmus' Prefaces and Ancillary Writings (Toronto: University of Toronto Press, 2019).

9 Richard Rex, "Humanist Bible Controversies," in Cameron (ed.), *New Cambridge History of the Bible*, 61–81.

10 See R. Loewe, 'The Medieval History of the Latin Vulgate,' in G. W. H. Lampe (ed.), *The Cambridge History of the Bible*, vol. 2 (Cambridge, 1969), 102–54; Pierre Maurice Bogaert, OSB, "La Bible Latine des Origines au Moyen Âge. Aperçu Historique, État des Questions," *Revue Théologique de Louvain*, 19 (1988): 137–59 and 276–314.

11 Frans van Liere, "The Latin Bible c.900 to the Council of Trent, 1546", in Richard Marsden and E. Anne Matter (eds.), *The New Cambridge History of the Bible, vol. 2: 600–1450* (Cambridge: Cambridge University Press, 2012), 106–107.

12 W. Schmidt and F. A. Schmidt-Künsemüller (eds.), *Johannes Gutenbergs Zweiundvierzigzeilige Bibel: Faksimile-Ausgabe nach dem Exemplar der Staatsbibliothek Preußischer Kulturbesitz Berlin. Kommentarband* (Munich: Idion, 1979), 9–31.

13 On the Paris Bible, see Laura Light, "French Bibles c. 1200–30. A New Look at the Origins of the Paris Bible," in Richard Gameson (ed), *The Early Medieval Bible: Its Production, Decoration and Use* (Cambridge: Cambridge University Press, 1994), 155–76; Laura Light, "Roger Bacon and the Origin of the Paris Bible," *Revue Bénédictine*, 111 (2001): 483–507; Lee Anderson Smith, 'What was the Bible in the Twelfth and Thirteenth Centuries?', in Robert E. Lerner and Elisabeth Muller-Luckner (eds.), ¨Neue Richtungen in der hoch- und spatmittelalterlichen Bibelexegese¨, *Schriften des Historischen Kollegs, Kolloquien* 32 (Munich: Oldenbourg, 1996): 1–15.

14 Van Liere, "The Latin Bible", 108.

scholastic educations in biblical exegesis. Luther's formative years from 1512 to 1519 at Wittenberg were spent expounding the Vulgate to his students.[15] The Erasmian call to bring the Bible to the people in their own languages did not, by any means, relegate the Vulgate to obsolescence. The Latin Bible played a crucial role in the formation of Protestant culture, honored as the inheritance of Christendom's greatest scholar, Jerome. The necessity of a Bible in Latin spoke to the centrality of the classical language for the nascent churches of the Reformation. German, Dutch, French, and English were the means by which the faith was preached to the people, and how they should worship, but Latin remained for the new churches the language of theological discourse and education.[16]

1 Erasmus and the Vulgate

Alongside other leading scholars of the late-medieval church, Erasmus advocated the urgency of revising the Vulgate, disfigured by the accretion of scribal errors, with the unhappy consequence that Jerome's translation was almost wholly lost.[17] The Dutchman considered the post-twelfth century form of the Vulgate to be in a deplorable condition. It was evident that prior to 1514 and his arrival in Basel, Erasmus had intended to produce the Greek text and annotations alongside the Latin Vulgate, and not a new translation.[18] Prior to the publication of the first edition in 1516 of his Greek New Testament, the *Novum Instrumentum*, Erasmus' working method was to make a careful comparison ('collation') of the Vulgate with the Greek texts he found in manuscript form, mostly of Byzantine provenance. His editions thus cannot be properly understood without the Vulgate as the third element alongside the Greek text and his own Latin translation. His first translation of 1516, prepared in less than a year, sailed close to the Vulgate text. It was only for the subsequent 1519 edition that his Latin become freer.[19] Although his editions, except the fourth (1527),

15 Ulrich Köpf, "Martin Luthers Theologischer Lehrstuhl," in Irene Dingel and Günther Wartenberg (eds.), *Die Theologische Fakultät Wittenberg 1502 bis 1602* (Leipzig: Evangelische Verlagsanstält, 2002), 71–86.

16 Bruce Gordon, "The Authority of Antiquity: England and the Protestant Latin Bible," in Patrick Collinson and Polly Ha (eds.), *The Reception of Continental Reformation in Britain. Proceedings of the British Academy, vol. 164* (London, 2010), 1–22.

17 On Erasmus' approach to the Vulgate, see Jan Krans, *Beyond What is Written. Erasmus and Beza as Conjectural Critics of the New Testament* (Leiden: Brill, 2006), 69–90.

18 Andrew J. Brown, "The Date of Erasmus' Translation of the New Testament," *Transactions of the Cambridge Bibliographical Society* 8 (1984): 374.

19 *Ibid.*

did not contain a Vulgate text, no contemporary reader could fail to notice that Erasmus' enterprise was centered around the correction or 'emendation' of the received Latin Bible.

Erasmus himself presented the project in the following way:

> I have translated the whole New Testament after comparison with the Greek copies, and have added the Greek on the facing pages, so that anyone may easily compare it. I have appended separate annotations in which, partly by argument and partly by the authority of the early Fathers, I show that my emendations are not haphazard alterations, for fear that my changes might not carry conviction and in the hope of preserving the corrected text from further damage.[20]

As Jan Krans has remarked, there was a fundamental flaw in Erasmus' approach in using the Vulgate and the Byzantine manuscripts as his base texts. Fundamentally, he regarded the Vulgate as a polluted source, while the Greek manuscripts were pristine.[21]

As Andrew Brown has written, "[Erasmus'] aim was to convey the meaning of the Greek more accurately and more clearly than the existing Latin Vulgate version, and at the same time to employ a more elegant classical Latin style, purged from linguistic barbarism."[22] Replying to those who wished that nothing would agree with the Vulgate, Erasmus argued in the preface to his 1527 Greek New Testament:

> I have not done this in order that the language would be more polished and refined (politior), but in order that it would be more correct (emendatior) and more clear (dilucilior). I have not tried to find problems unnecessarily ... We are dealing with a sacred subject matter, where it is ridiculous to boast of human erudition and also impious to make a show of human eloquence.[23]

Furthermore, describing his method of translation, Erasmus added: "I have rendered into Latin what I have found in the collated Greek manuscripts and, in doing so, I have, as far as possible, accommodated to the plain purity of the

---

20 Quoted in Krans, *Beyond What is Written*, 14.

21 Krans, *Beyond What is Written*, 16.

22 Cited in Josef Eskhult, "Latin Bible Translations in the Protestant Reformation," in Bruce Gordon and Matthew MacLean (eds.), *Shaping the Bible in the Reformation: Books, Scholars, and their Readers in the Sixteenth Century* (Leiden: Brill, 2012), 175.

23 Quoted in Eskhult, "Latin Bible Translations," 176.

Roman language."[24] Finally, when explaining his departures from the wording of the Vulgate, he maintained: "I have removed evident and conspicuous solecisms and everywhere, as far as possible, followed the elegance of the language in such a way that the simplicity, or plainness, does not turn out to be minor."[25]

Erasmus only offered modest claims to elegance. He had mastered classical Latin completely, but he disapproved of the Ciceronian approach to ecclesiastical subject matter.[26] In his version of the New Testament, the Latin vocabulary did not conform to the classicist norm, although the style displays fluency and ease. Furthermore, Erasmus held the Vulgate in high esteem and did not dissent from it without good reason. His disposition towards the Latin Bible, we shall we, was widely adopted by Protestant translators. Erasmus' deviations from the Vulgate found support in the exegesis of the Church Fathers. Nonetheless, he disapproved of those who claimed: "We are satisfied with the translation of Jerome." Opposing this attitude, and using his common metaphorical language about water, he countered that one must not neglect the Greek original; the Christian teaching was first and foremost to be drawn from the wellsprings rather than from the streams and pools. What is more, Erasmus pointed out that a great deal of Jerome's emendations from the Greek original had been lost, corrupted, or distorted by the faults of the copyists. Erasmus designated his efforts as a "castigatio," a complete revision of Jerome's translation.[27] In the end, as Erasmus made clear in his *Apologia*, he was wholly persuaded that Jerome was not in fact the translator of the Vulgate New Testament.[28] The church father had prepared the Old, but the New was largely a revision of existing translations. Erasmus followed a Renaissance effort to separate Jerome from the corrupted Latin Bible received in the Church. As Hilmar Pabel has written: "By liberating Jerome from the Vulgate translation of the New Testament, Erasmus not only cleared the way for his revision of the traditional translation of the New Testament but also enlisted for the benefit of his revision the authority of the authentic Jerome against the work of a counterfeit."[29]

---

24 *Ibid.*, 175.

25 *Ibid.*, 175–176.

26 H. C. Gotoff, "Stylistic Criticism in Erasmus' Ciceronianus," *Illinois Classical Studies* 7 (1982): 359–370.

27 Hank Nellen and Jan Bloemendal, "Erasmus's Biblical Project: Some Thoughts and Observations on Its Scope, Its Impact in the Sixteenth Century, and Reception in the Seventeenth and Eighteenth Centuries," *Church History and Religious Culture* 96 (2016): 600.

28 Hilmar M. Pabel, "St. Jerome's Exegetical Authority in Erasmus of Rotterdam's 'Annotations on the New Testament'," *Church History and Culture* 4 (2016): 582.

29 *Ibid.*, 583.

The *Novum Instrumentum* was primarily intended as a translation for those who had to engage with the Bible as theologians, that is, those who had to consult and interpret it professionally as university teachers, in schools and the church. These readers included priests and other clerics who needed to refer to a good translation of the Bible when composing their sermons. In short, the *Novum Instrumentum* was not a Bible for general use, but a type of study Bible. This declared purpose allowed Erasmus to claim repeatedly that his translation was never intended to supersede the Vulgate, but to be used alongside it, as an aid to understand the Vulgate better.[30] Nevertheless, his purpose was to produce a Latin text for the times that was purer, clearer, and more correct than the Vulgate.[31] His New Testament was foundational to his vision of a renewed church, in which people who had no access to the Greek would be able to read a faithful Latin translation. For this ideal, the Vulgate was not sufficient.[32]

Erasmus had a complex relationship to the Vulgate, and many of his critics were persuaded that his translation offered a direct threat to the authority of the established Latin Bible.[33] His esteem for the ancient text, together with his conviction that he was laboring to restore Jerome's monumental achievement, proved profoundly influential on Protestant attitudes towards the place of the Latin Bible in the life of their churches.

2 Lutherans and the Vulgate

The Lutherans did not reject the Vulgate, although they did not accept it as authoritative. The Latin Bible was widely used in the education of pastors in schools and universities, and early Lutherans continued to use the Vulgate in their scholarly work. The basis on which the Vulgate was used was its antiquity, although the text was frequently revised through comparison to ancient manuscripts and to Hebrew and Greek sources. Between 1521 and 1570,

30 Henk Jan de Jonge, "The Character of Erasmus' Translation of the New Testament as Reflected in his Translation of Hebrews 9," *Journal of Medieval and Renaissance Studies* 14 (1984): 81.

31 Henk Jan de Jonge, "Novis Testamentum a Nobis Versum: The Essence of Erasmus' Edition of the New Testament," *Journal of Theological Studies* 35 (1984): 400.

32 *Ibid.*, 406.

33 See Ronald K. Delph, "Emending and Defending the Vulgate Old Testament: Agostino Steuco's Quarrel with Erasmus," in Erika Rummel (ed.), *A Companion to Biblical Humanism and Scholasticism in the Age of Erasmus* (Leiden: Brill, 2008), 297–318. See also James K. Farge, "Noël Beda and the Defense of Tradition," in *ibid.*, 143–64.

Protestant (largely Lutheran) editors and printers issued fifty-eight editions of the Vulgate.[34]

The major figure among the Lutherans was Andreas Osiander (1496–1552), professor of Hebrew in Nuremberg. Osiander prepared an edition of the Vulgate in 1522, admitting that he had no access to manuscripts but had based his revisions on the Hebrew and the Greek of the Septuagint.[35] Where the Vulgate and the Hebrew did not seem to agree, he put the Hebrew words in marginal annotations. Vulgates were also printed in Basel and Strasbourg by Protestant typographers in 1522, although the texts were quite different. Five years later in 1527, the editor Johann Petreius issued a Vulgate in Nuremberg in which he corrected the text from a set of manuscripts.[36]

The most significant development among the Lutherans came in 1529 when a corrected partial edition of the Vulgate (the Pentateuch, Joshua, Judges, Samuel, and Kings, and the entire New Testament) was produced from the Hebrew and Greek.[37] The edition was printed in Wittenberg and was the work of a team of scholars consisting of Martin Luther, Philipp Melanchthon, Justus Jonas, Georg Spalatin, and others. In his preface, Luther remarked that his original intention was to correct scribal error and restore the Vulgate text to its pure form.[38] However, in examining the text they found it so corrupt that they had to return to the Hebrew, although they did not have any manuscripts. The result was an almost new translation into Latin from the Hebrew. The work was intended for theological students and not to be used in church worship or to be read publicly in place of the old Vulgate. Luther preferred to keep the traditional Vulgate because it was the text known by the people, despite its errors. Nevertheless, the edition had little influence as only a few copies were printed and it was never reprinted.[39]

---

34 John M. Lenhart, "Protestant Latin Bibles of the Reformation, 1520–1570: A bibliographical account," *The Catholic Biblical Quarterly* 8 (1946): 430.

35 Josef Eskhult, "Latin Bible Versions in the Age of the Reformation and Post-Reformation: On the Development of New Latin Versions of the Old Testament in Hebrew, and on the Vulgate as Revised and Evaluated among the Protestants," *Kyrkohistorisk Arsskrift* (2006): 35.

36 *Biblia Sacra Vtrivsqve Testamenti, iuxta uetere[m] tra[n]slationem, qua huiusq[ue] Latina utitur Ecclesia, ex antiquissimis ac rece[n]tioribus exe[m]plaribus diligentissime collatis & sicubi dissentieba[n]t co[n]sultis fontibus, hoc est, hebræis et græcis uoluminibus adhibitis, fidelissime restitute* (Norembergæ: Petreius Nürnberg, 1529).

37 *Pentatevchvs: Liber Iosve; liber Ivdicvm; liber Regnvm; Novvm Testamentvm* (Wittenbvrgae: Nicolaus Schirleitz, 1529).

38 Sig. Avr–v.

39 Eskhult, "Latin Bible Versions," 62 n. 27.

In 1544, Johannes Brenz published an emendated Vulgate that included Jerome's prolegomena to the different biblical books. Later, another edition was produced by Paul Eber (Hebrew professor in Wittenberg) and Georg Major.[40] The reason for the work was the decision of the Elector of Saxony to introduce a Latin Bible consistent with Luther's German translation in the schools.[41] The two bibles were to be harmonized theologically, and in 1565 a ten-volume edition appeared with parallel German and Latin texts. More editions of the Vulgate followed. During the 1560s, Victor Strigel in Leipzig produced another edition with extensive summaries and annotations.

Despite the number of editions based on revisions from the Hebrew, Lutheran scholars became aware of how problematic the text was. Numerous errors remained. Lucas Osiander the Elder (1534–1604) began work on the Vulgate by undertaking a new method. He emendated the text where he felt that it departed from the original Hebrew and Greek, but placed his changes in italics, thus preserving the original text.[42] Such was the extent of his work that virtually every biblical passage contained Osiander's italics revisions. In his preface, Osiander wrote that he chose the method of adding his own improvements to the Vulgate in order to demonstrate his corrections with the original text. His purpose, he wrote, was to make the original Vulgate clearer and plainer by removing obscure and ambiguous passages.[43] Often, he argued, Jerome had stayed so close to the Hebrew that his Latin was not entirely clear. In addition, Osiander provided marginal notes drawn from Luther's biblical commentaries in order to ensure a proper evangelical interpretation of the text. The heavily annotated edition came in seven volumes between 1574–1586, and reprinted in 1599.[44] Osiander's intention was to translate the Bible while

---

40 *Sacrae scripturae et divinarum literarum byblia universa, cum diligentia elaborata, deque sententia doctissimorum virorum Hebraicae linguae peritorum, plurimis in locis ultra priores editiones emendata atque correcta: et D. Erasmi roterod. Uersione Novi Testamenti, juxta priorem apposita. Praemissis prolegomenis, et insuper prooemio eximii Joannis brentii accessit Latina interpretatio, nominum Hebraeorum item, chosmographica locorum indicatio. Et index rerum sententiarumque* (Leipzig: ex officina Nikolaus Wolrab [impensis Sebastian Reusch], 1544 [1543]).

41 Eskhult, "Latin Bible Versions," 36.

42 *Quinque libri moysis juxta veterem seu vulgatam translationem, ad Hebraeam veritatem emendati, et brevi ac perspicua explicatione illustrati, insertis etiam praecipuis locis communibus in lectione sacra observandis. Lucas osiander D. Rationem totius nostri instituti ex altera praefatione huius primi tomi intelligens* (Tübingen: excudebat Georg Gruppenbach, 1573).

43 Eskhult, "Latin Bible Versions," 36.

44 *Biblia sacra veteris et Novi Testamenti, secundum vulgatam versionem, ad ebraeam veritatem in veteri; ad Graecam verò in novo testamento, à D. Luca osiandro perpurgata: et ad*

keeping the ancient version accepted in the church. The later Catholic scholar Richard Simon approved of Osiander's work because, on account of its antiquity and status, it did not reject the Vulgate completely.[45] Lucas Osiander, for his part, argued in his preface that it was not necessary to demonstrate that theological students and others greatly valued the Vulgate and that it was widely read, giving it a public authority. He decided to correct and expound the Vulgate because it remained widely used in schools and for theological exercises, venerated for its antiquity.

The work of Lucas Osiander on the Vulgate was continued by his son, Andreas, who became chancellor of Tübingen university. For the most part, Andreas augmented the annotations made by his father. Following developments in bibles elsewhere, Andreas set the pages of his Vulgates differently, with two columns of the Latin text surrounded by the dense theological commentary, mostly drawn from Luther and the *Formula of Concord* (1577–80). The first edition of his Latin Bible appeared in 1600, but the best-known edition was the fifth, which was printed in Frankfurt in 1618.[46]

3 Huldrych Zwingli

Zwingli had a high view of the Vulgate, which remained central to his exposition of scripture during the 1520s. During his times as priest in Einsiedeln (1516–1519), he intensively studied the Latin commentaries on the Psalms of Lefevre d'Etaples.[47] In 1516 he purchased a copy a copy of the *Octaplus*, which consisted of three Latin versions of the Psalms alongside Hebrew, Greek Arabic and Aramaic arranged in columns. His Greek was excellent and his Hebrew competent and he was a devoted advocate of Erasmus' call for a return to the original languages and the philological approach to the text.[48] Zwingli's copy

---

D. D. Lutheri versionem Germanicam collata, (Jena: excudebat Tobias Steinmann; Leipzig: sumtibus Henning Grosse, 1599).

45 Eskhult, "Latin Bible Versions," 37.

46 *Biblia sacra. Quæ præter antiquæ Latinæ versionis necessariam emendationem & difficiliorum locorum ... explicationem, ex Commentariis Biblicis ... Lucæ Osiandri ... depromptam, multas insuper vtilissimas obseruationes ... continent ... Studio & operâ Andreæ Osiandri, etc.* (Tubingæ: Typis & expensis G. Gruppenbachii, 1600).

47 Urs Leu and Sandra Weidmann, *Huldrych Zwingli's Private Library* (Leiden: Brill, 2018), 61.

48 On Zwingli's exegetical influences and approaches, see Christine Christ-von Wedel, "Erasmus und die Zürcher Reformatoren: Huldrych Zwingli, Leo Jud, Heinrich Bullinger and Theodor Bibliander," in Christine Christ von-Wedel and Urs Leu (eds.), *Erasmus in Zürich: Eine Verschwiegene Autorität* (Zurich: Verlage Neue Zürcher Zeitung, 2007), 77–166; Fritz Büsser, "Zwingli, the Exegete: A Contribution to the 450th Anniversary of the

of the Vulgate has survived, full of marginal notes demonstrating the care with which he read the Latin Bible after his emergence as a reformer. One remarkable survival is Zwingli's preaching Bible, which he seems to have taken with him to the battle at Kappel in 1531.[49]

The centrality of the Vulgate to the ecclesiastical life of the Zurich church was evident most days of the week with the meetings of so-called Prophezei in the Grossmünster church.[50] From the summer of 1525 Zwingli gathered with his colleagues to expound the Old Testament, beginning with the book of Genesis. The purpose was to provide the church with an Erasmian-inspired interpretation of the Hebrew scriptures based on the Vulgate, the Septuagint, and the Masoretic texts. The sessions would open with the Latin being read aloud by a student or by Zwingli's colleague Kaspar Megander, clearly identifying the close association of the interpretive work with the traditional Bible of the Western church. Zwingli would then expound (in Latin) the Septuagint while his close friend Konrad Pellikan took on the Hebrew.

The concept of prophecy as biblical interpretation was taken from 1 Corinthians 14. Bullinger describes how the meetings of the Prophezei were structured.[51] It met five days a week in the morning. After opening prayer, the scholars set to work on a book of the Bible, which they would examine line by line over a period of weeks and months. First read was the Latin Vulgate, reflecting the continuing Reformed esteem for the ancient Bible of the Church, followed by the Hebrew with interpretive commentary. Zwingli was responsible for the Septuagint, for which he had an especial fondness. Then the text was translated into Latin and discrepancies with the Vulgate were noted. The

---

Death of Erasmus," in Elsie McKee (ed.), *Probing the Reformed Tradition: Historical Studies in Honor of Edward A Dowey* (Louisville: Westminster, 1989), 175–196; R. Gerald Hobbs, "Zwingli and the Study of the Old Testament," in Edward J. Furcha (ed.), *Huldrych Zwingli (1484–1531): A Legacy of Radical Reform* (Montreal, McGill University Press, 1985), 144–178; G.Krause, "Zwinglis Auslegung der Propheten," *Zwingliana* 11 (1960): 257–265; E. Künzli, *Zwingli als Ausleger von Genesis und Exodus* (Zurich: Berichthaus, 1950); Marc Lienhard, "Aus der Arbeiten an Zwinglis Exegetica zum Neuen Testament: Zu den Quellen der Schriftauslegung," *Zwingliana* 18 (1990–1991): 310–328; George R Potter, "Zwingli and the Book of Psalms," *Sixteenth Century Journal* 10 (1979): 43–50.

49 Emil Egli, "Zwinglis Lateinische Bibel," *Zwingliana* 1 (1899): 116–120.

50 On the Prophezei, see Daniel Timmerman, *Heinrich Bullinger on Prophecy and the Prophetic Office (1523–1538)* (Göttingen: Vandenhoeck & Ruprecht, 2015), 118–123. Also, Traudel Himmighöfer, *Die Zürcher Bibel bis zum Tode Zwinglis (1531): Darstellung and Bibliographie* (Mainz: Verlag Philipp von Zabern, 1995), esp. 213–235; and Bruce Gordon, *The Swiss Reformation* (Manchester: Manchester University Press, 2002), esp. 232–239.

51 Heinrich Bullinger, *Reformationsgeschichte, vol. 1*, ed. J. J. Hottinger and H. H. Vögeli (rpt. Zurich: Nova-Buchhandlung, 1984), 289–91.

language of the exercise was Latin, and the final stage was the translation of the fruits of scholarship into the vernacular as a basis of a sermon to the people.

In his 1525 work *Von dem Predigtamt*, Zwingli distinguished two essential roles of the prophet: first, he must resist evil and sow what is good, and secondly, he must engage in the public exposition of Scripture.[52] As an interpreter of the Bible, Zwingli sought both to provide an exegesis that enabled readers to understand the text more fully and to remove himself as the mediating figure. In translating the biblical books into German and Latin, he emphasized lucidity and elegance over more literal renderings of the original languages. As Peter Opitz has commented, "... the goal of exegetical or translational work on a Biblical book is not an *Enarratio*, but the Zürcher Bibel."[53]

4 Sebastian Münster

The first Protestant to translate the complete Old Testament from Hebrew into Latin was Sebastian Münster (1488–1552) in Basel.[54] In the preface to his translation he called attention to the commotion that followed in the wake of Erasmus' Latin New Testament. He anticipated that he would arouse much the same reaction by his effort to present an Old Testament with the Hebrew and Latin on facing pages. Sebastian Münster was one of the leading Hebrew scholars in the early to mid-sixteenth century, professor of Hebrew in Heidelberg and Basel. His teacher in Hebrew was Konrad Pellikan (1478–1556), himself an autodidact. Both belonged to a circle of Bible scholars that has been called "the Rhineland school of exegesis."[55]

The *Hebraica Biblia* (1534) is distinguished by an idiosyncratic understanding of the importance of the Old Testament to Christians, and by its approach to Jewish scholars. The Bible also reflected how Münster positioned his text in relation to the Vulgate and to the imposing figure of Jerome. While the Vulgate

52 Peter Opitz, "Zwingli's Exegesis of the Old Testament," in Magne Sæbø et al. (ed.), *Hebrew Bible/Old Testament: The History of its Interpretation*, vol. 2 (Göttingen: Vandenhoeck & Ruprecht, 2008), 421.

53 *Ibid.*, 423.

54 *En tibi lector Hebraica Biblia Latina planeque noua Sebast. Munsteri tralatione ...* (Basileae: Ex officina Bebeliana, Impendiis Michaelis Isingrinij et Henrici Petri., 1534–1535). Referred to as the *Hebraica Biblia*. On Münster, see Matthew McLean, "Between Basel and Zürich: Humanist Rivalries and the Works of Sebastian Münster," in Malcolm Walsby and Graeme Kemp (eds.), *The Book Triumphant: Print in Transition in the Sixteenth and Seventeenth Centuries* (Leiden/Boston: Brill, 2011), 270–291.

55 See Bernard Rousell, "De Strasbourg à Bâle et Zurich: Une 'École Rhénane' d'Exégèse (ca.1525–ca.1540)," *Revue d'Histoire et de Philosophie Religieuses* 68 (1988): 19–39.

continued to be of tremendous importance in Zürich and Wittenberg alike, the Latin Bible of the medieval Church, the 'common edition' or the 'received edition' was, to Münster, wrongly revered.[56] Although he recognized that the Vulgate was deferred to because of its age, he regarded it as being of lesser antiquity than other texts and traditions, the Hebrew most notably.[57] Indeed, mere antiquity was no mark of verity, and Münster objected to this claim as arising from those who possessed considerable enthusiasm but little real learning.[58]

Münster further acknowledged that the style and quality of the Latin translation were established reasons for the Vulgate's absolute position, but found this claim equally flawed. In the eyes of its supporters,[59] the Vulgate was "*absolutissima & elegantissima*," both the most perfect and most elegant rendering of Scripture possible. Münster found such arguments unmoving: the traditional Latin Bible's supposed perfection was disproved by the number of corrections it required when compared to the Hebrew. Elegance, when it came at the expense of accuracy, was, he argued, inappropriate for the translation of Scared Literature. Münster held that the Vulgate translation had obscured the true Hebrew "no small amount," placing a barrier between Scripture and reader which time and human inconstancy had made ever harder to breach.[60] The final reason for the incorrect, indeed harmful, reverence of the Vulgate was its authorship: it was taken as axiomatic that this translation was the work of Saint Jerome and was therefore doubly beyond reproach, by virtue of its author's sanctity and his model scholarship. To fail to reverence his "*absolutam aeditionem*" in the established custom of the Church was to invite scathing derision and personal attacks.[61] In fact, Münster was quite willing to pay reverence to Jerome: it was the Vulgate for which he had criticism, and he disputed the traditional certainty that Jerome was the author of that translation.[62]

It seemed to Münster that the Vulgate was at odds in its translation with Jerome's commentaries, and that where the former erred, the latter were usually well-informed and correct. Jerome, indeed, was clearly possessed of a superior command of the Hebrew language than the translator of the Vulgate,

56 Emidio Campi, Simone De Angelis, Anja-Silvia Goeing, and Anthony Grafton (eds.), *Scholarly Knowledge: Textbooks in Early Modern Europe* (Geneva, 2008), 136.

57 Delph, "Emending and Defending the Vulgate Old Testament," 312.

58 *Hebraica Biblia*, α4v.

59 In this case, Erasmus' opponent Agostino Steucho, to whom Münster attributes the phrase. *Hebraica Biblia*, β1r.

60 The author of the Vulgate "*interdum non satis oculatum fuisse veritas Heb.*," *Hebraica Biblia*, α5v. On human inconstancy and its implications for the custodianship of Sacred Literature, *Hebraica Biblia*, α4r.

61 *Hebraica Biblia*, α6v.

62 *Hebraica Biblia*, β1r.

or "common," edition, and it seemed that Jerome's own Bible must be lost.[63] Who, then, had prepared the Vulgate? Münster mused that it was Theodotius, or Aquilius, or Symmachus, who cultivated stylish Latin but were unlearned in Hebrew.[64] Perhaps it was a person who assumed Jerome's name to "sell" a translation which had been greatly corrupted, rife with error.[65] It was not a question for which Münster was prepared to venture a definitive answer. Of greater interest was the removal of Jerome's support and protection from the champions of the Vulgate, and its reallocation to the Christian Hebraists.

Jerome was a model for Münster. The father had exerted himself to produce a sound Latin translation of the Old Testament, finding the Septuagint to be deficient. The Hebrew text from which Jerome worked was without vowel points in Münster's view, placing Jerome at great disadvantage, since these were necessary for non-native Hebrew linguists to correctly understand which of several possible readings of text was the correct one.[66]

Without the Masoretic text, Münster argued, Jerome would have struggled to find the sure meaning of the Hebrew text, a struggle for certainty with which Münster and his contemporaries would surely sympathize, even after the second Bomberg Bible had disseminated the Hebrew text with the vowel points widely.[67] Münster could at least turn to the Aramaic, a profound help in resolving ambiguities.[68]

If the problems with which he was forced to contend made Jerome a forebear of the Christian Hebraists, so too did his approach to solving those problems. Jerome took the path that Münster would later tread: to the door of Jewish teachers. Although Münster does not claim that Jewish scholars were at every turn keen to help Jerome master their languages and texts, he is emphatic that Jerome would not have been able to do so without their tuition.[69]

---

63 *Hebraica Biblia*, β3v.

64 *Hebraica Biblia*, β3r.

65 *Hebraica Biblia*, β3r.

66 *Hebraica Biblia*, β2r.

67 Instances of the corruption of the Masoretic text by Christians in order to make it conform with the Vulgate made even this tradition suspect: the textual problems of the Christian Hebraists were not to be resolved with a single stroke. Basil Hall, "Biblical Scholarship: Editions and Commentaries. Biblical Humanism and its Resources," in S. L. Greenslade (ed.), *The Cambridge History of the Bible. The West from the Reformation to the Present Day* (Cambridge, 1963) 52. David Steinmetz (ed.), *The Bible in the Sixteenth Century* (Durham and London, 1990), 96.

68 *Hebraica Biblia*, β5v.

69 Münster refers to Jewish efforts to deceive Jerome and ruin his holy work: *Hebraica Biblia*, α4v.

In the 1546 edition, the section of the preface which argues against Jerome's authorship of the Vulgate is removed; no clue for this excision remains. Nonetheless, the text and annotations of the 1546 *Hebraica Biblia* hold to the ideas apparent in those pages. Münster's Hebrew Bible was critical of the Vulgate, but gloried in the example of Jerome and his scholarship in the commentaries; it was immersed in the Hebrew and the Jewish exegetical traditions, and was opposed to simplifying them or presenting their contents as unproblematic or unchallenging.

5 Konrad Pellikan

The major reformed effort in revising the Vulgate was the work of Konrad Pellikan, the Hebraist who worked in Basel and then in Zurich.[70] Pellikan lived from 1478 to 1556 and was extremely close to both Erasmus and Zwingli.[71] His work on the Vulgate was part of a commentary on the whole Bible that he produced between 1532 and 1539 and which was reprinted in 1582.[72] With regard to the revision of the Vulgate, Pellikan maintained that he would have retained the Vulgate text if he had not been asked by his colleagues to emend it.[73] Pellikan says that he would himself all the better keep a translation of the venerable Vulgate unaltered and unchanged in the Christian congregations.[74] He shared with his student Sebastian Münster an extremely high view of Jerome, and in his discussion of the use of Rabbinic sources he singled out the father for praise. Although he recognizes problems with the Jewish sources, he argued that they were essential to the study of grammar. Jerome, he continued, had studied with Jewish teachers and had an excellent grasp of the language, which is why his translation was to be used. Most translators, he lamented, did

70 On Pellikan's *Commentaria*, see Conrad Zürcher, *Konrad Pellikans Wirken in Zürich, 1526–1556* (Zurich: Theologischer Verlag, 1975), esp. 85–152; R. Gerald Hobbs, "Conrad Pellican and the Psalms: the Ambivalent Legacy of a Pioneer Hebraist," *Reformation and Renaissance Review* 1 (1999): 72–99. See also *id.*, "Pluriformity of Early Reformation Scriptural Interpretation", in Magne Sæbø et al. (ed.), *Hebrew Bible/Old Testament: The History of its Interpretation*, vol. 2 (Göttingen: Vandenhoeck & Ruprecht, 2008), 482–484.

71 On Pellikan, see Zürcher, *Konrad Pellikans Wirken*, and Bruce Gordon, "Fathers and Sons: The Exemplary Lives of Konrad Pellikan and Leo Jud in Reformation Zurich," in Luca Baschera, Bruce Gordon and Christian Moser (eds.), *Following Zwingli: Applying the Past in Reformation Zurich* (Aldershot: Ashgate, 2014), 257–289.

72 *Commentaria Biblioru[m], id est XXIIII. Canonicorum veteris testament librorum, & illa brevia quidem & catholica* (Tiguri: Froschouerus, 1534–1539).

73 *Commentaria*, sig. B2v.

74 Hobbs, "Pluriformity," 484.

not have sufficient knowledge of Hebrew, which is why Jerome was such an exception.[75] In fact, Pellikan placed Jerome together with Nicholas of Lyra as the two scholars most capable of reading Hebrew.[76]

In the preface he states that in his revision he had rendered the Hebraisms more appropriately than the Vulgate, even though not translating them exactly. Pellikan held a high view of the Vulgate as the Bible of the church, commenting that his method was to use the Hebrew to make corrections. He did not, however, believe that he was correcting the great Jerome. The Zurich scholar expressed some ambiguity about the relationship between Jerome and the received Latin Bible that bore the father's name ("quae Hieronymi nomine in Ecclesiis recepta est").[77] Pellikan saw his task as correcting the falsified parts of the text; essentially, he sought to restore Jerome. The Fathers of the Church thought it more advisable, Pellikan argues, to permit a barbarism than to remove the smallest matter from the meaning of the divine prophecies. They did not think, he continues, that a legitimate method of translation of the Bible can be extended as far as in profane literature because the divine words conceal a mystery. He argues that he had changed the Hebrew forms of expression into words and terms sounding good in Latin. Pellikan says that he diverges from Jerome's wording only when the Hebrew original text appears to hint at something more.[78] However, in passages where the meaning of the Hebrew original is doubtful, Pellikan preferred to rely on the authority of the Fathers (Jerome and the Septuagint) and remain uncertain with them, rather than rely on the medieval Jewish exegetes and pretend the problems to be settled. Pellikan held an extremely high view of Jerome's authority.[79]

Pellikan revered the memory of Jerome and his translation, writing that it was good for the Church that there was a known and familiar version of the Bible. His own work, he was eager to claim, lay within a long tradition of biblical scholarship, and although he sought to correct errors he did not wish to cast aspersions on earlier fathers of the church. Famous interpreters of the divine law are not to be spurned because of mistakes.[80] Divine providence permitted some errors in order that humans should know their place, desiring not to earn more authority than the words of scripture. Being more specific, Pellikan argued that since the obscurity of divine eloquence ('eloquiorum divinorum obscuritas') is placed partially in the property of diction and partially in the

75 *Commentaria*, sig. A4r.
76 *Commentaria*, sig A5v.
77 *Commentaria*, sig. B3r.
78 *Commentaria*, sig. B3r.
79 *Commentaria*, sig. A4v.
80 *Commentaria*, sig. A5r.

nature of things, the force and nature of the words are to be discerned by the acumen of ingenium, trustworthy memory, sound judgment, the knowledge of sacred languages, expertise in the liberal arts, the observation of the circumstances and condition of things, the collection of different loci, the inspection of the author's particular diction, and the invocation of the Spirit.[81]

6 Theodor Bibliander and the Zurich Latin Bible of 1543

In 1531, Pellikan's student Theodor Bibliander arrived in Zurich from Basel.[82] A native Swiss, Bibliander had also studied with Johannes Oecolampadius, who was to prove an influential master. Oecolampadius was bold and polemical and insisted on translating from the Hebrew, creating fresh Latin versions. Pellikan, as we have seen, shared with Zwingli a reverence for the Vulgate.

Bibliander's distinctive voice was heard in 1534 when he produced a translation with commentary of the Old Testament prophet Nahum, very much in the style of Oecolampadius.[83] Quite arresting was Bibliander's attitude towards the Vulgate. Whereas Pellikan had made use of the Vulgate in his commentary, Bibliander set his own translation alongside Jerome's, as his teacher Oecolampadius had done, not with the intention of revision, but to present an entirely different rendering of the prophet. In his prefatory letter, Bibliander argued that Nahum had not been translated by learned men of his age.[84] In other words, it had not been treated by the humanists. This prophetic book, which speaks of God's judgment upon the nations, Bibliander added, was most appropriate for his own turbulent times, and should, therefore, be published in the interest of the church.

---

81 *Commentaria*, sig. A5r.

82 On Bibliander, see Christine Christ-von Wedel, "Theodor Bibliander in seiner Zeit," in *ead.*, *Theodor Bibliander 1505–1564: Ein Thurgauer im Gelehrten Zürich der Reformationszeit* (Zurich: Verlag Neue Zürcher Zeitung, 2005), 19–60. On Bibliander's teaching, see Anja-Silvia Goeing, "Vernünftig Unterrichten: Bibliander als Lehrer," in *ibid.*, 61–82.

83 On the text and Bibliander's translation method, see Bruce Gordon, "Christo testimonium reddunt omnes scripturae: Theodor Bibliander's Oration on Isaiah (1532) and Commentary on Nahum (1534)," in Bruce Gordon and Matthew McLean (eds.), *Shaping the Bible in the Reformation: Books, Scholars and their Readers in the Sixteenth Century* (Leiden: Brill, 2012), 107–142.

84 *Propheta Nahvm / Ivxta Veritatem Hebraicam, Latine redditus per Theodorum Bibliandrum; adiecta exegesi, qua uersionis ratio redditur, & authoris diuini sententia explicatur. Tigvri: Apvd Christoph Froscho., Mense Ivl. Anno M. D. XXXIIII*, sig 2r. Cf. Christian Moser, *Theodor Bibliander (1505–1564): Annotierte Bibliographie der Gedruckten Werke* (Zürich: Theologischer Verlag Zurich, 2009), B-3.

For Bibliander, the translator possessed a prophetic spirit, for he "raised his spirit to the divine explication of this writer [Nahum]." The translator acquires a distinctive voice, obliged both to achieve a fair rendering of the original Hebrew but also to provide the reader with good Latin. This claim distinguished his work, Bibliander argued, from the Vulgate occupying the other half of the page, which was neither entirely accurate nor appealing Latin. However, the relationship to Jerome's work was more complicated. A new translation, according to Bibliander, did not amount to a rejection of the Vulgate, which he freely declared to be the Bible of the Church. No one should think that he was attempting to replace the church father, though in a somewhat veiled critique he commented that Jerome was wont to remain a little too close to the Jewish sources. He concluded the letter to the reader with an appeal to a quote from Augustine found in the Zurich vernacular Bibles and later referenced by Bullinger in the 1543 Latin Bible. The divine Augustine held, Bibliander wrote, that it was useful to compare various translations, as well as to preserve what is familiar to the people, so that out of the collision of many versions the light of truth might spring forth more productively.[85]

The Zurich Latin Bible has a fascinating print history.[86] In early 1543 it appeared in folio from the press of Christoph Froschauer, followed the next year by quarto and octavo editions with much of the critical apparatus removed. The octavo *Biblia* has none of the prefatory material.[87] The whole text was produced again in Zurich in 1550. In 1545 the Zurich translation mysteriously appeared in Paris from the press of the royal Robert Estienne. The edition, designated a 'nova translatio' without attribution to Protestant Zurich, was alongside the text of the Vulgate. The only portions of the prefatory material retained were the Compendium and list of books. The work became known as the "Vatable Bible" on account of the extensive notes included from François Vatable's lectures by his students, and was reprinted in Paris by Estienne in 1565.[88] In 1546 Estienne produced an edition of the Psalms with the Vulgate and Zurich Latin

---

85 *Nahum*, sig 2v.

86 *Biblia sacrosancta Testame[n]ti Veteris & Noui: è sacra Hebraeorum lingua Graecorumque fontibus, consultis simul orthodoxis interpretib. religiosissime translata in sermonem Latinum: authores omnemq[ue] totius operis rationem ex subiecta intelliges praefatione. Tigvri: Excvdebat C. Froschovervs, Anno M. D. XLIII.*

87 Moser, *Theodor Bibliander*, B-8.2 (quarto 1544,), B-8.3 (octavo, 1544).

88 *Biblia quid in hac edition praestium sit, vide in ea quam opera praeposuimus, ad lectorem epistola. LUTETIA. Ex officinal Roberti Stephani, typographi Regii. M.D XLV. CUM PRIVELEGIO REGIS* (Moser, *Theodor Bibliander*, B-8.4.) Cf. Herbert Mayow Adams, *Catalogue of Books Printed on the Continent of Europe, 1501–1600 in Cambridge Libraries*, 2 volumes (Cambridge, 1967), 2: 1037.

translations, once more with the notes from Vatable's lectures.[89] Perhaps most astonishing was the printing of the Vatable Bible in 1584/5 in Salamanca. The parallel Vulgate and Zurich Latin translations appeared with the Vatable notes, which had been somewhat revised by Francesco Sancho and the theologians of Salamanca university. Whether the provenance of the Zurich translation was known to the Spanish scholars is not known.[90]

The translators of the Zurich Bible fully expected to be attacked for their efforts, but this response only justified their enterprise because it associated them with Jerome, who was fiercely criticized. The appeal to Jerome was subtle and multifaceted. Principally, Jerome was a model of scholarship and piety, and the Zurichers sought to cast their biblical work in his image. This action, however, was not without a degree of tension, as the status of the Vulgate was somewhat ambiguous. On the one hand, the Zurich scholars, like Münster, were wary of suggesting that the Vulgate as received was Jerome's work. Yet, on the other, they spoke of the common version of the Latin Bible that was to be honored. Indeed, the Vulgate continued to be printed in both Zurich and Basel.[91] Further, although Bullinger sought protection behind the words of Jerome and Augustine, there was a clear sense that the translation produced in Zurich was superior in terms of scholarship. This posturing was precisely what Bibliander had done in his Nahum commentary. The Zurich Bible was rooted in antiquity, but its quality was owing to the humanist scholarship of the sixteenth century.

The relationship between the Zurich Latin Bible and the Vulgate was complex. On the one hand, the historical justification for a new Latin translation rested on their argument that Jerome had not intended his Bible to be authoritative in the Church. There was little doubt, on the other hand, that the Vulgate was held in high esteem as the familiar Bible. The Vulgate embodied tradition, and the Zurich churchmen were struggling to position their humanist scholarship in relation to history. This ambivalence is evident when the preface addressed the ticklish question of whether the Vulgate could still be regarded as the work of Jerome. *The Catalogue of Ecclesiastical Writers* is cited where Jerome wrote that he translated "the New Testament with fidelity to the Greek and the Old Testament close to [iuxta] the Hebrew."[92] Nevertheless, the

---

89 *LIBER PSALMORUM DAVIDIS. Annotationes in eosdem ex Hebraeorum commentariis. LVTETIAE. Ex officinal Rob. Stephani typographi Regii. M.D. XLVI. CUM PRIVELEGIO REGIS.* (Moser, *Theodor Bibliander*, B-8.5.)

90 Moser, *Theodor Bibliander*, B-8.8.

91 See Urs Leu, "The Book- and Reading-Culture in Basle and Zurich During the Sixteenth Century," in Walsby and Kemp (eds), *The Book Triumphant*, 295–319.

92 *Biblia sacrosancta*, sig. A4v. The *Catalogue* was written by Epiphanius (310–403).

preface continues, there remained some skepticism: "whether that version which is today received as the Vulgate, and is called Jeromian [Hieronymiana], is the very version that he mentioned, is not for us to say. Indeed, his books cry out against it not a little, especially his *Questions* (On Genesis) or the *Hebraic Traditions*."[93] The Zurich scholars adopted the familiar line that Jerome's own commentaries bear witness against the veracity of the Vulgate, yet unlike Münster and others they were not prepared to take a firm stance. This reflected the enduring reverence for the Bible in Zurich, where great stock was placed in historical continuity.

Clearly the matter of the Vulgate was not resolved and the preface returned to the question and Jerome, "to follow his example." The Zurich scholars did not, they claimed, wish to quarrel with others on account of their edition and version, nor had they sought to slight Jerome in any way. Further they had not sought to decree imperiously that their version should be received and others "spat out." Those who do not like the Zurich Bible still have the Vulgate, which "we do not condemn by our version at all, although nevertheless we openly admit that it does not always and everywhere agree with the truth of the Hebrew and Greek."[94] This is very much the spirit of Bibliander: respect for the Vulgate, coupled with a pervasive sense of superiority.

7 Conclusion

For Protestants of the first generations of the Reformation, the Vulgate remained pregnant with authority. It was also a symbol of that which they had emphatically rejected. Central to their strategies was to uncouple Jerome from the Latin Bible inherited from the medieval church, but their success was limited. The corruption of the text, which in many ways served as an emblem of the church of antichrist, was balanced by their acknowledgement of the Vulgate, however disfigured, as the Bible of the Church. The robust Protestant engagement with the ancient Latin Bible, together with its veneration of Jerome as the greatest of Christian scholars, was part of a complex relationship to the nexus of scripture, tradition, and identity that troubled religious reform. That struggle would only be augmented when the cherished tools of humanist *ad fontes* themselves began to cast doubts on the reliability of the biblical texts.

93 *Ibid.* See C. T. R. Howard, *Jerome's Hebrew Questions on Genesis: Translated with an Introduction and Commentary* (Oxford, 1995).

94 *Biblia sacrosancta*, sig. A5r.

CHAPTER 3

Waiting for the Miracle: Uncertainty, Superstition, and Trust in Jean Gerson

Matthew Vanderpoel

Jean Gerson (1363–1429), chancellor of the University of Paris and one of the most prolific authors of the later Middle Ages, has long been studied as a mirror of his age,[1] the so-called "siècle de Gerson."[2] For his homeland of France, however, the later fourteenth and early fifteenth centuries resist any nostalgic retelling. People lived amid ongoing waves of the Black Death pandemic, the long shadow of the Hundred Years' War, and the ecclesial confusion of competing papal claimants in Avignon, Rome, and eventually Pisa. While the question of crisis has long dogged historiography of the era,[3] the late-medieval period has also been looked to as the cradle of the modern age. As a result, Gerson

1 A version of part of this essay was previously presented at the American Society of Church History's annual meeting in 2017. I would like to thank Mark M. Lambert for organizing the session, Constance Furey for giving a substantive and generous response, and the audience for their questions and feedback.

2 This phrase was coined by Étienne Delaruelle: *L'Église au temps du grand schisme et de la crise conciliaire (1378–1449)*, 2 vols. (Paris: Bloud & Gay, 1962–1964), 837. More recently, Daniel Hobbins has described Gerson as standing "at the intersection of nearly every major intellectual, spiritual, and social current of [his] time" and further asserts, "All the cultural traffic of the fifteenth century runs through him." *Authorship and Publicity before Print: Jean Gerson and the Transformation of Late Medieval Learning* (Philadelphia: University of Pennsylvania Press, 2013), 5 & 218.

3 The fraught, yet rewarding, starting point remains: Johan Huizinga, *The Autumn of the Middle Ages*, trans. Rodney J. Payton and Ulrich Mammitzsch (Chicago: University of Chicago Press, 1996). A more measured assessment of the interlocking crises of the fourteenth and fifteenth centuries, particularly for the history of Christianity, can be found in: Heiko A. Oberman, "The Shape of Late Medieval Thought: The Birthpangs of the Modern Era," in *The Dawn of the Reformation: Essays in Late Medieval and Early Reformation Thought* (Grand Rapids, MI: William B. Eerdmans Publishing Company, 1986), 21 ff. The lens of "crisis" has been criticized as both inaccurate to the fourteenth and fifteenth centuries and as shaped primarily by twentieth-century anxieties. See, respectively: Howard Kaminsky, "From Lateness To Waning To Crisis: the Burden of the Later Middle Ages," *Journal of Early Modern History* 4, no. 1 (2000); Peter Schuster, "Die Krise des Spätmittelalters: Zur Evidenz eines sozial- und wirtschaftsgeschichtlichen Paradigmas in der Geschichtsschreibung des 20.Jahrhunderts," *Historische Zeitschrift* 269, no. 1 (1999).

 | DOI:10.1163/9789004527843_004

has been regularly investigated to assess to what extent he may foreshadow features of early-modern thought, particularly that of Martin Luther.

Scholars have generally interpreted Gerson as pushing back on earlier scholasticism in a number of innovative ways, but not as any standard-bearer of an incipient modernity. Hans Blumenberg exemplifies this consensus, casting Gerson as a pious skeptic digging in his heels against the stirrings of (modern) curiosity.[4] Somewhat analogously, the ample scholarship on Gerson's views on the discernment of spirits has characterized him as similarly suspicious of new, more popular forms of mystical practice—especially that of women.[5] Within the history of theology, Gerson has been read as a precursor to Luther, though one who fails to anticipate the full force of the latter's interventions.[6]

---

4 Gerson's hard line against *curiositas* is contrasted to his fellow conciliarist Nicholas of Cusa's more sympathetic view of the human desire to know insatiably: Hans Blumenberg, *The Legitimacy of the Modern Age*, trans. Robert M. Wallace, Studies in Contemporary German Social Thought (Cambridge, Mass.: MIT Press, 1983), 354–56. In a somewhat similar vein, later studies of the Cusan as a pivotal figure in the history of modernity's emergence tend to reduce Gerson to a conciliar forebear or omit him entirely. See, respectively: Simon J. G. Burton, Joshua Hollmann, and Eric M. Parker, *Nicholas of Cusa and the Making of the Early Modern World* (Leiden: Brill, 2019), 151; Karsten Harries, *Infinity and Perspective* (Cambridge, Mass.: MIT Press, 2001).

5 Dyan Elliott describes Gerson's maneuvering to police theological method as simultaneously aiming to curtail "the female mystic's parallel curiosity and love of novelty," *Proving Woman: Female Spirituality and Inquisitional Culture in the Later Middle Ages* (Princeton, N.J.: Princeton University Press, 2004), 274. Wendy Love Anderson notes, however, that Gerson's "misgivings" about women visionaries should not be conflated with a desire to punish women pursuing contemplative lives: *The Discernment of Spirits: Assessing Visions and Visionaries in the Late Middle Ages* (Tübingen: Mohr Siebeck, 2011), 223. More recently, Nancy McLoughlin has called for rhetorical analyses of Gerson's misogynist polemics, rather than reducing his statements to merely personal prejudice. See: *Jean Gerson and Gender: Rhetoric and Politics in Fifteenth-Century France*, Genders and Sexualities in History Series (Houndmills, Basingstoke Hampshire; New York, NY: Palgrave Macmillan, 2015), 2–3.

6 Steven Ozment's study on Luther's reliance upon Tauler, via Gerson, in his theological anthropology, is exemplary; e.g., while Gerson may rightly perceive the noetic weight of sin, he fails to appreciate its impact upon the affective faculties: *Homo Spiritualis. A Comparative Study of the Anthropology of Johannes Tauler, Jean Gerson and Martin Luther (1509–16) in the Context of Their Theological Thought*, Studies in Medieval and Reformation Thought, (Leiden,: Brill, 1969), 73. Likewise, Mark S. Burrows sees Gerson's exegetical privileging of a *sensus litteralis* as fully in line with Luther's own hermeneutics, though Gerson still relies upon the Church to dictate the bounds of the literal sense: "Jean Gerson on the 'Traditioned Sense' of Scripture as an Argument for an Ecclesial Hermeneutic," in *Biblical Hermeneutics in Historical Perspective. Studies in Honor of Karlfried Froehlich on His Sixtieth Birthday.*, ed. Mark S. Burrows and Paul Rorem (Grand Rapids, MI: William B. Eerdmans Publishing Company, 1991), 158–59. Sven Grosse, while conceding a superficial resonance between Gerson's description of hope as certain and Luther's conception of faith, has argued that their approaches to relating sapiential and existential theology are nevertheless fundamentally incompatible: "Existentielle

Put simply, Gerson's uncontested historical importance remains difficult, if not downright ambiguous, to parse as one gets to specifics.

This essay poses a modest intervention, taking as a perhaps unintuitive starting point Gersonian texts that do not represent the commonplaces of Gerson studies: mystical theology, the discernment of spirits, or conciliarist reform. Instead, we will consider a number of polemical works of Jean Gerson's—on differing topics and from all major periods of his career—that are united by their concern with superstition: *De erroribus circa artem magicam* (1402), a cancellarian address to medical licentiates recapitulating the University of Paris's theses condemning necromancy among educated elites; *Contra sectam Flagellantium* (1417), a firm rejection of self-flagellation as a devotional practice written on behalf of the Council of Constance; and *Contra superstitionem sculpturae leonis* (1428), an occasional treatise critiquing popular Lyonnais reverence for an image of a lion said to treat renal maladies.[7] Unsurprisingly, these texts diverge from each other in a number of ways, illustrating Gerson's enduringly perspectival approach to writing and pastoral care. Nevertheless, set side by side, these treatises bring into focus a Gersonian account of superstition that foregrounds the problem of uncertainty and considers how faith and hope could prove remedial thereto.

We will consider each treatise in turn, aiming to articulate the account of superstition presupposed within, drawing connections between them to see

---

Theologie in der vorreformatorischen Epoche am Beispiel Johannes Gerson: Historische Überlegungen zum ökumenischen Disput," *Kerygma and Dogma* 41 (1995): 108 ff.

One important exception to this trend of making Gerson an underwhelming Luther *avant la lettre* that demands further study is the extent to which Martin Luther's moral theology relies upon that of Gerson. On this topic, Rudolf Schuessler asserts, "Martin Luther and the reformation were as much influenced by Gerson as early modern Catholic moral theology," "Jean Gerson, Moral Certainty and the Renaissance of Ancient Scepticism," *Renaissance Studies* 23, no. 4 (2009): 448. After all, Luther describes Gerson as giving the first responsible theological treatment of scruples: see Sven Grosse, *Heilsungewissheit und Scrupulositas im späten Mittelalter: Studien zu Johannes Gerson und Gattungen der Frömmigkeitstheologie seiner Zeit* (Tübingen: J. C. B. Mohr, 1994), 1.

7 These works are included in the tenth volume of Palémon Glorieux's *opera omnia* of Gerson: *De erroribus circa artem magicam*, in *Jean Gerson. Œuvres complètes: vol. 10, l'œuvre polémique*, ed. Palémon Glorieux, (Paris: Desclée & Cie, 1973); *Contra sectam Flagellantium*, in *Jean Gerson. Œuvres complètes: vol. 10, l'œuvre polémique*, ed. Palémon Glorieux, (Paris: Desclée & Cie, 1973); *Contra superstitionem sculpturae leonis*, in *Jean Gerson. Œuvres complètes: vol. 10, l'œuvre polémique*, ed. Palémon Glorieux, (Paris: Desclée & Cie, 1973). On pages 73–76 of the same volume Glorieux provides a dossier of Gersoniana "contre le magie, l'astrologie, les superstitions, etc." One cluster of those texts comprises Gerson's back and forth with his mentor Pierre d'Ailly on astrology. The standard study remains: Laura Ackerman Smoller, *History, Prophecy, and the Stars: the Christian Astrology of Pierre d'Ailly, 1350–1420* (Princeton, N.J.: Princeton University Press, 1994).

that, for Gerson, superstition represents the realm of the suspect. The suspicion raised by superstition gives a new vantage point onto the problem of certainty within Gerson's oeuvre. Accordingly, in a change of emphasis from recent scholarship on superstition in Gerson,[8] I will argue that Gerson gives us something like a premodern hermeneutics of suspicion, wrapped in the language of superstition, that aims ultimately to discern a faithful way of life.

1 *De erroribus circa artem magicam*

De erroribus circa artem magicam explicates a series of condemned propositions on magical practice issued by the faculty of theology at the University of Paris in September of 1398. It was initially a collation given by Gerson to licentiates in the faculty of medicine; the edited lecture circulated with the faculty's condemnations appended as a stand-alone anti-magical treatise under its present title. The audience, educated and elite, is noteworthy. After all, the evidence suggests most of the era's highly structured magical practice (e.g., necromancy) occurred in clerical and/or academic circles.[9] Specific arguments raised in the course of the treatise demonstrate this point further, insofar as they suggest that Gerson's opponents offered relatively sophisticated defenses of their magical practices. For instance, many of the condemned propositions are cognizant of the typical theological arguments brought to bear against magical rites. Some contest the charge of idolatry: "that attempting by magical arts to bind, compel, and constrain demons in [various objects] ... may not be idolatry."[10] Ethical arguments are invoked: "that it is permissible to use magical

8 Michael Bailey gives Gerson pride of place in his article on the relation of superstition to conceptions of "crisis" in the later Middle Ages: "A Late-Medieval Crisis of Superstition?," *Speculum* 84, no. 3 (2009). Bailey argues, compellingly, for continuity in views of superstition between the medieval and early-modern eras, suggesting that disparaging superstition as qualitatively distinct from proper reason is a feature of modern, secular epistemologies. Superstition has been addressed in treatments of lay devotion and/or contemplative practice in Gerson too. See: Daniel Hobbins, "Gerson on Lay Devotion," in *A Companion to Jean Gerson*, ed. Brian Patrick McGuire (Leiden: Brill, 2006); Bernard McGinn, "Academics and Mystics: the Case of Jean Gerson," in *Desire, Faith, and the Darkness of God: Essays in Honor of Denys Turner*, ed. Eric Bugyis and David Newheiser (South Bend: University of Notre Dame Press, 2015).

9 See: Richard Kieckhefer, *Magic in the Middle Ages* (Cambridge: Cambridge University Press, 1989), 151–72.

10 Gerson, *De erroribus*, 88. "4us articulus.—Quod conari per artes magicas daemones in lapidibus, annulis, speculis aut imaginibus nomine eorum consecrates, vel potius execrates, includere, cogere et arctare, vel ea velle vivificare non sit idolatria."

arts or some other superstitions, prohibited by God and the Church, for the sake of a good end," or "that it is permissible—or even should be encouraged—to resist witchcraft by means of witchcraft."[11] There are attempts to describe even magical practice as reliant on divine power: "that God, by magical arts and witchcraft, is prompted to compel demons to obey invocations."[12] The condemned propositions, as a whole, try to articulate a mediating position that on the one hand takes advantage of the purported powers of the magical arts and on the other wards off any charges of demonolatry.

Gerson's unpacking of the issue aims to explain how these practices are still superstitious, still transgress the bounds of proper Christian religion, even if one has good intentions in pursuing them. The underlying logic of his argument moves backward from the commission of an idolatrous practice to its root cause: worshipping or serving a demon is illicit, any such activity would take place within the bounds of a pact, and any pact depends on the establishment of trust (*fides*). Thus, Gerson suggests, trust becomes a litmus test by which one can deduce the presence of superstition and thereby condemn any associated magical practice as idolatrous.

The first step in his argument, defining superstitious practice as demonolatrous, is largely presupposed in the treatise and the cited articles of condemnation—though Gerson does acknowledge those "who now mock theologians when they make mention of demons."[13] Nonetheless, Gerson asserts that ritual practices of magic can be seen as demonic worship. He remarks: "A demon is honored through the prayers, sacrifices, and censing called for in the magical arts."[14] Interacting in this way with demons, as Gerson sees it, constitutes a pact. He explains: "Seeing something happen which cannot rationally be expected to come about by God's miraculous working or by natural causes must be considered, by Christians, to be superstitious and suspected of being a secret pact—implicit or explicit—with demons."[15] Deploying the language

---

11 Gerson, *De erroribus*, 88. "5us articulus.—Quod licitum sit uti magicis artibus vel aliis quibusdam superstionibus a Deo et Ecclesia prohibitis, pro quocumque bono fide;" "6us articulus.—Quod licitum sit aut etiam permittendum maleficia maleficiis repellere."

12 Gerson, *De erroribus*, 88. "9us articulus.—Quod Deus per artes magicas et maleficia inducatur compellere daemones suis invocationibus obedire."

13 Gerson, *De erroribus*, 79. "... qui theologos derident mox ut de daemonibus sermonem faciunt."

14 Gerson, *De erroribus*, 81. "Colitur praeterea ipse daemon per orationes sacrificia et thurificationes iussas fieri in artibus magicis."

15 Gerson, *De erroribus*, 79. "Observatio ad faciendum aliquem effectum qui rationabiliter exspectari non potest a Deo miraculose operante nec a causis naturalibus, debet apud christianos haberi superstitiosa et suspecta de secreto pacto implicto vel explicito cum daemonibus."

of concealment, Gerson casts an image of superstition as fundamentally suspect because it relies on connections between cause and effect that could not be reasonably predicted. These occult causalities are not open questions to be considered further empirically, but rather are red flags precisely because of their essential uncertainty.[16]

With this established, Gerson proceeds to unpack what is entailed in a pact. For Gerson, a pact is not simply a formal contract, but any sort of transaction. The prototypical example he gives is King Asa, who "in his illness did not seek the Lord but rather trusted (*confisus est*) more in the art of physicians."[17] Gerson suggests that this transaction—hoping for bodily recovery from a miraculous art in exchange for payment—represents an implicit agreement between Asa and demons. And, even if it turned out that these demons made good on the bargain and healed the body, they certainly would only do so by harming the soul. In this instance, one would be literally selling one's soul for mere bodily health.[18] Although a demon may not be present to shake on it, Gerson suggests any magical practice constitutes a pact, a contract governed by exchange, conditionality, and mutual trust.

Gerson's treatise does not rest here. It gives another reason for why a pact is so troubling: what it reveals about hope and faith. Gerson sees these theological virtues as motive forces. By looking back at them, one can determine the moral rectitude of a course of action. For instance, Gerson summarizes the story of Asa with a powerful question: "Who does not see it as a great crime if one should place hope in such superstitions?"[19] By placing hope in something uncertain, regardless of whether or not it bears out, one reveals—so Gerson's thinking goes—a relative lack of trust in more apparent causalities, namely those of nature and divine promise.

Following this line of thought, hoping in an illicit pact cuts against the Christian faith itself. Those who suggest magic may be employed for good ends are acting "foolishly against the faith."[20] Such people "having recognized

16 Gerson, *De erroribus*, 82. Gerson refers to "haec empirica vel methodica superstitiosa."

17 Gerson, *De erroribus*, 82. "Nam inculpatur rex Aza, II Paral. xvi, quia in infirmitate sua non quaesivit Dominum sed magis in medicorum arte confisus est."

18 Gerson, *De erroribus*, 82. "Profecto daemones etsi sanarent corpora, illa sanarent Deo irato. Quomodo Deo irato? Quia certe necarent animas, et deterius tandem variis incommodes suos cultores et invocatores afficerent. Denique odienda prorsus esset corporalis valetudo quae animae pretio et morte venderetur."

19 Gerson, *De erroribus*, 82. "Quis non videat majoris criminis esse si quis in talibus superstitiosis spem apponat?"

20 Gerson, *De erroribus*, 85. "Non igitur sunt maleficia maleficiis repellanda; aliter sapere est contra fidem desipere."

God, do not then glorify God but rush into all the impiety of idolatry"[21] and are dragged like "Solomon into idolatry and Dido into magical practice."[22] The faculty's condemnation of such practices is, in contrast, reliable because it has "hope in the Lord and not in getting things from vanities and raving falsehoods."[23] Trust, for Gerson, is zero sum. Regardless of what one is looking for when one puts some trust in something unknown that holds great promise, one is growing accustomed to putting licit faith aside in favor of getting a fix of superstition. The person waiting for the miracle is actually waiting for their man.

Over the course of *De erroribus*, Gerson has tried to move debate from speculating on the specific mechanics of unknown, obscure causes and effects—the preferred terrain of debate for advocates of magical practice in the orbit of the University of Paris. Instead, Gerson roots the entire discourse in the question of trust, encompassing both hope and faith. Trust is the grounds for a moral hermeneutic that cuts the knot of occult processes.

In the case of superstition, one puts one's "primary hope" in things that lack clear causality, setting God aside.[24] First described in *De erroribus*, this definition of superstition recurs throughout Gerson's writings.[25] Superstition opts to trust in suspect, empty causality over rational inquiry and divine revelation. Hoping in something unclear or vague, definitionally for Gerson, cuts against proper Christian faith.

---

21 Gerson, *De erroribus*, 86. "… qui cum cognovissent Deum non sicut Deum glorificaverunt sed in omnem idolatriae impietatem … corruerunt."

22 Gerson, *De erroribus*, 87. "… Salomonem ad idola et Didonem ad magicas artes pertraxit effrena voluptas."

23 Gerson, *De erroribus*, 86. "… facultas theologiae in alma Universitate parisiensi, matre nostra, cum integro divini cultus honore spem habere in Domino ac in vanitates et insanias falsas non recipere."

24 Gerson, *De erroribus*, 84. "Hauc autem est intentio ut talia suscipiantur aut fiant non tamquam necessario efficacia aut tamquam spes principalis in talibus posita sit, Deo postposito; sed quod pietas fidei per ista nutriture et augetur et exaudiri meretur."

25 Some (non-exhaustive) examples: "Sed nulla causarum istarum sufficiens est aut rationabilis ut haec ponatur observation, nec omnes simul. Talis ergo observation vana est reprobanda," Jean Gerson, *Contra superstitiosam dierum observantiam*, in *Jean Gerson. Oeuvres complètes.*, ed. Palémon Glorieux, (Paris: Desclée & Cie, 1973), 117; "… hoc vanum est et superstitiosum ac sine aliqua ratione," Jean Gerson, *De observatione dierum quantum ad opera*, in *Jean Gerson. Oeuvres complètes.*, ed. Palémon Glorieux, (Paris: Desclée & Cie, 1973), 129; "Convincitur ergo superstitiosum, frivolum et vacuum, immo nocivum, talia et taliter asserere," Jean Gerson, *Adversus superstitionem in audiendo missam*, in *Jean Gerson. Oeuvres complètes.*, ed. Palémon Glorieux, (Paris: Desclée & Cie, 1973), 142.

2 *Contra sectam Flagellantium*

Nearly fifteen years later, Gerson penned *Contra sectam Flagellantium* on behalf of the Council of Constance, in response to the spread of self-flagellation among lay followers of the Dominican preacher Vincent Ferrer. The popular spread of the devotional practice, especially coupled with the charismatic authority of Vincent, emitted an aura of sacrosanctity. However, previous papal condemnation of the practice in the wake of the plague was clear and explicit. Moreover, Vincent was one of the most visible proponents of Avignon's Pope Clement VII, and thus there was a political imperative that Constance not alienate him as they sought to resolve the schism amicably. Complicating matters further, Vincent was not actively endorsing the practice, and so he could not be brought to account for it directly. Thus, Gerson was left to thread a needle in this treatise that required a new response to flagellation.

Gerson's strategy is signaled in his anaphoric use of the phrase "the law of Christ" to introduce each section within his text. As becomes clear, there is the proper practice of the Christian religion, and then there is everything else. Similar to his tack in *De erroribus*, Gerson argues that loyalty to the law of Christ precludes any alternative trust. Gerson wastes no time getting to this point, raising the question of superstition in the second sentence:

> The law of Christ must avoid in its worship the superstitions of the Gentiles and idolaters, especially cruel and horrendous ones, against which the old law moreover makes a prohibition ... [in the gloss on Deuteronomy 13:] 'You must not be similar to idolaters in any regard.'[26]

The concern with "cruel and horrendous" practice is contrasted with the law of Christ, defined most basically as "the law of love."[27]

Gerson goes on to propose a general rule for interpreting novel religious movements (e.g., Beghards and Beguines): they "present an appearance of great religiosity and of many spiritual fruits in the soul" and yet are followed by "many evils which come about under this pretext."[28] Something good may be twisted to a more perverted purpose. Gerson sees superstition as something

26 Gerson, *Contra sectam Flagellantium*, 46. "Lex Christi non minus debet in cultu suo vitare superstitiones gentilium et idololatrarum, praesertime crudeles et horrendas, quam antiqua lex in qua tamen prohibitio fit per expressum Deut. xiii ubi ... glossa: non debetis in aliquot idololatris assimilari."

27 Gerson, *Contra sectam Flagellantium*, 46. "Lex Christi dicitur lex amoris."

28 Gerson, *Contra sectam Flagellantium*, 47–48. "Lex Christi frequenter prohibuit multas observations, sicut Begardorum et Begardarum, quae in prima sui introductione

that necessarily escalates. Accordingly, in perhaps the most vivid passage of a text laden with violent and gruesome imagery, Gerson notes the danger of new practices, even and especially if they are ostensibly enhancements to licit church practice:

> ... by a similar logic [sc. not considering the good of the whole body] it is possible for a person to brand themself with a fiery sword—which up until now no one has allowed or permitted—except indeed idolaters and false Christians, such as are found in India, who deem that they must be baptized in fire.[29]

The specious example notwithstanding, Gerson believes that even within the context of the church superstitious practices outstrip proper Christian worship, ultimately straining sacramental logic until it becomes something else. Superstition is not simply something one can take advantage of *ad hoc* and ignore otherwise. For Gerson, superstition will erode and warp even the most-traditional Christian practice if left unchecked.

In like fashion, spilling blood by self-flagellation may appear to be an act of piety that comports with biblical sacrifice, but it also echoes the self-mutilating priests of Baal in 1 Kings 18. Gerson warns that "both murderers and apostate demons are desirous for the spilling of blood, especially that of humans."[30] The stated aim of piety and the pretext of devotion become overshadowed by the violent transaction actually taking place. Demons delight in any gruesome rite as they are actually getting a cut.[31] Whereas in *De erroribus*, Gerson argued from one's trust to a suspect pact, here Gerson derives the transactional pact from a resemblance to known instances of demonolatrous practice. The upshot is the same: superstitious practice means trust is misplaced and vice versa.

However, Gerson raises the stakes at the conclusion of *Contra sectam Flagellantium*, returning to the questions of suspicion, concealment, and

---

praetendebant speciem magnae religionis ac multis fructus spirituales in animabus ... prohibuit, inquam, propter sequelas malas et multas quae sub hoc pretext fieri sunt inventae."

29 Gerson, *Contra sectam Flagellantium*, 50. "... alioquin simile ratione posset se homo cauterizare per ignitum ferrum, quod adhuc nemo posuit vel concessit nisi forsitan idololatrae vel falsi christiani, quales reperiuntur in India, qui se putant baptizari debere per ignem."

30 Gerson, *Contra sectam Flagellantium*, 46. "Compertum siquidem est et traditum homicidas illos et apostatas daemones esse cupidos effusionis sanguinis, praesertim humani."

31 Gerson, *Contra sectam Flagellantium*, 46. "Lex aliquo quanto est iniquior et daemoniis obsequentior, tanto semper invenitur crudelior et amarior. Patet in illis qui filios suos et filias immolabant daemoniis."

unknowing in an apocalyptic framework. He proposes that Christians can and should only speak generically about the final judgment and Antichrist. On such topics, "one can only have an approximate and uncertain opinion."[32] While these are true events, specifics are not known. When people dare to give specifics, like Gerson's contemporaries who allege that miraculous happenings point to the Antichrist's imminent appearance, they fail to keep in mind that "the decaying world suffers the illusions of false miracles, just as an elderly person imagines things in dreams."[33] These illusions and phantasms are empty and occluded; they are superstitions. They "must be held in great suspicion, unless they have been first examined diligently."[34] While the specific example is that of last things, Gerson proffers a general principle for his age: the miraculous is uncertain and suspect. Observation is insufficient grounds for knowledge. Superstition, whether by putting stock in irrational hope or in observable wonders with unknown causes, reveals its problematic basis. Once again, for Gerson, the issue boils down to what one trusts in.

Yet Gerson goes further in this treatise than he did in his 1402 account of the anti-magic condemnations of the university. The infidelity of superstition runs amok, affecting other spheres of life. Specifically, Gerson asserts, flagellating one's body analogously harms the body politic and the bonds of trust upon which it depends.

The body is multivalent. There are human bodies; there are bodies politic and ecclesiastic. Gerson invokes a sound medical principle, namely that one should not harm parts of the body except for the health of the whole.[35] The axiom has more general applications too. If one is to flagellate an ecclesial or political member, one needs to make sure it is for the balance and good of the whole body. As *Contra sectam Flagellantium* moves to this macrocosmic scale, Gerson's vocabulary crescendos from obedience and discipline—typical touchstones for discussing devotion—to the more politically charged terms of sedition and violence.

---

32 Gerson, *Contra sectam Flagellantium*, 51. "Proinde si praedicandum fuerit de finali judicio vel Antichristo, fiat hoc in generali, concludendo quod in morte quilibet habet suum judicium proximum et incertum."

33 Gerson, *Contra sectam Flagellantium*, 51. "Quod si quis inducer voluerit miracula nova super Antichristi adventu proximo, notet quod mundus senescens patitur phantasies falsorum miraculorum, sicut homo senex phantasiatur in somno."

34 Gerson, *Contra sectam Flagellantium*, 51. "… sunt nunc habenda miracula valde suspecta, nisi fact prius examinatione diligenti."

35 Gerson, *Contra sectam Flagellantium*, 50. "Immo sicut non licet hominem seipsum propria auctoritate mutilare vel castrare nisi pro sanitate totius corporis consequenda, sic non licet … quod a seipso quis sanguinem violenter ejiciat nisi causa medicinae corporalis."

Especially since "Gallic blood is being shed," even secular authorities ought to intervene to curb lay self-flagellation.[36] Gerson gives a dizzying catalogue of the tribulations afflicting society, from ongoing fighting in the Hundred Years' War to illness spreading unchecked. The scope of these afflictions does indeed signal that greater penance is demanded (the typical justification for penitential flagellation), but doing so through something violent will only fuel the violence endemic across Europe. The only logical outcome of whipping oneself bloody is that one "cuts and rends oneself to death, piece by piece."[37] Gerson is deliberately coy about whether he means individual Christians or the social order itself.

3 *Contra superstitionem sculpturae leonis*

Appearance and observation come into sharper focus in Gerson's *Contra superstitionem sculpturae leonis*, written at the end of his life while exiled in Lyon away from Burgundian-controlled Paris. The text examines a peculiar, local case.

A large medallion, bearing the image of a lion, was crafted under the oversight of Nicolaus Kolne, dean of the storied Faculty of Medicine in Montpellier. Gerson describes Kolne as "renowned,"[38] and he at no point accuses Kolne of superstition. Moreover, Gerson himself acknowledges the famous case of Arnau de Vilanova ("a most Christian doctor"),[39] who had cured Pope Boniface VIII of kidney stones by using a talisman bearing an astrological image of a lion without incurring any papal censure. Given the use of astral lion medallions in successful treatments by doctors above reproach, Gerson affirms that such images "designed by an astrologer and properly executed according to his specifications" may have medicinal value for kidney pains.[40]

However, the plot thickens. Gerson also cryptically refers to another doctor, who, driven by professional envy over Kolne's successes treating kidney

36 Gerson, *Contra sectam Flagellantium*, 48. "... immo et principes, quod sectam hujusmodi cruentam et sanguinolentem, gallice sanglante, student et laborent destruere seu compescere."

37 Gerson, *Contra sectam Flagellantium*, 50. "... quam si manens iracundus et impatiens nedum flagellaret seipsum ad sanguinem, sed lacerat et discerperet membratim ad mortem."

38 Gerson, *Contra superstitionem*, 131. "... doctor eximius."

39 Gerson, *Contra superstitionem*, 131. "Arnoldus de Villanova, christianissimus doctor."

40 Gerson, *Contra superstitionem*, 131. "... in certis amphorismis, quos [Arnoldus] fecit, fugat renum illico dolorem, scilicet recte secundum regulas suas sculptum et praeparatum astrologice."

stones, apparently coordinated the transfer of the talisman from Montpellier to Lyon.[41] Gerson pivots to an unsurprising incipit, "Whose image and epigraph is this?" drawn from Matthew 22:20.[42] The biblical story referenced, wherein Christ tells the disciples to render unto Caesar what bears his image, implies a straightforward hermeneutic principle: the image shows the referent of the object. Gerson then asserts his thesis, which strains against the earlier concessions offered on behalf of Kolne and Arnau: "The crafting and use of images that are called 'astrological' is highly suspect of superstition and idolatry or magical practice."[43] He follows this up with a quick nod to ecclesial condemnation of crafting magical images and even calls for the craftspeople who worked on the medallion to be interrogated carefully—under threat of condemnation—about the specific astrological principles they adhered to.

Gerson moves from these bold claims to the substance of his argument. He concisely recaps the substance of *De erroribus* in the fourth proposition: "Any observation, of which an effect is expected to happen other than by a natural process or by a divine miracle, must be reasonably condemned and held firmly suspect (*suspecta*) of a pact with demons, whether explicit or implicit."[44] The strong conclusion on *suspecta* in the Latin is stylistically pronounced.

The next proposition provides a gloss on what it means to be suspect. Gerson notes that many practices can, in actuality, be worthwhile in any number of aspects. However, if any facet of it cannot be clearly explained, "it must be considered *totally suspect* and infected."[45] Uncertainty, in any regard, demands suspicion and, in turn, total rejection. (Gerson does concede that this rejection may be provisional, should further discernment clarify what is in doubt.)[46] This notion, a superstition of the gaps, is particularly well suited to the specifics of the lion case, which in many regards appeared to be above board given the pedigree of the talisman. After all, any open question, any lack of certainty—in

41 Gerson, *Contra superstitionem*, 131. "Sed ista delatio [a Montepessulano] processit ex invidia cujusdam alterius physici, sinister deferentis auto diose, de dicto sigillo leonis."

42 Gerson, *Contra superstitionem*, 131. "Cuius est imago haec et superscriptio. Matth. 22. 20."

43 Gerson, *Contra superstitionem*, 131. "Imaginum quae astrologicae nominantur fabricatio et usus, suspectus est plurimum de superstitione et idolatria seu magica observatione."

44 Gerson, *Contra superstitionem*, 132. "Omnis observatione cuius effectus expectatur aliter quam per rationem naturalem aut per divinum miraculum debet rationabiliter reprobari et de pacto daemonum expresso vel occulto vehementer haberi suspecta."

45 Gerson, *Contra superstitionem*, 132. "Omnis observatione quantumcumque sancta est salubris videatur in decem aut viginit aut centum particulis, si habeat unicam particulam de idolatria vel haeresi vel de apostasia suspectam aut infectam, debet tota suspecta et infecta reputari." Emphasis mine.

46 Gerson, *Contra superstitionem*, 132. "[A suspect observance must be rejected] … nisi fiat manifesta separatio pretiosi a vili."

part or in whole—points toward the spiritually dangerous. Those who superstitiously expect healing from a sigil of a lion, particularly if they are common folk or even doctors who do not fully understand the natural-scientific mechanisms relied on, decidedly lack certainty about what they are invoking.

Interestingly, Gerson turns to the philosophical nitty-gritty of cause and effect to further his case. He gives an account of signification:

> Characters or figures or letters do not have or receive their efficacy from a purely natural or corporal cause ... Characters or figures or letters do not have by their own reason an effect on other things, except by means of a rational or intellectual substance, for to signify something is to constitute it in the intellect. So, if characters of such a kind should have or be believed to have efficacy, it is clear that this is from a spiritual cause, not from a purely natural or corporeal cause.[47]

Symbols function through the activity of a mind, either that of a human or that of a spiritual entity. If something does not then have a natural cause, it must be due to the work of some supernatural force. Given that the church has not endorsed leonine medallions for renal ailments nor—he wryly notes—are physicians and astrologers qualified to discuss supernatural forces,[48] demons become not just a possible cause, but a probable one. Things must be rationally explained or divinely revealed, or else they must be held suspect of demonic activity.

To entertain superstitions is to forfeit a proper relationship between cause and effect and to threaten one's own standing with God. Gerson contends, "All deception consists in this: that, by conceding one problematic thing for the sake of some principle, it becomes necessary that many other things are

---

47 Gerson, *Contra superstitionem*, 132. "Characteres seu figurae vel litterae non habent vel sortiuntur ex causa pure naturali et corporali efficaciam, sicut nec entia mathematica cujusmodi sunt figurae et characteres, sunt de potentiis activis, et in eis secundum Philosophum non est bonum neque finis. [Propositio octava]—Characteres seu figurae vel litterae non habent de ratione sua quod ordinentur ad aliquos effectus, nisi mediante rationali vel intellectuali substantia; significare enim est rem in intellectu constituere. [Propositio nona]—Characteres hujusmodi si habeant vel habere credantur efficaciam, oportet quod hoc sit a causa spirituali, non a pure naturali et corporali, qualis causa est coelum cum suis influentiis in corpora."

48 Gerson, *Contra superstitionem*, 132. "Constat quod talis observatio non est posita ab Ecclesia et sacris doctoribus, tanquam eveniat effectus speratus per miraculum divinum ... et medicus seu astrologus verus non habent multum se intromittere de actionibus sanctorum angelorum circa homines."

consequently conceded and thence drawn on."[49] With one misstep, signification is liable to spiral away from its starting point deceptively. Superstition unravels the semiotic foundations of knowledge itself. In this way, analogous to the proliferation of violence from body to body explored in *Contra sectam Flagellantium*, superstition outstrips itself to render signification a battlefield between the Christian faith and demonic adversaries. Signs, poised between God and the Devil, are subject to being hijacked for concealed ends. Gerson reiterates that the standard of reasonability, of clarity, must be affirmed to avoid the multifarious confusion presented by superstition.

Though superstition starts small, it does not remain that way for long.

4 Gerson, Prism of His Age

Gerson's intense, sustained anxiety over superstition is of a piece with larger late-medieval shifts toward greater supervision, if not active policing, of forms of popular religiosity. Yet, the later circulation of Gersonian discernment treatises alongside inquisitorial texts like the *Malleus Maleficarum* notwithstanding, Gerson's particular concerns do not always map directly onto the broader contours of his contemporaries' thought. In this way, perhaps, he may be better described as a prism of his age, rather than a mirror. With Gerson, we find the image of late-medieval Latin Christianity refracted into a spectrum, wherein certain elements are isolated, cast into relief, and ordered anew.

This refraction is apparent in how Gerson offers a nuanced rethinking of received medieval traditions of faith. For much of the scholastic tradition, faith is keyed to the intellect and hope to affect. While, to be sure, these two faculties interface and may reinforce each other in the Christian life, they are distinguished by relating to cognition and to volition respectively. Sven Grosse has situated Gerson within such a framework, noting that Gerson himself distinguishes the certainty of hope's striving and the intellective certainty of faith.[50] While this is the case, such a formulation may elide the degree to which Gerson sees faith and hope as potentially fungible.

49 Gerson, *Contra superstitionem*, 134. "Tota deceptio stat in hoc quod concesso uno inconvenienti pro alicuius principio, concedi oportet plura alia consequenter inde elicita." Interestingly *elicio, -ire* bears technical usage as a term for ritual conjuration.

50 Grosse, "Existentielle Theologie in der vorreformatorischen Epoche am Beispiel Johannes Gerson: Historische Überlegungen zum ökumenischen Disput," 86. "Die eigene Gewißheit der Hoffnung ist aber von der des Glaubens dadurch unterschieden, daß sie nicht eine Qualität eines Verstandesurteils ist wie—auf übernatürlichen Grundlagen

That is to say, a superstitious hope always exists only at the expense of faith in God. The same transactional logic that Gerson sees as structuring pacts is echoed in how faith and hope operate. Misguided affect subverts faith. Thus, although faith is strictly speaking specified by Gerson as an intellective virtue, its presence requires that one's hope is properly aligned toward God. In practice, faith is always a personal trust for Gerson. The threat of superstition is how poised it stands to interject itself into a licit concordance of hope and faith.

More provocatively, perhaps, Gerson's sustained, animated concern toward superstition may be seen as a hermeneutics of suspicion: uncertainty must be analyzed, latent meaning discerned, and only then may *authentic* knowledge emerge.[51] This rather wary posture is necessary, Gerson suggests, because rationality and signification constitute a demonic battlefield. Contrary to some more recent formulations,[52] Gerson sees suspicion as working hand-in-hand with faith against the threat of diabolic deception, rather than as an accomplice to impious doubt. Without suspicion, trust in God will prove undermined by superstition's creeping advance. It is by attentively interpreting personal attachments and desires that the Christian may detect and resist superstition.

This refracted arrangement of hope and faith, resting upon a suspicion oriented against the superstitious proclivities of the fallen mind, aligns Gerson with Martin Luther's redefinition of faith more closely than has been previously appreciated. Faith's dependence on a matrix of personal, experiential trust in God rather than superstition looks ahead to the subjective certainty claimed for faith in the magisterial Reformation. To be sure Heiko Oberman has linked nominalism, broadly construed and explicitly including Gerson, with an emergent sensitivity to the place of experience in epistemology, though he

ruhend—auch die Glaubensgewißheit, sondern eine Eigenschaft des Strebevermögens, zu dem die Hoffnung gerechnet wird."

51 The turn of phrase, of course, was established by Paul Ricœur to refer to Nietzsche, Marx, and Freud's congruent forms of suspicion: "Beginning with them, understanding is hermeneutics: henceforward to seek meaning is no longer to spell out the consciousness of meaning, but to *decipher its expressions*," Paul Ricœur, *Freud and Philosophy: An Essay on Interpretation*, trans. Denis Savage (New Haven: Yale University Press, 1970), 33.

52 For instance, Ricœur explicitly opposes suspicion in this context to faith: "The contrary of suspicion, I will say bluntly, is faith. What faith? No longer, to be sure, the first faith of the simple soul, but rather the second faith of one who has engaged in hermeneutics, faith that has undergone criticism, postcritical faith." *Freud and Philosophy: An Essay on Interpretation*, 28. Whereas Ricœur sees a place for suspicion, as part of the hermeneutic, perhaps in propaideutic terms to the emergence of a robust, postcritical faith, Gerson imagines a continuingly suspicious habit as prophylactic.

warns against overemphasizing this in Luther's own formation.[53] And Gerson gives no sign of seeing faith as the medium for receiving the righteousness of Christ.[54] Yet, we have seen that Gerson does not relegate faith simply to the mental assent to "data."[55] It requires the cultivation of habits of suspicion, an affective striving of hope, and a radical trust in God even amid adversity. While Gerson does not share Luther's insistence on a tower experience as requisite for the emergence of critical faith, he does call for a faith that is prosecuted, personal, and critical.

In conclusion, Gerson's reconstrual of the scholastic tradition's definitions of hope and faith—a refraction captured by the prismatic notion of superstition—does resonate *avant la lettre* with Luther's subsequent redefinition of faith, if not the reformation insight. Further, it suggests the need for further research about how nominalist skepticism toward strong forms of epistemic confidence endemic to earlier scholastic theology may lie behind Luther's own rigorous critiques of reason. The problem of superstition, for Gerson, underscores the necessity of suspicion to the maintenance of upright faith. The only fideists, as he sees it, are those waiting for a miracle.

53 Heiko A. Oberman, "Headwaters of the Reformation: Initia Lutheri—Initita Reformationis," in *Dawn of the Reformation: Essays in Late Medieval and Early Reformation Thought* (Grand Rapids: William B. Eerdmans Publishing Company, 1992), 54–61.

54 Though, even here, Gerson emphasizes the way hope and faith look to the promise of God's salvific work. See: Mark S. Burrows, "Jean Gerson after Constance: 'Via Media et Regia' as a Revision of the Ockhamist Covenant," *Church History* 59, no. 4 (1990).

55 *Pace* Heiko A. Oberman, *The Harvest of Medieval Theology: Gabriel Biel and Late Medieval Nominalism* (Cambridge: Harvard University Press, 1963), 334. It should be noted, however, *pace* Erikson, that Gerson's faith does require critical analysis and suspicion in contradistinction to a facile fideism. Erik H. Erikson, *Young man Luther: A Study in Psychoanalysis and History* (New York: Norton, 1962), 184–85.

PART 2

The Reformation

CHAPTER 4

Early Modern Protestants and the "Hard Knots" of the Epistle to the Hebrews: A Study of Reformation Certainty

Ronald K. Rittgers

According to Susan Schreiner, the early modern era was marked by a "search for certitude," above all, religious certitude, and the Reformation played a crucial role in motivating this feverish quest.[1] Schreiner locates the origins for this search in the intellectual and spiritual concerns of the later Middle Ages, but she insists, "The era of the Reformation … transformed the [existing] questions about certitude into the central issue of the age."[2] The mutually exclusive truth claims of the various Protestant confessions, along with their shared critiques of many inherited certainties, presented a challenge to the possibility of religious truth itself. Protestant reformers developed various means for dealing with this threat, none of them finally satisfactory in Schreiner's mind.[3] Anxiety about certainty, doubt, and diabolical deception is, indeed, everywhere in the relevant sources, as are attempts to deal with this anxiety by appeals to the Holy Spirit and prophetic authority,[4] especially among Protestants. As Schreiner has shown, nowhere was this truer than in the realm of scriptural exegesis.[5] This chapter examines one very interesting attempt by early modern Protestants to deal with the issue of certainty in their interpretation of the Bible. It focuses on the exegesis of the Epistle to the Hebrews, especially its passages that seem to allow for the loss of salvation through serious sin (2:1–4, 6:4–12, 10:26–29, 12:16–17). Such passages posed important challenges to Protestant claims of salvific certitude and thus threatened to undermine the very foundation of the evangelical movement itself, which was based in large part on such claims.

1 Susan E. Schreiner, *Are You Alone Wise? The Search for Certainty in the Early Modern Era* (Oxford and New York: Oxford University Press, 2011), ix.

2 *Ibid.*, 15.

3 *Ibid.*, ix, 83, 302, 321.

4 See G. Sujin Pak, *The Reformation of Prophecy: Early Modern Interpretations of the Prophet and Old Testament Prophecy* (Oxford: Oxford University Press, 2018); and Ronald K. Rittgers, "The Word-Prophet Martin Luther," *The Sixteenth-Century Journal: The Journal of Early Modern Studies* XLVVIII/4 (Winter 2017 [2018]): 951–976.

5 Schreiner, *Are You Alone Wise*, 79–129.

 | DOI:10.1163/9789004527843_005

1 Hebrews Exegesis in the Reformation

The Epistle to the Hebrews was a pivotal text in the Reformation, and Protestant pastors and theologians expended a great deal of effort in their works to interpret it for their times and purposes.[6] For example, Protestants found in Hebrews important support for their critiques of the Catholic view of the priesthood and the Mass. They argued that because Hebrews teaches that Christ's sacrifice for sin was unique and singular in occurrence (9:24–28), Catholic priests could not offer Christ as a sacrifice for sin again and again in the Mass.[7] They also believed that Hebrews supported their insistence on the centrality of faith in the Christian life. Luther was especially impressed with Abraham, the man of faith (11:8), who "gave a supreme example of an evangelical life, because he left everything and followed the Lord. Preferring the Word of God to all else and loving it above all else, he was a stranger of his own accord and was subjected every hour to dangers of life and death."[8]

But Hebrews also presented difficulties to Protestant interpreters. In fact, according to Kenneth Hagen, for Protestants, "among the epistles, the one to the Hebrews was the most controversial."[9] For example, there were inter-Protestant debates about the twin issues of canonicity and authorship. Protestant interpreters were quite familiar with the ancient controversy about these matters.[10] Some, such as Zwingli, claimed Pauline authorship, but others, following the lead of Cajetan and Erasmus, rejected it, arguing for an alternative such as Apollos, or simply choosing to leave the issue of authorship open. Both Luther and Calvin denied Pauline authorship. No one questioned the canonical status of Hebrews, but Luther and some of his followers did consign the epistle to a

6 For a helpful overview of the exegesis of Hebrews in the Reformation period, see Craig R. Koester, *Hebrews: A New Translation with Introduction and Commentary*, The Anchor Bible, vol. 36 (New York, London, Toronto, Sydney, Auckland: Doubleday: 2001), 33–40. See also Ronald K. Rittgers, *Reformation Commentary on Scripture: Hebrews and James* (Downers Grove, Illinois: Intervarsity Press Academic, 2017), xliii–xlviii. Hereafter, RCS-HJ.

7 For the contemporary Catholic view of the matter, see Session 22, Council of Trent, chs. 1–2, in Norman P. Tanner, S.J., *Decrees of the Ecumenical Councils*, vol. 2: Trent to Vatican II (London and Washington, D.C.: Sheed & Ward and Georgetown University Press, 1990), 732–734.

8 *Hebräervorlesung/Lectures on Hebrews* (1517–1518), WA 57/3: 236.4–7; LW 29: 238. Unless otherwise noted, Luther quotations are from the LW.

9 Kenneth Hagen, *Hebrews Commenting from Erasmus to Bèze, 1516–1598* (Eugene, OR: Wipf and Stock, n.d.; originally published by JCB Mohr, 1981), 97.

10 On early Christian debates about the authorship and canonicity of Hebrews, see Koester, *Hebrews: A New Translation*, 19–24.

kind of New Testament apocrypha.[11] Luther placed it after 3 John, explaining, "we cannot put it on the same level with the apostolic epistles," yet he could still refer to it as "a marvelously fine epistle."[12] Protestants also debated the Christological statements in Hebrews, especially Christ's session at the right hand of the Father (1:13) and what it meant for the nature of His presence in the Lord's Supper.[13]

The most controversial aspect of Hebrews for Protestants was the passages noted above that appear to teach that salvation can be lost through serious sin. (These passages also troubled Erasmus, who based his argument against Pauline authorship in part on the way Hebrews denied repentance to apostates; he could not believe that the apostle who hoped for the salvation of an incestuous man in 1 Cor. 5:1–2 could adopt such a position.)[14] Luther observed in his typically expressive language, "there is a hard knot in the fact that in chapters 6[:4–6] and 10[:26–27] it flatly denies and forbids to sinners any repentance after baptism; and in chapter 12[:17] it says that Esau sought repentance and did not find it. This [seems, as it stands, to be] contrary to all the gospels and to St. Paul's epistles; and although one might venture an interpretation (*eyn glos*) of it,[15] the words are so clear that I do not know whether that would be sufficient."[16]

Such passages in Hebrews posed a direct threat to the assurance of salvation that Protestants believed they had discovered in justification by faith alone. Protestant theologians thought they were delivering their contemporaries from a false and unbiblical understanding of salvation that provided no enduring assurance of forgiveness, because it was based on the uncertain foundation of "man-made" doctrine and human good works, rather than on the solid foundation of the divine promises of unconditional forgiveness and grace in the Word. These promises were to be believed by faith, itself a divine gift of the Word. Protestants argued that "works-righteousness" necessarily produced great anxiety in the hearts of the faithful, because one could never be sure if one had done enough to placate the divine Judge. By way of contrast, in the eyes of most Protestants, a truly biblical salvation was a secure salvation, because

---

11 Ibid., 35–36.

12 "Die Epistle an die Ebreer"/"Preface to the Epistle to the Hebrews," (1522/46), WA DB 7:344.20; LW 35:395. Cited in Koester, *Hebrews: A New Translation*, 35–36.

13 See RCS-HJ, 26–27.

14 See Koester, *Hebrews: A New Translation*, 34.

15 Luther appears to have had Heb. 12:17 in view here.

16 "Die Epistle an die Ebreer"/"Preface to the Epistle to the Hebrews," (1522/46), WA DB 7:344.13–17 [1522 edition]/7:345.13–17 [1546 edition]; LW 35:394–5. The LW includes additions to the 1546 section in brackets.

it rested entirely on God's character and agency and not at all on human character and agency. Thus, for most Protestants, an uncertain salvation was an unbiblical salvation that directly contradicted their most cherished theological and pastoral convictions.[17]

Yet Protestants also saw Scripture as the ultimate authority in matters of doctrine and practice, and so when portions of it—such as the passages in Hebrews under consideration here—appeared to challenge their central beliefs, they faced a real crisis. How could they claim against "papists" to base their beliefs on divine revelation in the Word, if Scripture opposed foundational aspects of their teaching? For Protestants, salvific certitude rested upon another certitude, namely, their confidence in the clear teaching of Scripture on matters of salvation. If this teaching was not clear, or if it contradicted their understanding of salvation, the threat to their overall certitude was potentially lethal.

2 Ancient and Modern Rigorist Interpretations

Early Protestants were by no means the first Christians to wrestle with these difficult passages in Hebrews.[18] Adherents of the third-century Novatian movement cited them to argue against the possibility of repentance after serious post-baptismal sin, reflecting a rigorist position that had precedents in the second century, if not earlier. Novatian (d. 257–58) was a Roman presbyter and then rival bishop of Rome who argued for this position following the Decian persecution (AD 249–250), in which a number of Christians apostatized. Owing to the efforts of Cornelius, bishop of Rome, and Cyprian, bishop of Carthage, Novatian's rigorist views were eventually deemed heretical and the lapsed were permitted to return to Communion after penitence. A similar conclusion

17 On the importance of certainty of salvation in the Reformation movement, see Robert J. Bast, ed., *The Reformation of Faith in the Context of Late Medieval Theology and Piety: Essays by Berndt Hamm* (Leiden and Boston: Brill, 2004), 200–201. For Hamm's larger discussion of "normative centering" in the later Middle Ages and Reformation period and how concerns for certainty were central in it, see 1–49.

18 For a brief overview of early Christian debates about Hebrews, including its statements about apostasy, see Koester, *Hebrews: A New Translation*, 19–24; and Erik M. Heen and Philip D. W. Krey, eds., *Ancient Christian Commentary on Scripture, New Testament, vol. X, Hebrews* (Downers Grove, Illinois: InterVarsity Press, 2005), xvii–xxvi (especially xvii), 83–4. For a brief discussion of attitudes toward post-baptismal repentance in the early and medieval church, see Ronald K. Rittgers, *The Reformation of the Keys: Confession, Conscience, and Authority in Sixteenth-Century Germany* (Cambridge, Mass.: Harvard University Press, 2004), 29–30. The following discussion is based on these sources.

emerged in the wake of the later and much more widespread Donatist movement of the fourth and fifth centuries. The Early Church generally interpreted Hebrews to forbid rebaptism but not repentance after serious sin, provided the lapsed were penitent, a position that contributed to the admission of the book into the canon.[19] Medieval exegetes followed this ancient tradition, interpreting Hebrews to prohibit rebaptism but to allow that impenitent Christians could permanently fall from grace.[20]

It is important to note that leading modern biblical scholars support the early sterner interpretations of the troubling texts, although they do not think this means that the author of the book was a thoroughgoing rigorist. Commenting on 6:4–8, Harold Attridge writes, "While for apostates there is no hope, our author expresses confidence in his addressees that they will not fall away."[21] A little later, Attridge expands, stressing that it is important to be clear on the purpose of this passage:

> There is no indication that apostates have any hope of redemption. The stance is a rigorous one, but its presuppositions are not unique in the early church. Yet, on the other hand, there is no formulation of a general or carefully considered doctrinal position on the impossibility of post-baptismal repentance. While the rigorous attitude that our author represents lies behind the controversies on the subject of repentance in the early church, he is not addressing systematically the problem of penitential discipline. His aims are rhetorical and the accent in his treatment falls on the second, more hopeful, part of the exhortation [cf. 6:9].[22]

Attridge sees those who are in danger of lapsing as full members of the Christian community—they are not quasi-Christians—and the sin of which they are guilty is "clearly the extreme sin of apostasy." Attridge also does not see a prohibition of rebaptism in this and similar passages in Hebrews; at least he does

---

19 Koester, *Hebrews: A New Translation*, 318.

20 See *Glossa Ordinaria*, "Epistola ad Hebraeos," PL 114, Cols. 0646C, 0653C–D; *Saint Thomas Aquinas, Commentary on the Letter of Saint Paul to the Hebrews*, trans. F. R. Larcher, O.P., eds., J. Mortensen and E. Alarcón, Latin/English Edition of the Works of St. Thomas Aquinas, vol. 41 (Lander, Wyoming: The Aquinas Institute for the Study of Sacred Doctrine, 2012), 46 (paragraph 91), 128–29 (paragraph 291), 224 (paragraph 516); and Nicolaus of Lyra, *Postilla super totam Bibliam* (1488), http://www.umilta.net/NL5.pdf, 182/319 and 194/319 [=pdf page numbers].

21 Harold W. Attridge, *The Epistle to the Hebrews: A Commentary on the Epistle to the Hebrews*, edited by Helmut Koester, Hermeneia—A Critical and Historical Commentary on the Bible (Philadelphia: Fortress Press, 1989), 166.

22 *Ibid.*, 167.

not want to limit these passages to such a prohibition. According to Attridge, the author simply could not conceive of how someone who had rejected Christ, the only and decisive sacrifice for sin, could be restored to repentance.[23]

William Lane largely agrees with Attridge. In 6:4, he maintains that the danger of apostasy—of a "decisive moment of commitment to apostasy"—is real and not merely hypothetical; the passage should also not be limited to considerations of rebaptism.[24] Lane refers to 6:4–6 as a "stern warning" but says the author is finally "positive" in outlook, hoping for better from his audience.[25] Lane interprets 10:26–27 along similar lines.[26] Craig Koester is of the same mind. He insists that in 6:4 "impossible" means impossible and describes the entire passage as presenting an "uncompromising warning" against the very real dangers that apostasy presents to the Christian.[27]

As we will see, for theological, exegetical, and, especially, pastoral reasons, most early Protestants looked for alternatives to such rigorist understandings of the difficult passages in Hebrews. As we will also see, when Protestants attempted to undo the "hard knots" of the Epistle to the Hebrews, important exegetical differences emerged between them, which reflected key theological differences among Protestants. It will therefore be helpful to consider their exegesis of the difficult passages in Hebrews by confession: Lutheran, Reformed Protestant, and Radical (i.e., Anabaptist and Spiritualist).

3 The "Hard Knots": Hebrews 2:1–4

In their wrestling with Heb. 2:1–4, a number of Protestant commentators seized on the nautical image suggested by the Greek term *pararuōmen* (drift away) in 2:1,[28] urging spiritual vigilance on their readers and auditors, even as they sought to assure them of divine mercy. For example, in his commentary on Hebrews, the Lutheran Lucas Osiander (1534–1604), a pastor and court preacher in Stuttgart, remarks,

---

23 See Attridge's helpful "Excursus: The Impossibility of Repentance for Apostates," *ibid.*, 168–69 (quotation, 169).

24 William L. Lane, *Word Biblical Commentary*, vol. 47a, *Hebrews 1–8* (Dallas, Texas: Word Books, Publisher, 1991), 142. There is also a second volume: Lane, *Word Biblical Commentary*, vol. 47b, *Hebrews 9–13* (Dallas, Texas: Word Books, Publisher, 1991).

25 Lane, *Hebrews 1–8*, 145.

26 Lane, *Hebrews 9–13*, 291.

27 Koester, *Hebrews: A New Translation*, 318.

28 See Attridge, *The Epistle to the Hebrews*, 64; and Lane, *Hebrews 1–8*, 35. The Latin term *pereffluamus* (Vulgate), which was also in the minds of Protestant exegetes, similarly connotes "drifting away" or "flowing through," but also "to forget."

> And the similtude has been adduced of a human being who has fallen into a swift stream and is snatched away by the strength of the stream [and who] soon is about to perish ... [H]elpers go before to the bank in the lower part of the stream, and they stretch out helping hands to that one, but he himself, as he flows by, does not give heed to them, and so perishes in the stream. Thus, the Lord by the ministry of the gospel longs to help sinners who are in danger with respect to their eternal salvation. But many neglect the gracious offer and by their own guilt flow past the gate of salvation, where they would have been able to be extracted and kept if they had wanted. Therefore, let us embrace with great gratitude the salvation that has been offered, lest we also, whether through errors or pleasures and the cares of this sunken world, flow past and fall away from the heavenly inheritance.[29]

Osiander here appears to allow for the possibility that baptized Christians can drift away from salvation. There is not much human agency in his comment—the lost simply "flow past the gate of salvation," rendered incapable by the temptations of the flesh and the world of embracing or being embraced by the Lord's helping hand—but it does seem that Christians have some minimal role to play in responding to divine grace. Osiander says that neglectful Christians could have been extracted from the stream "if they had wanted." His comments also seem to amount to more than a mere threat or preaching of the law. Despite the Lutheran monergistic understanding of salvation, many Lutheran theologians said much the same thing in other places. Elsewhere, I have argued that, in their works of consolation, sixteenth-century Lutherans could be "limited synergists" when it came to sanctification, but certainly not with respect to justification. Owing to their belief in the potentially overpowering force of the world, the flesh, and the devil, and motivated in large part by their adherence to the law-gospel dialectic and its appreciation for the ferocious strength of sin, Lutheran theologians took the threat of drifting away from salvation seriously and therefore urged their contemporaries to active vigilance.[30] One can find a similar emphasis in some early Reformed Protestant theologians.

---

29 Lucas Osiander, *Epistola ad Hebraeos*, ... Gruppenbachius, 1584, 11–12 (digital copy online at books.google.com); RCS-HJ, 29. Unless otherwise noted, I have followed the RCS-HJ translations or updated English versions throughout.

30 See Ronald K. Rittgers, *The Reformation of Suffering: Pastoral Theology and Lay Piety in Late Medieval and Early Modern Germany* (Oxford and New York: Oxford University Press, 2012), 197–99 (quotation, 199). See also Article XII of the Augsburg Confession in Robert Kolb and Timothy J. Wengert, eds., *The Book of Concord: The Confessions of the Evangelical Lutheran Church* (Minneapolis: Fortress Press, 2000), 44.

In his exegesis of 2:1, the Swiss-German reformer and theologian of Basel, Johannes Oecolampadius (1482–1531), offered an interpretation akin to Osiander's, although it predated the Lutheran's by fifty years. The Basel theologian opines,

> But note the emphasis of the words, for he says, "If we neglect"—*amelēsantes*—that is, if we should have transgressed in the smallest way, we will be punished heavily, just like those who did not believe the words of the angels. And what offense is smaller than to be neglectful? Who then will absolve himself? Therefore, there is need for great zeal among Christians. Anyone who has not fulfilled the law has an escape with Christ the mediator; but how will anyone restore himself who neglects Christ and the word of faith? Whom else will he invoke as mediator?[31]

"Great zeal" was required on the part of Christians lest they neglect the Word and thus endanger their salvation. Like Osiander, Oecolampadius does not specify here how such neglect and its dire consequences could take place, only that it can.

Similarly to Osiander, the puritan divine and sometime divinity reader at St. Paul's in London, Edward Dering (ca. 1540–1576), explored the watery imagery of 2:1, but took a rather different approach. He explains,

> After this, the Apostle adds his reason to persuade us to this special carefulness above all other people, to hearken to the voice of Christ; and that is, of the peril that ensues, "lest" (he says) "we run out" [i.e., "lest we drift away"]. The Apostle uses a metaphor, taken of old tubes, which run out at the joints, and can hold no liquor. In such a phrase of speech one says of himself: "I am full of crevasses or little holes, and I flow out on this side and on that," meaning thereby, that every vain thing which he heard, he would blab it out. So we, if we take into us the sweet wine of the word of Christ, as into old bottles and broken vessels, that it run out again, we become then altogether unprofitable, all goodness falls away, and we are as water poured upon the ground.[32]

---

31 Johannes Oecolampadius, *In Epistolam ad Hebraeos Explanationes* ... Strasbourg, Mathias Apiarius, 1534, 23v–24r (digital copy online at books.google.com); RCS-HJ, 30.

32 Edward Dering, *27 Lectures or Readings on the Epistle to the Hebrews*, in *M. Derings workes. More at large then euer hath heere-to-fore been printed in any one volume*, London, 1590, F5 v–F6 r (digital copy online at books.google.com); RCS-HJ, 28–29. Cardinal Cajetan (Thomas de Vio) had also referred to "cracked vessels that leak" in his comments on Heb. 2:1. See "In Epistolam ad Hebraeos commentarii," in *Epistolae Pavli et aliorvm*

Dering does not explain here how a Christian could become a leaky tube, but, like Osiander and Oecolampadius, he seems to allow for the complete loss of living water or divine wine (i.e., grace). Still, we should be careful about pushing this metaphor too far, especially in light of what Dering says about the other "hard knots" in Hebrews (see below). Dering's mention of hearing the "sweet word of Christ" is also significant, as Reformed Protestants tended to relate this warning in Hebrews (2:1) to the importance of attending closely to sermons, the most important way of avoiding such unwanted spiritual porosity.

The English theologian and minister at East Bergholt in Suffolk, William Jones (1561–1636), reflected this theme. He comments on 2:1, "It is said of the people, that they hung on Christ, watching the words that came from his mouth, ready to receive them before they came: so with all care and diligence we must hang on the Preacher, mark his words, and be ready to receive them into our ears and hearts, even before they are delivered, so eager should we be of the Word."[33] Jones goes on to explain, "We must let the Word slip at no time though we have never such weighty business: One thing is necessary. This one necessary thing is to be preferred before all others: Never let a sermon slip from you without some profit."[34] Such comments greatly extolled the office and the responsibility of the Protestant preacher, who served as the mouthpiece for Christ in Protestant theology.[35]

4 The "Hard Knots": Hebrews 6:4–12

Undoing the hard knot of Heb. 6:4–12 was especially challenging for many Protestant exegetes, who struggled with its assertion in v. 4 that it is "impossible" (*adunaton*) to restore to repentance those who have fallen away. Whereas the Catholic Cajetan (1469–1534) reflected the traditional position, that a prohibition of rebaptism was in view in this passage (and also in 10:26–29), most Protestants opted for other interpretations.[36] Luther opposed those who, in

---

apostolorvm ad graecam veritatem castigatae, Venice: Luca-Antonio Giunta, 1531, 158 v (digital copy online at www.e-rara.ch); RCS-HJ, 28. Dering may well have been familiar with Cajetan's work.

33 William Jones, *A Commentary upon the Epistles of St Paul to Philemon and the Hebrewes …*, London, 1636, 78 (digital copy online at books.google.com); RCS-HJ, 29.

34 *Ibid.*, 79; RCS-HJ, 29.

35 See Ronald K. Rittgers, "Pastoral Theology and Preaching," in K. Appold and N. Minnich, eds., *The Cambridge History of Reformation Theology* (Cambridge University Press, forthcoming).

36 Cajetan, "In Epistolam ad Hebraeos commentarii," 162 r, 167 r; RCS-HJ, 87, 145.

an effort to avoid the error of the Novatians, sought to replace "impossible" of the Vulgate (*impossibile*) with "difficult" (*difficule*). He argues, "But because it is dangerous to twist clear words of Scripture into a different meaning, one should not readily permit this, lest in the end the authority of all Scripture vacillate, except where the context demands it." Luther insisted, based on other passages of Scripture (2 Cor. 12:21–22, 1 Cor. 5:5, 1 Tim. 3:5, 2 Tim. 2:25, Titus 1:7, Titus 3:10, the entirety of Galatians), that there is repentance for those who fall into sin, including the sin of unbelief. He also cited the examples of the adulterous and murderous David, the fratricidal brothers of Joseph, and the Christ-denying Peter. According to Luther, a very particular (and very evangelical) sin is in view in this section of Hebrews:

> Therefore one must understand that in this passage the apostle is speaking about the falling of faith into unbelief, namely, because of their opinion that they can be saved without Christ by their own righteousness, which is altogether impossible. For this reason he says at the beginning (6:1) that he will omit the words about faith and the elementary doctrines of Christ. This means that it is "impossible" for him to be restored who at one time began with Christ and, after backsliding, seeks someone else.

The cause for lapse here is the sinner's perceived ability to be able to save himself through his own efforts instead of relying fully on Christ. In other words, in Luther's mind, the unforgivable sin is rejection of justification by faith alone, although he does not describe how this could actually happen for someone who "began with Christ." Luther concedes that the writer of Hebrews speaks harshly in this passage, but he says the author does so because the early church needed to protect the "newly planted faith" that was still fragile at this stage in its development.[37]

Luther's colleague at the University of Wittenberg, Johannes Bugenhagen (1485–1558), emphasized that forgiveness of sin, including serious sin, is possible according to Scripture. He thought there was support for this view throughout Hebrews, especially its references to Christ as a high priest (7:25, 9:24).[38] In order to understand the seemingly contrary position in Heb. 6:4–6, he compared it to discussions of the sin unto death in 1 John 5:16–17 and the

37 *Hebräervorlesung/Lectures on Hebrews* (1517–1518), WA 57: 181.9–182.24; LW 29: 181–183. In his *Lectures on Hebrews*, Luther attributed the epistle to the Apostle Paul, a position he would later revise.

38 Johannes Bugenhagen, *Annotationes ... in epistolas Pauli ad ... Hebraeos*. Strasbourg: Johann Knobloch, 1525, 147 r–v [images 327–28] (digital copy online at www.gateway-bayern.de); RCS-HJ, 87–88.

unforgiveable sin in Mark 3:29. Regarding the fatal sin in view in all three passages, Bugenhagen concludes,

> It happens when the truth which God has revealed is evident, so that you are overcome within your very being in your heart and conscience, because it is the way things really are, and it cannot be otherwise. And nevertheless you dare to speak impiously, and contend to the contrary that this is not true, it is not from God, it is perverse, it is from the Devil. By this horrible blasphemy you show no reverence for the sword of the Lord who testifies to the contrary, as though it were lawful for someone like you to fight deliberately against God without fear of punishment. You can see this in Mark 3[:22–30], where in violation of conscience they attributed the manifest work of God to Beelzebub. This is why after Christ's statement, "Whoever blasphemes against the Holy Spirit will not be forgiven in eternity," the Evangelist adds, "because they were saying, 'He has an unclean spirit.'"

Bugenhagen continues by stressing that Christians can commit this unforgivable sin:

> But if Christ said this regarding others who were ungodly and refused to receive the truth, but fought against something so manifest that they could not deny it, why do we accuse this our author because he condemns those who were illuminated not only in external words or external miracles, but inwardly in the heart, who had tasted the heavenly gift, received the Holy Spirit, and tasted the goodness of the word of God, and the influences and power of the kingdom of God, and nevertheless fall away from all these things and blaspheme against the grace which had been made evident by so much testimony from the Spirit?[39]

Loss of salvation for the baptized is clearly possible for Bugenhagen.

The Danish Lutheran theologian, Niels Hemmingsen (1513–1600), who taught for many years at the University of Copenhagen, averred that Heb. 6:4–6 refers not to a particular lapse but to a universal one: "The universal lapse is not simply to transgress against one or many or even all the commandments of the Decalogue; rather, it is when one who has known Christ and his gospel renounces it utterly. Such a person not only does not believe in Christ any longer, but condemns him, is full of anger against him, mocks him, and becomes

39 *Ibid.*, 147v–148r [images 328–29]; RCS-HJ, 86–87.

a tyrant against him, as the Pharisees and Julian the Apostate did."[40] As with Luther and Bugenhagen, Hemmingsen allows for someone who once believed in Christ to commit this universal lapse and forfeit salvation.[41]

Reformed Protestant exegetes were far less willing than their Lutheran counterparts to apply Heb. 6:4–6 to Christians, at least not to true Christians, which in their minds meant the elect. Zwingli argues that it is not possible for "a believer and lover of true godliness to depart from the faith. For if one did fall away, it would show that it was a counterfeit and hypocritical faith." Thus, Zwingli concludes that the author of Hebrews—in his mind, Paul—was either addressing false Christians or speaking hyperbolically to true Christians in this passage: "Thus by this exaggeration Paul not only intends to divert us from sins, but to deter us from falling back into our original blindness or wickedness."[42]

According to Calvin, the reprobate are clearly in view in this passage. Such people can taste heavenly things, but they are not true members of Christ's flock.[43] Calvin acknowledged how the Novatian heresy had turned many in the early church against Hebrews, but he thought this was a mistake, for when properly understood, he saw nothing in the epistle that threatened the gospel's offer of mercy to sinners. "The knot of the question," according to him, "is in the words 'fall away.'" Similarly to Hemmingsen, who wrote after Calvin and therefore may have been influenced by him, Calvin taught a twofold lapse, particular and general: the former referred to specific sins, such as theft, murder, or adultery; the latter, to "a total defection or falling away from the gospel, when a sinner offends not God in some one thing, but entirely renounces his grace." According to Calvin, the author of Hebrews mentions apostasy here not because it is a possibility for the elect: "The elect are also beyond the danger of finally falling away." Rather, the author wishes to keep the elect "on their guard"

---

40 Niels Hemmingsen, *Commentaria In Omnes Epistolas Apostolorvm ... et In Eam Qvae ad Hebraeos inscribitur ...* Leipzig: Ernst Schneider, Andreas aus Ortrant und Vögelin, 1571, 859 [image 883] (digital copy online at www.gateway-bayern.de); RCS-HJ, 83.

41 Veit Dietrich (1506–1549), the Lutheran preacher in Nürnberg, held the same view (see RCS-HJ, 89), as did Johann Gerhard (1582–1637), the Lutheran theologian at Jena. See *Johann Gerhard, Theological Commonplaces, VIII–XI: On Creation and Angels, On Providence, On Election and Reprobation, and On the Image of God in Man Before the Fall,* trans., Richard J. Dinda, ed., Benjamin T. G. Mayes and Joshua J. Hayes (St. Louis: Concordia Publishing House, 2013), 166 (paragraph 113).

42 Ulrich Zwingli, *In Evangelicam Historiam ... Adiecta est Epistola Pauli ad Hebraeos ...*, edited by Leo Jud and Kaspar Megander, Zurich: Christoph Froschouer, 1539, 571–72 (digital copy online at books.google.com); RCS-HJ, 85–86.

43 Inst. 3.2.11, 3.3.21, 3.3.23.

and by this "bridle" to promote "fear and humility" in them and thus to avoid "foolish confidence."[44]

Edward Dering followed suit. For him, "it does not matter at all what this great and heinous sin should be of which the Apostle says, one can never repent of it. Whatever it is, it is none of ours." It relates only to those who despise knowledge of Christ, condemn the cross, and make the world their God. Dering insists, "I do not say this out of my own head, but by good warrant of the Apostle himself, and by the word of the Holy Spirit, for after this heavy threatening, does not the Apostle say to them immediately [6:9–12], and does he not say it to us this day, that because we have loved God's saints and have rejoiced to glorify his name, our state is faster knit unto salvation, and these heavy things shall never come near to us? ... And thus far the purpose of the Apostle has been to confirm that though we should fall through many infirmities, yet we can never fall away."[45] A little later, Dering asserts, "This then is the sin against the Holy Spirit; it is a continual apostasy and a general falling from God." It is the sin committed by Satan himself, and also by Cain, the scribes and the pharisees, and the Roman emperor, Julian the Apostate. Dering again explains, "This sin is a mocking and scoffing at the Son of God; it is not a weeping and mourning, lest you should fall into it."[46] Clearly, he was seeking to deliver the devout among his hearers from worry about committing this unforgiveable sin.[47] The worry itself was the sign that the dire warnings of this passage did not apply to them. The opposite possibility—that the passage did apply to true Christians—was apparently too unsettling for Reformed Protestants to entertain as it threatened their sense of salvific certainty.

While both Lutherans and Reformed Protestants believed in predestination and the perseverance of the saints, only the latter did so in a way that precluded the possibility of the elect falling from grace. This difference may be attributed to a number of factors, including divergent understandings of predestination itself and its place in the *ordo salutis*, along with the alternative views of grace and salvific certainty that informed and followed from these

---

44 John Calvin, *Commentaries on the Epistle of Paul the Apostle to the Hebrews* (1549), translated and edited by John Owen, in the Calvin Translation Society [hereafter CTS] edition of *Calvin's Commentaries*, 46 vols., Edinburg, 1843–1855, here vol. 40 (1853), pp. 37–40 (reprinted 2005 by Baker Books, Grand Rapids, Michigan; digital copy online at www.ccel.org); RCS-HJ, 83–84.

45 Dering, *27 Lectures or Readings on the Epistle to the Hebrews*, Cc r–Cc2 r; RCS-HJ, 82.

46 *Ibid.*, Cc 7 v–Cc 8 r; RCS-HJ, 83.

47 William Jones had a similar purpose in his exegesis of this passage. See RCS-HJ, 88.

respective understandings.[48] Such differences help to explain why Lutherans and Reformed Protestants sought to unravel the hard knot of Heb. 6:4–12 as they did.

The Anabaptist leader Dirk Philipps (1504–1568), who ministered in northern Germany and the Netherlands, saw no need to try to untie this hard knot, as his other Protestant contemporaries did, for he took it at face value: Christians who squandered divine grace and produced no fruit but lived according to the flesh would suffer eternal flames. Philipps asserts, "This will happen to all false Christians, who have fallen away from the truth (which they have once known and received)." Christ had commanded His followers to shun such "false brothers" who persist in sin: "For he who wishes to reach life eternal with Christ must love him with true faith, cleave to him, suffer and die with him, i.e., to be with him in one spirit, and to be one body with his church, persevering therein perpetually."[49] Those who have begun with Christ and who then arrogantly reject Him, refusing to bear the cross, especially the cross of persecution, would be consigned to hell; there was no possibility of repentance for them. Like many Anabaptists, Philipps was squarely in the rigorist camp.[50]

5 The "Hard Knots": Hebrews 10:26–29

We have already seen how pastoral concerns could inform the Protestant exegesis of the "hard knots" in Hebrews. These concerns are especially evident in the way many interpreted Heb. 10:26–29. Luther understood the passage along the same lines as he did 6:4–6, namely, as a warning against works righteousness or seeking salvation in oneself rather than in Christ,[51] an interpretation shared by Bugenhagen. But Bugenhagen also went to great lengths to comfort those sensitive Christians whom he thought were inclined to despair at this

48 For the Reformed Protestant perspective, see the "Fifth Head of Doctrine: Of the Perseverance of the Saints," in the Canons of the Synod of Dort (1618–19), digital copy online at www.ccel.org. For the Latin and Dutch text, see J. N. Bakhuizen van den Brink ed., *De Nederlandse belijdenisgeschriften in Authentieke Teksten* (Amsterdam: Bolland, 1976), 266–77. For the Lutheran perspective, see "The Solid Declaration of the Formula of Concord," art. xi, paragraphs 13, 20, 23, 26, 28, 32, 33, 42, 52, and 83, in Kolb and Wengert, *The Book of Concord*, 647–48. See also, *Johann Gerhard, Theological Commonplaces*, 200 (paragraph 152, II), cf. 207 (paragraph 161), and 217 (paragraph 176).

49 "Evangelical Excommunication," (1567) in Cornelius J. Dyck, trans. and ed., *The Writings of Dirk Philips, 1504–1568*, (Scottdale, PA; Herald Press, 1992), 596; RCS-HJ, 82.

50 See George Huntston Williams, *The Radical Reformation*, third edition (Kirksville, Missouri: Truman State University Press, 2000), 84, 242, 418.

51 *Hebräervorlesung/Lectures on Hebrews* (1517–1518), WA 57: 182.13–20; LW 29: 182–83.

passage's warning about there no longer being a sacrifice for sin for those who sin deliberately. While Lutherans could allow for the loss of salvation, they were keenly interested in assuring their contemporaries of divine mercy and grace. Bugenhagen writes, contrasting the plight of the godly with the ungodly, "But if you are in Christ, no matter how great a sinner you are, now you have a sacrifice and you cannot be other than pleasing to God for the sake of Christ, with whom he is well-pleased, for the sake of this High Priest, who always stands for us before the Father, so that he may intercede for us." Bugenhagen continues, "Take this description of the people of whom he speaks as referring, surely, to those who blaspheme the Gospel and Christian truth, not to those sinners who are indeed in Christ, for what person is there upon the earth who does not sin?" Finally, in a pointed effort to comfort the faithful, he writes, having just condemned those who reject Christ and rely on their own works, "But since I should not overlook how easily the delicate and weak consciences of some people are injured and driven to despair, I assert that whoever returns to God from the heart has the certain testimony that never, as God preserves him, will he be liable to this sentence, even when he may seem to have fallen away. For those who actually do fall away can never recover. For they are blinded, either by open wickedness or feigned righteousness, just as we see the Jews perish."[52] Here Bugenhagen clearly seeks to protect the sense of salvific security that he and his fellow Lutherans thought was so important to the consolation they offered to their contemporaries.

Niels Hemmingsen also displayed pastoral concerns in his exegesis of this hard knot, offering a novel interpretation of the specific sin in view. After observing that it is essential to remain within the church, for outside the church there is no sacrifice for sin, the Danish Lutheran explains, "For here the apostle is not speaking about just any kind of lapse or about voluntary sin, but only about those who, having known this Priest, repudiate Christ and exclude themselves from the church and from the priesthood of Christ, renouncing all the benefits of Christ." Hemmingsen historicizes this lapse, taking it to refer specifically to Jewish Christians in the writer's context who renounced Christ because they did not want Gentiles to share in the gospel. Hemmingsen then seeks to reassure his readers: "But those who remain in the church, although they often fall, whether knowingly or unknowingly, nevertheless, when they repent, they are most certainly received in grace." Defection from the church is possible for Christians, something Hemmingsen makes clear. But his primary

52 Bugenhagen, *Annotationes*, 148 v–149 r; RCS-HJ, 144.

concern is to comfort his readers lest they think this passage applies directly to them in their daily struggle with sin.[53]

Turning to Reformed Protestant interpretation of this hard knot, as we have seen in other Protestant exegetes, Zwingli argued that Paul was referring to a very specific sin in this passage, not to any and every sin: "For there is no sin, no matter what kind of deliberation or brashness were involved in its commission, which would not encounter grace and mercy in the sight of God, if only the transgressor were to repent. Therefore, this is said with reference to the sin against the Holy Spirit, which is nothing else than brazenly and abominably despising, spurning, rejecting, and opposing the truth when it is fully understood." The person who commits this sin is probably not a true Christian in Zwingli's mind, but the person does know the truth of the gospel, which he or she then spurns. Similarly to Luther, Zwingli has in mind those who rely on "papistical satisfactions" rather than on the sacrifice of Christ for forgiveness of sin.[54]

Heinrich Bullinger (1504–75), Zwingli's successor in Zurich, also limited the sin in view in Heb. 10:26 to the intentional suppression of the truth of the gospel, that is, of Christ's sacrifice for sin, which the sinner knows to be the only source of forgiveness. Bullinger seeks to assure his readers, "we must understand that the people who 'sin deliberately' are not those who sin as a result of any weakness, or who succumb to the desires of the flesh."[55] One finds the same in Calvin. He describes this unforgivable sin as "complete turning away from God and, so to speak, apostasy of the whole man."[56] As in 6:4–6, Calvin thinks only the reprobate are capable of this sin, only one who is "possessed by the devil."[57]

Oecolampadius shared the concern of Protestant interpreters to comfort sensitive consciences and also to argue for the canonicity of Hebrews against those who had been tempted to reject it based on false understandings of its difficult passages. Oecolampadius, however, offered a unique exegesis of the author's intent in 10:26–27:

---

53 Hemmingsen, *Commentaria*, 886; RCS-HJ, 146–47. Lucas Osiander shared the same concerns. See RCS-HJ, 148.

54 Zwingli, *In Evangelicam Historiam*, 580; RCS-HJ, 145.

55 Heinrich Bullinger, *In piam et eruditam Pauli ad Hebraeos epistolam ...*, Christoph Froschauer, Zurich, 1532, 110 r [image 239] (digital copy online at www.e-rara.ch); RCS-HJ, 145.

56 Inst., 3.3.23.

57 Inst., 3.3.21. One finds the same perspective in William Jones: see RCS-HJ, 147.

> But this, in brief, is what he means to say: henceforth, Christ will not come again to save, but to judge. By these words he spurs into action the reluctant and the idle. But he does not at all say, "No opportunity for repentance is left once the truth is known," but, "No other sacrifice for sins is left"; take note of this! For no one else after Christ may be expected as redeemer and savior.[58]

For the Basel theologian, the purpose of the passage is to encourage greater faithfulness in Christians, not to deny them divine mercy when they sin.

We find a different approach to this challenging passage in the northern German Anabaptist leader, Melchior Hoffman (1495?–1543). He referenced Heb. 10:26–27 in the context of railing against those who teach the bondage of the post-lapsarian will to sin, which in his mind made God the author of sin, a terrible blasphemy. Hoffman asserts, no doubt with Lutherans and Reformed Protestants in mind,

> Of all such intentional sins [e.g., blasphemy] against the High Holy Spirit of God, the Lord Jesus Christ says [Mark 3:29] that neither now nor in the next world nor in all eternity can they ever attain forgiveness. Saint Paul also says the same in Hebrews [10:26 f.], namely, that no more sacrifice remains over for such sins but rather fearful revenge and ordeal of fiery indignation. In this manner God also speaks through Moses [Num. 25:8] that one shall without any mercy root out from the congregation all such willful sinners against the Spirit of God and shall accept for them no further sacrifices, for they will forever have no forgiveness.[59]

While Hoffman could allow readmission of sinners into the Christian community via repentance,[60] he at times promoted a more rigorist position that would allow no forgiveness for serious post-baptismal sin, as he took baptism—that is, rebaptism—to signal the death of the seed of sin within the Christian. As he puts it, "for he who has been born of God has the upper hand and victory, and therefore no sin can issue."[61] This position, which bordered on spiritual perfectionism, appears to have influenced the Radicals who took over the northern German city of Münster for a time (1534–35). According to

---

58 Oecolampadius, *In Epistolam ad Hebraeos Explanationes*, 113 r–v; RCS-HJ, 147–48.

59 Hoffman, "The Ordinance of God," in George H. Williams and Angel M. Megal, eds., *Spiritual and Anabaptist Writers* (Philadelphia: The Westminster Press, 1957) 199; RCS-HJ, 147.

60 Hoffman, "The Ordinance of God," 197.

61 *Ibid.*, 188 (cf. n. 12).

Obbe Philipps (1500–1568), the older brother of Dirk and leader of Anabaptism in the Netherlands, some of the Münsterites denied pardon for serious post-baptismal sin, operating with a rather broad definition of apostasy.[62]

6 The "Hard Knots": Hebrews 12:16–17

Commentary on the final hard knot is not as plentiful, but Protestants still had important things to say about the troubling case of Esau in Hebrews. Bugenhagen saw in this passage an important distinction between true and false penitence:

> The repentance and lamentation of Esau is properly understood as the repentance of the ungodly, which in the sight of God is no repentance at all if they only feel sorrow for their painful circumstances and the distress of their soul, into which they perceive they have fallen at present through the judgment of God, while, if they could be released from their distress, they would despise God forever. Esau's story openly teaches this very thing, for after he had wept before his father with great lamentation, he went out and, in pure contempt of his father, he took a third wife whom his father had never seen.[63]

True penitence was not such an easy matter, according to Bugenhagen. Viewed within the context of Catholic penitential theology, which allowed imperfect sorrow for sin (attrition) motivated by fear of punishment to suffice for forgiveness, his position could be seen as a rigorist one. Most late medieval Catholic theologians taught that priestly absolution could transform attrition into contrition—sorrow for sin motivated by the love of God—and thus merit divine mercy,[64] although there were limits to just how imperfect a sinner's sorrow could be and still qualify as acceptable attrition.[65] Still, Bugenhagen's rigorist position had a decisively Lutheran dimension to it, for he was not

62 Obbe Philipps, "A Confession," in Williams and Megal, *Spiritual and Anabaptist Writers*, 220.

63 Bugenhagen, *Annotationes*, 157v–158r; RCS-HJ, 177–78.

64 See Rittgers, *Reformation of the Keys*, 38–46.

65 Commenting on Heb. 12:16–17, Aquinas argued that Esau's sorrow was completely unacceptable because it was entirely motivated by anger at being rejected, as with those who were in hell. See *Aquinas, Commentary on the Letter of Saint Paul to the Hebrews*, 299 (paragraph 694).

advocating for greater moral exertion; rather, he stressed that true penitence was a "work of God" that could not be demanded but only humbly received.[66]

For his part, Bullinger taught that this passage did not actually address the matter of post-baptismal sin and therefore was not such a troubling text:

> For of course no one understands this as referring to repentance from sins, but rather to change of fortune. For it was not permissible for Esau to recover his birthright after he had once sold it with such carelessness. Therefore, those who argue from this passage whether repentance is denied to those who have fallen away undergo contortions uselessly. For *metanoia* in Greek is turning around and correcting, or rather changing any matter at all, not only in the sense of repentance which is in use among theologians. But we find no mention of the forgiveness of sins, but rather we speak of the right of primogeniture, or how great an evil it is to despise holy things.[67]

Oecolampadius agreed but offered a different interpretation: Esau represented those in hell upon whom the divine sentence of condemnation had already been pronounced and who were beyond salvation; had Esau repented from the heart before Isaac gave his blessing to Jacob, Esau would not have been rejected by God.[68]

7 Conclusion

Protestant interpreters of Hebrews viewed its challenging passages from the perspective of their respective confessions, which is not surprising. Lutherans could understand the unforgivable sin as rejection of justification by faith alone; Reformed Protestants frequently taught that only the reprobate—not the elect—could apostatize; and Anabaptists, whose exegesis largely agreed with ancient (and modern) rigorist views, sought to exclude all false Christians from their communities of pure apostolic Christianity. More surprising, and more significant, is how the concern for consolation, for comforting anxious consciences, shaped the Lutheran and Reformed Protestant engagement with

66 Bugenhagen, *Annotationes*, 157v–158r; RCS-HJ, 177–78. Luther had the same view, as did Catholic theologians such as Johann von Staupitz (ca. 1468–1524), Luther's spiritual mentor. See Rittgers, *Reformation of Suffering*, 102–103, and Rittgers, *Reformation of the Keys*, 49, respectively.

67 Bullinger, *In piam et eruditam Pauli ad Hebraeos epistolam*, 130r–v; RCS-HJ, 178.

68 Oecolampadius, *In Epistolam ad Hebraeos Explanationes*, 156r–157r; RCS-HJ, 178–79.

the troubling texts of Hebrews, although they went about providing this solace in different ways. Whereas the biblical passages seek to warn, Lutheran and Reformed Protestant exegetes, while sharing this concern, finally wished to console. In other words, many evangelical interpreters were first and foremost pastors who wanted to protect Christians from despair, especially the despair they believed that insecurity about salvation produced. Magisterial Protestants wanted to promote assurance of divine forgiveness and mercy among their contemporaries; they were interested in defending salvific certitude, which they took to be central to the evangelical movement itself.

Was this a futile effort, that is, was it simply part of the larger failure of Protestants to provide an adequate basis for religious certitude that Schreiner has asserted?[69] Schreiner's provocative argument is based on the fact of Protestant (and Catholic) bickering, backbiting, and bloodshed throughout the early modern period and also on normative claims she makes about the importance of finite human beings embracing the "ethic of incompleteness" as we seek to understand the divine.[70] This microcosmic study of Protestant biblical exegesis and the concern for salvific certainty that informed it obviously cannot speak to Schreiner's larger thesis about epistemological certainty as such in religious matters. Still, this study does provide compelling evidence for Schreiner's assertions about the abiding Protestant interest in certainty, at least among Lutheran and Reformed Protestant theologians when they thought believers' confidence in divine mercy and grace was under threat. Their interpretive choices were driven by the persistent concern to promote certitude of salvation. The sources under consideration here cannot tell us if common pastors and lay people shared this concern or not, as they consist mainly of scholarly commentaries on Hebrews that were directed to a learned audience.

Most surprising is how relatively conservative Lutherans and Reformed Protestants were in their interpretation of Hebrews. When viewed within the larger context of Christian reflection about the possibility of repentance for serious post-baptismal sin, with the notable exception of Anabaptists, Protestant interpreters were rather conventional in their conclusions, that is, they followed tradition in avoiding rigorist understandings of the difficult texts in Hebrews, although they did so in uniquely Protestant ways. Despite their significant theological differences with Catholic exegetes, including on the challenging passages in Hebrews, many Protestants exegetes still preserved the long-established trend of greatly restricting the application of these passages to the lives of Christians. This fact is indicative of some of the defining

69 Schreiner, *Are You Alone Wise*, ix.

70 *Ibid.*, 354.

tensions of the evangelical movement itself. The Protestant Reformation was a fascinating and perplexing amalgam of both thoroughly conventional and radically unconventional impulses, now complementing each other, now at complete loggerheads, a fact that helps to account for its incredible complexity, creativity, and dynamism. The Protestant Reformation is itself a hard knot that scholars will likely never fully undo, at least not with any final certainty.

Acknowledgement

For helpful comments and corrections, I am grateful to Scott Manetsch and to my former colleagues in the Theology Department of Valparaiso University.

CHAPTER 5

Melanchthon and the Utility of the Liberal Arts

Ralph Keen

1 Praeceptor as Founder

One of the products of late nineteenth-century investigation into German cultural and educational history was a quest for origins, specifically the native origins of German institutions. Karl Hartfelder in his 1890 study of late-medieval universities states that academies in the German-speaking territories were imitations (*Nachahmungen*) of foreign models.[1] Among the founders of a national system of gymnasia and studia in the early-modern period, Melanchthon stands out as a builder and reformer, and Hartfelder's major contribution to our understanding of German education was his study of Melanchthon's role as the Preceptor of Germany.[2]

In naming the Reformer the *praeceptor Germaniae*, Hartfelder designated Melanchthon the inaugurator of the educational tradition of Protestant Germany, a claim arguably more correct for the Gymnasium system than for the 19th-century university. (Hartfelder was himself a Gymnasium instructor.) From the perspective of institutional history, universities associated with Melanchthon stand out: Marburg, Jena, Königsberg, as well as Wittenberg itself. Few did more than Melanchthon in promoting the natural sciences and the classical canon. Although Melanchthon recognized the division of the sciences, he understood them as unified rather than distinct. The disciplines or *artes* were components of an integral whole, not mutually independent.

Institutional continuity notwithstanding, the Enlightenment or Humboldtian ideal of higher education renders questionable the claim that Melanchthon should be regarded as the founder of a tradition of learning that extended into modernity. The ideal of academic freedom, both as *Lehrfreiheit* and

1 Karl Hartfelder, "Der Zustand der deutschen Hochschulen am Ende des Mittelalters," *Historische Zeitschrift* 64 (1890), 50–107; here, p. 50.

2 Karl Hartfelder, *Philipp Melanchthon als Praeceptor Germaniae* (Berlin: Monumenta Germaniae Paedagogica, 1889; rpt. Nieuwkoop: De Graaf, 1971). The epithet had belonged to the Carolingian encyclopedist Rabanus Maurus. The title would be used frequently during the 1897 commemorations of his birth, and again on the 500th anniversary: Hans-Rüdiger Schwab, *Philipp Melanchthon, der lehrer Deutschlands: ein biographisches Lesebuch* (Munich: Deutscher Taschenbuch Verlag, 1997).

 | DOI:10.1163/9789004527843_006

Lernfreiheit, is a modern one and a conscious deviation from the premodern concept of education for the sake of particular ends. In the following discussion we wish to point to some passages in Melanchthon's work that identify the criterion determining the canon of subjects in the Melanchthonian program of education.

In the discussion that follows I offer an account of Melanchthon's work closely associated with the Humanist tradition. As a careful expositor of the ethical works of Aristotle and Cicero, Melanchthon occupies a place in a tradition of interpretation theologically independent of the evangelical movement originating in Wittenberg and elsewhere, some of whose leaders in turn viewed with skepticism claims that the classical tradition could be constructively fused with the truth revealed in scripture. Although Melanchthon's efforts in reviving the study of the classics have been associated with his insistence on the importance of clarity and rigor in language, little attention has been devoted to his understanding of the value of classical thought.[3] Closer study of Melanchthon's humanistic or ethical work reveals a nuanced and original construction which subordinates classical learning to evangelical dependence on scriptural revelation. In short, alongside the positive benefits that classical study yields, reading the moral tradition of pagan antiquity also reveals the limitations of reason while serving as a guide, a *paedagogus* to use Melanchthon's word, to revelation.

2 Common Themes in the Rhetoric of the Revival of Learning

The recovery of classical study in Northern Europe at the end of the fifteenth century was heralded in writings both protreptic and encomiastic intended to declare that the dawn of a new era would be shaped by the literature of an earlier one. Denunciations of Scholastic barbarism, both in Latinity and the alleged futility of the philosophical exertions of these thinkers, are a common, even arguably defining, theme of these pieces. Given the centrality of style in the Humanist project and the conscious emulation of classical authors by some of these writers, the topos of praise of classical study was a field in which they strove to display their own most refined Latinity. While imitation of classical models was a common exercise among students and notable humanists

3 I argue that Melanchthon's defense of the study of Greek and Hebrew are necessary for clear and true theology, and for resolution of dogmatic disputes, in Ralph Keen, "Melanchthon as Advocate for Trilingual Humanism," in *The Impact of Learning Greek, Hebrew and Oriental Languages*, ed. Raf Van Rooy et al. (Turnhout: Brepols, forthcoming).

alike regardless of the position presented, within the tradition one finds arguments for the merit of the study of antiquity quite apart from the aesthetic value of a superior prose style. Arguing for the practical benefit, either alongside the aesthetic or independently, of such study would become an inaugural exercise of sorts for the humanists of the early sixteenth century.

An early Northern specimen in the genre is the oration "In laudem philosophiae & reliquarum artium" (1476) by Rudolph Agricola (1444–85), best known for his manual of dialectic and one of the luminaries of Heidelberg whose influence Melanchthon may have known through his conversations with the theologian Pallas Spangel.[4] In Agricola's oration, the study of the humanities and philosophy are the guide to life, so necessary that common views about difficulty cannot seriously be entertained.[5] Philosophy, he states, is the "investigatrix" of celestial and eternal matters and the "scrutatrix" into those things inaccessible to mortal minds (h2ᵛ); it is a study reserved for few: "O how great this is and how truly divine that which reaches so few persons."[6] Philosophy, says Agricola, calls souls away from vices and both teaches and purges, not by fear but by means of its own virtue (h3). "It is certain," he adds, "that the practices of good and evil cannot coexist in one breast any more than health and illness can coexist in one member."[7] Among the virtues that the study of philosophy imparts is fortitude in the pursuit of truth and indifference to external conditions (h6–6ᵛ); the philosopher is attached to the best of human concerns (*summum in rebus humanis*) so as to have no worldly need (h6ᵛ). Regarding the particular arts, Agricola corrects the impression that grammar, dialectic, and rhetoric are separate disciplines: while each has its own method, they serve the single goal of ensuring eloquence, without which philosophy is ineffective as a guide to life (h8).

Although Agricola remains bound to the trivium and quadrivium and offers conventional comments on the merits of each discipline, his description of philosophy as the study that shapes life and custom (*vitam atque mores hominum*

---

4 Wilhelm Maurer, *Der junge Melanchthon zwischen Humanismus und Reformation*, vol. 1 (Göttingen: Vandenhoeck & Ruprecht, 1967), 24. For Agricola's influence on contemporaries and successors, see James Michael Weiss, "The Six Lives of Rudolph Agricola: Forms and Functions of the Humanist Biography," *Humanistica Lovaniensia* 30 (1981), 19–39; and for Agricola's role in introducing the loci method, Lodi Nauta, "From Universals to Topics: The Realism of Rudolph Agricola, with an Edition of his Reply to a Critic," *Vivarium* 50 (2012), 190–224.

5 Rudolph Agricola, *Nonnulla opuscula* (Antwerp: T. Martinus, 1511), sig. h2.

6 *Nonnulla opuscula*, sig. h2ᵛ: "O quantum hoc est & quam vere diuinum quod tam paucis hominibus contingit."

7 *Nonnulla opuscula*, sig. h3: "[C]ertum est bonarum malarumque atrium non magic esse posse vno in pectore consortium quam in vno membro morbi & sanitatis."

formand[*a*], i3) points toward the practical emphasis that later humanists would adopt as the authentic substance of the study. The great effort required to study the moral part of philosophy yields the insights of the most learned persons; and there is hardly a sentence from them that has not generated a multitude of differing opinions (i3^{v}). Thus, according to Agricola, one needs to be diligent in seeking the great impulse in it, its great power for living well and rightly, for without it persons live without guidance.[8] Agricola's oration, delivered in the presence of Ercole d'Este (1431–1505), is (as its title implies) an encomium of the humanities that ends with a panegyric of Ferrara, a city allied with Naples after d'Este's 1473 marriage to the daughter of Ferdinand I, the embattled King of Naples.

Arguably more influential as a contribution to the discourse, Agricola's letter to Jacobus Barbirianus (Jacques Barbireau, 1455–91) of June 1484 on the formation of studies offers a program for drawing practical benefit from the disciplines.[9] The letter offers a program of study for Barbireau, who evidently had wished to study with Agricola, then at Heidelberg. Agricola explains to his would-be student that studies should be arranged by their matter (*res*) and method (*natura*) and that one should pursue the field one thinks best for oneself, selecting as auxiliary disciplines those that will help in the student's particular pursuit.[10] Each subject, he adds, has its own body of knowledge and style of learning: "thus civil law has one sort of learning, pontifical rulings another, medicine another art of learning."[11] This letter being contemporaneous with the oration on the liberal arts, we find here similar language about the practical value of moral philosophy: every plan for living correctly is contained in that part of philosophy called moral philosophy (204–06; d1).

8 *Nonnulla opuscula*, sig. i3^{v}: "Est ex hac hominum diligentia circa ipsam [sc. philosophiam] perspicere, magnum in ipsa momentum esse / magnam vim positam ad bene recteque viuendumm & necesse esse sine suo ductu fluctuare res nostras & passim tanquam sine gubernaculo, since rectore iactari, ad quam solam respicientes vitae nostrae tranquillum in offensum dirigimus cursum."

9 Rudolf Agricola, *Letters*, ed. and tr. Adrie van der Laan and Fokke Akkerman (Bibliotheca Latinitatis Novae, 216; Assen: Royal Van Gorcum, 2002), 202–19 (no. 38); in context, see Elly Kooiman, "The Letters of Rodolphus Agricola to Jacobus Barbirianus," in *Rodolphus Agricola Phrisius 1444–1485*, ed. F. Akkerman and A. J. Vanderjagt (Brill's Studies in Intellectual History, 6; Leiden: Brill, 1988), 136–46; for analysis, see Jürgen Blusch, "Agricola als Pädagoge und seine Empfehlungen *De formando studio*," in *Rudolf Agricola 1444–1485 Protagonist des nordeuropäischen Humanismus*, ed. Wilhelm Kühlmann (Bern: Peter Lang, 1994), 355–85.

10 Agricola, *Letters*, 202–204; *Nonnulla opuscula*, sigs. c8–8^{v}.

11 Agricola, *Letters*, 204/5–6; *Nonnulla opusula*, sig. c8^{v}: "Ergo ciuile ius alius [aluis in 1511 text] / alius pontificum sanctiones: alius medicinae artem discendam sumit."

Agricola articulates an expansive view of the literature that bears on moral philosophy. He states that moral precepts should not just be sought from those philosophers who treat it explicitly, such as Aristotle, Cicero, Seneca, and others, but also from historians, poets, and orators. Authors in these other traditions do not teach so much as offer examples, as if holding up a mirror.[12] All the others, he adds, have errors intermixed with whatever good they hand down and thus are unreliable as guides to correct living (204; d1). Only sacred literature, to which these pursuits aim, is free of error since God has handed it down (204–06; d1). All other subjects are defined by their content and their pursuit is determined by a mission appropriate to the content. Aware that he is deviating from the view that a common set of skills provides access to all subjects, Agricola advocates order in these studies. "I praise them all but would surely praise them more if they were treated correctly and in order."[13]

If Agricola represents the first generation of humanists north of the Alps, Martin van Dorp (1485–1525) may be placed among the second.[14] In a 1513 oration at Leuven in praise of all the arts, Dorp presents the trivium as a group of siblings, dialectic being the "sister" of grammar and the "solid food" after the "milk" of grammatical study.[15] Dialectic, he says, is the touchstone for distinguishing true from false in every branch of learning (30). Rhetoric, the third "sister," is the one who, with the other two, produces the "progeny" of eloquence (32): "then rhetoric, like a mistress and leader supported by the two, lays the final hand on a polished oration."[16] Dorp exhorts his listeners to apply themselves to eloquence, for it is an ornament that gives "light and propriety" (*lumen ac decus*) to one's learning (35/33–34).

---

12 Agricola, *Letters*, 204/29–206/1; *Nonnulla opuscula*, sig. d1: "[H]uius prima nobis & praecipua habenda est ratio: hec autem est petenda tibi non modo a philosophis: qui litteris eam tradidere, vt sunt Aristoteles, Cicero, Seneca: & si qui sunt alii vel latini vel latine ita redditt, vt digni sint qui legantur, sed ab historicis etiam & poetis & oratoribus quoniam hi & benefacta laudando: & que contra contra facta sint vituperanda. Non docent quidem: sed quod efficacissimum est, exemplis propositis que recte secusue fiant, velut in speculo ostendunt per hec gradus ad sacras litteras faciendus est." (The transcription, which differs in punctuation, is from the *Opuscula*.)

13 Agricola, *Letters*, 204/12–13' *Nonnulla opuscula*, sig. c8v: "Laudo eas omnes tamen plus certe laudaturus si recte ordineque tractarentur."

14 For a detailed summary of Dorp's career and a contemporary account of his life, see "Gerard Morinck's Life of Martin van Dorp," *Humanistica Lovaniensia* 4 (1934), 123–348. For his role in dialectic, see Demmy Verbeke, "Maarten van Dorp and the Teaching of Logic at the University of Leuven," *Humanistica Lovaniensia* 62 (2013), 225–46.

15 Martinus Dorpius, "Oratio in laudem omnum atrium," in *Orationes IV*, ed. Joseph IJsewijn (Leipzig: Teubner, 1986), 29–30.

16 *Orationes IV*, 32/14–15: "[D]emum rhetorica quasi domina ac princeps duabus innixa ultimam manum absolutae orationis imponit."

The most honorable and praiseworthy branch of study, for Dorp, is moral philosophy, the one that "many prudent persons and those gifted with the highest wisdom have alone considered worthy."[17] It is from this branch of philosophy that one learns how to live calmly and to maintain an orderly political existence as well as "religion toward the gods, piety toward parents, justice for all and the whole spectrum of the other virtues."[18] It is thus a discipline freighted with a range of tasks, at least one of which, religion toward the gods, points to a contested boundary between moral conduct and pious practice. Yet Dorp explains that all of these are contained within higher laws (43). Since all persons share the same light and air, says Dorp, they should live according to the laws of God, those laws being "the expunger of all evils and the donors of nothing that is not good."[19]

Erasmus's *De ratione studii* (1512) describes an ordered program in good letters grounded in the distinction between words and things and the importance of exact correspondence between them. No one disputes over words, he says, "more than those who boast that they don't care about words but consider only the thing."[20] One approaches the desired understanding of "things" (presumably what is revealed in scripture and how the Fathers understand these terms) by acquiring a sound knowledge of Greek and Latin (A2–2v). Erasmus is blunt with his critique of recent authorities and direct in his recommendations. Those with good memories should read and reread certain authors (A3v); and he favors Terence for being pure, terse, and the nearest to everyday speech (A2v) while one should learn dialectic from Aristotle and not from the "extremely verbose of class of sophists" then reigning.[21] Moreover, no matter what the subject, there is no discipline in which the poets and the ancient orators are not useful (A5).

17 *Orationes IV*, 43/2–3: "[H]anc plerique prudentes viri et summa sapientia praediti solam censuere dignam."

18 *Orationes IV*, 43/10–15: "eiusmodi dico homines mansuete suaviterque composuit, rectum politicae vitae ordinem monstravit, humanitatem, comitatem, benignitatem, affabilitatem, amicitiam, individuam vitae societatem, religionem erga deos, erga parentes pietatem, erga omnes iustitiam ceterarumque hominis virtutum agmen universum invexit."

19 *Orationes IV*, 44/32–36: "quod vivimus et omnino communi hoc aere, hac luce fruimur, cui quaeso secundum Deum debemus nisi praeclarissimis legibusomnium malprum expultricibus, nullorum non bonorum datricibus?"

20 Erasmus, *De ratione studii libellus aureus* (Strasbourg: Matthias Schuster, 1516), sig. A2: "Postremo videas nullos omnium magis vbique de voculis cauillari, quam eos qui iactitant sese verba negligere, rem ipsam spectare."

21 *De ratione studii*, sig. A3: "Modo ab Aristotele eam [sc. dialecticam] discat, non ab illa loquacissimo sophistarum genere."

Regarding the method of teaching, Erasmus in his related work *De pueris instituendis* advocates a comprehensive preparation for the instructor, who can only know what is best from being well-read, for one cannot know what is best without knowing much that is not (A4). Erasmus recommends not being satisfied with ten or a dozen authors, but wants "the whole world of teaching," so that the instructor overlooks nothing, "even the slightest details."[22] He recommends Plato, Aristotle, and Theophrastus among philosophers, and among theologians, Origen, Chrysostom, and Basil (A4). Following the model of Quintilian (*Inst.* 10, whom he mentions at A5), Erasmus offers a reading list of classical authors in an early effort to create a canon from the body of literature newly available via the printing press. For teaching such authors, Erasmus expects an instructor to be both diligent and learned (*diligentem ac doctum praeceptorem requiram*, A6^{v}).

Melanchthon's 1517 oration on the liberal arts is a contribution to a genre that reaches beyond Agricola to models like Pier Paolo Vergerio and before that to Plutarch and Quintilian. Melanchthon's own entry to the tradition is a praise of wisdom, prodigiously erudite and sharp in its critique of those still reserved toward the new learning. Framing the discussion with mythological images, Melanchthon describes the arts as originating from philosophy in the way Mercury emerged from the head of Zeus, to the sound of a lyre with seven chords. These are the seven arts "that have flowed from the mind above, by which all knowledge of nature is comprehended."[23] Melanchthon's comments about the liberal arts are more poetic than insightful, yet it is worth noting that he calls logic the discipline that encompasses grammar, dialectic, and rhetoric (21–22). The subjects of the quadrivium are the other four chords in the lyre, all meant to play in harmony.

While the 1517 piece may be considered an exercise in the genre, the *Inaugural Oration* of 1518 is a lucidly nuanced position on the place of learning at the dawn of a new age, one characterized by its rejection of what he considered the fractious speculations of the various Scholastic schools. Throughout the declamation Melanchthon scorns the "sophists," whom he calls "eunuchs rather than philosophers" (γάλλους μᾶλλον ἢ φιλόσοφους, MWA 3, 36/30). The bitter disputes over insoluble questions instill only a spirit that tarnishes the pursuit of advanced subjects like law or theology (38). While some of his scorn for Scholastic culture is drawn from common Humanist critique, some surely

22 *De ratione studii*, sig. A4: "In hoc non ero contentus decem illis, aut duodecim authoribis, sed orbem illum doctrinae requiram, vt nihil ignoret, etiam qui minima paret doctrinae."

23 MWA 3, 20/21–23: "Septem hae sunt artes, ut agam historica fide, supera defluxae mente, quibus omnis naturae Scientia comprehenditur."

is grounded in his own experience in the two *viae* in which he was trained at Heidelberg and Tübingen. He praises his new Wittenberg colleagues for making sure that students "draw from the very wellsprings of the arts from the leading authors" (*fontes ipsos artium ex optimis auctoribus hauritis*, 38/19–20).

Melanchthon sees the trivium (which he calls *progymnasmata*, harking back no doubt to Agricola's Latin translation of Aphthonius's work of that title) as necessary preparation for philosophy, understood as the "human disciplines" learned best from Aristotle and Plato (the *Moralia* and *Laws*), the poets Homer, Virgil and Horace, and history (39). He would hold this conception of philosophy, with its extended canon that includes the orators as well, consistently over the years. Melanchthon declares that his own contribution to the curriculum will be pedagogical and (to use an anachronistic term) philological: to identify the proper authors for each subject while also elucidating Greek authors (41–42).

In his exhortation to return to the sources and his praise of particular classical authors for their practical (rather than ornamental) value, Melanchthon establishes his place among the humanists of his time. In his sprinkling of Greek and Hebrew phrases in an address to students who would have known neither language, he displays uncommon erudition in an earnest appeal to pursue the good and the true. In its focus on the moral value of classical literature, Melanchthon's oration bears certain similarities to Basil's oration on the benefit (ὄφελος) of studying Greek literature. Acknowledging that the range of behavior chronicled in the pagan canon includes material not suitable for imitation by students intent on a virtuous life, Basil nevertheless encourages his hearers to emulate bees and draw from it the honey that will be a benefit for their soul (ὠφέλειαν ... εἰς τὴν ψυχήν, 4.7). In the pursuit of virtue, according to Basil, the foremost sources are among the poets and historians as well as the philosophers (4.10). Study of virtue is almost incomplete without attention to Hesiod and Homer (5.5–6), authors whom Basil considers useful (χρήσιμα, 6.2). Attention to practical utility in the moral sphere, while not absent from the language of later humanists, is not ubiquitous and is not a defining mark of the topos.

3 The Uses of Ethics

Despite Melanchthon's evident distaste for metaphysical speculation, his regard for Aristotle as a master of method is manifest in unexpected areas of his work. For example, in presenting his own moral philosophy he offers an explanation of the utility of ethics according to the four Aristotelian causes.

Aristotle himself offered no such causal analysis for ethics. His thought on causality is found in *Met.* 1.3 (a text Melanchthon tended to ignore) and is meant to be applied to material objects. The evidently peculiar use of *causa* in its application to a segment of a system of thought should not obscure the intention of Melanchthon's analysis of the purpose of moral philosophy.

In his commentary on selected books of the *Nicomachean Ethics*, Melanchthon not only offers a defense of the place of moral philosophy alongside the gospel (CR 16, 7) but explains his conception of ethics as part of the divine law (278–79). In seeking to know God's will for persons, according to Melanchthon, reason itself demonstrates that it is not enough simply to know the law.[24] One must know that the end of such knowledge, the wellbeing that Aristotle calls εὐδαιμονία and that Melanchthon translates as *beatitudo*, is knowledge and obedience of God (283). Melanchthon describes *beatitudo* as the ultimate good, the state in which nothing is lacking (297), one that philosophy itself cannot explain despite Aristotle's discussion of virtue as the means to happiness at *EN* 1.10 (1100a10–1101a21). The present life is never without troubles, but in true blessedness there are no troubles (304). Melanchthon's appreciation of Aristotle is anchored in the fact that Aristotelian thought operates by induction from material examples; it is, in other words, a method of understanding the material world in its finitude and imperfection.

In thus subordinating moral philosophy to Christian doctrine and asserting that human minds are in doubt about the final good for persons, Melanchthon defines the end as obeying and celebrating God (281–82, 288). This, he says, is common to all: although each form of life has its own value and virtuous practices, the end of all is to obey God, each in their own vocation (290). Hence the common good transcends particular callings. Moral philosophy points toward the end but cannot disclose it (282). In Melanchthon's words, reason spurs the pursuit of the best: *ratio hortatur ad optima* (308). These are Aristotle's words as well; but Aristotle was unaware of the ultimate good to which reason points.[25] "If reason shows that is best, what need would there be for the Gospel?"[26]

The study of Aristotelian ethics at an early age is useful, as Melanchthon states in his prefatory letter to Arnold Burenius, as a guide to the explanation of the greatest matters (9–10). His word for guide, χειραγωγία, has interesting connotations: it is used by Basil and others for spiritual guidance toward higher

24 CR 16, 308: "Ratio monstrat ut lex, nec satus est legem nosse, cum quaerimus de voluntate Dei erga nos."

25 *EN* 1.13, 1102b16: ὠρθῶς γὰρ καὶ ἐπὶ τὰ βέλτιστα παρακαλεῖ.

26 CR 16, 308: "Si ratio monstrat optima, quid opus est Evangelio?"

matters.[27] Students, he hopes, will find Aristotle's text (especially Book 5) not only pleasant to read but also useful in interpreting "many controversies both theological and forensic."[28] The commentary, however, never loses sight of the "great matters" to which he feels Aristotle's text points. The first virtue, as Melanchthon states it, is reverence for God, which as he explains is understood in Latin as "religion" or "piety."[29] As Melanchthon implies in the maxim *ratio hortatur ad optima*, it is in the character of classical *ratio* to point to higher things in a way to make one desire them; but it is also the limitation of classical thought to be unable to do more than exhort, *hortari*.

Central to Melanchthon's argument that Christian doctrine supplies what is lacking in classical moral thought is the discussion of justice in Bk. 5 of the *Nicomachean Ethics*. The seemingly coherent yet (for Melanchthon) incomplete conception found in the Aristotelian text addresses civil justice without attention to the way it participates in the divine law. The latter is that form of justice that binds persons to God and that reveals the divine will for obedience and the correct distinction of good from evil so that persons may know which duties to cultivate.[30] In the church, Melanchthon states, the word refers to "diligence, faith, tolerance, and other virtuous duties." Moreover, the justice articulated both in divine books and in the works of philosophers and jurists within the church is understood as the divine voice, "for the true demonstrations and explanations of customs are part and explication of the divine law."[31]

---

27 *A Patristic Greek Lexicon*, ed. G. W. H. Lampe (Oxford: Clarendon Press, 1961), s.v. χειραγωγία. Burenius (1485–1566) was professor of rhetoric at Rostock who reformed the Arts faculty; see Johannes Grave, "Der Humanist Arnold Burenius. Ein Emsländer macht Gelehrtenkarriere," *Osnabrücker Mitteilungen* 104 (1999), 91–106.

28 CR 16, 9–10: "Sed polliceor studiosis non tantum iucundam fore hanc lectionem, sed etiam valde utilem in explicatione multarum controversiarum theologicarum et forensium." The same letter is found at CR 2, 849–54.

29 CR 16, 321: "Prima igitur virtus est reverentia erga Deum, quam vel religionem, vel pietatem Latini vocant."

30 CR 16, 365: "Erudite inchoavit hanc doctrinam a consideratione partium hominis, sed eruditior definitio es set, dicere, iustitiam universalem esse obedientiam Deo debitam, iuxta discrimen honestorum et turpium, quod impressit Deus humanae naturae, ut et ipsum agnoscamus, et intelligamus quibus officiis coli velit."

31 CR 16, 365: "Utinam igitur eam placide audiamus, et vere sentiamus, hos nostros coetus praecipuam Ecclesiae divinae partem esse, et in hac statione divinitus collocatos, ut iustitiae vocem, id est, doctrinam de rebus bonis conservemus, et in eo munere diligentiam, fidem, tolerantiam, et caetera virtutis officia praestemus. Concionatur autem iustitia, cum in libris divinis, tum in philosophorum et iurisconsultorum doctrina, quae etiam est vox divina. Nam verae demonstrationes et conclusiones de moribus sunt pars et explicatio legis divinae."

From this perspective we gain a more informed understanding of Melanchthon's approach to the Aristotelian account of virtue in Bk. 2. In his commentary he describes "spiritual virtue" (something distinct from the civic virtues that Aristotle describes) as the product of four causes: the word of God, the working of the Holy Spirit, the assenting mind, and the obedient will.[32] The will, when strengthened and impelled by the Holy Spirit, coerces the external members and hence ensures virtuous action (311). Melanchthon recognizes that for Aristotle civic virtue is the product of right reason (mind judging correctly) and the will obeying.[33] What Melanchthon describes is virtuous action performed in a conscious desire to obey the divine will.

For Melanchthon, there are three causes of virtuous action in general: the mind judging according to the word of God; the will assenting to this; and the Holy Spirit impelling both mind and will, these being weakened on account of sin.[34] What is missing from Aristotle and the rest of pagan thought, as this implies, is awareness of the limitation on human understanding that results from the Fall. As Melanchthon understands the causes of virtue, Aristotle is not incorrect; but the immense weakness of humans (*ingens imbecillitas hominum*) impedes the attainment of a virtue in most persons (326). Hence divine guidance is needed for directing both mind and will, for, as Melanchthon asserts, right reason conforms to the law of God, and voluntary actions follow a rule, which is the law of nature (314–16).

Melanchthon understands the Decalogue as a codification of the divine law and thus as something universally known, even if not uniformly observable. Because they govern civil society, the laws (or virtues, as he calls them) of the second table of the Law are better known than those of the first (322);

---

32 CR 16, 310, using the example of Joseph in Gen. 39: "Has sententias et similes observent studiosi, et ut causas virtutis considerent, et se quisque accuratiore disciplina regat. Illud etiam hic monendi sunt studiosi, Aristotelem loqui de civilibus virtutibus, aliquanto aliter de spiritualibus dicitur, ut in Ioseph concurrunt quatuor causae. Verbum Dei, Spiritus sanctus, mens assentiens, et voluntas obtemperans." Joseph considers (*cogitat*) the commandment against adultery (despite it not yet having been revealed), "et Spiritus sanctus inclinat mentem, ut assentiatur praecepto, et colligat multas causas, cavendum, ne Deus iratus, prorsus te abiiciat, puniat praesentibus et futuris poenis, eripiat praesentia dona, habenda est et scandali ratio, parcendum item alienae conscientiae. His argumentis movetur voluntas et confirmat spem Spiritus sanctus, ut obtemperet legi" (310–11).

33 CR 16, 311: "Nunc in secundo capite nominat causam, scilicet rectam rationem, qua appellatione complectitur mentem recte iudicantem, et voluntatem obtemperantem."

34 CR 16, 327: "In doctrina christiana sic traduntur causae actionum, ut sint tres: Mens iudicans iuxta verbum Dei, voluntas assentiens, Spiritus sanctus impellens mentem et voluntatem, et has infirmas vires adiuvans, et exitum gubernans, sicut inquit Christus (Ioann. 15, 5.): Sine me nihil potestis facere, ut, cum Ioseph repugnat illecebris dominae."

yet the presence of deity in classical literature indicates consciousness of the demands of the first table.

Without an awareness that sin has disrupted human emotions, Aristotle applied the rule of moderation, something within persons' natural ability (338, 353). Because of humanity's weakened state, all persons sin, according to Melanchthon (333); and it is impossible to comprehend, much less to attain, the true end (345). He makes these comments in reference to *EN* Bk. 3, and they serve as a critique of Aristotle's conception of virtue as something attainable by a person's natural abilities and habits. Whereas Aristotle claims that virtue and evil are within human powers (ἐφ' ἡμῖν δὴ καὶ ἡ ἀρετὴ, ὁμοίως δὲ καὶ ἡ κακία, 1113b6–7), Melanchthon holds that according to Christian doctrine, "the will is not turned toward God, and the heart strays and has wandering impulses: excessive self-love, neglect of God, and love for the pleasures of the body."[35] Aristotle, he states, only saw a great confusion of emotions without knowing its cause (353).

4 Freewill

Given that the Commentary is a selective one, covering only *EN* 1–3 and 5, it is evident that Melanchthon was not interested in recovering the whole of Aristotle's ethical work; and the commentary he does provide is as much critique as appropriation. In contrast to the notion that the worldly realm is autonomous and that classical thought is sufficient for preserving order and understanding the work of its institutions, Melanchthon subordinates the social order to the transcendent one and argues that a knowledge of the divine law is the necessary complement to Aristotle's account of behavior and the norms that govern it. He understands the "exhortation to the best things" mentioned above to signal the incompleteness of the understanding available only in the classical tradition. The "guidance" (χειραγωγία) that the tradition offers is its ability to lead the faithful reader to the *optima* to which authors like Aristotle point.

Because it participates in the divine law, ethics leads persons to God. In the first book of his Commentary, Melanchthon distinguishes two paths of learning: the transmission of naked precepts without causes, such as when a physician instructs a feverish patient not to drink wine; and the explanation of causes, the δι' ὅτι or *propter quod* (288). While philosophy is able, he says, to

35 CR 16, 353: "Voluntas non est conversa ad Deum, et cor vagatur, et habet errantes impetus, amorem nostril nimium, neglectionem Dei, et amorem voluptatum corporis."

identify the first two causes of virtuous actions (the mind judging and the will obeying, which Melanchthon calls truly divine, *vere divini*, sources of virtue), it is unable to supply the instrumental cause: the Holy Spirit impelling the mind and will (326–27). In a comment to the discussion of voluntary actions at the beginning of *EN* Bk. 3, Melanchthon states that the will sins when it neglects divine and human law, and that contempt of God is a voluntary sin. The will sins, he explains, when it fails to inquire after what it needs to know; and all are meant to know human and divine law.[36] Melanchthon's critique of Aristotle's view of the causes of virtuous action allows him to identify the Holy Spirit as the agent in the working of the virtuous will.

Hence we find Melanchthon, when commenting on the Aristotelian conception of justice in in Bk. 5, not only articulating the distinction between universal justice and particular justice (equity) but also describing the orders of justice in such a way as to define moral philosophy as a part of divine law.[37] It is the first form of justice, the instinct to do what is commanded and avoid that which is prohibited, that orders—we might say binds—persons to God (365). Because it has been implanted in all persons by God, this first formal principle of justice is *a priori*, individual actions conforming to or deviating from positive law.[38]

Although this discussion has focused on a small part of the Melanchthonian corpus, it may serve as evidence that the humanistic dimension of Melanchthon's work is not only not independent of his theological concerns, but in service to them by leading like a guide (χειραγωγία) to the "best things." Melanchthon understands the virtues distributed according to the precepts of

36 CR 16, 332: "Estque usitata regula: Ignorantia facti excusat non iuris. Non excusat ignorantia Evangelii eos, qui adversantur verae doctrinae. Peccat enim voluntas, cum id, quod homo scire debet, non inquirit. Omnes autem scire debent ius divinum et naturale. Id negligere, est Deum contemnere. Ideo recte dicitur ignorantiam iuris, praesertim divini et naturalis, esse dolum. Contemptus autem Dei voluntarium peccatum est. Et hic honestissime inquit Aristoteles: Affectatam ignorantiam non esse involuntariam, sed malitiam." Thus Aristotle himself is held to account for his ignorance.

37 Universal justice, according to Melanchthon, is justice in the formal sense of avoiding that which is prohibited and doing what is commanded, while particular justice is a specific instance such as Joseph not betraying his wife. The third meaning is what Paul describes as reconciliation, divine acceptance, and the imputation of righteousness (CR 16, 364–65). Melanchthon states (CR 16, 365) that he will not describe this third type. However, the three meanings cohere: "Hic tantum congruunt appellationes ad iustitiam, quae vocatur legis iustitia, ut constat philosophiam moralem esse legis divinae partem" (365).

38 For Melanchthon's place in the Natural Law tradition, see John Witte, Jr., "'The Natural Law Written on the Heart': Natural Law and Equity in Early Lutheran Thought," in *The Legal Teachings of the Protestant and Catholic Reformations*, ed. Wim Dekock (Göttingen: Vandenhoeck & Ruprecht, 2014), 231–265.

the Decalogue, a position that does not permit relegating works of piety to a realm separate from the realm of moral action conventionally understood. All action falls under the rubric of moral philosophy, seen as a part of the divine law. As Melanchthon states in connection with Aristotle's enumeration of the virtues at *EN* 2.6:

> A learned, rationally congruent, and very true distribution of the virtues can be taken from the order of the precepts of the Decalogue. Just as an image is meant principally to represent its model, so might human nature principally be an image of God: that is, so that that an awareness of God shines in us—or that we become examples of God, as it is said, "And each one is an example of God in miniature"; it can be easily understood that the highest end for persons is to recognize, obey, and celebrate God.[39]

5 The "Pedagogical" Mode in the Study of Moral Philosophy

Two works by Melanchthon are systematic treatises in his moral philosophy: the *Philosophiae moralis epitome*, first issued in 1538, and the *Ethicae doctrtinae elementa* (1550). The titles suggest different audiences but the *Elementa* is an expansion of the *Epitome* rather than a completely new composition.[40] Melanchthon draws on classical sources, but these are not commentaries and do not assume deep familiarity with canonical authors in the moral tradition. Nevertheless, in Mads Langballe Jensen's words, they "arguably contain Melanchthon's most sustained engagement with moral and philosophical questions, as well as his most systematic formulation of a theory of the law of nature."[41]

The foregoing examples point to a central and distinguishing aspect of Melanchthon's thought regarding the study of the classical tradition. Alongside his oft-repeated distinction between *philosophia* and *evangelium* is a view that

39 CR 16, 321: "Erudita, rationi congruens, ac verissima distribution virtutum sumi potest ex ordine praeceptorum decalogi. Ut effigies praecipue fit, ut repraesentet archetypum, ita cum humana natura praecipue condita sit, ut sit imago Dei, hoc est, ut in nobis luceat Dei notitia, seu, ut simus exempla Dei, ut dicitur:
Exemplumque Dei quisque est in imagine parva,
Facile intelligi potest, summum hominis finem esse agnoscere Deum, ei obtemperare, et eum celebrare." The classical line is Manilius, *Astronomica* 4.407.

40 Mads Langballe Jensen, *A Humanist in Reformation Politics: Philipp Melanchthon on Political Philosophy and Natural Law* (Leiden: Brill, 2019), 97.

41 Jensen, 98.

the former leads to the latter, and that the moral life is fulfilled in life under the gospel: that is, in grace. If this be true, the structural concept of two kingdoms in irresolvable dialectical tension is alien to the Melanchthonian system. The relationship as Melanchthon understands it is instead anagogical, with the moral realm participating in the divine mind or *mens aeterna*, with the same end as revealed scriptural law.

Such a seemingly impossible conception of classical thought sharing in the same *usus* as biblical law does have scriptural warrants, according to Melanchthon. For him, the impression of divine law on human minds signifies that moral reasoning across cultures is the exercise of reason addressed to that *lex divina* (CR 16, 23). Moreover, he sees the classical tradition as evidence of the divine illumination of humanity: a statement such as "Hesiod is a kind of Decalogue among the gentiles" can refer either to the place of the *Works and Days* in Greek literature or to the divine source of the poet's inspiration. In Melanchthon's view it is both.[42] In stating that moral thought in its various forms is grounded in the *lex divina*, Melanchthon means that non-biblical traditions participate in divine law, its imperfection due only to the obscurity resulting from the weakness of human nature (16, 23). Stated another way, the authors of moral works employ a faculty divinely bestowed but working within the imperfections of humanity's fallen state.

In his *Epitome of Moral Philosophy* (1538), Melanchthon both describes and defends the study of this branch of philosophy, in the context of the question of whether Christians are permitted to use the teachings of moral philosophy. In answering in the affirmative (more in rebuke of the Radicals than for the illumination of his Wittenberg community) he makes the point not only that this is a mandated "pedagogy" but that the law that governs "external and civil conduct in life" (*externam et civilem consuetudinem vitae*) is a *paedagogus* in the sense meant in Gal. 3:24.

---

42 CR 17, 661: "Hesiodus est quidam decalogus apud gentes." This is found in his *Enarratio* to Quintilian 10.52 (where Quintilian offers moderate praise for the poet: "Raro adsurgit Hesiodus ... tamen utiles circa praecepta sententiae"). Melanchthon's estimation is more expansive: "Deinde addit decalogum, quia haec duo debent docere sacerdotes. Caeterum non est opus oratorium scilicet, in principio de Prometheo et Epimetheo. Duae sunt partes in homine. Mens seu ratio, λόγος. Deinde ὁρμή [CR: ὅρμη], affectus. Multa praedicit Prometheus; sed Epimetheus non obtemperat. ἐπιμηθεὺς, id est, post deliberans. Pandora est voluptas, quae decipit affectus. Voluit autem poeta describere imbellicitatem humani animi. Lex naturae est decalogus. Ideo Deus excitavit quorundam summorum virorum ingenia, qui perspexerunt illas leges, et descripserunt, ut extaret lex naturae in toto orbe."

> First of all there is no doubt [that Christians may use law], since God demands and teaches the pedagogy, that is, that persons are to be controlled by external discipline and conform to honorable habits. Also, as is written (Gal. 3, 24): the law is a pedagogue, and God adorns this pedagogy with rewards, as the text (Ex. 20:12) says: Honor your father and mother so that you may live long on the earth; and punished license. Thus this pedagogy is not to be contemned. Secondly, scripture teaches (Rom. 13:1) that we should obey the laws of the magistrates. Moreover, philosophy agrees with the laws of magistrates, since each category originates in the law of nature.[43]

In the *Epitome*, Melanchthon cites Rom. 1:19–20 in support of the proposition that the law of nature is the law of God, revealed to all and hence placing all under its demand. In his opening discussion of the nature of moral philosophy he states that "the ability to tell good from bad is the most obvious vestige of God in nature, since it demonstrates that persons did not appear by accident but are directed by some eternal mind that discerns good from bad."[44] Moral philosophy, being apart from the gospel, is part of the divine law and God's wisdom; and it is precisely in not being confused with the gospel that the distinction between revealed and human ceases to be operative. In his commentary to Aristotle's *Politics*, Melanchthon states (following Arist. *Pol.* 3.7–9) that each state has the form of government best suited to it, and that the form suited to one might be wholly inappropriate to another (16, 439). Thus Israelite polity, while a form of social organization suited to that people at that time, has no normative claim on any other people except as a set of moral examples. In the *Epitome* he writes that rulers who know that the moral values of Mosaic law apply to rulers in every age should consider the examples of the kings of Judah

---

43 *Philosophiae moralis epitomes* I, CR 16, 24: "Primum autem non dubium est, quum Deus requirat, et praecipiat paedagogiam, id est, ut coherceantur homines externa disciplina, et assuefiant ad honestos mores. Item ut doceantur, sicut scriptum est (Galat. 3, 24): Lex est paedagogus, et hanc paedagogiam ornat Deus praemiis, sicut textus (Exod. 20, 12) ait: Honora patrem et matrem, ut sis longaevus super terram, et punit licentiam. Ideo haae paedagogia non est contemnenda. Secundo scriptura (Rom. 13, 1) praecipit, ut obtemperemus legibus magistratuum. Consencit autem philosophia cum legibus magistratuum, quia utrumque genus oritur ex lege naturae."

44 *Philosophiae moralis epitome* I, CR 16, 23: "Hoc est evidentissimum vestigium Dei in natura, quod testatur homines non extitisse casu, sed ortos esse ab aliqua aeterna mente, quae discernit honesta et turpia."

and Israel and apply their minds to the horrible punishments for authors of idolatry.[45]

Melanchthon's interest in positive law is a recognized aspect of his work, yet it has not consistently been woven into the broad fabric of his religious thought. Following Aristotle (and Plato's *Laws*), Melanchthon calls positive law "what nature cannot teach but which has force because of the authority of the magistrates," adding that obedience to such magistrates is a natural trait: that is, one divinely encoded in human nature as part of natural law.[46] In his 1550 declamation on laws, delivered at the promotion of the jurist Michael Deuber, Melanchthon cites Paul's proposition (Gal. 3:24) that the law is a "pedagogue" leading persons to Christ.[47] The punishments under secular law, he states, are the beginnings of "celestial wisdom," slowly opening persons to learning about Christ.[48]

In the *Elementa*, a more mature work than the *Epitome*, Melanchthon defends the discipline of moral philosophy with an argument that corresponds to one in his commentary to Aristotle's *Ethics* 3.5. In both texts, Melanchthon states that the discipline is important for four reasons, or *causae* as he terms them: 1, because it is divinely commanded; 2, in order to avoid punishment; 3, to preserve the common peace; and 4, because it is a *paedagogia* to Christ, "since God does not work in those who persist in pleasures contrary to conscience."[49]

---

45 CR 16, 88: "Porro boni principes proponant sibi mandata Dei, quae supra citavimus, deinde exempla, quae commemoravi, tertio considerent etiam exempla regum Iuda et Israel, quae sciant non esse propria politiae Mosaicae, cum sint moralia sed pertinere ad omnes principes omnium aetatum. In his animadvertent horribilibus poenis affectos esse autores idololatriae." Commas after "regum" and "omnes" have been removed for the sake of sense.

46 CR 16, 393 (from the extended discussion of positive law found in the 1532–44 editions): "Postea vero ius positivum habet autoritatem multo magis propter autoritatem magistratus, quam propter rationem, quia natura praecipit magistratui parere. Itaque cum leges magis valeant propter autoritatem magistratus, quam propter rationem, non sunt calumniandae leges, etiam ratio non statim cerni potest."

47 The audience would probably have known Isidore's definition (*Etym.* 10.206), according to which the pedagogue both guides and restrains the young: "Paedagogus est cui parvuli adsignantur. Graecum nomen est; et est compositum ab eo quod pueros agat, id est ductet et lascivientem refrenet aetatem."

48 CR 11, 910: "Etsi igitur iuventus ferocior est, tamen ideo haec ipsa gubernatio politica instituta est, ut doctrina, impreiis, carcere erudiat iuventutem, et cicuratam ac domitam flectat ad agnitionem Dei, ut gravissime Paulus inquit, Lex est paedagogus, et additur laus amplissima, cum inquit esse paedagogum, ut Christum agnoscamus, id est, docendo et castigando rudibus instillat initia sapientia coelestis, et paulatim provehit discentes, et compescit errantes impetus, ut mentes admittant doctrinam de filio Dei."

49 *Ethicae doctrinae elementa* 1 (1550), CR 16, 169 (under the locus "Quid est philosophia moralis?"): Ibi etiam discimus, propter quas causas disciplina praestanda sit, videlicet

In his commentary Melanchthon adds that "these four causes should always be in view to stir persons to controlling their ways for the sake of gaining 'true penance and faith.'"[50]

Throughout this body of Melanchthon's work we find references to the noetic effect of sin on the ability to discern right from wrong in the moral sphere. In the *Elementa* he states that the mind has an implanted awareness of moral goodness, and the will possesses a certain amount of freedom, because God wants evidence of God and of God's nature to "shine" in persons. Moreover, Melanchthon adds, God "wants discipline about these things to be common."[51] At the beginning of the earlier *Epitome* he had said, while affirming that the law of nature is the law of God concerning virtues consonant with reason, that although the divine law is impressed on human minds, it is obscured in the weakness of humanity's fallen nature, "so that it is not possible to see clearly the precepts that seek to establish the will of God and teach the perfect obedience of the heart."[52] If human nature were pure, he adds, the light of God would shine more brightly and the image of God would be more distinct (23).

We have noted above Melanchthon's use of the Pauline idea that law is a *paedagogus* to Christ, an orthodox claim within evangelical thought when said of revealed law. Melanchthon does not, however, restrict this function to the Mosaic Law but extends it to the civil systems of other societies, all of which expose human imperfection. As he states in the commentary to Aristotle's *Pol.* 5

propter quatuor: Primo, propter mandatum Dei. Secundo, ad vitandas poenas. Tertio, ut aliorum tranquillitati serviamus. Quarto, quia est paedagogia in Christum. Quia Deus in his, qui perseverant in delictis contra conscientiam, non est efficax." We may compare this with this part of his discussion of free will at *EN* 3.5 (CR 16, 340): "Ac saepe monemus quatuor esse causas, propter quas haec diligentia necessaria est. Prima est propter mandatum Dei, secunda ad vitandas poenas, quia non dubium est externa delicta, ordine a Deo instituto, sequi poenas in hac vita, propter duas causas, ut ostendat se Deus irasci delictis, deinde ut tueatur politias, quas vult conservari, ideoque vult hominum mores regi et poenis coherceri. Ideo manifestis cladibus punit periuria, seditions, iniustas caedes, incestas libidines, atrocia furta, usuras etc. Tertia causa, ut aliorum tranquillitati serviamus. Quarta, ut sit paedagogia in Christum, quia Spiritus sanctus non est efficax in his qui perseverant in delictis contra conscientiam."

50 *Comm.Eth.Arist.* 3.5, CR 16, 340: "Hae quatuor causae semper sint in conspectu, ut nos ad regendos mores exuscitent, hoc cum fit, addamus etiam veram poenitentiam et fidem."

51 *Eth.Doctr.Elementa*, CR 16, 184 (on the question "Quid est virtus?"): "Etsi autem post depravationem naturae, ingens et tristis imbecillitas secuta est, tamen et mens retinet insitas notitias, et voluntas aliquam libertatem, quia Deus vult lucere in nobis testimonia, quod sit, quails sit, et quod iudicaturus sit, et vult disciplinam commonefactionem esse de ipso."

52 *Phil.Mor.Epit.* 1 (CR 16, 23): "Nam lex divina hominum mentibus impressa est, sed in hac imbecillitate naturae obscurata est, ut non satis perspici possint illa praecepta, quae iubent statuere de voluntate Dei, et de perfecta obedientia cordis praecipiunt."

mentioned above, it is part of the natural law to obey the governing authorities; and of course Melanchthon endorses the Pauline notion (Rom. 13:1) that all governing authorities have been instituted by God. While Paul is referring in Galatians to the ceremonial law which is no longer binding upon those justified by grace, Melanchthon applies the "pedagogical" imagery to law in its regulatory use: that is, the kind to which Rom. 13:1 refers. In Melanchthon's view, the law under which Paul says Israel was restrained (ἐφρουρούμεθα = *custodiebamur*, Gal. 3:23) included both the civil and ceremonial dimensions of revealed law. As he states as early as the 1521 *Loci communes*, it is the ceremonial aspect that is no longer in force (MWA 2/1, 154–57).

Melanchthon's understanding of the "pedagogical" function of law calls for attention. Although the Vulgate for Gal 3:24 has the wording *lex paedagogus noster fuit in Christo*, the Greek ὁ νόμος παιδαγωγὸς ἡμῶν γέγονεν εἰς Χριστόν, implies that the law *leads to* Christ.[53] For Melanchthon, awareness of the divine origin of law, combined with a sense of human imperfection due to sin, opens the mind to receiving the gospel. A similar interpretation of εἰς Χριστόν is found in Luther's 1519 Galatians commentary (LW 27, 278–79), where he criticizes the Vulgate wording *in Christo*. By 1535 Luther reads the preposition in a temporal sense: the law was a caretaker *until* Christ (LW 26, 346). Luther understands the law as the Decalogue and describes its purpose as revealing sin and driving the afflicted conscience to Christ (347–48). Hence the Law of which Luther speaks in 1535 is that which "discloses sin and threatens death and the eternal wrath of God," from which there is no refuge and in which there is no comfort (337).[54]

The *usus theologicus* is as pronounced, if not always so stridently presented, in Melanchthon as it is in Luther. As he states in the 1521 *Loci*, Christian doctrine is knowing what the law demands, and law is said to be the knowledge of sin (MWA 2/1, 21, 55). Yet within the same locus Melanchthon reads Rom. 2:15

53 In this reading Melanchthon is following Erasmus (*Novum instrumentum omne*, Basel: Froben, 1516), who translates Gal. 3:23–24 as "Caeterum antequam uenisset fides, sub lege custodiebamur, conclusi in eam fidem, quae erat reuelanda. Itaque lex paedagogus fuit noster ad Christum, ut ex fide iustificaremur." In his Annotations he comments (sig. uu5) "Melius hoc loco, in Christum, siue ad Christum. εἰς Χριστόν atque ita leget Hieronymus, in secondo dialogo aduersus Pelagium."

54 Bugenhagen, like Luther, understands law as revealed law: see *Annotationes Io. Bvgenhagii Pomerani in epistolas Pauli ad Galatas, Ephesios, Philippenses, Colossenses, Thessalonicenses primam et secundam, Timotheum primam et secundam Titum, Philemonem, Hebraeos. Ab ipso autore nuper recognitae* (Strasbourg: Johann Knobloch, 1525), sig. B7[v]: "Haec est recta & finalis responsio ex praedictis illata. Scriptura, id est, lex conclusit omnia, id est, quicquic est hominum & uirium humanarum sub peccatum, quia omnes reos morte fecit, ut agnoscerent illud. Omnes peccauerunt & egent gloria dei, gloria nostra & nostrarum uirium ignominia nostra est & damnatio."

as attributing to gentile law the power to accuse: "there is among the nations a conscience either defending or accusing a deed; it is therefore law."[55] For Melanchthon, worship is part of the natural law and the existence of God is evident in the order of the cosmos (57), and even if the magistrate's domain extends only to punishing and preventing wrongs, that power according to Rom. 13:1–3 is from God (71). While human weakness makes the laws necessary, we do not yet have in 1521 a sense that civil law is a *paedagogus* leading to Christ.

The threefold division of laws (natural, divine, and human) is present in the second version of the *Loci*; and once again Melanchthon holds that the Decalogue is the foundation of the moral law, hence binding all persons to the first Table as well as the second (CR 21, 390, 392). The second version speaks of the pedagogical function of law in the context of humans' natural faculties and their inability to satisfy the divine demand. Those who rely on their own abilities yet never seek the help of God, he says, will never practice faith or have knowledge of God (CR 21, 279). Nevertheless, he adds, it is necessary to know honorable discipline as civil good works required by God, even though they do not make one righteous before God. Melanchthon continues:

> Paul adorns this with an outstanding declaration when he states that law is a pedagogue to Christ. If discipline is a pedagogue, and one that leads to Christ, it should never be neglected. The pedagogy is strong so that, accustomed to good habits, we may hear and learn the gospel. Then the Holy Spirit is efficacious through the gospel.[56]

Elsewhere in the same version Melanchthon states that civil duties are demanded of all, even those who are not sanctified; they are not useless, for these may be made ready for piety. Quoting Gal. 3:24 once again, Melanchthon explains that "this pedagogy is useful so that persons may be taught, and hear, the word of God. And since God is efficacious through the word, so through these exercises [of civic duty] many are called to true piety."[57] They are made

---

55 MWA 2/1, 56/2–4: "Est in gentibus conscientia factum defendens vel accusana; est igitur lex."

56 CR 21, 279–80: "Paulus ornavit eam [sc. disciplinam] egregio praeconio cum ait. Lex est paedagogus in Christum. Quodsi disciplina est paedagoga, et quidem In Christum, nequaquam negligenda erit. Valet enim paedagogia ut assuefacti bonis moribus, audiamus et discamus Evangelium. [P]ostea spiritus sanctus efficax est per Evangelium."

57 CR 21, 377: "Et hanc disciplinam requirit Deus etiam in his, qui nondum sunt sanctificati. Nec nulla est eius utilitas. Nam externa delicta poenis corporalibus et aeternis puniuntur. Ad haec Paulus inquit [Gal. 3, 24], Legem esse Paedagogum in Christum. Prodest enim

ready for piety by having their imperfection, both in knowing the law and fulfilling it, exposed; and classical thought as well as Mosaic law is, for Melanchthon, sufficient for this "pedagogical" end.[58]

6 The Person

Generalizations about Melanchthon's supposed Aristotelianism, not infrequently made by confessional theologians with polemical intent, have overshadowed a rich eclecticism that represents the fusion of schools of thought both classical and Patristic. Attaching a single term to Melanchthon, be it Aristotelian or Erasmian or even Lutheran, is to attribute a dominant tendency to his thought, and calls for effort to reconcile—or dismiss as deviant—influences from other authors and traditions.

Melanchthon's anthropology is a case in point. The fallen human condition is marked by the inability to fulfill the demands of the law: not the law revealed by Moses, but the moral law written on the minds of all persons. In an undated disputation Melanchthon condemns the "well-worn and erroneous" (*usitata et falsa*) distinction that there are three laws: natural, Mosaic, and Evangelical (CR 12, 444). Instead, Melanchthon asserts that there is one moral law across time that endures as long as human nature remains; and this law is known "naturally" in various ways ([*e*]*aque lex aliquo modo naturaliter nota est*, 445). Such law, he states elsewhere, does not endure because it was given by Moses, but because it is divinely written on the soul (478).

In the vision of Melanchthon's works, the *Liber de anima* is classified among his philosophical efforts, understandably but wrongly considered an inquiry remote from his theological corpus. If one centers the latter on questions about scripture and grace, the generic classification is understandable yet anomalous given the centrality of anthropology in the *Loci* and other more explicitly theological writings. And although the work first appeared with "Commentary" in the title, it was always an independent work, not a commentary on an ancient text.

---

haec paedagogia, ut doceantur homines et audient verbum Dei. Et quia Deus est efficax per verbum, ideo per haec exercitia multi vocantur ad veram pietatem."

58 One notes for comparison Augustine, *De Spiritu et littera* 51 to the effect that the righteousness of the law is the ability to recognize one's infirmity: "Ideo quippe proponitur iustitia legis, quod qui fecerit eam, vivet in illa; ut cum quisque informitatem suam cognoverit, non per suas vires, neque per litteram ipsius legis, quod fieri non potest, sed per fidem concilians iustificatorem perveniat et faciat, et vivit in ea."

The *De anima* addresses matters ostensibly physiological, such as sensation and the four bodily humors, as well as the emotions, which Melanchthon understands as the responses of the nerves to stimuli (MWA 3, 309–19). Melanchthon's treatise represents both a recovery of classical sources and a critique, such as we find in his refutation of Stoic teaching about the emotions. Against the view that the emotions are opinions and thus controllable by reason, Melanchthon argues that hunger and thirst, and pain and pleasure, are inclinations present without deliberation in animate beings, such as the natural affection (στοργή) that parents have for their children.[59]

The Melanchthonian counterargument to the Stoic view of the emotions is grounded in examples from scripture. The divine law, says Melanchthon (321–22), teaches the best things. Among these are love of God and family and all persons, as well as joy in good things, sadness in bad ones, and contempt for enemies. Moreover, the fruits of the spirit are the emotions enumerated in Gal. 5:22–23. In Melanchthon's view, the emotions are part of creation, and thus it is impossible to consider them evil. In his words, they are the natural affections that have been implanted to be "reminders of the love of God for his son and for us."[60] The reason the Stoics saw the emotions as bad, Melanchthon explains (323), was their inability to grasp the reason for the disruption of the emotions: namely, the effect of humanity's fallen condition.

The limitations of reason have also, according to Melanchthon, diminished the capacity to discern the divine order, even though there is clarity in some things, such as numbers (327). "Now let us consider the actions that separate us from beasts, and which are testimonies of God, and govern life and produce all honorable arts." The disciplines, that is, originate in that part of human nature that is a witness to God and the particular property of humans. The rational faculty, he adds, is the highest power of the human spirit (*summa vis humanae animae*, 328/13), even though compromised.

> Now the extent of our infirmity is to be deplored when we notice that there is such a gap between the two highest powers and knowledge. In this case God's plan must be considered: why he wished knowledge of law to remain in us, and what freedom of will means. Perception remains

---

59 MWA 3, 320/18–21: "Postremo et hoc argumentum ostendit affectus non esse opinions, quia quidam affectus seu inclinations natura insunt animantibus sine deliberatione, ut στοργαὶ φυσικαὶ in parentibus erga sobolem."

60 MWA 3, 322/18–23: "Praeterea nihil a Deo conditum in natura hominum, suo genere malum est. Ut autem lumen in oculis a Deo conditum est, ita cordi insitae sunt στοργαὶ divinitus, et quidem ideo insitae sunt, ut sint commonefactrices de dilectione Dei erga filium et erga nos. Non sunt igitur suo genere vitiosae."

> so that there be evidence of God and that sin be reproached; also, so that there be a director of external discipline. For there remains a level of liberty.[61]

For Melanchthon, there is one ultimate object of the intellect: God and the totality of things (*Deus et tota rerum universitas*, 332/28–29), and persons are created for that end. Melanchthon's frequent claims that the moral law inscribed in all persons includes the first table implies that piety, the "light of awareness of divinity" (*lu*[*x*] *notitia*[*rum*] *divinitus sparsa*[*rum*], 333/32) is a divine demand binding upon all but imperfectly, indeed idolatrously, fulfilled by most.

Melanchthon holds that the divine will is for God to be known, and known with the defining attributes of wisdom, goodness, justice, and "a judge of persons and punisher of sins" (*iud*[*ex*] *hominum, punien*[*s*] *scelera*, 340/6). (The presence of other conceptions throughout history indicates that the existence of deity has never been in question, but these attributes call for a particular understanding of God.) God, says Melanchthon, is the eternal mind (*mens aeterna*, 341/17): wise, true, just, pure, maker and preserver of order, and the punisher of sins; and the human mind is God's likeness. Thus humanity is meant to be true, just, generous, and pure (341). Likewise, the object of the will is also God (345). The will, he states, is free, yet was created "in order to want what is good."[62] This divine object of the will, in Melanchthon's thought, is infinite good, and all "other things are to be sought in their proper order" (*cetera bona suo ordine appetenda*, 348/5).

In the course of his discussion of free will, Melanchthon presents his four reasons or "causes" that moral conduct does not merit forgiveness of sin or count as evangelical righteousness. These are familiar from other texts we have considered, particularly his discussion of freedom of the will in his commentary to *EN* 3.5 at CR 16, 340. The causes are: first, it has been commanded by God; second, it guides persons in avoiding punishment; third, it helps preserve the common peace; and fourth, "external modesty is a pedagogy to Christ: that is, the Holy Spirit is not active in persons who persevere in sin against their

61 MWA 3, 229/21–28: "Iam hic magnitudo humanae infirmitatis deploranda est, cum tantum dissidium esse duarum summarum virium et cognatarum cernimus. Deinde et consilium Dei considerandum est, cur notitiam legis in nobis reliquam esse voluerit, et quails sit in voluntate libertas. Notitia manet, ut sit de Deo testimonium, et ut arguat peccatum. Praeterea ut sit rectrix externae disciplinae. Nam hic gradus libertatis manet."

62 MWA 3, 346/239–30: "Etsi enim est aliqua voluntatis libertas, tamen sic ordinata est, ut velit bonum."

consciences, since conversion is included in divine judgment."[63] Melanchthon continues:

> But since this governing of external actions is to some extent in our power, God wants us not to be slothful or sluggish, but to force our limbs by his law and the fear of punishment as if they were harsh chains. And this diligence among the regenerate and in those who recognize the Son of God with true faith, pleases God. These are clear and plain, and benefit both habits and piety when properly understood.[64]

The will, compromised by the weakness of human nature and the intentions of the devil, can be corrected and guided by the Holy Spirit in those who, aware of these hazards, call prayerfully for help (353). For Melanchthon it is the awareness of imperfection that humbles a person to allow the Holy Spirit to work; thus law, regardless of historical conditions, can reduce a person to that state of need.

We need not pursue the more intricate details of Melanchthon's psychological doctrine, some of which continues Scholastic systems of the faculties, humors, and emotions. Of more interest for our purposes is his conception of the divine image in persons and his view that humanity is meant to correspond to divinity, i.e., that God wants the person to be an image of God and able to perceive and understand the likeness (*similitudinem cerneret et intelligeret*, 362/5–6):

> Therefore [God] bestowed knowledge of human perception which show both the existence and nature of God. For similarity or dissimilarity cannot be judged if we completely ignore what God is like. And the first stage of likeness is to have intellectual ability and congruent wisdom.[65]

---

63 MWA 3, 8–12: "Quarta causa est, quia haec externa modestia est paedagogia in Christum, id est, Spiritus sanctus non est efficax in his, qui perseverant in sceleribus contra conscientiam, quia in iuramento divino comprehenditur conversio." This final explanation is not found in the *Comm.Eth.Arist* 3.5 (CR 16, 340), although the rest of the wording is similar.

64 MWA 3, 353/15–21: "Cum autem haec gubernatio externarum actionem sit aliquot modo in nostra potestate, vult Deus nos non ignavos et segnes esse, sed sua lege et metu poenarum, tamquam vinculis acriter coercere membra. Et quidem haec diligentia in renatis, et filium Dei vera fide agnoscentibus, placet Deo. Haec sunt perspicua et plana, ac prosunt moribus et pietati recte intellect."

65 MWA 3, 362/10–14: "Indidit igitur menti humanae notitias, quae monstrant et esse Deum, et quails sit. Nam similitude vel dissimilitudo non posset iudicari, si prorsus nesciremus

More significant for our understanding of Melanchthon's anthropology is his definition of the soul as an "endelecheia" and his attribution of that term to Aristotle. At the beginning of *De anima*, Melanchthon defines the soul as "the first 'endelecheia' of the organic physical body, the *potentia* of one with life."[66] In point of fact the word Aristotle uses is ἐντελέχεια, fulfillment or completion (*De anima* 412a27), not ἐνδελέχεια (continuity) which is found in Cicero, *Tusc.Disp*. 1.10.22. The Ciceronian passage describes the workings of the mind, something Cicero says is separate from the soul, which he calls "a kind of continuous and perennial movement" (*quasi quaedam continuata motio et perennis*, *Tusc.disp*. 1.10.22, cases altered). Whereas the Aristotelian word accentuates completion, the Ciceronian term places the accent on indefinite duration. As Johann Stigel would explain it in his 1570 commentary on Melanchthon's text, the soul is the formal substance and always in motion; Stigel also defends the word ἐνδέλεχεια and argues strenuously that Aristotle spelled it with a δ and not τ.[67] The difference signifies Melanchthon's understanding of the soul not as its own τέλος but as the imprint of the divine mind and that which participates in it.[68]

This reading of Melanchthon's description of the soul as the productive tension of potentiality and actuality bears certain affinities with Nemesius's view, in *De natura hominis* (99), that the soul (as Aristotle defines it) is the motive power of the body while itself remaining unmoved.[69] For Nemesius, the soul

---

quails sit Deus. Et primus gradus similitudinis est, habere potentiam intelligentem et congruentem sapientiam."

66 CR 13, 12: "Anima est Endelechia prima corporis physici organici, potentia vitam habentis." Cf. Arist. *De an*. 2.1, 412a27–28: "διὸ ἡ ψυχή ἐστιν ἐντελέχεια ἡ πρώτη σώματος φυσικοῦ δυνάμει ζωὴν ἔχοντος." As W. D. Ross explains, "soul is not a substance separate from the body, but an added condition of body, a condition which not all bodies have. When he comes to define soul (in 412^{a}27), he says that it is the *first* ἐντελέχεια of a natural (i.e. not manufactured) body which potentially has life, which without soul potentially has life, and with soul actually has life" (Aristotle, *De anima*, ed. David Ross [Oxford: Oxford University Press, 1961], 15; italics his).

67 Johann Stigel, *De anima Commentarii ... Philippi Melanchthonis, explicatio* (Mühlhausen: Georg Hantzsch, 1570), sig. A6^{v}.

68 In contrast to the completeness implied by the Aristotelian term, Cicero (*Tusc.disp*. 1.10.22) describes the "fifth nature" (*quinta quaedam natura*) as that from which the mind comes and the source of "cogitare enim et providere et discere et docere et invenire et tam multa [alia] miminisse, amare odisse, cupere timere, angi laetare, haec et similia eorum in horum quatuor generum inesse nullo putat," these functions being among (if not exhaustively) those which Melanchthon holds as distinctive to humanity as the image and likeness of God.

69 *Nemesii Emeseni De natura hominis*, ed. Moreno Morani (Leipzig: Teubner, 1987), 28/18–20: "πόθεν οὖν τῷ σώματι τὸ κινεῖσθαι, εἰ μὴ ἀπὸ τῆς ψυχῆς; οὐ γὰρ αυτόκινητόν ἐστι τὸ σῶμα."

is the first entelechy (the ἐντέλεχεια ἡ πρώτη of Ar. *De an.* 412a27) in continuous motion, a movement represented by the Ciceronian alteration of the term. Whether Melanchthon was familiar with Nemesius (whose work had appeared in 1512 and 1538[70]) is beyond our current scope; the concept of participation in the divine mind, long seen as a mark of his Neoplatonist tendencies, illuminates this aspect of Melanchthon's doctrine of the soul. To his earlier definition Melanchthon adds "the definition used in the church," which identifies the soul as an intelligent spirit: "The rational soul is the intelligent spirit, which is the other part of the substance of a person, and is not extinguished when it leaves the body but is immortal."[71]

This soul, says Melanchthon, is a single presence in all persons, the source of breath (*spiraculum*) and at the same time conveying the divine light (*vehens lucem divinam*) and bringing the appropriate life (*vitam congruentem*) to all parts (17). The awareness that Melanchthon describes is not, however, complete or precise. The Melanchthonian concept of the human soul participating in the divine mind accentuates the salience of original sin in his theological anthropology. Like a light apprehended from a distance, the *lux divina* is something that, like a precise understanding of nature, is obscured.

> But let us acknowledge that we cannot distinctly perceive the amazing work of God's wisdom and power in the creation of the world. Let us all the more give thanks to God that we can observe nature in some way and understand a part of it, and discern the traces of God in nature, the culmination of which is certainty.[72]

---

70 Nemesius's work is found in *Divini Gregorii Nyssae episcopi libri octo. I De homine. II. De anima. III. De elementis. IIII. De viribus animae. V. De voluntario et involuntario. VI. De fato. VII. De libero arbitrio*, translated by Burgundio of Pisa and revised by Johannes Cuno (Strasbourg: Matthias Schürer, 1512), with a prefatory letter by Beatus Rhenanus (among others) at xlv–lx. The translation by Georgius Valla appeared separately as *Nemesii philosophi clarissimi De natura hominis liber utilissimus* (Lyons: Sebastian Gryphius, 1538). For Beatus Rhenanus's preface to Jacques Lefèvre d'Étaples, on the value of Nemesius (and of the Fathers generally), see Eugene F. Rice, "The Humanist Idea of Christian Antiquity: Lefèvre d'Étaples and his Circle," *Studies in the Renaissance* 9 (1962), 126–60, esp. 137–39.

71 CR 13, 16 (Definitio Animae usitata in Ecclesia): "Anima rationalis est spiritus intelligens, qui est altera pars substantiae hominis, nec extinguitur, cum a corpore discessit, sed immortalis est."

72 CR 13, 17: "Sed fateamur, nos mirandum opus sapientiae et potentiae Dei in creatione mundi non penitus perspicere. Agamus potius Deo gratias, quod aliquo modo aspicimus naturam, et aliquam partem intelligimus, et vestigia Dei in natura cernimus, quorum summa est certitudo."

In contrast to any assumption that unaided reason is sufficient for understanding things of the material world, Melanchthon's *Liber de anima* offers yet more evidence that the realm of *philosophia*, juxtaposed with *Evangelium* throughout Melanchthon's work, is one in which human capacity is obscured by sin. Although Melanchthon recognizes that mathematical and scientific inquiry is marked by exactitude, matters of human nature and conduct, notwithstanding the rigorous exertions of the foremost classical thinkers, can be understood only imperfectly as a result of sin. For Melanchthon, it is illusory to imagine these disciplines as both complete and autonomous: they are inexact and reveal the limitations of unaided human understanding.

7 Certitude

The comment in the previous section to the effect that exactitude and certainty are possible in the mathematical and natural-scientific realms but not in the arena of moral philosophy and anthropology points to an epistemological distinction essential for understanding the unity of Melanchthon's thought. To these disciplines we must add logic, which for Melanchthon was less a subject in itself than a tool applicable to all subjects. Dialectic treats "all matters or questions about which persons are to be taught, just as arithmetic deals with all things that have to be counted."[73] In the course of his work in ethics, Melanchthon applied dialectics in refuting positions he considered erroneous; and described syllogistic reasoning as certain. The proper task of dialectic, as he states at the beginning of his *Erotemata*, is "to teach correctly, in proper order, and clearly" ([*r*]*ecte, ordine, et perspicue docere*, CR 13, 513). The formal nature of dialectic guarantees its rigor regardless of the validity or speciousness of the propositions under consideration.

The prefatory letter to the *Initia doctrinae physicae*, dated September 1549 and addressed to Michael Meienburg, extols the cosmos as a highly beautiful theater (*pulcherrimum theatrum*) displaying God's work, which exists for the sake of displaying the order and beauty of the "architect" (CR 7, 472–73). In Melanchthon's words, even if the nature of things cannot be completely perceived, and the causes of such admirable works cannot be understood,

73 *Erotemat*[*a*] *dialectices* I, CR 13, 514 (Circa quas res versatur Dialectica?): "Circa omnes materias seu quaestiones, de quibus docendi sunt homines, sicut Arithmetica versatur circa omnes res numerandas."

> Nevertheless now too in this dimness of ours, a certain kind of observation and contemplation of the order of the most beautiful bodies in the world has been given [us] both for recognizing God and for virtue: that is, for loving and preserving order and moderation in all actions. For this whole body of teaching, which the medical art contains, is a great gift to life.[74]

Although the "dimness" (*caligo*) Melanchthon mentions is the limited human understanding of the divine will, he singles out for comment those who disparage natural science because of its seeming inexactitude as exemplified by being unable to predict the duration between comets (473). Such "tenuous and pointless" (*tenuia et ieiuna*) criticism, he says, goes only to Aristotelian foundations and fails to see the full realm of the disciplines (*totus artium orbis*) encompassing medicine and mathematics which ground demonstrations about the shapes and motions of bodies (473–74). Students are to pursue the arts not through Democritean materialism or the corrupted language of Scotus and others, but to take their starting-points from examples whose usefulness (*utilitas*) is evident (475). From the foundations set by Plato, Aristotle, and Theophrastus one should see that these ancient investigators are praiseworthy not just for their scientific work but for their desire to shed light on "this marvelous work of God, namely all the bodies of the world"—to which Melanchthon adds that it is useful to contemplate the divine wisdom and the "traces" (*vestigia*) of the divine architect in nature (476). "In this darkness of the human mind, [God] wants sparks of divine wisdom to shine, and wants persons to apply this teaching, once discovered, to their lives for caring for their health and governing their behavior, indeed for celebrating God the builder."[75]

---

74 CR 7, 473: "Etsi autem natura rerum non potest penitus perspici, nec caussae tam mirabilium operum prius intelligi poterunt, quam ipsius architecti aeterni patris, filii et spiritus sancti deliberationem coram audiemus, tamen nunc quoque in hac caligine nostra qualiscunque aspectio et consideratio ordinis pulcherrimorum in mundo corporum aditus est et ad agnitionem dei, et ad virtutem, hoc est, ad amandum et conservandum ordinem et modum in omnibus actionibus. Deinde magnum vitae praesidium est illa tota doctrina, quam ars medica complectitur."

75 CR 7, 476: "Et gratia debetur omnibus, qui partem aliquam recte et simpliciter monstrant, ac praesertin iis, qui, cum multi audacissime corruperint simplicem doctrinam, ut Democritus, Epicurei, Stoici, Pyrrhonii, et horum similes, monitores sunt iunioribus, ut vitent monstrosas opinions et recta atrium via quaerant versa sententias, nec putent ingenii decus esse ludere praestigiis opinionum, nec acquiescent in veritate, ac deo gratias agant, quod in hac caligine humanae mentis aliquas tamen scintillas suae sapientiae vult lucere, et inventam doctrinam ad usum in vita transferant ad tuendam valetudinem

Physics itself (a term more inclusive in scope than it would be later) is the discipline of investigating and explaining, "as much as possible in this darkness of the human mind" (*quantum in hac caligine humanae mentis*), the movement and cycles of the elements and allows the mind to admire all of nature, since it is in this system of nature that one can discern, within limits, the divine architect whose will for humans is not "to be born to the enormous miseries of this life" (*ingentes miserias huius vitae nasci*) but to see the perfection of which humanity is a (flawed) part (CR 13, 179–80). And evidence of human inability to understand is the confusion of scientific theories: Empedoclean uncertainty, Democritus on the elusiveness of truth, and the denial of certainty in the senses by philosophers of the later "Academy," possibly the Florentine school (180). The dissonance of views is itself evidence for Melanchthon of the inability to understand the *sapientia divina* and the ultimate causes and end of the material universe.

Grounds of certainty are a question raised early in the *Initia*. Melanchthon raises and answers the question of whether there is any certainty in the study of physics by stating that God wants certain governing principles (*rectrices*) in life, shown to be sure and firm, without which—even if they are ultimately uncertain and contain nothing firm—God could not be revealed, nor would there be laws for life.[76]

Methodological skepticism and the denial of intrinsic authority to tradition would leave Melanchthon with no ground for asserting that earlier thinkers, whether in science or thought, had been mistaken. For Melanchthon, certainty in natural science is grounded in three criteria or rules of judgment, which establish certitude: principles, universal experience, and understanding of the consequent, "as the dialectitians teach that these are the criteria for certainty in all disciplines."[77] Principles like those that govern valid consequences in syllogisms, he adds, are what determine proper consequences from experience. Experience shows clearly (*manifeste ostendit*) that there are various qualities and movements in lower bodies: heat in fire, coldness in land and water, and the contrast between these (186). The greater part of physics, he explains, is

---

et regendos mores, imo ad celebrandum deum opificem." Few texts raise questions about natural theology in Melanchthon quite like this letter to Meienburg.

76 CR 13, 185: "Vult Deus artes aliquas vitae rectrices, imo ipsum quoque aliquo modo monstrantes, certas et firmas esse, ut dixit Plato, gratam Dei famam in artibus sparsam esse, quae si prorsus incertae essent, et nihil firmi continerent, nec Deum monstrarent, nec vitae leges essent."

77 CR 13, 186: "Sunt autem κριτήρια tria, id est, regulae iudicii, quae certitudinem ostendunt, scilicet principia, universalis experientia, et intellectus consequentiae, ut Dialectici moment haec esse κριτήρια certitudinis in omnibus artibus."

drawn from experience, which "for the most part" (*plerunque*) permits being led from effects and signs to causes (194).

What Melanchthon means by this *plerunque* unfolds in the locus on God in the *Initia*. Melanchthon orders the topics of physics from the "first efficient cause" (*prima causa efficien*[s], 195) to the goal of human existence (*de fine hominis*, 197), in the process setting natural science within a theological frame. Knowledge of the physical world, he explains, is knowledge of Law as opposed to Gospel. "Here in fact is the dignity of the builder of the entire world, and particularly of humanity, made conspicuous."[78] "There shines in the human mind," he adds,

> [A] knowledge which not only affirms that there is one God, creator of the whole world and of the order in all of nature, but which even teaches what God is like, namely wise, benevolent, just, giving equitably, truthful, a lover of chastity, wishing for our obedience to conform to God's will, and punishing with horrific punishments those who atrociously violate this order, as the whole history of the human race attests, since it clearly shows that all murderers are finally brought to death, while perjurers and those polluted with incestuous and adulterous lusts are ultimately crushed by fatal punishments in a certain divine order.[79]

Resorting to Rom. 1:31 for evidence that knowledge of the divine attributes is universally present yet obscured, Melanchthon states that the nations possessed a knowledge of God even in their unrighteousness, and were able to perceive the power of God through the construction of the world (198). For Melanchthon, knowledge of the physical world falls within Law, and hence would seem to participate to some extent in the function traditionally assigned to it.[80] The order of nature reveals God as the *mens aeterna et architectatrix*

78 CR 13, 198: "Hic vero dignitas universi opificii mundi, ac praecipue hominis conspicitur."

79 CR 13, 198 "Fulget in mente humana noticia, quae adfirmat non solum esse unum Deum, opificem totius mundi et ordinis, in tota natura, sed etiam docet quails sit, scilicet sapiens, beneficus, iustus, aequalia aequalibus tribuens, verax, amans castitatis, postulans ut hanc suam voluntatem nostra obedientia congruat, et puniens horribilibus poenis hunc ordinem atrociter violantes, sicut universa historia humani generis testatur, quae manifeste ostendit homicidas omnes tandem rapi ad supplicia, periuros etiam, et pollutos incestis libidinibus et adulteriis, tandem fatalibus poenis divino quodam ordine opprimi."

80 CR 13, 198: "Ut autem in doctrina Ecclesiae, necesse est saepe commonefieri homines de discrimine Legis et Evangelii, ita hic praemoneo auditores, physicam de Deo noticiam, esse Legis noticiam, non Evangelii." This is to my knowledge the only place in which Melanchthon associates the study of nature (which, given his broad conception of natural inquiry, includes philosophical anthropology) with Law as the counterpart to Gospel.

(200–201), an order from which persons deviate on account of their own freedom. The scientific investigator, upon recognizing the order of causes, must acknowledge that there is one first cause of infinite power. "For if there were several first [causes], there would be no order of causes."[81] In the order of thought, though not in the comprehensiveness of understanding, there is precision.

The working of Providence in the natural order is evidence of this sovereignty and justice. The punishment of the wicked is evidence of providence, for Melanchthon, of a providential order that governs human experience and displays God's care (*cura*) for humanity, evidence for which is completely certain (*certissima*, 204–205.). However, God's absolute sovereignty means that the realm of experience is one of contingency rather than absolute necessity, the latter being understood as the impossibility of contradiction—such as denying God's existence or attributes.[82] Because of God's freedom, the natural order follows its own laws but is subject to interruption by divine intervention: "for what would prayer be like if the mind judged that God is not able to interfere with secondary causes?"[83] Human freedom, likewise, introduces a degree of uncertainty that renders experience unpredictable (209–10).

These two elements, rational exactitude and the inability to perceive the world completely (*penitus*) and predict events, are related: the former provides certainty to the latter. In order to establish beyond question the incapacity of unaided reason to know the divine will, Melanchthon underscores the need for rigorous disciplines like physics and logic. As he states as early as the 1520 *Compendaria dialectices ratio*, for example, logic adds the "sure and exact" (*certa et exacta*) element to the "splendid" (*splendida*) wording of rhetoric (CR 20, 711). "The benefit of dialectic is to be able to speak properly and exactly, and in an order suited for teaching, about any subject."[84] The tension between

His promise to expand on this point (*haec suo loco copiosius declarantur*, 198) remains unfulfilled in this text. In his ethical works, he contrasts *philosophia* and *evangelium* in such a way as to allow him to draw on classical moral thought.

81 CR 13, 202: "Nam si plures essent primae, nullus ordo esset causarum."

82 CR 13, 207: "Necessitas absoluta est, cuius contradictorium simpliciter est impossibile. Sic necessariae sunt hae propositiones: Deus est, Deus est intelligens, iustus, bonus, liber agens." By locating these attributes within the category of absolute necessity, Melanchthon denies any validity to any affirmation of deity that does not include the qualities of intelligence, justice, goodness, and freedom. Hence any assertion of God's existence without these properties stated or implied is incomplete or misguided.

83 CR 13, 206: "Qualis enim erit invocatio, si mens existimet Deum non posse impedire causas secundas?"

84 CR 20, 712: "Fructus dialecticae, est proprie et exacte, de quocunque themate, idque ordine ad docendum accommodato posse dicere." This is also substantially the beginning of the *Erotemata dialectices* (CR 13, 513).

the certainty made possible by rational precision and the incompleteness of human understanding of the divine will, a relationship that characterizes Melanchthon's work, also illumines his recovery of rigorous classical authors. They display rationality in its clearest form while also revealing the limit of human comprehension. Sensibility of this limitation is part of the "pedagogical" function discussed above.

In a 1556 Tübingen disputation, Jakob Beurlin (1520–61) discusses Melanchthon's conception of certainty as it is presented in the *Loci* (obviously not the final version, which did not appear until 1559). Beurlin explains that the church has different grounds (*causae*) of certainty than philosophy. In philosophy, he explains, there are three grounds of certainty: universal experience, innate principles, and the demonstrations, either mathematical or empirical, that are derived from them. To these are added the ground of certainty in the church: divine revelation.[85] Moreover, divine revelation is a ground for certitude independent of the philosophical grounds for truth (A3–3^{v}). For Beurlin, a philosopher who required philosophical corroboration for an article of faith, dismissing revelation as sufficient, would be *plane absurdus*, plainly absurd, and cites Col. 2:8 (a favorite verse of Melanchthon's) against the danger of being deceived by what he calls "inane philosophy" (*inanis philosophia*, A3^{v}).

Beurlin is primarily concerned with certainty in doctrinal disputes and thus with the authority of scripture, and holds both that scripture admits only one correct interpretation and that this was recognized by the Fathers. He attributes discord within the tradition to confusion of civil and ecclesiastical forms of judgment (*iudici*[*a*]). Rulings in the civil realm, he states, are to be obeyed on account of the governing authority, for the principal end of such judgments is the peace of society (*societatis tranquilitas*, A7). The "pedagogical" function of law that we find in Melanchthon's own approach to civil governance is absent from Beurlin's discussion. Equally telling perhaps is his view that the authority of rulers inheres in their office rather than in the finality of their judgment. There is nothing to suggest that the application of philosophy (as he and Melanchthon understand it) yields cogency to affairs of the civil realm;

85 Jakob Beurlin, *Disputatio de causis certitudinis doctrinae ecclesiae Dei, desumpta ex praefatione in Locos Communes D. Philippi Melanthonis* (Tübingen, 1556), sig. A3: "In Philosophiae enim haec tres omnino certitudinis causae numerantur. Experientia universalis. Nobiscum nata principia, & quae ex his conficiuntur demonstrationes: Vt ignem esse calidum, certum est experimento sensus. Bis duo esse quatuor, certum est ueritate principiorum. Animam esse immortalem, certum est euidentia demonstrationum. Sed praeter has alia est causa certitudinis in doctrina Ecclesiae, Philosophiae plane ignota, nempe Reuelatio diuina."

for Beurlin it is thus not more exact than determinations of doctrine and likely less so:

> From all these things which we consider not at all obscure, a certain method must be preserved in handing down the teaching of the church, and it particularly needs to be distinguished from philosophy and its method, because of its different ground of certitude, by which sure and uncertain teachings of the church are discerned: namely divine revelation. Since this remains forever the unique ground of certitude for doctrine and Christian faith, so should the holy and canonical scriptures be considered divine revelation, with none of the obstructive rationality of inane theology.[86]

8 Conclusion

Melanchthon's work has been compartmentalized in ways that have obscured its unity and his place as a religious thinker in the Reformation era. Due to arguably anachronistic divisions of theological disciplines, Melanchthon's "humanism," his "ethics," and his "theology" have been investigated in relative isolation, separated by boundaries that Melanchthon himself would most likely not have recognized as legitimate. Without denying that these are discrete bodies of thought, each with its own coherence, we should recognize that these subdisciplines are systematically interrelated and that Melanchthon's thought cannot be understood except as a unified whole. The interpreter's task is to determine the point of Melanchthon's greatest originality and from that point to argue for the coherence of his thought.

The subordination of the material to the spiritual that the Reformers inherited and sustained in the dual realms of divine governance and, with Melanchthon, in the distinction between *philosophia* and *evangelium*, meant that the divine will was the ordering principle for the secular realm. This is not a new insight into Melanchthon's thought, and Melanchthon is in accord with the broad tradition in this. Although the assignment of the visible church

86 *Disputatio*, sig. A8v: "Ex his obmibus, cum minime obscurum existimemus, Methodum quondam etiam in tradenda Ecclesiae doctrina seruandam esse, eamque potissimum a Philosophia & ipsius method discernendam, diuersa certitudinis causa, qua in Ecclesiae doctrina certa ab incertis internoscuntur, nempe reuelatione diuina. Quae sicut perpetuo mane tunica certitudinis doctrinae & christianae Fidei causa, its nihil obstantibus rationibus inanis Theologiae, solae sacrae & canonicae scripturae, pro diuinis Reuelationibus sunt habendae."

to the temporal realm was central to the institutionalization of evangelical reform, the finitude and contingency of the material universe are fundamental elements of traditional Christian thought.

For Melanchthon, as for much of the tradition, the study of noncanonical and particularly of classical writings has instrumental value: these texts have practical as well as aesthetic benefit, the former outweighing the latter. One rarely finds a Melanchthonian encomium of a classical author that does not point to the usefulness of that figure's work. The orators are models of eloquence, Aristotle is a master of method, and Cicero is an example of the statesman-philosopher. When Melanchthon speaks of the utility of classical study, he is unambiguous in identifying its benefit in the practical realm.

What we find throughout Melanchthon's work is evidence suggesting a protreptic function, specifically an evangelical one, alongside the propaedeutic value that has provided the ground for the customary explanation of his advocacy for humanistic study. Without denying or diminishing the utilitarian value of classical authors for training in logic and eloquence (the propaedeutic use), we can see in his own humanistic writings an undercurrent of affirmations of the value of the classical tradition for piety.

The inescapable implication of Melanchthon's thought concerning the regulating and pedagogical function of positive laws is that biblical law and secular law alike point to the divine will in which, according to Melanchthon, they participate. Thus, while Melanchthon was emphatic in preserving the distinction between philosophy and gospel, and in warning of the risk of confusing the two realms, the moral tradition broadly understood that governed the worldly realm participates in the work of the spiritual world to an extent hitherto unrecognized.

CHAPTER 6

Distinguishing Divine and Human Speech: Idolatry and the Words of Institution in the Eucharistic Debates

Daniel Owings

The Eucharistic debates in early sixteenth-century Europe, as in other times and places,[1] often bled into questions of idolatry: if the real presence of Christ's body and blood in the sacrament was denied, it was naturally a very short step to portraying veneration of the elements as the idolatrous worship of mere bread and wine. Scholarship has long rightly pointed out the deep distrust of material religion operative in this connection: most recently, the analyses of Lee Palmer Wandel[2] and Amy Nelson Burnett,[3] though divergent in many respects, have both reiterated the fact that the impossibility of conveying spiritual benefit through material means provided a central sticking point for many of the Protestant theologians who rejected the bodily presence.[4] Such insights build on the observation that much early Protestant rhetoric cast Roman Catholic practice as external rather than internal, material rather than spiritual, and therefore cheap and insincere rather than heartfelt and truly pious. It is undeniably the case that both anxiety about idolatry and the polemical casting of one's foes as idolaters is shot through with worries about carnal materiality.

---

1 The literature on the history of Eucharistic doctrines and controversies is voluminous. For a general history of the development of the Eucharist in the Latin church (as well as the Roman Catholic developments during and after the age of reform), see Edward J. Kilmartin, s.j. (ed. Robert J. Daly, s.j.), *The Eucharist in the West: History and Theology* (Collegeville, Minn.: The Liturgical Press, 1998). For a history of the rite in the Eastern church, see Hugh Wybrew, *The Orthodox Liturgy: The Development of the Eucharistic Liturgy in the Byzantine Church* (London: SPCK, 2013 [1989]).

2 *The Eucharist in the Reformation: Incarnation and Liturgy* (Cambridge: Cambridge University Press, 2006).

3 *Karlstadt and the Origins of the Eucharistic Controversy: A Study in the Circulation of Ideas* (Oxford and New York: Oxford University Press, 2011) esp. ch. 3.

4 This is not to suggest that all Protestants who rejected or limited Christ's bodily presence in the sacrament can be grouped into a single homogenous category; cf. Wandel's sharply worded, but well-heeded, objections to the category of "spiritual presence" in her review of Burnett (*Journal of Religion* 92.3 [July 2012]: 428–29).

 | DOI:10.1163/9789004527843_007

However, there is some danger in supposing that this worry regarding materiality amounts to the single most important aspect of "idolatry" and the determinative foundation of Eucharistic doctrines that denied Christ's bodily presence in the sacrament.[5] In particular, the differences between Luther and Zwingli in their Eucharistic doctrines (especially in combination with their respective positions on images) can at times be reduced to different attitudes regarding materiality. Carlos Eire, for instance, asserts:

> Zwingli was adamant that true religion could not admit any meditation [sic] through matter ... This principle shaped Zwingli's interpretation of rituals and symbols, and especially of the sacrament of the Eucharist, which for him could never be understood literally as a 'real' communion with the body and blood of Christ. In his eyes the Catholic doctrine of transubstantiation was wrong not only because it was unbiblical, but also because it was the greatest of all affronts to God's transcendence. The Mass, therefore, was itself the worst idol of all, and adoration of the consecrated host the grossest insult to God.[6]

On such an account, the fault line between Reformed and Lutheran that culminated in an irreparable division at Marburg in 1529, dashing all hopes of Protestant unity, came down to a disagreement over a "core metaphysical issue that defined their approach to rituals and symbols." Because Zwingli and his allies couldn't let go of their conviction that "spirit is far superior to matter," they left the Marburg Colloquy unable to muster a much needed political and military unity.[7]

Without minimizing the role that metaphysics played in this debate, I submit that such an explanation obscures, more than it reveals, what was actually at stake for both Luther and Zwingli in their rival conceptions of the

---

5 Wandel and Burnett both steer clear of this danger, but a particularly egregious recent example of this sort is Robert Orsi's *History and Presence* (Cambridge, MA: Harvard University Press, 2016). Orsi, drawing primarily on Wandel's account, paints the various Protestant views of the Eucharist as arising from an emphasis on divine absence over a "grossly material" and thus "disgusting ... " presence (32, *et passim*). This sixteenth-century denial of presence, driven by disgust at the material and bodily, then becomes for him the great tragedy of Christianity and Western civilization writ large—and it is the lens through which he approaches his nineteenth- and twentieth-century case studies.

6 *Reformations: The Early Modern World, 1450–1650* (New Haven: Yale University Press, 2016), 233–34.

7 *Ibid.*, 243.

sacrament.[8] The aim of this essay will thus be to document the manner in which the Eucharistic debates among Protestants were driven on all sides by a fear of idolatry understood not—or at least, not merely—as the use of material elements in worship, but as the fallen mind's *creation* of a false god meant to replace the true. My analysis will focus on the positions and disagreements of Karlstadt, Luther, and Zwingli. In so restricting my focus, I do not mean to suggest that these three are the only theologians in the debate whose voices are worth considering, but merely to draw attention to certain aspects of these figures' rhetoric that has been overlooked in scholarly analysis of their thought.[9] Close attention to the language of these debates will reveal that these three theologians framed their arguments about the rightness or wrongness of doctrine around the question of whether that doctrine encouraged or discouraged the innate tendency of fallen humanity to *speak over God*—that is, to attempt not only to disguise their own human words as divine words, thereby usurping divine authority for them, but in so doing to *un*say the true Word of God. In the Eucharistic debates (and more generally throughout the Reformation), idolatry was one of the names given to this sin of presumption.

At root, the charge of idolatry represents an anxiety about human agency passing itself off as divine agency, and though it is often expressed in the language of material creativity—the idol as the work of a human craftsman—I submit that castigations of materiality *per se* should primarily be seen in the service of a distrust of materiality *as a site of human creativity within the realm of religion*. Because the unifying complaint against Roman Catholicism was that it putatively failed to adhere to God's word and substituted a human institution in its stead, human creativity or invention in worship came to be understood *eo ipso* as deviation from divine rule, and thus as evidence of hubristic rebellion against God. Where Luther, Karlstadt, and Zwingli disagree about Christ's corporeal presence in relation to the bread and wine, they are fundamentally disagreeing about how best to stifle human meddling in the sacrament—and, perhaps more importantly, they are all tacitly in agreement that such human interference is the chief problem to be solved.

---

8 John A. Maxfield has made a parallel case regarding Luther's views of images, arguing against Eire's similar characterization of the distinction between Luther and Zwingli regarding images: "Martin Luther and Idolatry," in Anna Marie Johnson and John A. Maxfield, eds., *The Reformatio as Christianization: Essays on Scott Hendrix's Christianization Thesis* (Tübingen: Mohr Siebeck, 2012), 141–68.

9 A more complete investigation, which space constraints prohibit here, would examine additional contributors to the debate, including Oecolampadius, Bucer, Melanchthon, and Bugenhagen. Each of these, Wandel would remind us, had their own nuanced views of what "real presence" entails.

In arguing thus, I seek to confirm and refine Susan Schreiner's insights regarding the epistemological anxiety undergirding the Eucharistic debates. Schreiner has demonstrated quite conclusively that certainty was such a compelling desideratum of the age that it was used as a hermeneutical test by both Luther and Zwingli; if one's doctrine or reading of a text introduced any uncertainty, it was *eo ipso* false.[10] Highlighting the place of idolatry in these debates helps us to clearly see why this equation of uncertainty with falsity was persuasive. Because all parties agreed that idolatry amounted to replacing the clarity and certainty of the Divine Word with murky, equivocating, deceiving, and deceived human words, it was therefore obvious that uncertainty in a crucial point of doctrine was direct evidence of human (or human-*cum*-demonic) speech passing itself off as God's speech. In this way, attention to the conceptual role of idolatry in the Eucharistic debates helps us to understand why Luther, Karlstadt, and Zwingli differed with each other so vehemently and irreconcilably.

While all three agreed that idolatry was human speech passing itself off as divine speech, they all disagreed about what kind of human speech—and speaker—was most inclined to commit this fraud, and for what reasons. For Luther, the paradigmatic idolater was the Pelagian caught up in works-righteousness to exalt his own self-image to the detriment of God's grace; for Karlstadt, it was the individual who sought to weasel his way out of obedience to the clear command of God; and for Zwingli, it was the malevolent priest who abused his office by teaching the wicked inventions of his own mind rather than the salutary doctrine of God. Each paradigm arose from its originator's view of the primary problem with Roman Catholicism; each, in turn, caused controversy because the others thought it left too much leeway for what they considered the principal problem. Their respective exegeses of the words of institution were thus driven by their ideas about who was most likely to misuse those words, how, and for what end.

1 Luther's Critique of the Mass: Idolatry as Failure to Trust in the Promise

We begin with Luther's understanding of the mass as idolatrous. Luther characterized the Roman mass as a species of works-righteousness. Works-righteousness was, for Luther, equivalent to idolatry insofar as it elevated

10 Schreiner, *Are You Alone Wise? The Search for Certainty in the Early Modern Era* (Oxford and New York: Oxford University Press, 2011), 112–23.

the individual's conscience to the status of divine command while inciting the individual to distrust the true word of God, the promise of salvation. We may loosely sum up his position by stating that all ethical injunctions may be divided between law and gospel; the law kills because it entices us to think we may earn God's favor, while ignoring—indeed, actively avoiding—the life-giving gospel, which reveals that the only truly achievable means of salvation is the grace that God freely bestows through the crucified Christ.

We avoid trusting in this grace for two related reasons. First, our fallen reason is utterly baffled by the offer of free grace; it seems quite obvious to us that our salvation should not come freely but must be earned through some meritorious efforts on our part. But more fundamentally, the free grace of the crucifixion is an affront to our pride, because its most basic meaning is that we are fundamentally incapable of earning our own salvation. Our latent desire to prove to ourselves that we are capable of doing sufficiently meritorious work to obtain justification motivates us to assume that free grace is unreasonable, whereas our earning salvation through obedience to the law is more reasonable. To the fallen mind, faith seems like blasphemy insofar as it abandons works-righteousness. But in fact, Luther says, faith is true piety because it takes God's promise of grace at face value, as opposed to the veiled hubris of the sinner who insists *over God's explicit denial* that they can attain righteousness by their own power. In Luther's view, this repudiation of the promise of free salvation amounts to the creation of a new god, an idol who demands, and can be appeased by, good works.

This is the basic insight that governs Luther's early critique of the mass. It is perhaps most clearly visible in *The Babylonian Captivity of the Church*, his 1520 treatise attacking the sacramental system of the church, of which the Eucharist performed in the mass was the centerpiece. Luther's critique of the mass as the Roman church practiced it names three "shackles" (*captivitates*) that he claims have been imposed on the sacrament in his own time. The first shackle is the administration of the sacrament to the laity in one kind, that is, giving only the bread/body to the laity while reserving the wine/blood for the priests alone. Luther argues that the church can offer no justification for thus emending Christ's clear instructions at the last supper where he says "drink, *all of you*."[11]

While this reasoning sounds similar to the kinds of argument that Karlstadt and Zwingli will make, where the complaint is primarily that Roman teaching deviates from the divine commandment and therefore must be human

11 Mt. 26:27. Cf. John Dillenberger, ed., *Martin Luther: Selections from his Writings* (New York: Anchor, 1962), 257; WA 6.502.

innovation, we will see that Luther's grounds are somewhat more complicated. He is quite insistent, here and elsewhere, that what matters is not whether one performs the sacrament precisely as Jesus did, but whether one *requires* that it be performed in any one particular way. The requirement that the laity receive both kinds, equally with the requirement that the wine be withheld, makes a law of the gospel. It incites the recipients to think that their own correct performance of the sacrament is responsible for the sacrament's effectiveness, rather than recognizing that the sacrament conveys God's saving grace to them with no regard for their just desserts (which is, in every case, death).[12]

The second shackle is the doctrine of transubstantiation *as a necessary article of faith*. Luther makes clear that he regards as less than persuasive the opinion of "the Thomists" that the accidents of bread and wine remain while the substance is changed to body and blood. He prefers instead the suggestion of d'Ailly that the wine and bread remain wholly there in addition to the body and blood, since this requires fewer miracles.[13] Nevertheless, Luther wants only to "allow anyone to hold whichever opinion he prefers. The only thing I aim at ... is to banish scruples of conscience, so that no one may fear being called a heretic if he believes that the bread and wine on the altar are real bread and wine."[14] The phrase "scruples of conscience" is quite telling here, as it refers to a condition often developed in monasteries from which Luther

12 Dillenberger, 264. Cf. WA 6.507: "Prima ergo captivitas huius sacramenti est quo ad eius substantiam seu integritatem, quam nobis abstulit Romana tyrannis, Non quod peccent in Christum qui una specie utuntur, cum Christus non preceperit [1 Cor. 11:24] ulla uti, sed arbitrio cuiuslibet reliquit dicens 'Quotiescunque haec feceritis, in mei memoriam facietis', Sed quod illi peccant, qui hoc arbitrio volentibus uti prohibent utranque dari: culpa non est in laicis, sed sacerdotibus. Sacramentum non est sacerdotum sed omnium, nec domini sunt sacerdotes sed ministri, debentes reddere utranque speciem petentibus, quotiescunque petierint. Quod si hoc ius rapuerint laicis et vi negaverint, tyranni sunt, laici sine culpa vel una vel utraque carent, fide interim servandi et desyderio integri sacrament ... Itaque non hoc ago, ut vi rapiatur utraque species, quasi necessitate praecepti ad eam cogamur, Sed conscientiam instruo, ut patiatur quisque tyrannidem Romanam, sciens sibi raptuni per vim ius suum in sacramento propter peccatum suum ... "

13 Dillenberger, 265. Cf. WA 6.508: "Dedit mihi quondam, cum Theologiam scholasticam haurirem, occasionem cogitandi D. Cardinalis Cameracensis libro sententiarum quarto, acutissime disputans, multo probabilius esse et minus superfluorum miraculorum poni, si in altari verus panis verumque vinum, non autem sola accidentia esse astruerentur, nisi Ecclesia determinasset contrarium." D'Ailly argues this at length in book IV, question 6 of his Sentences commentary; cf. *Quaestiones super libros Sententiarum Petri Lombardi* (Lyon: Nikolaus Wolf, 1500), Biblioteca Nazionale Centrale di Firenze, MS Magl. M.7.32, accessible through ProQuest Early European Books.

14 Dillenberger, 266. Cf. WA 6.508: "Permitto itaque qui volet utranque opinionem tenere: hoc solum nunc ago, ut scrupulos conscientiarum de medio tollam, ne quis se reum haereseos metuat, si in altari verum panem verumque vinum esse crediderit, sed liberum

appears to have suffered, in which the penitent, seeking to make a full confession of all sins committed since one's last absolution, is overcome by an endless stream of internal sins of doubt or omission. We can easily imagine a tortured Luther having spent a good many hours fretting about precisely how many times he had wondered in just the last week whether the substance of bread and wine might remain on the altar—and fearing the wrath of God if he did not explicitly and contritely confess each moment of doubt. But regardless of whether Luther himself struggled with this problem, it is nevertheless the way in which he frames his critique of the doctrine. Thus, the Luther of 1520 is perfectly satisfied if one's righteousness before God is completely unyoked from one's belief about the status of the bread; that is, "no one may fear being called a heretic," since Christ's promise of salvation overrides one's full intellectual assent to any opinion about the bread.

The third shackle that Luther treats, the concept of the mass as a good work or sacrifice, gives us the clearest statement of Luther's general principle here—as Luther himself indicates when he calls this "the most wicked abuse of all." He leads off with the revealing claim that "this abuse has brought in its train innumerable other abuses; and these, when faith in the sacrament has completely died away, turn the holy sacrament into mere merchandise, a market, and a business run for profit."[15] Here he makes the financial abuses dependent on, but ultimately secondary to, the loss of faith that is the key issue. He is, of course, aware that the financial abuses weigh heavily on the minds of his audience; still, he manages to incorporate those concerns into—and subordinate them to—his overriding theological framework of faith in the promise.

He does this by defining the mass as a promise. Following Luke and Matthew, he notes that Christ refers to the sacrament as "the new testament [διαθήκη] in my blood." Luther then states that "testament" here must be understood as a last will and testament. In other words, it is "a promise made by a man in view of his death."[16] The promised inheritance we receive is the forgiveness of our sin. The problem is that, whereas we ought to heed that word of promise,

esse sibi sciat, citra periculum salutis, alterutrum imaginari, opinari et credere, cum sit hic nulla necessitas fidei."

15 Dillenberger, 271. Cf. WA 6.512: "Tertia captivitas eiusdem sacramenti Est longe impiissimus ille abusus, quo factum est, ut fere nihil sit hodie in Ecclesia receptius ac magis persuasum, quam Missam esse opus bonum et sacrificium. Qui abusus deinde inundavit infinitos alios abusus, donec fide sacramenti penitus extincta meras nundinas, cauponationes et quaestuarios quosdam contractus e divino sacramento fecerint."

16 Dillenberger, 273. Cf. WA 6.513: "Testamentum absque dubio est promissio morituri, qua nuncupat haereditatem suam et instituit haeredes. Involvit itaque testamentum primo mortem testatoris, deinde haereditatis promissionem et haeredis nuncupationem."

instead we bring "prayer, self-preparation, good works, outer signs, and genuflections." By relying on these works, we fail to hear the promise and thereby tell ourselves that our salvation ultimately relies on our own efforts rather than on the word God has already spoken. This is the core issue for faith: "these two, promise and faith, are necessarily yoked together. No one can believe if there is no promise. If there is no faith, a promise is useless, because faith is its counterpart and completion." While Luther was clearly worried about attributing too much goodness to our abilities and warned against those who "think they have a right of access to the altar," he was more worried about those like himself who troubled their consciences about unimportant details:

> How many priests you may see everywhere and every day offering the sacrifice of the mass, who, if they have made some error in vestment, or have unwashed hands, or if they stumble in the prayers, or blunder in some small way, make themselves very miserable, as if guilty of a great crime! But, on the other hand, they are not in the least conscience-stricken if they do not reverence or believe the mass itself, i.e., the divine promise.[17]

Thus, Luther frames sin in terms of failing to listen to God, but with the very important qualification that the only divine Word that ultimately matters is the promise. This allows Luther to schematize all human speech acts[18] into

---

17 Dillenberger, 277–78. Cf. WA 6.517: "Quilibet enim facile intelligit, quod haec duo sunt simul necessaria, promissio et fides: sine promissione enim credi nihil potest, sine fide autem promissio inutilis est, cum per fidem stabiliatur et impleatur. Ex quibus itidem facile quivis colligit, Missam, cum sit aliud nihil quam promissio, hac fide sola adiri et frequentari, sine qua quicquid precularum, praeparatoriorum, operum, signorum, gestuum, affertur, irritabula sunt impietatis magis quam officia pietatis, cum fere fiat, ut his paratis existiment sese legitime altaria accedere, et revera non fuerint ullo tempore vel opere magis inepti propter infidelitatem quam secum afferunt. Quantos passim videas et quotidie sacrificulos, qui, si vel inepte vestiti vel illotis manibus vel inter precandum titubantes quid leviuscule erraverint, ingenti sese miseri crimine reos faciunt, at, quod missam ipsam, id est, divinam promissionem, neque observant neque credunt, prorsus ne tantillum quidem habent conscientiae." Thus Quentin Skinner (*The Foundations of Modern Political Thought, Volume 2: The Age of Reformation* [Cambridge: Cambridge University Press, 1978], 6) is not quite on the mark when he says that Luther's primary motive for his innovations were his Augustinian anthropology and low view of human nature. These, indeed, were not at all new but were well-established orthodoxy within many strains of Latin Christianity. The thing newly motivating Luther, rather, was the focus on the voice of the conscience as something idolatrously opposed to the voice of Christ.

18 J. L. Austin's term, although anachronistic, is I think quite applicable here, because the effect of Luther's approach is to reduce all "human reasoning" regarding God—and thus all human speech regarding God—to the *action* of distrusting or turning away from God, in a re-enactment of Adam's fall into original sin. Faith, on the contrary, is reduced to the

two categories: those which point toward the promise of salvation from sin and drive the individual toward faith, and those which help prop up our delusions of the possibility of human merit before God's justice. The former are marked as essentially divine, the latter as essentially human/diabolical (these two forces being understood as always cooperating in sin).[19] This means that idolatry for Luther is not restricted to the priest. Anyone, clergy or lay, who grounds their salvation in obedience to the law rather than in the free promise, is guilty of setting up a false god that will be appeased by that obedience.

2 Karlstadt's Critique of the Mass: Lack of Faith as Disobedience

Early in Luther's reforming career, he was closely allied with Andreas Bodenstein von Karlstadt, a colleague at the University of Wittenberg. After the Diet of Worms in May 1521, when an order for his arrest and prosecution as a heretic was issued from Rome, Luther was hidden away in the Wartburg castle under the protection of the elector Frederick. As a result, Karlstadt was left as the *de facto* religious leader in Wittenberg.

There is much that we might say of Karlstadt's views of the problem with the mass, but the most important task for our purposes is to show his difference with Luther. To that end, we may examine the sermon he preached soon after he performed his first "evangelical eucharist," on Christmas Day of 1521. There is certainly much that sounds very similar to Luther in this work,[20] but already we can begin to see the fault lines that would come to divide the two. From the beginning of the sermon, it is clear that Karlstadt practically treats

---

action of trusting and therefore honoring God, though Luther would characterize this not as a human action but a negation of the same through the intervention of the Holy Spirit. It should be remembered here that the "speech acts" Luther is concerned with are restricted to the "vertical" interaction between God and the individual sinner; he theorizes the "horizontal" interactions among humans as liberated, but essentially unaltered, by faith (although he is somewhat inconsistent on this point).

19 Cf. Heiko Oberman's *Luther: Man between God and the Devil* (New Haven: Yale, 1989). A clear illustration of this conjunction can also be seen in Luther's commentary on Genesis 3, where he makes clear that Eve's sin is only possible as a form of cooperation with Satan.

20 Cf. Ronald Sider's introduction to his translation of the text in *Karlstadt's Battle with Luther: Documents in a Liberal-Radical Debate* (Minneapolis: Augsburg Fortress, 1971 [repr. Wipf and Stock, 2001]), p. 6: "The simple but powerful sermon Karlstadt preached on this historic occasion shows how similar his and Luther's theology were at this time. Although the phrase is not used, the sermon contains a clear, forceful declaration of justification by faith alone."

faith as the fulfillment of a commandment. Karlstadt addresses himself to "what makes one unworthy of this venerable sacrament."[21] He notes that it is a complete lie and invention when someone names something that makes a recipient unworthy of the sacrament if they don't cite scripture. Based on this critique of the standard liturgy as inventing various markers of "unworthiness," Karlstadt structures his sermon around the question of what in fact makes a recipient of the sacrament worthy or unworthy. In discussing how one ought to approach the altar, he exhorts his audience:

> Remember only that you shouldn't approach with unbelief when you want to receive the sacrament, for God will say to you, "Because you haven't believed, you aren't worthy of my comfort and won't see the fruit and increase" ... You can show no greater scorn to God in this sacrament, you can't injure and diminish him more strongly than when you don't believe him.[22]

Clearly Karlstadt joins Luther in yoking the authority of the church to the honor of God that is implicit in a trusting faith; his attack on the prevailing piety is unambiguously rooted in the claim that distrust of the promise of free forgiveness amounts to blasphemy. However, we can see also that this faith is *meritorious*, insofar as it the only thing needed to make one "worthy" of the sacrament. To be sure, Karlstadt thinks the injunction to faith is a commandment distinct from all others. When the sinner trespasses any of the other commandments, "God is gracious, kind, merciful, forbearing ... and does not reproach any believer with his guilt and villainy," whereas the sin of unfaith is far more grave.[23] Karlstadt perceived faith as a fulfillment of the most important law and thus as the key to becoming "worthy" of receiving the sacrament.

While unfaith is a sin of the highest order, Karlstadt does not equate it with idolatry. The site of idolatrous human creation that overturns God's law is the

21 Burnett, 80. Cf. *Predig Andresen Boden. Von Carolstatt zu Wittenberg, Von empfahung des heiligen Sacraments* (Wittenberg: Nickel Schirlentz, 1522), §1: "Welcher wissen un[d] lernen will/ was ihn disses hoch wirdigen sacraments unwirdig macht/ der muß ach-tung haben auff die historien/ geschicht/ und schriffte altes gesetzes/ und fleissig auff sehen/ was die Juden unwirdig gemacht hat gotlicher zusagunghen ... "

22 Burnett, p. 83, §13. Cf. *Predig*, §13: "Gedenck nur dastu nit mit unglauben zu gehst/ wa[n] du das sacrament wilt empfahen/ dan got wirt dir sagen: Drumb dastu dit glaubt hast/ bistu meines trostes un-wirdig/ und wirdest frucht un[d] gedeyhen nit sehen ... Du magst got in dißem sacrame[n]t keine[n] grosser hon thun, du kanst ien nit hefftiger beleydi-gen/ und vorkleinen/ dan wan du ym nit gleubest ... "

23 *Ibid.*, §12: "Nein, got ist gnedig/ gu[o]tig/ barmherzig/ gedultig/ unnd vergibt boßheiten. Jone. 4. [i.e., Jonas 4:2]."

priestly list of things *other than unfaith* to make the sinner unworthy of the sacrament. So here Karlstadt distinguishes himself from Luther, insofar as he still practically makes obedience to (one) law the primary issue. While the two agree that the Roman church's authority is specious and illegitimate because it drives believers to dishonor God through unfaith, Luther had conceptualized the faith that honors God as categorically distinct from obedience; it rather signified a complete surrender of the attempt at obedience, a clinging to God in pure fear and desperation that was a free gift of God's grace infused entirely from without. Karlstadt, on the contrary, seems here to speak as though faith is within the power of the sinner. This is perhaps most evident in his claim that the one who partakes of the sacrament without believing not only "diminishes Christ's honor" but "injures him and mocks him when he sits at his table and remembers the Lord as the Jews and Judas Iscariot remembered him."[24] By comparing the unbeliever to Judas, Karlstadt makes the unfaithful a willful traitor of Christ rather than someone who is blindly caught up in an idolatrous delusion of ethical self-grandeur.

Again, while the recipient of the sacrament who doesn't faithfully hold fast to the promise is, on Karlstadt's telling, guilty of calling God a liar, he is not an idolater: the sin of human creation that usurps God's authoritative voice falls not on the shoulders of the layman, but of the priest who proffers such empty things as "prayer, fasting, confession, chastisements and the like"[25] as ways to make the sinner worthy. The layman's failure to believe the promise is equated not with idolatry but with simple blasphemy. In other words, unlike Luther, Karlstadt does not conflate the dishonor of God in unfaith with the creation of a new false god.

If unfaith is not idolatry for Karlstadt, then what is? And more importantly, in what way might the mass fall under that heading for him? While he does not directly make the connection between mass and idolatry in his early writings, Karlstadt hints at his later view when he says,

> It is a lamentable and horrible thing that I believe a priest when he absolves me and I can't believe him when he speaks the word of Christ

24 Burnett, p. 84; cf. *Predig*, §16: "Welcher disse wort nit ym glawben ergreufft/ der ist disses sacraments gantz unwirdig/ und schneidet Christo/ seine eere ab/ er verlezt ihn/ un[d] spot seiner/ ßo er zu seinem tusch sizet. Und gedenket des hern/ wie seiner die Juden un[d] Judas Iscariota gedacht haben/ nit wie die Junger."

25 Burnett, p. 83; cf. *Predig* §7: "Derhalben soll niemand dencken wie er sich dieses sacraments wirdig unnd empffencklich konn machenn/ durch Betten/ Fasten/ Beychten/ Casteyhen/ unnd der gleychen/ dan ob du disse stuck allsampte/ un[d] aller weltt rew und gut ubung hettest/ un[d] mangelt dir der glawb/ ßo bisttu disses Sacraments unwirdig ... "

> in the manner, form, and way that Christ says it for the forgiveness of sins. It is nothing but a devil's game and anti-Christian teaching that I shouldn't grant the word of the cup as much validity as the invented formula of a wretched priest, especially since they have heard only the form of their authority from Christ, which says "What you bind is bound and what you loose is loosed." [Mt 16:19] This is a form and word of authority that they and laypeople may and can absolve and bind. But I would gladly like to see or hear that they can show me the formula and words for their absolution.[26]

The principal suspect is the priest,[27] who usurps Christ's all-encompassing formula of forgiveness by making the priest's own words of absolution, uttered in the sacrament of penance, the necessary ingredient in forgiveness. The *word* of Christ is unfavorably contrasted to the *game* and *invented formula* of the priest-*cum*-devil. The believer is unquestionably at fault for trusting the latter over the former, insofar as they ought to respect the orders of the highest general, Christ himself, far above those of any mere lieutenant. There is no doubt that Karlstadt holds the believer at fault for not bothering to investigate what Christ actually said and thus not discovering the tension between the words of the two. Nevertheless, the priest is the one who invents a word to drown out God's word.

Regardless of whether we may yet say that this constitutes *idolatry* in Karlstadt's view, it was without a doubt already the center of his critique of the mass. To put it simply, the mass was a conspiracy to encourage the laity to abandon trust in God for trust in rituals invented and performed by human priests. As Karlstadt makes clear in a pamphlet published in November of 1521, a central part of this ploy is dividing the two forms of the sacrament in what is administered to the laity: "the gospel says clearly, 'You should all drink from it,' … It follows that all who have eaten the bread should use the cup, and if they

26 *Ibid.*, §22. Cf. *Predig*, §22: "Es ist ye ein yemerlich und greulich dingk/ das ich eynem pfaffen gleube/ ßo er mich absoluirt/ und kan im nit glauben/ ßo er das wort Christi in seiner art/ form/ un[d] weiß spricht/ wie das Christus/ zu vergebung der sunden spricht/. Es ist nichst dan des Teuffelß spihl und Endchristis laher das mir das wortt des kelches nit ßo vil gelten soll/ alß eyn erdicht form eyn-nes elenden pfaffen. Angesehen das sie allein form yrer macht von Christo verhort/ Welche alßo laudet. Waß yr pindet/ das ist gepunden. Waß yr ablößet/ das ist geloset. Daß ist ein form und wort der macht das sie/ und leyhen/ mogen und kunden absoluiren und pinden. Aber gern wolt ich sehen oder horen/ das sie mir form un[d] wort/ yrer absolution zeigten."

27 This accords with his depiction of idolatry in relation to images in another pamphlet, *On the removal of images*. There he argues the primary agent responsible for the illicit introduction of images into churches were the priests who sought financial gain thereby.

don't, then they divide the mass and the venerable sacrament."[28] Both clergy and laity sin in deviating from the prescribed order of the last supper, although the sin of the clergy is far greater because they are responsible for leading the laity astray. This eventually became the clear meaning of the term "idolatry" for Karlstadt as he wielded it against Catholic and Lutheran understandings of the real presence in the Eucharist.

3 Luther's Clash with Karlstadt

Luther grew increasingly agitated at the lack of control his seclusion imposed, and the cracks between his own views and Karlstadt's that had been so easily spackled over in the face of common opposition to Rome quickly grew to unbridgeable chasms in Luther's eyes. In early March of 1522, Luther re-entered Wittenberg to regain control of the situation. Within days, he was preaching a series of eight sermons indirectly attacking Karlstadt's position. These sermons, known as the *Invocavit Sermons*, essentially accused Karlstadt's hardline position of idolatrous works-righteousness. (Luther later reiterated these same arguments in his 1525 treatise *Against the Heavenly Prophets*.) His basic move was to make Karlstadt's prohibitions, against both images and reception of the sacrament in one kind only, equivalent to the Pope's requirements of the same. Both amount to a human claim on righteousness originating in one's own ultimately indifferent actions. God couldn't care less whether we take the sacrament in one kind or two, so long as we understand that our salvation is utterly dependent on His unmerited grace; but it is precisely this insight that is lost in insisting that the believer must take the sacrament in both kinds.[29] In the fifth *Invocavit* sermon, Luther puts it as follows:

> Although I hold that it is necessary that the sacrament should be received in both kinds, according to the institution of the Lord, nevertheless it

28 E.g.,"On Both Forms of the Holy Mass" §21, in Burnett, *Eucharistic Pamphlets*, 68.

29 Burnett is thus not quite correct to say that "Luther rejected [Karlstadt's utraquist view] because he believed that this placed too much emphasis on an external act" and "The issue dividing Karlstadt and Luther therefore ... [was a] fundamental disagreement on the relationship between external actions and internal disposition ... " (*Origins*, 32–33). Luther was not concerned with the exteriority or interiority of the act, nor can Luther's faith simply be mapped on to the internal. As we saw in *Babylonian Captivity*, insistence upon an internal act of belief about the substance of the Eucharist could be just as opposed to faith as the demand that believers externally commune in both kinds. The sticking point was rather the *necessity* of the act for salvation, which Luther considered opposed to faith insofar as it made the believer, rather than God, the ultimately responsible party.

> must not be made compulsory nor a general law. We must rather promote and practice and preach the Word, and then afterwards leave the result and execution of it entirely to the Word, giving everyone his freedom in this matter ... I was glad to know when someone wrote me, that some people here had begun to receive the sacrament in both kinds. You should have allowed it to remain thus and not forced it into a law. But now you go at it pell mell, and headlong force everyone to it.[30]

Within a few months, Karlstadt was *persona non gratis* in Wittenberg. He moved to Orlamünde in 1523 and was formally banished from Saxony in September of 1524.[31] Luther's position of dominance within the new capital city of Church Reform was beyond question as soon as he returned.

In response, Karlstadt more fully developed his own understanding of the mass as idolatrous so as to prove that it was Luther's views, rather than his own, that were still enveloped in the Pope's errors. In October of 1524, in response to a public confrontation with Luther at the Black Bear Inn in Jena,[32] Karlstadt published five separate tracts attacking various aspects of Luther's Eucharistic teaching and practice. The theme of idolatry became more pronounced in these writings as Karlstadt sought to smear Luther as a "new Papist." In each of these tracts, Karlstadt makes clear that what marks both Lutheran and Catholic doctrines as idolatrous is their claim to summon Christ's body into the sacramental elements, thereby appropriating to their own ritual actions the efficacy and honor that rightfully ought to belong only to Christ's actions on the cross. While many of Karlstadt's arguments focus on the bread, and seek (with varying exegetical success) to make the bodily presence of Christ in the sacrament equivalent to the presence of bread on the cross,[33] what is at stake

30 LW 51:90–91. Cf. WA 10/III: 45–46: "Nun woellen wir von den zweyen gestalten sagen. Wiewol ichs darfür halte, Es soltte sein von noetten, das mann das Sacrament under beyder gestalt nemen nach der auffsetzunge des herrn, jedoch sol man keynen gezwang darauß machen noch in eyne gemeyne ordnung stellen, sonder das wort treyben, uben und predigen, dannocht darnach die folge und treibunge dem worte heym geben oder stellen und jederman hierjnnen frey lassen ... Und hoertte es gantz gerne, Do es mir geschrieben wardt, das ettliche alhie angefangen hetten, das Sacrament in beyderley gestalt zunemen. In dem braüch haettet jrs soellen lassen bleyben, jn keyn ordnunge gezwungen haben. Nůn fart jr aber purdi purdi hin zů und wolt mit den koepffen hindurch und wolt jederman hinzů dringen."

31 Cf. Sider, *Andreas Bodenstein von Karlstadt: The Development of His Thought 1517–1525* (Leiden: Brill, 1997), 174–201.

32 Sider summarizes the events and provides a translation of the record of the dispute in *Karlstadt's Battle with Luther*, 36–48; cf. WA 15.323–340.

33 E.g., "Exegesis of this word of Christ, etc.," in Burnett, *Eucharistic Pamphlets*, 148.

in these arguments is not the worship of a material element, but the question *who gives Christ's body*—Christ himself, or the priest passing out the bread?

> If Christ gave his body to the disciples in the bread, then Christ also gave his body in the bread for his disciples [i.e., was crucified in the form of bread] and further, will give his body in the future for all those to whom he should give his body today in the sacrament. But this is anti-Christian, for it would be as if to say that Christ was crucified and died for us in the bread ... It would also follow that *Christ must die as often as a priest gives him to a Christian in the sacrament.*[34]

It is on this basis that Catholics and Lutherans "should know that they are judged and handed over by these words, that they have no more help or excuse for their idolatry, and that they should be avoided as subtle enemies of Christ's cross." Christ's words, *This is my body, given for you,* must refer to the body given on the cross, and "it is absolutely impossible that Christ thought about the giving of his body and shedding of his blood that is supposed to happen in this sacrament."[35]

In another pamphlet, Karlstadt refers to the ciboria which hold the consecrated host as "prisons" in which priests try to lock up Christ, as well as to the bread itself (citing Hebrews 9) as a "temple built by human hands."[36] Thus, it is not simply the adoration of a creature, bread, which constitutes the mass as

---

34 *Ibid.*, 149 (emphasis mine). Cf. Andres Carolstat, *Auslegung dieser wort Christi, etc.* ([Basel: s.n.,] 1524) b.i verso "Wenn nu[o]n Christus seinen leyb in dem brodt/ den iün-geren geben herr/ so het auch Christus seinen luyb/ in dem brodt für seyne iünger gegeben/ unnd würdt fürter/ für seynen leib heüttiges tages in dem sacrament geben sal. Das aber ist endchristisch. Denn es were so vil gesagt. Christus ist für unß in dem brodt gekreüzi-gen unnd ge-storben. Christus hatt seyn bul[o]th inn dem kelch ver-gossen. Es würdt auch volgen/ das Christus so offt ster-ben müst/ so offt jnen eyn pfaff/ eynem Christen/ inn dem sacraement gybet/ das aber stünd wider Petrum unnd Palum [sic]/ so sprechen/ Das Christus nicht mehr sterben würdt."

35 *Eucharistic Pamphlets*, 156–57. Cf. *Auslegung dieser wort*, d.1 recto and verso: "Da-rumb ist es ganz unmo[e]glich/ das Chistus vo[n] der gebu[n]g seines leybes/ unnd vergiessung seines blu[o]thes/ so in dem sacrament sollen geschehen sein/ gedacht hab ... Darumb sollen die papisten wissen/ das sie/ obgemelte wort richten un[d] überwesen werden/ das sie irer abgo[e]t-terey keine behelff oder endschuldigu[n]g mehr haben mo[e]ge[n]. Das sie auch als subtile feind des kreüzess Christi/ zu[o]flie-hen seind."

36 "Dialogue on the Horrible, Idolatrous Misuse of the Most Worthy Sacrament," in Burnett, *Eucharistic Pamphlets*, 198–99. Cf. *Dialogus oder ein gesprechbüchlin Von dem grewlichen vnnd abgöttischen mißbrauch des hochwirdigsten sacraments Jesu Christ* (Basel: 1524), f.4.v–g.1.r, where protagonist Petrus refers to the bread as "gefenknüssen" as "eine[n] tem-pel ... den mensche[n] hende gewir-cket habe[n]."

idolatry; the most idolatrous element is the moment of consecration, in which a human priest falsely claims to have captured God within the ciborium in the form of bread.

This line of argument largely went unanswered by Luther. In *Against the Heavenly Prophets*, his 1525 response to Karlstadt, he maintained the line that Karlstadt was making a gospel-killing law out of his insistence that no symbols should be employed in the Eucharist that could possibly imply that it was a sacrifice (e.g. calling it "mass," elevating the host, and so forth). He didn't remark on the claim that the priest was seizing Christ's honor through the ritual because he was too preoccupied with the notion that all parties involved might dishonor Christ through failing to trust in his promise of free forgiveness by attaching too much importance to the ritual in whatever form it took.

4 Zwingli on the Mass: The Elevation of Human Law over Divine Law

While all these developments were coming to fruition in the north, a related but separate Reformation was underway in the south, led in Zürich under the direction of Huldrych Zwingli. Loosely inspired by Luther's writings, Zwingli nevertheless insisted that his own reform efforts were entirely *sui generis*. His reform is said to have begun during Lent in 1522—around the time Luther was preaching the *Invocavit* sermons—when Zwingli preached in support of a printer and some of his workers who had broken the Lenten fast by eating sausages, contrary to canon law. By October of 1523 he had convinced the town council to hold a public disputation regarding reform, at which he won a decisive victory. One of the articles debated there—the 18th article, to be precise—was an early statement of Zwingli's doctrine of the Eucharist.

If we begin by simply looking at the thesis itself, we may note a couple of interesting emphases. The text of the thesis reads:

> That Christ who offered himself up once as a sacrifice is a perpetual and valid payment for the sin of all believers; from this it follows that the mass is not a sacrifice, but a memorial of the sacrifice and a seal of the redemption which Christ has manifested to us.[37]

---

37 HZW 1:92; cf. Z 2.111: "Das CHRISTUS sich selbs einest uffgeopfferet, in die ewigheit ein wärend und bezalend opffer ist für aller gleubigen sünd; daruss ermessen würt, die mess nit ein opffer, sunder des opffers ein widergedächtnus sin und sichrung der erlösung, die CHRISTUS uns bewisen hat."

The primary focus here, as for Karlstadt, rests on the question of sacrifice in relation to the Eucharist. Zwingli restricts both the agency and the substance of the sacrifice to Christ, who "offered himself up once," and implies that making any other party a participant in that single sacrifice should be seen as an attack on the "perpetual and valid" nature of Christ's sacrifice. From this reading, Zwingli draws the conclusion that the mass is not a sacrifice, but a "memorial" and "seal" of the single effective redemption Christ worked upon the cross.

Already we can see that the question of "materiality" was not important enough for Zwingli to raise to the byline summarizing his point. Indeed, Zwingli implicitly maintains the importance of the material reality of what Christ underwent on Calvary when he refers all Eucharistic piety back to that event. The question is not whether God can be materially present to the believer—as yet, the issue of presence has not even come into view—but whether the work of the priest performing the mass should be considered a sacrifice, that is, a work which offers God some gift which is pleasing to Him and which might be credited to the merit and authority of the priest performing it. It is this which Zwingli vehemently denies, insisting instead that the merit and authority conferred by the name of "sacrifice" belong properly only to Christ.

To this sacrifice, he contrasts the elements of bread and wine as *aides-mémoires*, thereby suggesting the parallel contrast between Christ as unique high priest and human ministers of the sacrament. The latter are not, or should not be, defined by their ability to broker a quasi-economic transaction with God; they derive any authority they hold solely on the basis of their ability to point back to the unique high priest's single sacrifice. Any attempt to highlight the importance of their own role in the sacrament—including any doctrines, liturgical practices, gestures, metaphysical claims, or the like that might work to persuade the congregation of their special status before God—detract from their proper task, insofar as they thereby point to themselves rather than back to Christ. While Zwingli's opponents will eventually bring the debate to center on his characterization of the bread, the heart of the matter for Zwingli is the human priest standing over the bread: what claims he makes, what power he wields as a result, and whether this power enables him to lead his flock to, or away from, God.

This basic assessment of the article is confirmed by the explanation for it that Zwingli offers, and particularly by its exegetical basis. The first section of the explanation cites the epistle to the Hebrews almost exclusively. Here the contrast between Christ as the one, eternal, spotless high priest and the Old Testament's many, temporal, faulty priests is carried over to the contrast between Christ and priests who claim to offer sacrifice in the mass. Especially noteworthy is the use Zwingli makes of the difference between the two temples in Hebrews: the priests of the old covenant "went into a temple ... which was temporal; for it was *made by human hands* ... But Christ did not enter such a temple, but heaven which cannot be destroyed since it is not made by human hands."[38] Materiality, locality, or metaphysics are not what Zwingli points to as making heaven the proper realm for Christ's bodily presence, but rather the fact that the heavenly temple is not made by human hands; this designation hearkens back to discussions of idolatry, of course, by pointing to the absence of human agency so as to guarantee exclusively divine agency. Thus, for priests to claim the prerogative of repeating the sacrament daily not only leads the flock astray; it belittles and degrades Christ.[39]

In all this, Zwingli sounds very close to Karlstadt. The priests are the prime suspect when it comes to idolatry because they are so easily tempted to make the Eucharist a buttress for their own authority to impose laws on their congregations, rather than a reminder of Christ's sacrifice. However, when Zwingli comes into open conflict with Luther, he will articulate a somewhat different understanding of why the doctrine of the bodily presence of Christ in the sacrament is such a dangerous one. He will regard it as a lie that the priests officiating the sacrament *make the recipients tell themselves*.

5 Zwingli's Clash with Luther: The Bodily Presence

Zwingli's *Letter to Matthew Alber* was the first published tract in which Zwingli specifically positioned himself vis-à-vis other reformers with regard to the Eucharist. He was prompted by Karlstadt's five treatises of 1524 to publish the letter as a statement of his own position. It was well-known that the views Karlstadt expressed in these were similar to Zwingli's own, so Zwingli was obliged to defend his views against Luther's excoriation while distinguishing

---

38 HZW I:93, emphasis mine. Cf. Z 2.112: "Diser worten [d.h., Hebr. 9:11f.] meinung ist kurtzlich: Christus ist vil ein krefftiger obrester priester, dann die im alten testament xin [gewesen] sind. Dieselben sind in einen tempel oder tabernackel ingegangen, der abgenglich was; dann er von menshcen henden gemacht, und habent imm selben tempel vihenblu[o]t uffgeopfret. Aber Christus ist nit in ein sölichen tempel, sunder in den himel inggangen, der nit zerbrochen mag werden; dann er nitt von menschenhenden gmacht ist."

39 HZW I:94; cf. Z 2.114: "Und so er für und für mu[o]ßte widrumb uffgeopfret werden, hette er ein gstalt glych wie die opffer inn dem alten testament, die ouch umb ir unvolkommnus willen mu[o]ßten gewidret werden. Das wäre ie ein mindrung und schmach der volkummenheit des opffers, das Christus ist, der sich selbs durch sinen tod hat got für aller menschen sünd uffgeopfret, die ye warend und immer me werdend."

himself from the black sheep of the reform movement.[40] Though he doesn't specifically name Luther, it is clear that he has his writings in mind. Zwingli does, however, name Karlstadt.[41] Damning him with faint praise, he says that Karlstadt is substantially correct in his Eucharistic doctrine but bunglingly puts it forward "in such a way that it offends rather than edifies" the unenlightened. Zwingli inserts himself so as to more capably handle such an intricate and subtle theological matter, although he is quick to caution that even his own powers of explanation are useless if God should not aid him.[42]

Zwingli begins with a consideration of John 6:35–59 to argue for a basic exegetical distinction between the "spiritual," "metaphorical" meaning of Christ's words and the "obtuse," "Jewish" interpretation of them. He asserts that Christ, in calling himself the bread of life, is quite plainly talking about his coming death, and is offering an image to help his audience more easily understand what he is saying. Belief in his sacrifice for humanity grants life, in the same way that eating bread grants life. Zwingli simply takes the image "bread of life" to be a very clear illustration of what faith in Christ would offer. But due to the Jewish audience's attachment to the senses, they insisted on taking the metaphor literally, thereby totally missing the point: "The Jews, inasmuch as they are ignorant of the spirit, failed to comprehend that Christ meant 'eats me' to be understood as 'believes in me' … "[43] This is self-evident to Zwingli because a carnal eating could produce only carnal results, whereas Christ clearly indicates a spiritual result, an inward refreshing.

Importantly, Zwingli points again to the senses to bolster his point. He argues that if we were to eat Christ's physical body according to the fleshly sense, then we would *see* the body in the bread, precisely because vision is a bodily sense: "Is there any other physical body than that which is perceived? Yet what is perceived is an object of the senses. Since the senses perceive nothing here [i.e., perceive only bread in the sacrament], and whatever is done takes place inwardly, what need is there of talking of the body insofar as it is the body, since it is not in this way that Christ is the food of the soul … " It is

---

40 Cf. H. Wayne Pipkin's account in his introduction to the letter, HZW II:129, as well as Burnett's account in *Origins*, 92–101.

41 Cf. Wandel, *The Eucharist in the Reformation*, 62.

42 HZW II.131; cf. Z 3.335–36. Note that Zwingli's phrasing of the standard humility topos has the convenient rhetorical benefit of implying that his own explanation is divinely inspired if the reader so much as understands it clearly.

43 HZW II.134; cf. Z 3.338–39: "Porro Iudaei sensum hunc, utpote rudes spiritus, non adsequti [sic], ut pro 'me edit' sentirent Christum 'in me credit' velle intelligi, sic non modo rustice, verum etiam contumeliose respondebuant [Jn 6:52]: Quomodo potest hic nobis carnem suam dare ad manducandum?"

the very fact of a discord with our sensation that produces Zwingli's conviction that God must have meant something other than what the surface of the text indicates. With this, Zwingli can conclude, "Why, then, are we asking about eating the body? His body is eaten when it is believed that it was slain for us. It is faith, therefore, not eating, about which Christ is speaking here."[44]

In other words, Zwingli identifies the primary problem with the doctrine of the bodily presence as its insistence that the laity disbelieve their eyes. Whereas their eyes and common sense tell them it is bread on the altar, the priest who would claim to consecrate the host into Christ's literal body and blood must demand that his congregation trust his own proclamation against every other piece of evidence. This same basic complaint recurs throughout the back-and-forth with Luther over the next five years. Insisting on the bodily presence is not only a red flag of a priest on a power trip; it must be a human invention because, to Zwingli's mind, this claim is only conducive to reinforcing the priest's own power of consecration and does nothing to make Christ's actual sacrifice on the cross more effective. There is an obvious and clear reading of the words of institution which does not require us to believe that the ordinary powers of our perception have been suspended at the daily behest of a priest. When Christ says, *this is my body*, he is simply speaking metaphorically: the "is" simply means "represents," as it does in countless of his other sayings. No one would insist that "I am the true vine" necessitates understanding Christ to be a literal vine. That anyone would insist on reading Christ's words at the last supper in a strictly literal fashion when such a straightforward alternative interpretation is available can only indicate the basest malfeasance or diabolical deception.

Most importantly for our purposes, this is how the substitution of human creation for divine creator is most likely to occur, in Zwingli's view, and so it is what makes the real presence theologically dangerous. While the distinction between spiritual interior and carnal exterior is an important piece of evidence that Zwingli musters in support of his argument, he is not simply opposed to the intermixture of spirit with matter from a detached Platonic sensitivity. Rather, he makes clear that his primary concern is the theological danger that such a doctrine will do nothing to direct believers to the true

---

44 HZW II.134; cf. Z 3.339: "An ne corpus aliud est, quam quod sentitur? Quod autem sentitur, organorum est obiectum. Organa igitur, qum [sic] hic nihil aliud sentiant, sed intus fit, quicquid agitur: quid opus est de corpore, quatenus corpus est, loqui? qum sic Christus non sit cibus animae (alioqui Iudaei non tantopere ab eo abhorruissent); sed quatenus iuxta hoc corpus necatus est, sic est animae cibus ... Quid igitur de corporis manducatione quaerimus? Tunc editur corpus eius, qum pro nobis creditur caesum. Fides ergo est, non manducatio, de qua Christus hic loquitur."

miracle of the true God's crucifixion, instead only lending support to priests who would lead their flocks toward a false miracle and a false human-made god. This idol is not primarily manufactured in the baking of bread, but in the specious interpretation of the words of institution.

Luther viewed the matter in precisely opposite terms: rather than seeing the attack on reason as a sign that a human priest was attempting to create a false god for his congregation, he saw human reason itself as the crucible in which idols were forged. Already in the *Babylonian Captivity*, Luther had framed the matter thus: "When I fail to understand how bread can be the body of Christ, I, for one, will take my understanding prisoner and bring it into obedience to Christ; and, holding fast with a simple mind to His words, I will firmly believe, not only that the body of Christ is in the bread, but that the bread is the body of Christ."[45] It was precisely the unreasonableness of the doctrine that guaranteed its veracity for Luther. We will remember that Luther associated reason with the law; it was fallen reason that was bewitched into thinking it had anything worthwhile to offer to God, and reason that thus insisted on rejecting the promise of free grace as eminently unreasonable.

Luther took the bodily presence of Christ in the sacrament to be the token of that promise. Thus, it was to be expected that reason should balk at accepting the sacramental presence as absurd. Zwingli was not accusing the *priest* of deception, then, but accusing *Christ himself* of lying when he promised to be there in the bread and wine. But to call Christ a liar was the very definition of idolatry for Luther, and it was ultimately reducible to a reliance on one's own righteousness to save oneself without needing Christ's help. Zwingli's exasperated compilation of all the other places in the gospels where Christ used figurative language was for this reason a red flag for Luther: it seemed obvious that Zwingli was just grasping for any possible explanation other than the plain clear meaning of Christ's words, just as reason looks for any possible meaning for the crucifixion except the obvious fact that we are hopelessly lost without it.

Luther's vehement response to Zwingli (and other "sacramentarians" such as Oecolampadius and Bucer) came clearly enough in his 1527 treatise, "That These Words of Christ, 'This is my body,' etc., Still Stand Firm Against the Fanatics." There he cast all who would oppose his understanding of the real presence as wanting to make God weak. In the first place, he takes claims

---

45 Dillenberger, 269. Cf. WA 6.511: "Ego sane, si non possum consequi, quo modo panis sit corpus Christi, captivabo tamen intellectum meum in obsequium Christi, et verbis eius simpliciter inhaerens credo firmiter, non modo corpus Christi esse in pane sed panem [1 Cor. 11:23ff] esse corpus Christi."

about the impossibility of the bodily presence to be reason's feeble challenge to an omnipotent God:

> It is not necessary in this matter for them to teach us that Christ is seated at the right hand of God, having left the earth and ascended into heaven, and that our hearts should cling to him there and not to earthly things—and a host of other such arguments; for by God's grace we know all these things perfectly well. Rather, what is necessary is to prove convincingly how these two points are contradictory: *Christ's body is seated at the right hand of God, and is at the same time present in the supper*; how it may come to pass that God's power could become so weak that it is unable to accomplish this, and how all this may be proven by sound argument and clear Scripture. Here is where we should be instructed, here is the real need, to convince us that the words "This is my body," are dark and obscure and need to be understood otherwise than the way they read.[46]

He then goes further, supposing that the "sacramentarians" are attempting to insult the body of Christ itself:

> Similarly, you need not teach us that flesh is of no use, and that we must eat, live, and do all things spiritually, and that without the spirit nothing is of use. This we realize already. We should like to know more—namely, how the statement "FLESH IS OF NO USE" is contrary to the statement "CHRIST'S BODY IS IN THE BREAD." Again, we should like to be assured that "FLESH IS OF NO USE" is said concerning Christ's body; again, that Christ's body is a perishable, useless, corruptible food, though he himself says in John 6[:51] that it is an imperishable food which gives life.[47]

---

46 Trans. Burnett, "That These Words of Christ ... Still Stand Firm," in Paul W. Robinson, ed., *The Annotated Luther. Vol.3: Church and Sacraments* (Minneapolis: Fortress, 2016), 270 (emphasis Luther's). Cf. WA 23.274: "Es ist nicht not zu dieser sachen, das sie uns leren, wie Christus zur rechten Gotts sitzt, die welt verlassen hat, gen hymel gefaren ist und unser hertzen daselbst hin sollen hengen, nicht auff yrdisch ding geben und des gleichen viel, denn wir solchs alles von Gotts gnaden wol wissen. Sondern das ist not, das sie gewis machen und beweisen, wie die zwey stuck widdernander sind, CHRISTUS LEIB SITZT ZUR RECHTEN GOTTS UND IST ZU GLEICH YM ABENDMAL. Wie es zu gehe, das Gotts gewalt so schwach worden sey das sie solchs nicht vermuege, und das solchs alles mit gutem grunde und heller schrifft uberwunden werde. Hie sol man uns leren, da ligt die not, auff das wir sicher muegen sein, das die wort, 'Das ist mein leib' tunckel vnd finster seyen, vnd anders zuverstehen denn sie lauten."

47 Burnett, "That These Words ... ", 271 (emphasis Luther's). Cf WA 23.274: "Desselbigen gleichen duerfft yhr uns nicht leren, wie fleisch kein nuetze sey, und wie man muesse

Luther sees all of Zwingli's arguments as reducible to distrust in God's power. Time and again throughout the treatise, he positions himself as defending God's ability to do the impossible, such as to be both in heaven and in the bread, over against Zwingli's insistence that this is absurd. At one point, Luther claims to have found the root cause of his opponents' caviling in the *difficulty* of believing that the bread is God's body.[48] Luther paints Zwingli as doing battle against God and arguing with God about what is or isn't reasonable for God to do.

This not only misrepresents Zwingli's own objection; it glosses over a very crucial insight from Zwingli. Zwingli does not see himself as fighting against God, but rather as fighting against the priest who would deceive his congregation and use the name of God to further his own standing. For instance, in the *Subsidium sive coronis de Eucharistia* (1525), while he does complain about how some "urge that there are many things in the divine writings which are inconsistent with all sense, which you must yet believe or you are an infidel,"[49] his point is not simply that it is difficult to believe. The problem is rather that the believer is being *compelled* to believe something impossible, which he himself cannot make sense of, and *therefore* human deception rather than Divine truth must be doing the compelling.

Zwingli is naming a danger that Luther doesn't quite recognize because Luther so strenuously restricts the matter of true religion to the relation between the individual believer and God. For Luther, the Roman church is a problem only to the extent that it puts itself in the way of that relation, but to his mind this always ultimately entails thrusting the believer back upon herself and her own powers; other abuses of power are secondary and derivative.

---

geistlich essen, leben und alles thun, und wie on geist nichts nuetze sey, Solchs koennen wir schon. Wir wolten gerne mehr wissen, nemlich, Wie der spruch FLEISCH IST KEIN NUTZE sey widder den spruch CHRISTUS LEIB IST YM BROD, Item das wir gewis werden, das von Christus leib gesagt sey FLEISCH IST KEIN NUTZE. Item des Christus leib eine vergengliche unnuetze vermesenliche speise sey, so er doch selbst Johan. vi. spricht, Es sey eine unvergengliche speise, die das leben gebe."

48 "They have one argument, however, which I regard as the strongest of all; they are in earnest about it too, and I believe it is true. It is this: such articles, they say, are burdensome to people. For it is difficult to believe that a body is at the same time in heaven and in the Supper ... [O]ut of this argument spring all their other arguments ... Here we have caught the fanatics in their own confession that they are enemies of the sacrament and feel spite, aversion, repugnance, and loathing in their hearts toward it; ... [but] there's no fighting against God's wisdom; God is bound to win." Burnett, "That These Words ... ", 219. Cf. WA 23.161.

49 HZW II.217; cf, Z 4.492: "Secundo sic instat: multa esse in divinis scripuris, quae ab omne sensu abhorreant, quae tamen nisi credas, perfidus sis ... " This is one of the places Burnett names as a possible source for Luther's accusation: "That These Words ... " 219, note J.

Zwingli, by contrast, considers the institutional usurpation of God's authority to be primary. He views the baser motives of clergy as the greatest theological threat—not because he is incensed by the social injustice they entail, but precisely because they incentivize both human pastors and congregations to look away from God and toward the pastor.

6 Conclusion

The arguments of these three theologians all revolved around a single desire: to separate the idolatrous human voice proclaiming itself as divine from God's own true voice. While they all deployed arguments about the material presence or absence of God, the stakes of the argument should not be mistaken for metaphysical commitments about the way God interacts with things. Rather, each was aiming to prevent what he saw as unruly human nature usurping the honor due to God alone. The disagreements between them arose from differences, largely unrecognized, in how they thought about which humans were most likely to usurp this honor, how, and with what motives. Whereas Luther continued to insist that the primary idol was the individual believer's delusions of ethical merit before God, Zwingli and Karlstadt largely agreed in viewing priestly hubris exerted over their flock as the source of idolatry. The Eucharistic debate between these characters thus ought to be read as a direct result of these differences.

CHAPTER 7

The Reformation of Doubt: Incredulity, Faith, the Body, and the Search for Certitude in Early Lutheran Interpretations of John 20:24–31

Barbara Pitkin

1 Introduction

Thomas the apostle might well be considered the patron saint of religious skepticism. Appearing in all four canonical gospels and associated with various non-canonical texts, he is best known from a singular episode in chapter 20 of the Gospel of John. When his fellow disciples tell him that they have seen the risen Lord, Thomas asserts that he will not believe them unless he not only sees for himself but also puts his finger in the marks of the nails in Jesus's hands and his own hand into Jesus's wounded side. When Jesus appears and shows the wounds and offers his body for touching, Thomas overcomes his incredulity and confesses Jesus to be his Lord and God. Jesus's response to him, "Have you believed because you have seen me? Blessed are those who have not seen and yet have come to believe" (John 20:29, NRSV), seems to diminish the exemplary character of the doubting apostle's apparent repentance and conversion to faith.

Yet in the Gospel of John as a whole and in this episode in particular, the relationship between faith and external evidence apprehended through the senses is complicated, even paradoxical. Chapter 20's ensuing verses explain that the signs or miracles contained in the Gospel of John were recorded precisely to bring those who heard them or read them to believe that Jesus is the Messiah and the Son of God (John 20:30–31). John's singular account of this resurrection appearance inspired later Christian interpreters to ponder the nature and source of Thomas's incredulity, the means of his conversion, and the role of human bodies in the story. Naturally, over the course of nearly two millennia of interpretation, readers have drawn different and often contradictory conclusions about the meaning of this puzzling episode.

Since themes of religious doubt and faith and the relationship between faith and external evidence are inherent in the biblical text, they attract the attention of virtually all commentators on the Fourth Gospel. However, as Susan Schreiner's pioneering work has shown, a "common anxiety about certitude"

 | DOI:10.1163/9789004527843_008

was pervasive throughout the early modern period and especially permeated the thought-world created by the Protestant Reformation.[1] Schreiner argues that the competing epistemological certainties that exploded in the transitional sixteenth century, which she contends were articulated primarily in religious terms, fueled an inherited crisis over certainty through their "drive toward immediacy, the appeal to experience, and the search for the reliability of knowledge."[2] The case of the incredulous apostle led by evidentiary experience to certain faith seems tailor-made for testing Schreiner's contention that questions surrounding certainty were foregrounded by sixteenth-century thinkers in new ways. Artistic renderings of Thomas in the same period likewise underwent an evolution that came to prioritize the certainty of the sense of touch but also betrayed an "emerging dichotomy between belief and empirical modes of thought." This metamorphosis suggests the widespread cultural significance in the early modern era of the paradoxes at the heart of Thomas's story.[3]

Closer investigation into Protestant engagements with John 20:24–31 is all the more necessary in light of recent examinations of early modern reception of the figure of Thomas that have argued for novelties in Reformation exegesis of the passage. Glenn Most engages in broad investigation of premodern Christian traditions about Thomas and the narrative, exegetical, pictorial, and material elaborations they inspired. He claims that Lutheran and Reformed interpreters offered an innovative reading of Thomas's story that called into question a thousand years of virtual consensus holding that Thomas actually touched Jesus (a point that is left open in the biblical text itself). Most acknowledges that Protestant readings were not monolithic, continued to reflect and perpetuate some traditional concerns and insights, and, with respect to the issue of touch, were anticipated by exactly four earlier interpreters who entertained the possibility that Thomas had not touched Jesus.[4] Nevertheless, he contends that Protestants generally denied the reality of Thomas's touch or read it allegorically or metaphorically. Moreover, Most asserts that Catholic

1 Susan E. Schreiner, *Are You Alone Wise? The Search for Certainty in the Early Modern Era* (New York: Oxford University Press, 2011), 391.

2 Schreiner, *Are You Alone Wise?*, 12, 15.

3 Erin E. Benay and Lisa M. Rafanelli, *Faith, Gender and the Senses in Italian Renaissance and Baroque Art: Interpreting the* Noli me tangere *and Doubting Thomas* (Burlington, VT: Ashgate, 2015), 7; see also Erin Benay, "The Pursuit of Truth and the Doubting Thomas in the Art of Early Modern Italy," (Ph.D. Diss., Rutgers—The State University of New Jersey, 2009).

4 Glenn W. Most, *Doubting Thomas* (Cambridge, MA: Harvard University Press, 2005), 139–41. The interpreters identified by Most are Augustine, Euthymius Zigabenus, Albert the Great, and Thomas Aquinas.

interpreters "responded vigorously and polemically to the Protestant challenge" and vociferously defended the reality of Thomas's touch.[5] Jörg Frey follows Most's argument, citing liberally from Most's examples, to maintain that Reformation interpreters broke with the exegetical tradition in advancing a more massive critique of Thomas's behavior and intensifying criticism of the idea that Thomas actually touched Jesus.[6]

Benjamin Schliesser has identified some key problems in Most's portrayal of early modern interpretations of Thomas. Schliesser contends that Protestant views on the question of Thomas's physical contact with Jesus are more often in continuity with traditional views, and, drawing on a dissertation by Ulrich Pflugk, he notes that medieval exegesis presupposed Thomas's touch, but did not emphasize it in the way that Most suggests.[7] Schliesser explores several key Reformation and post-Reformation interpretations of Thomas, to show that, *pace* Most, Martin Luther and John Calvin both affirmed that Thomas touched Jesus, and that whereas the Lutheran theologian Johann Gerhard agreed with them, the Reformed theologian Theodore Beza held that Thomas made his confession without touching Jesus. Schliesser also lists the following representatives of different Protestant confessional traditions as affirming the traditional (and it seems, majority) Protestant view that Thomas touched Jesus: the Lutheran Hugo Grotius, the Reformed Abraham Calov, the Remonstrant Arnold P. Poelenburg, and the Pietist Johann Albrecht Bengel.[8] According to Schliesser, it is only with the rise of historical criticism in the eighteenth century that the trend "which deems Thomas's physical verification of Jesus's wounds as improbable or inappropriate" emerges.[9]

If there is novelty in early modern Protestant interpretations of the doubting apostle, it can be discovered only through a broader consideration of the existing exegetical literature. As a first step toward this reevaluation, this investigation concentrates on Lutheran interpretations, viewed in the context of

---

5 Most, *Doubting Thomas*, 149.

6 Jörg Frey, "Der zweifelnde Thomas (Joh 20,24–29) im Spiegel seiner Rezeptionsgeschichte," *Hermeneutische Blätter* 1, no. 2 (2011): 18–23.

7 Benjamin Schliesser, "To Touch or Not to Touch? Doubting and Touching in John 20:24–29," *Early Christianity* 8 (2017): 78, 79n43. See Ulrich Pflugk, "Die Geschichte vom ungläubigen Thomas (Johannes 20:24–29) in der Auslegung der Kirche von den Anfängen bis zur Mitte des sechzehnten Jahrhunderts" (PhD diss., University of Hamburg, 1965), 226.

8 Schliesser, "To Touch or Not," 81. Pflugk also concluded from his analysis of Luther, Calvin, Erasmus, Melanchthon [in actuality, Caspar Cruciger the elder], Bugenhagen, Erasmus Sarcerius, Musculus, Antonius Corvinus, Johann Mathesius, Veit Dietrich, and Johann Spangenberg, that Protestant interpreters assumed that Thomas touched Jesus; "Die Geschichte vom ungläubigen Thomas," 181–220, 226.

9 Schliesser, "To Touch or Not," 82.

the pre-Reformation exegetical tradition. Treatments of Thomas produced between 1523 and 1556 by major early Lutheran exegetes will show that their innovation did not center on understandings of John 20:27 and whether or not Thomas acted on Jesus's invitation to touch his wounds. Instead, they focused on the object of his doubt and what and how he came to believe through his encounter with the risen Christ. As Schliesser observes, "Reformation commentators are less concerned with christological controversies, such as the materiality of the body of Jesus, but rather with the impact of the appearance and words of Jesus."[10]

Following a recent trend in interpretation of the Fourth Gospel inaugurated by Philip Melanchthon, early Lutheran exegesis thus evidences a shift in emphasis from reading the Gospel of John as proving orthodox christological doctrine to emphasizing soteriology—not so much who Christ is as what he does, or in Schliesser's words, his impact.[11] Regarding the story of Thomas, their great innovation is not the abandonment of a traditional (but by no means universal) conviction of and emphasis on Thomas's actual touching of Jesus's risen body. Some Lutheran interpreters retained the idea that Thomas touched Jesus, but among those who did, there were varying judgments about the purpose and effects of haptic experience and its relationship to doubt and faith. Nevertheless, all assumed Thomas to be making more of a soteriological than a christological claim. This shift in emphasis in turn occasioned reevaluations of Thomas's doubt that reflected both a traditional diversity of opinion on the role of empirical experience in faith and a heightened concern for the certitude of faith that emerged in the early modern era. These Lutheran innovations were not only anticipated in part by Catholic humanist approaches to John, but also found a surprising afterlife in a mid-century Catholic commentary on the Fourth Gospel by Claude Guilliaud (1493–1551). These cross-confessional connections further complicate a picture of rigid and predictable confessional divisions—particularly in the pre-Tridentine period—and signal the broad appeal of questions of doubt and certainty in the early sixteenth century.

2 Exegetical Traditions Prior to the Reformation

A complete picture of the treatment of the figure of Thomas would require attending to a wide range of Christian literature and material culture. This

10 Schliesser, "To Touch or Not," 79.

11 On this trend, see Barbara Pitkin, *Calvin, the Bible, and History: Exegesis and Historical Reflection in the Era of Reform* (New York: Oxford University Press, 2020), 68–96.

section focuses on the major exegetical treatments of the episode in John 20 by interpreters whose works were available in published editions in the early sixteenth century.[12] The aim is not to demonstrate influence (though in some cases there are connections between interpreters) but rather to provide a broad overview of the questions, themes, and emphases that dominated patristic and medieval readings of the passage. It is important to acknowledge that oft-repeated traditions also originated in non-exegetical literature. For example, later reflections on the meanings of the name Thomas as "twin" or "abyss" originated in Jerome's discussion in his book on the interpretation of Hebrew names.[13] Mentions of Thomas elsewhere in the gospels and extra-biblical traditions about him—particularly his missionary activity to India—also implicitly informed some exegetes' work. To the extent that these traditional ideas are echoed in commentaries, sermons, and biblical glosses on John 20:24–31, they become part of the body of "exegetical lore" that shaped later interpretations.[14]

The treatments by John Chrysostom (ca. 349–407), Augustine (354–430), and Cyril of Alexandria (ca. 376–444) represent the variety of early interpretation of the pericope, showing a wide range of judgments about the character of Thomas, the nature of his doubt, and the overall meaning of the episode.[15] Chrysostom paints the most negative portrait, emphasizing Thomas's obstinate doubt of the other disciples' testimony, his demand for confirmation through not one, but two senses, and the Lord's merciful but reproachful condescension to his crass materialism. Augustine also indicates Thomas's incredulity but without speculating on its origins. Rather, he focuses his brief treatment on the belief concerning Christ's divine nature that Thomas gains principally by seeing, whether or not he actually touched Jesus's body. Cyril, in contrast, gives an extended treatment of the passage that claims that Thomas

12 For a listing of commentaries on John published between 1470 and 1555, see Timothy J. Wengert, *Philip Melanchthon's* Annotationes in Johannem *in Relation to Its Predecessors and Contemporaries* (Geneva: Droz, 1987), 235–54. Citations are from English translations when available; in cases where no modern English version exists, translations are my own.

13 Jerome, *Liber interpretationis hebraicorum nominum*, in vol. 72 of *Corpus christianorum, series latina* (Turnhout: Brepols, 1959), 138, 149.

14 The term "exegetical lore" comes from David C. Steinmetz, *Calvin in Context*, 2nd ed. (New York: Oxford University Press, 2010), 73.

15 John Chrysostom, *Commentary on Saint John the Apostle and Evangelist, Homilies 48–88*, trans. T. A. Goggin, vol. 41 of Fathers of the Church (New York: Fathers of the Church, 1960), 458–78; Augustine, *Tractates on the Gospel of John 112–24; Tractates on the First Epistle of John*, trans. John W. Rettig, vol. 92 of Fathers of the Church, (Washington, DC: Catholic University of America Press, 1995), 60–62; Cyril of Alexandria, *Commentary on the Gospel According to S. John*, 2 vols. (Oxford: James Parker, 1874), 2: 678–92. See Pflugk, "Die Geschichte vom ungläubigen Thomas," 39–47, 51–59, and 107–36.

only affected incredulity because of his overwhelming grief. Asserting that Thomas had already received the Holy Spirit even though he was away when Jesus first appeared, Cyril calls him wise for demanding evidence and designates his slight want of faith beneficial for teaching us the true mystery of the bodily resurrection. It was appropriate for Thomas to touch the Lord, says Cyril, since he had already received the Spirit, and in so doing, he dispelled the doubt about the resurrection lingering in his fellow disciples. Cyril cites the post-resurrection appearance in Luke 24:35–43 in which Jesus offers his body to all for touching to bolster this point.

Bequeathing to the later tradition a diversity of judgments about Thomas's character and his incredulity, these early interpreters make two other points that are echoed in later engagements with the passage. The first has to do with how Thomas overcame his doubt and what it was that he came to believe. Augustine's brief comments put forth the idea of sight as a generic sense, so that whether or not Thomas actually touched Jesus, it was through seeing that he came to believe; moreover, he saw (and possibly touched) Christ's humanity, and through this was led to his divinity: "He saw and touched the man and confessed the God whom he did not see and did not touch, but through this which he saw and touched, with doubting now removed, he believed that."[16] The idea that Thomas is moved by Christ's humanity from doubt to explicit faith in his divinity will emerge as a consensus interpretation of Thomas's confession in pre-Reformation exegesis.

A second point concerns the role of divine providence in the episode. The conclusion calling those blessed who have not seen and yet believed (John 20:29) suggests that Thomas's example serves as divinely intended instruction for later generations of believers, and interpreters point to different elements that indicate the divine hand. For Chrysostom, Jesus waited eight days before returning, so that Thomas would be taught by the others, his desire would be inflamed, and his later belief would be stronger. For Cyril, the divine purpose is evident in that Christ returns after eight days, exposes his wounds, and allows them to be touched, not just for the sake of Thomas and the other disciples (who were still weak in faith), but for later generations. Thomas's want of faith was, says Cyril, "extremely opportune and well-timed, in order that, through the satisfaction of his mind, we also who come after him might be unshaken in our faith" in Christ's bodily resurrection.[17]

Two influential papal voices echo and expand these insights, identifying other points besides the timing of Christ's reappearance and the preservation

16 Augustine, *Tractates on John*, 61.

17 Cyril, *Commentary on John*, 2: 681–82; cf. 686.

of the wounds of the crucifixion as signs of divine dispensation. In a sermon preached in 444, Leo the Great (d. 461) stresses the divine plan that governed the reactions of all of the disciples, who were afraid and doubted but saw, heard, and touched to establish the foundations of faith for later generations.[18] In a sermon from the early 590s, Gregory the Great (ca. 540–604) singles out Thomas and distinguishes his experience and its benefits. He underscores that it was not by chance but through the divine dispensation that Thomas was absent, that he refused to believe, and that when he was cured of this, he benefited us more than the other disciples who believed: "Divine compassion brought it about in a wonderful way that when the doubting disciple touched the wounds in his master's body, he cured the wounds of our unbelief."[19] This idea finds many echoes in the later tradition, as do two more of Gregory's observations. Like Chrysostom, he references Hebrews 11:1 when discussing Thomas's confession, and he links this passage's description of faith as the proof of unseen things to Augustine's notion that Thomas saw the man but believed the God whom he did not see with carnal eyes.

Medieval exegetes built on these early foundations concerning Thomas's character, whether and why he doubted, how he overcame his incredulity, and what he came to believe. In his commentary on John, the Bulgarian archbishop Theophylact (ca. 1050–1108) engages with Chrysostom and, to a lesser degree, Cyril. Like Chrysostom, Theophylact explains that Thomas doubted not because he thought the other disciples were lying to him but because he thought the resurrection was impossible. He wanted to have confirmation from two senses. Also like Chrysostom, Theophylact suggests that Jesus delayed his appearance to Thomas by eight days to awaken his desire as he was being instructed by the others. However, Theophylact softens slightly the harshness of Chrysostom's portrayal of Thomas's stubbornness, noting Jesus's accommodation to his demand. At the same time, he criticizes Cyril's opinion that Thomas feigned his doubt, asserting that Thomas doubted out of a lack of faith and not because he was careful not to believe too easily.[20] Having thus

---

18 English translation in Leo I (Pope), *Sermons*, trans. Jane Patricia Freeland and Agnes Josephine Conway, vol. 93 of The Fathers of the Church (Washington, DC: Catholic University of America Press, 1996), 322–23.

19 Gregory I (Pope), *XL homilarium in evangelia libri duo*, *Patrologiae cursus completus, series latina*, ed. J.-P. Migne (Paris, 1841-1855), 76:1201; hereafter abbreviated PL and cited according to volume and column numbers. English translation in Gregory I (Pope), *Forty Gospel Homilies*, trans. David Hurst (Spencer, MA: Cistercian Publications, Inc., 1990), 206–7. See Pflugk, "Die Geschichte vom ungläubigen Thomas," 140–43.

20 Theophylact, *In quatuor evangelia enarrationes*, trans. Johann Oecolampadius (Basel: A. Cratander, 1524), 218r; English translation in Theophylact, *The Explanation of the Holy Gospel According to John*, trans. Christopher Stade (House Springs, MO: Chrysostom

cautioned that Thomas's doubt was real and serious, however, Theophylact immediately embraces the spirit of Cyril's highly favorable reading of Thomas's confession, and goes beyond both Chrysostom and Cyril in detailing its christological dimensions: "But as soon as Thomas touched the Lord's side, he was revealed as a superb theologian, proclaiming the two natures and single hypostasis of the one Christ."[21] Whereas Cyril seems to understand the confession "Lord and God" to pertain to Christ's divine nature, Theophylact, like Augustine and Gregory, understands Thomas to profess here the two natures doctrine as defined at Chalcedon.[22] The *Glossa ordinaria* in the Latin Bible also transmitted some of the key early points: the common consensus that Thomas was originally absent by divine dispensation; Jerome's explanation of the meaning of his name; from Augustine, the idea that sight is a generic sense; and, from Augustine and Gregory, the idea that through the action of seeing and (perhaps) touching, Thomas confessed what he did not see, that is, he saw Christ as man but believed him to be God.[23]

Theophylact's contemporary, the Latin bishop Bruno of Segni (ca. 1045–1123), offers a brief exegesis of the episode with expanded observations on the meaning of this latter point. After noting the frequently appearing idea that by doubting Thomas confirms others and frees them from doubt, Bruno asks what his confession means. His robust answer represents a more personalized profession of Christ's entire salvific work that echoes a passage from the Psalms and the articles of the creed:

> Now I doubt nothing; I am certain, affirm the resurrection, proclaim immortality. You are my Lord, my teacher; I am your servant and the son of your handmaid [Psalm 115:16, Vulgate]. You are indeed my God, who created me, took up flesh for me, was handed over to death to redeem me and now have been resurrected from the dead to raise me up with you. This is my faith; thus I perceive and thus I believe.[24]

Bruno's rendering of Thomas's confession, which arguably constitutes the centerpiece of his comments on the passage, is somewhat unusual even

Press, 2007), 301. The Greek version is found in vols. 123–124 of *Patrologiae cursus completus, series graeca,* ed. J.-P. Migne (Paris: Migne, 1857–1866). See Pflugk, "Die Geschichte vom ungläubigen Thomas," 85–89.

21 Theophylact, *Explanation of John*, 301; cf. Theophylact, *In quatuor evangelia*, 218r.

22 Cyril, *Commentary on John*, 2: 690.

23 [*Biblia Latina ... cum glossa ordinaria ... et interlineari ... et cum postillis ac moralitatibus Nicolai de Lyra*], 6 parts in 6 vols. [Basel: Froben and Petri, 1498], DOI 10.3931/e-rara-16208.

24 Bruno (Bishop of Segni), *Commentaria in Joannem*, PL 165: 596.

when compared to later Latin interpreters who synthesize and elaborate on earlier readings. It does, however, find an echo in the influential *Life of Christ* by Ludolph of Saxony (1295–1378), for whom Bruno's commentary served as a source (in this case, unattributed).[25]

Ludolph's meditative depiction of the life of Christ drawn from the gospels synthesized many borrowings from patristic and contemporary biblical commentary and theology, including, in his discussion of Christ's appearance when Thomas was there, material from Augustine, Leo, Theophylact, Gregory, and Chrysostom. This synthesizing approach is also found in the exegetical treatments of John 20:24–31 in the high and late Middle Ages. Interpreters such as Thomas Aquinas (1225–1274), Nicholas of Lyra (1270–1349), and Denis the Carthusian (1401–1471) perpetuate traditional insights, probe certain points in greater depth, and introduce some new perspectives, including different levels of meaning, applications, or doctrinal precision. For example, Aquinas, Ludolph, and Nicholas add novel dimensions to the traditional explanations of Thomas's name. Whereas earlier medieval interpretations briefly related "twin" and "abyss" to Thomas's doubting nature, these three exegetes expand the pool of meanings. In his lectures on John delivered between 1270 and 1272, Aquinas observes that "Thomas was an abyss because of the darkness of his disbelief" and relates this via a cross reference to Psalm 41:8 (Vulgate; cf. Ps. 41:7 NRSV) to the abyss that is the depths of Christ's compassion.[26] Ludolph observes that "abyss" applies well because Thomas penetrated the heights of divinity by a certain faith.[27] Aquinas also speculates that he may have been called "twin" because "he was from the tribe of Benjamin, in which some or all were twins."[28]

25 Ludolph of Saxony, *Vita Iesu Christi ex evangelio et approbatis ab ecclesia catholica doctoribus sedule collecta*, ed. L. M. Rigollot, 4 vols. (Paris: Palmé; Brussels: Lebrocquy, 1878), 4: 222. See also the prayer that concludes this chapter, 4: 225.

26 Thomas Aquinas, *In Joannem evangelistam expositio*, in volume 10 of *Opera omnia* (1860; reprint, New York: Musurgia Publishers, 1949), 632. English translation in Thomas Aquinas, *Commentary on the Gospel of John: Chapters 13–21*, trans. Fabian Larcher and James Weisheipl, intro. and notes Daniel Keating and Matthew Levering (Washington, DC: Catholic University of America Press, 2010), 274–81. Aquinas's lectures utilize, among other things, the exegetical work of Augustine, Chrysostom, and the *Glossa ordinaria*. On Aquinas's sources, see the introduction to Thomas Aquinas, *Commentary on the Gospel of John: Chapters 1–5*, trans. Fabian Larcher and James Weisheipl, intro. and notes Daniel Keating and Matthew Levering (Washington, DC: Catholic University of America Press, 2010), xvii–xxx. For reflections on the abyss in Bede and Hugh of St. Cher, see Pflugk, "Die Geschichte vom ungläubigen Thomas," 143; Murray, *Doubting Thomas*, 43.

27 Ludolph, *Vita Christi*, 4: 222; cf. Aquinas, who attributes this to Alcuin in the *Catena Aurea*. Thomas Aquinas, *Catena super Joannis evangelium*, in vol. 12 of *Opera omnia* (1860; Reprint, New York: Musurgia Publishers, 1949), 437.

28 Thomas Aquinas, *In Joannem evangelistam expositio*, 632; *Commentary on John*, 274.

In his literal commentary on the passage, Nicholas mentions this idea, and distinguishes it from the view of other interpreters, who say he received the name because he doubted the resurrection.[29]

Denis does not show the same interest in the different meanings of Thomas's name, repeating only that it means he was a doubter since he was incredulous toward the claims of Christ's resurrection. However, elsewhere he demonstrates a similar synthesizing approach when he reports earlier interpretations and identifies sources such as Augustine, Gregory the Great, Bede (ca. 672–735), and even Thomas Aquinas. Moreover, he recognizes a diversity of previous opinions regarding the matter of whether or not Thomas touched Jesus: "It is not certain if he touched Christ's side or hand, or whether out of reverence he passed this by; this cannot be determined from the text, and there are various opinions about this."[30] Denis does not venture his own opinion on this point, and his formulation signals that the question was far more open in medieval discourse than Most's study has alleged.

In addition to transmitting and embellishing traditional questions and themes regarding Thomas's doubt, these high and late medieval interpreters probe more deeply two aspects of the story. First, Aquinas and Nicholas intensify criticism of Thomas's request and show a more marked interest in the epistemological function of the senses. Nicholas judges that Thomas's demand was laughable and, echoing Chrysostom, says it demonstrates his obstinacy, since he wanted to be confirmed by two senses. However, Nicholas also gives this a positive spin when he continues that sight and touch are the two senses that are least likely to be deceived. He references the opening of Aristotle's *Metaphysics* to assert that among all the senses sight reveals the differences among things. Then, referencing the philosopher's *De anima*, Nicholas adds that the sense of touch is more certain or precise in human beings, whereas other senses (such as the sense of smell) are more robust in other animals.[31]

Citing Sirach 19:4, Aquinas observes that Thomas would have been justified for not believing the word of the others immediately, but, referring to

29 Nicholas, [*postilla literalis*], in [*Biblia Latina*], comments on John 20.

30 Denis the Carthusian, *Enarratio in evangelium secundum Joannem*, in vol. 12 of *D. Dionysii Cartusiani opera omnia*, 42 volumes in 44 (Mostrolii: S. M. de Pratis, 1901), 611.

31 Nicholas returns to the question of the relative certainty of these two senses when he discusses how Jesus invites Thomas to "see" his hands. Here he echoes Augustine's idea of sight as a generic sense and says that here sight is taken for touch. He repeats that another reason for coupling this with the invitation to touch his side was because Thomas wanted to have proof from two senses. Nicholas, [*postilla literalis*], in [*Biblia Latina*], comments on John 20. The relevant discussion is in *De anima*, book 2, chapter 9; see Aristotle, *De anima*, trans. Christopher Shields (Oxford: Clarendon Press, 2016), 41.

Proverbs 25:27 and Sirach 3:22, Aquinas cautions that his demand was harsh and unreasonable for insisting on sensible evidence.[32] Like Nicholas, Aquinas offers conflicting opinions about the epistemological role of the senses and the propriety of touch. He gives a mystical (in this case, tropological) interpretation to Thomas's finger: "A finger signifies knowledge [*discretio*], and a hand signifies our works. Thus when Thomas is told to put his finger and hand into the wounds of Christ, we are being told to use our knowledge and works for the service of Christ."[33] But as far as answering the question of whether or not literal touch of Christ's body brought Thomas to faith, Aquinas, like Denis, acknowledges there are different opinions. Following Augustine, it could be that Thomas perceived through touch, or, alternatively, perhaps he became flustered (*confusus*) when he saw Christ's wounds and made his confession before he touched Christ, though Gregory had said that because he touched, he also confessed that he saw.[34]

A second development can be seen in the way that Aquinas and Denis supplement the traditional view that aspects of or even the entire episode happened by divine dispensation with heightened emphasis on God's mercy and Christ's compassion. Chrysostom had noted the Lord's mercy in appearing to show his wounds for the sake of one soul, and Gregory memorably attributed to divine compassion the universal effects of Thomas's touch: "Divine compassion [*clementia*] brought it about in a wonderful way that when the doubting disciple touched the wounds in his master's body, he cured the wounds of our unbelief."[35] In addition to citing Gregory verbatim, Aquinas, as mentioned earlier, offers a novel connection between Thomas's name and Christ's compassion (*miseratio*) grounded in Psalm 41:8 (Vulgate), "Abyss calls to abyss": "In compassion, the deepest depth (namely, Christ) calls to the depth of darkness (namely, Thomas), and in confessing, the depth of stubbornness (namely, Thomas) calls out to the deepest depth (namely, Christ)."[36]

A similar reciprocity appears in Aquinas's comments on how God showed mercy (*pietas*) and rescued Thomas. Citing two verses from the psalms that

---

32 "One who trusts others too quickly has a shallow mind" (Sir. 19:4, NRSV); Thomas Aquinas, *In Joannem*, 633; *Commentary on John*, 275–76.

33 Thomas Aquinas, *In Joannem*, 634; *Commentary on John*, 279. Cf. Ludolph of Saxony, *Vita Christi*, 4: 222.

34 Thomas Aquinas, *In Joannem*, 634; *Commentary on John*, 280. Cf. Thomas Aquinas, *Catena*, 457–58.

35 Chrysostom, *Commentary on Saint John*, 458; Gregory, PL 76: 1201; Gregory, *Forty Gospel Homilies*, 206–7. Cf. Aquinas, *Catena*, 437 (citing Chrysostom).

36 Thomas Aquinas, *In Joannem*, 632; cf. *Commentary on John*, 274 (translation altered). For the citation from Gregory, see *In Joannem*, 632; *Commentary on John*, 275.

praise God's sustaining hand, Aquinas contends that Christ meets Thomas's conditions: "And so our Lord quickly puts his hand under the fallen Thomas so that when Thomas said, 'Unless I see … I will not believe,' our Lord rescues him, saying, 'Put your finger here.'"[37] There is also a mutuality between Thomas's need and Christ's merciful condescension evident in Denis's commentary. Although Denis repeats the stock criticisms of Thomas's harshness, crassness, and desire for confirmation from two senses, he adds a new speculation that after Thomas heard from the other disciples, he remained with them more often than he had earlier because he feared that he would miss Jesus's return.[38] Like Aquinas, Denis underscores Christ's compassion in condescending to Thomas's demand for sensible proof: "Behold how much Christ did for the conversion of just one person, how kindly [*pie*] and lovingly [*caritative*] he showed himself to the incredulous Thomas! For even if Thomas had sought additional and more certain proofs of the resurrection, the savior would not have denied these to him."[39]

The expanded attention to Christ's merciful treatment of Thomas has the effect of rendering Thomas's doubt even less culpable. Though he is still described as obstinate, hard, and crass, the heightening of the theme of divine compassion softens his image overall and accents the result to which this merciful accommodation leads: Thomas's profession of christological orthodoxy. Here these interpreters agree: Thomas confesses Christ's divinity, and he sees one thing (a human being) and believes another (God). Moreover, for Nicholas and Denis, Thomas does so in order that later Christians also might believe this with a faith formed by love.[40] Through God's mercy, Thomas shows himself to be a good theologian, professing the certain truth that Christ is both human and divine, overcoming heresies like Arianism and Manicheism. Even Nicholas of Lyra, who does not emphasize divine compassion and is the most critical of Thomas's incredulity, portrays him as seeking a certain faith and proclaiming a robustly orthodox christological teaching, aligning his profession of Christ's divinity with what Nicholas takes to be the overall aim of John's Gospel from the beginning.

The heightened interest in balancing the image of Thomas the doubter with Thomas the believer is evident in aspects of medieval culture beyond the

---

37 Thomas Aquinas, *In Joannem*, 633–34; *Commentary on John*, 278. Thomas cites Ps. 36:24 (Vulgate; cf. 37:24 NRSV) and Ps. 93:18 (Vulgate; cf. 94:18 NRSV).

38 Denis, *Enarratio*, 610.

39 Denis, *Enarratio*, 611.

40 Thomas Aquinas, *In Joannem*, 634; *Commentary on John*, 279; Nicholas, [*postilla literalis*], in [*Biblia Latina*], comments on John 20; Denis, *Enarratio*, 611. Cf. Thomas Aquinas, *Catena*, 458 (citations from Augustine and Theophylact on verse 28).

world of biblical exegesis. Medieval artists portrayed the climactic moment at which Thomas's doubt vanished as he moved his hand to touch Jesus's body or, in depictions beginning in the thirteenth century, actually penetrated his wounded side. Murray has noted the connections between this more graphic iconography, the formalizing of Christ's eucharistic presence in the doctrine of transubstantiation, and the rising devotion to the eucharistic elements in high and late medieval spirituality.[41] Benay and Rafanelli trace the appropriation of images of Thomas in and around Tuscan courthouses and other civic spaces in Renaissance Tuscany "as emblems of empirical evidence." In this new incarnation, Thomas's incredulity is reinterpreted as a positive icon of rational and juridical inquiry and demonstration of truth.[42]

Thus, over the course of the Middle Ages, Western Christianity saw the beginnings of a reformation of Thomas's doubt. In biblical commentary, preaching, and visual culture, the doubting disciple became a representative of certainty.[43] There was universal agreement as to the certain knowledge he proclaimed—namely, orthodox christological doctrine—and regarding the ultimately beneficial role played by his incredulity. However, questions of exactly how Thomas overcame his doubt were still open, with the role of the human senses and divine agency still unresolved.

This ambivalence toward the grounds of faith's certitude finds an echo in two early modern reformist Catholic interpreters, Desiderius Erasmus (1466–1536) and Jacques Lefèvre d'Étaples (1450–1536). Moreover, in their exegesis of Thomas's confession of faith, these two Catholic reformers and humanists repeat the traditional opinion that Thomas proclaimed Christ's divinity and humanity, but their comments about Thomas's move from doubt to faith anticipate some aspects of the interpretive shift that becomes manifest in evangelical engagements with the passage.

Erasmus gives a short synopsis of the episode in his *Paraphrases on John* (first published in 1523) that reiterates traditional topics such as Thomas's demand for confirmation through multiple senses (Erasmus stresses the role of hearing in addition to sight and touch); that divine dispensation made Thomas's disbelief strengthen the faith of later believers; and that despite his rather stubborn disbelief, he proclaimed Christ to be God and man more

---

41 Murray, "Doubting Thomas," 39–40, 50–52, 57, 67–68.

42 These public images also at times reflected non-biblical traditions about Thomas, such as his missionary activity in India; see Benay and Rafanelli, *Faith, Gender and the Senses*, 10, 123–46.

43 On Franciscan art and preaching, see Benay and Rafanelli, *Faith, Gender and the Senses*, 10, 97–122; Murray, *Doubting Thomas*, 53–58.

clearly than anyone.[44] More than many earlier exegetes, Erasmus gives even greater weight to haptic experience as a component of faith, saying explicitly that Thomas touched Christ's body, and that it was by touching that he came to believe that Jesus's true humanity had been raised. In addition, Erasmus attributes Thomas's incredulity to weakness rather than wickedness, offering therewith the most positive image of this since Cyril of Alexandria.[45] Finally, although in his comments on verse 28 he understands Thomas's christological profession to proceed from the full faith he received by seeing and touching, Erasmus earlier hints that the object of faith implied by Thomas's story is broader than christological doctrine. He paraphrases the closing admonition to Christ's invitation to touch in verse 27, "Do not doubt but believe" (NRSV), as follows: "And from now on do not be so disbelieving in other matters, but have faith in my promises, however unbelievable in the accepted human sense."[46]

Lefèvre provides a more extensive treatment in his commentary on John, which was also published in Basel in 1523.[47] At first, like Chrysostom and those after him, Lefèvre underscores Thomas's obstinacy and stubbornness, but he also embraces the medieval trend that expanded the theme of divine compassion and mercy. He stresses divine agency not just in orchestrating the episode (noting that Thomas was only temporarily abandoned to himself) but also in creating true faith. For Lefèvre, God imparts another faith to Thomas.[48] In this process, as for Erasmus, the sense of touch is central, and the three senses of vision, hearing, and touch are all involved in the way that God, who "knows

---

44 Desiderius Erasmus, *Erasmi opera omnia emendatiora et auctiora,* 10 vols., ed. I. LeClerc (Leiden: Peter Van der Aa, 1703–1706), 7: 645; hereafter abbreviated LB. In English in *Paraphrase on John,* vol. 46 of *Collected Works of Erasmus,* trans. and ann. J. E. Phillips (Toronto: University of Toronto Press, 1991), 219–21. These both provide the 1535 edition, which was scarcely changed from the 1523 version published first by Froben: *Paraphrasis in euangelium secundum Joannem* (Basel: J. Froben, 1523); the endnotes to the English translation identify a number of places where Erasmus echoes traditional comments of earlier interpreters (see *Paraphrase,* 344). On Erasmus's paraphrases on John, see Albert Rabil, Jr., "Erasmus' Paraphrase of the Gospel of John," *Church History* 48 (1979): 142–55. On his treatment of Thomas, see Pflugk, "Die Geschichte vom ungläubigen Thomas," 198–99.

45 Christopher Boyd Brown points out that Cyril's commentary was unknown to the Western medieval tradition but was translated into Latin by George Trebizond and published in 1508 (LW 69: xix); for a listing of editions, see Wengert, *Philip Melanchthon's* Annotationes, 242–45, 251.

46 Erasmus, LB 7: 645; *Paraphrase,* 220.

47 Jacques Lefèvre d'Étaples, *Commentarii initiatorii in quatuor evangelia* (Basel: A. Cratander, 1523); the first edition was published at Meaux in 1522 (Wengert, *Philip Melanchthon's* Annotationes, 244).

48 Lefèvre, *Commentarii in evangelia,* 403v.

how to turn bad things to good[,] ... especially [shows] his mercy" in acceding to Thomas's demand.[49]

After a substantial digression on the nature of Christ's resurrected body that includes references to the transfiguration, Lefèvre offers a new perspective on Thomas's touch. Commenting that sight and hearing were not sufficient to create faith that Christ's true body had been raised, he concludes that vision, hearing, and touch simultaneously were active in this. He then continues: "But by touching, Thomas was himself more deeply touched. For when he touched the Lord's body, he was touched by divinity; and that peace was fulfilled, with which the Lord had greeted them when he entered, and fulfilled also was the command, 'Be not disbelieving but believing.'"[50] Thus reversing the widely repeated Augustinian dictum that Thomas touched Christ's humanity but believed and confessed the divinity that he did not see (or touch), Lefèvre lays stress instead on God touching Thomas and creating faith.

In addition to giving new emphasis to God as the author of Thomas's faith, Lefèvre also sees divine agency in Thomas's confession and, because of this, views Thomas's faith as certain. He repeats the consensus view that Thomas here expresses his belief that Christ had been truly raised and confesses Christ's two natures. Yet Lefèvre adds that Thomas is the first of the apostles chosen to proclaim that Christ is God (which was a traditional observation) and that, in making this profession, "the Spirit of the Father was speaking through Thomas, the Spirit who speaks lofty truths in those who are believing."[51] Echoing the unusual interpretive focus of Bruno of Segni that was echoed in Ludolph of Saxony, Lefèvre also explores the significance of the possessive pronoun: "And as to the other item that Thomas joins to 'Lord' and 'God,' namely 'my'—this small particle indicated his state of mind and expressed his great faith."[52] Finally, after a long discussion of Thomas's missionary work and the general spread of the gospel, he concludes his commentary on the pericope by underscoring the certainty of Thomas's faith: "This faith is most certain and true, which no human being but only God infuses. If we can have this faith from the Word of Christ, which is true, we are blessed. And we can, if we understand that we can do nothing, but God can do all things."[53]

On the eve of the Reformation, the treatments of Thomas by Erasmus and Lefèvre show a marked intensification of earlier interest in empirical, sensory

49 Lefèvre, *Commentarii in evangelia*, 404r.
50 Lefèvre, *Commentarii in evangelia*, 404r.
51 Lefèvre, *Commentarii in evangelia*, 404r–404v.
52 Lefèvre, *Commentarii in evangelia*, 404v.
53 Lefèvre, *Commentarii in evangelia*, 405r.

knowledge and a deeper appreciation of Thomas's coming to profess Christ's divinity and humanity as a multi-sensory event involving sight, hearing, and, most importantly, touch. The Augustinian claim of sight as the most generic sense, and that it was ultimately seeing Christ's humanity that grounded Thomas's claim that he was also God, has been eclipsed; for these two interpreters, Thomas arrives at sure and certain christological doctrine through visionary, auditory, and haptic evidence. Traditional interest in a positive assessment of Thomas's physical verification of the evidence and recognition by some interpreters that the sense of hearing also must have been involved become more prominent in these early modern readings.

In addition, Erasmus and, especially, Lefèvre take the content and character of Thomas's faith in new directions that foreshadow the Protestant readings to come. While both embrace the tradition's virtual unanimity in understanding Thomas's confession as a profession of the reality of the bodily resurrection and Christ's two natures, each augments discussion about the nature of his faith and, by implication, his doubt. Erasmus connects Thomas's doubt about the resurrection to a broader attitude of incredulity when he has Jesus urge Thomas going forward to "have faith in my promises, however unbelievable in the accepted human sense."[54] He suggests that Thomas's doubt is not entirely overcome, and the obstacle to his faith is not simply doubt about Christ's resurrection but a broader attitude of mistrust toward the divine promises.

Lefèvre takes a different approach that also transforms traditional views of Thomas's faith and doubt. That true faith is a divine gift was not an explicit point of discussion in earlier interpretations, though it is implicit when Nicholas and Denis identify his faith or the faith of later believers as *fides formata*. When Lefèvre makes divine infusion of faith central to his interpretation of the passage, he extends the earlier discussions of divine compassion to their logical conclusion and makes the divine activity the ground of Thomas's certitude. Also echoing the reciprocity and mutuality in Aquinas's interpretation, Lefèvre offers a new reading of Thomas's touching as being touched. Combined with the emphasis on Thomas's use of the possessive pronoun "my," the focus of Thomas's confession of faith is altered. Thomas's exclamation is more than a proclamation about Christ's unique identity that forms the certain ground for the faith of later believers. Rather, it is as much a confession of what God has done through Christ for Thomas, transforming his incredulity into a personal and certain faith.

---

54 Erasmus, LB 7: 645; *Paraphrase*, 220.

3 Lutheran Readings: Melanchthon, Bugenhagen, Brenz, Luther, Sarcerius, and Cruciger

In 1523, Basel publishers not only printed Erasmus's *Paraphrases* and Lefèvre's commentary on the Gospels, but also issued the first Protestant commentary on John, by Philip Melanchthon (1497–1560). The book was both popular and influential. It was reprinted ten times in 1523 alone, and three more times the following year.[55] Even though Melanchthon does not treat the Thomas episode in this commentary, his approach to John 20 as a whole provides the foundation for assessing subsequent Lutheran interpretations, here represented in the work of Martin Luther (1483–1546), Johannes Bugenhagen (1485–1558), Johannes Brenz (1499–1570), Erasmus Sarcerius (1501–1559), and Caspar Cruciger the elder (1504–1548).

In his 1523 commentary, Melanchthon does not pursue a line by line exposition, but focuses his comments on verses that he judges constitute the underlying structure of this biblical text. The annotations originated in university lectures, and the format reflects this setting; Melanchthon raises questions about and comments on selected issues and particular verses, all aimed at supporting evangelical preaching by highlighting key elements of the scriptural message. In his treatment of John 20, he clusters his comments on Christ's words in verses 17, 21, and 23.[56] Here he addresses traditional areas of interest, such as why Christ forbade Mary Magdalene from touching him, the significance of Christ's greeting of peace and impartation of the Holy Spirit, and apostolic authority over sin. But Melanchthon also advances three central ideas that reflect and further some of the novel concerns that featured in the contemporary treatments by Erasmus and Lefèvre. Also incorporating several of Luther's key theological principles, Melanchthon takes traditional approaches to John 20 as a whole in a new direction.

---

55 Philip Melanchthon, *In evangelium Ioannis, annotationes Philippi Melanchthonis* (Basel: [A. Cratander], 1523); modern edition in *Philippi Melanchthonis opera quae supersunt omnia*, 28 vols., ed. C. G. Brentschneider and H. Bindseil, vols. 1–28 of *Corpus Reformatorum* (Halle: C. A. Schwetschke and Son, 1834–1860), 14: 1047–1220. Hereafter abbreviated CR and cited according to volume and column number. On the origins of the commentary and its printing history, see Wengert, *Philip Melanchthon's* Annotationes, 25–54, 259–63. Froben was the publisher of Erasmus's *Paraphrases*, while Cratander published the commentaries of Lefèvre as well as the annotations by Melanchthon.

56 Most is correct in noting that the reformers' emphasis on justification by faith led them to focus not on what Thomas did or did not do but rather on what Jesus did or did not do (*Doubting Thomas*, 148). But the foundation for this is Melanchthon's focus on what Jesus *said*.

First, Melanchthon's choice to comment only on some of the words of Christ in chapter 20 reflects a main concern throughout his entire exposition of John to identify the promises of God and build up certain faith in the gospel. Although he briefly contextualizes each of Christ's statements in the narrative storyline, Melanchthon's exclusive focus on Christ's words highlights and universalizes them, making the sole point of the passages' timeless doctrinal lessons that Christ not be worshipped carnally, that the preached gospel brings peace to the conscience, and that consciences derive certainty from the Word alone. Second, Melanchthon stresses that Christ is touched only by faith and that he himself effects proper devotion; Mary's attempt to touch represents human beings' efforts to worship God on their own terms. Third, he underscores that only God can forgive sin, but that Christ in verse 23 entrusts remission to the apostles, who through the proper preaching of the gospel render consciences certain of divine forgiveness. Moreover, he asserts that the ground of certain faith lies only in the Word: "Let the one who announces the gospel not seek anything else besides the very same Word, whether signs or miracles, by which to render the remission of sins more certain."[57]

Given this indication of what his position likely would be on the traditional question of the role of the senses in overcoming Thomas's doubt, Melanchthon's failure to treat the Thomas episode, or at least Christ's words to Thomas, may seem to be a missed opportunity. However, hazarding a guess as to why he does not address this passage here helps to pinpoint the novelty in Melanchthon's approach that will underlie subsequent Lutheran readings. As we have seen, pre-Reformation readings are virtually unanimous in understanding the Thomas episode as a proof of the resurrection and orthodox christology. Melanchthon's treatment of John 20, however, shifts the focus of this chapter to its soteriological implications, and particularly to the issue of how all humans come to true and certain faith.[58] In this shift, the traditional interest in epistemology is heightened and becomes the main theme Melanchthon seeks to elucidate, but he does so by completely ignoring the traditional locus for discussing such matters. Instead, he finds this theme articulated especially in verses 17, 21, and 23, and uses his comments there to explicate the text's main theological and hermeneutical principles: Word, faith, and certainty. Treating Thomas might have provided opportunity to reinforce these

---

57 Melanchthon, *In evangelium Ioannis*, 148v; CR 14: 1217.

58 In his annotations on John as a whole, Melanchthon shows far less interest in the trinitarian and christological dogmas that featured so prominently for earlier interpreters and prioritizes how the Word creates faith and certitude; see Wengert, *Philip Melanchthon's* Annotationes, 93, 113, 149–50, 152–55.

points, but it would add nothing to what Melanchthon has already outlined as the main structure and point of John 20.

This remains the case for Melanchthon's later treatment of John 20:19–29 (the gospel reading appointed for the first Sunday after Easter) in a postil collection assembled from his Sunday morning lectures for foreign students, which was published in Latin in 1544 and which appeared in a sometimes loose German translation by Johannes Pollicarius a year later.[59] Melanchthon's postil identifies five *loci*, or topics, in the reading. Though an edition of the German translation from 1549 contains a woodcut illustration of Thomas touching Jesus's side, Melanchthon does not make any reference to this part of the pericope. Instead, he mentions in passing under his fourth locus Thomas's claim that Christ is God as a proof of the Trinity (the other being the fact that he imparts the Holy Spirit). Under his fifth locus, Melanchthon addresses Christ's words in verse 29, finding here a great comfort for believers that their faith, like that of the apostles, rests only on the very same gospel: "We should remember this and believe it and not look beyond it for new revelations, as the Anabaptists foolishly pretend."[60] Melanchthon follows this up with discussion of the difficulty of adhering solely to the Word, but instead of referencing Thomas's doubt and his demand for supplemental proof, he supplies the contrasting examples of Saul and David: "Saul thinks that even though God is merciful, he will not have mercy on him."[61] David, however, trusts in the promise of the remission of sins. In this way, Melanchthon again shifts the focus away from the resurrection and christology to the promise of forgiveness. Divine mercy is not merely the motive for healing doubt. Rather, mercy becomes itself the object of Thomas's doubt. This represents a crucial shift in emphasis that manifests itself in other Lutheran engagements with the story of Thomas.

Melanchthon's new approach to John 20 in the *Annotationes* and the postil collection from the 1540s would have been most influential on his contemporaries and is reflected in their new emphases in the readings of the passage. An explicit discussion of Thomas's doubt and his confession assembled in a collection of manuscript notes from Melanchthon's later Sunday Bible lectures remained unpublished until the end of the sixteenth century, but it should be noted before considering his interpretive legacy.[62] This later postil on John 20

59 On this collection, see John M. Frymire, *The Primacy of the Postils: Catholics, Protestants, and the Dissemination of Ideas in Early Modern Germany* (Leiden: Brill, 2010), 87–89; Wengert, "Philip Melanchthon on Bible Translation," 28; see also Georg Buchwald, "Zur Postilla Melanthoniana," *Archiv für Reformationsgeschichte* 21 (1924): 78–89.

60 Philip Melanchthon, *Postill Philip Melanchthons Deudsch: Uber die Evangelia von Ostern bis auffs Advent*, trans. Johannes Pollicarius (Erfurt: Stürmer Brothers, 1549), 17r; CR 14: 261.

61 Melanchthon, *Postill*, 17r–17v; CR 14: 261.

62 This collection was published by Christopher Pezel in 1594–1595 as *Postillae Melanthonianae* and appears in CR 24–25.

also has five *loci*, and Thomas is the subject at the start of the fourth. On the one hand, there are elements in Melanchthon's treatment that are quite traditional: Thomas's stubborn doubt concerns the resurrection, Christ deigns to heal him, Thomas touches Christ's body, and he confesses Christ's divinity (and is the first of the apostles to do so). Yet, on the other hand, Melanchthon gives greater weight to the obstacle of doubt, refines the way Christ removes it, and draws a different lesson from Thomas's example. For Melanchthon, Thomas's doubt is grave and stubborn; indeed, it is a great darkness and sin, which the Lord heals by leading him to the Word and to visible proofs of it. In the same moment that Thomas touches, the Holy Spirit efficaciously awakens in him a new disposition, and he makes his profession.[63] Melanchthon then launches into a detailed (and learned) explanation of how this formulation distinguishes the way of calling on the true God from pagan invocations of their gods. He concludes by summarizing: "When Thomas says, 'my Lord and my God,' this is an example of true invocation. The name 'Lord God' points us to the true God; the particle 'my' applies the promise of grace."[64] Thus, Thomas's story teaches that sin remains even in the saints, and that Christ wants to heal this. Moreover, it shows that all people are weak, and that Christ receives everyone this way. For Melanchthon, all people need to be instructed by the Word and led by the Spirit to receive the promise individually and personally.

Even though Melanchthon here appears to grant some positive epistemological role to Thomas's touch (when, as for Lefèvre, it is combined with Christ's Word and the inner work of the Spirit), in the final locus (commenting on verse 29) he emphasizes that faith comes from hearing: "External beholding, or external touch, alone does not help ... God wants to be grasped by us in this life by faith. We must be satisfied with this apprehension and rest in God grasped through faith and conclude with certainty that we are accepted by him, that we will be heard, and that we will have eternal life."[65] This is, he says, a different route to certainty than found in philosophy, medicine, and other natural studies, in which proof precedes assent. In faith, the path is reversed: first hear and assent to the Word, and then proof, i.e., the experience of consolation, will follow.[66] Despite the many traditional interpretive elements, Melanchthon's treatment of Thomas in this postil shares the central emphases that governed his comments on John 20 in the 1523 annotations: focus on the Word, on faith as the proper avenue to Christ, and on certainty of divine forgiveness.

Melanchthon's Lutheran colleagues by and large follow his lead and adapt these principles and concerns explicitly to the story of Thomas and his doubt.

---

63 CR 24: 758–60.

64 CR 24: 763.

65 CR 24: 763–64.

66 CR 24: 765.

Their treatments likewise range over a variety of genres. There are commentaries that pursue either the *loci* method (Cruciger) or a largely continuous exposition (Brenz and Sarcerius). There are also outlines for sermons, notes from sermons, postil collections, and other published sermons, such as those by Luther, Bugenhagen, and Sarcerius. These preaching materials often encompassed Christ's original appearance to the other apostles as well as his second appearance with Thomas present a week later, as these both featured in the appointed reading. Across this diverse literary corpus, there are nevertheless unifying themes. Moreover, there is a unity of purpose. All of these materials are designed to foster preaching and therefore a common practical focus guides their interpretation of Thomas. As Wengert points out, Wittenberg exegetes "interpreted texts by determining what a biblical text says *and* what it does to its hearers—terrifying the sinner and comforting the believer in God's mercy."[67] This interest in addressing the application of scriptural teaching can be seen particularly in how these Lutheran interpreters speak about the character of Thomas, the nature of his doubt, the means by which he overcomes it, and what the text does to its readers and auditors.

As we saw in his later postil, Melanchthon intensifies the tradition's harsher judgments toward Thomas's doubt by extending this condition to all human nature: "This instructs us that in this life great weakness, much darkness, error, and doubt remain even in the saints."[68] Other Lutherans also underscore how Thomas's example represents a universal human failing. In his commentary from 1528, Brenz writes that Thomas speaks with the "voice of the flesh, which is not in Thomas alone, but truly in all people, for we are all from the same mass, and God has subjected everyone to incredulity in order to show mercy to all."[69] Sarcerius contends that one of the main points taught by the start of the passage concerns fallen human nature, which, having abandoned the simple Word, wants to be led by external means and signs.[70] Luther comments in a sermon from 1540 that through the example of Thomas, "the Holy Spirit

67 Timothy J. Wengert, "Philip Melanchthon on Bible Translation and Commentaries," *Lutheran Quarterly* 33 (2019): 35.

68 CR 24: 759.

69 Johannes Brenz, *In D. Iohannis evangelion, Iohannis Brentii exegesis, per autorem primum diligenter revisa, ac multis in locis locupletata* (Hagenau: J. Setzer, 1528), 345v. Brenz's discussion of this pericope is unchanged from the first edition of his commentary, which was published in 1527. All citations are from the 1528 edition.

70 Erasmus Sarcerius, *Expositiones in evangelia festivalia, ad methodi formam ferè absolutae* (Frankfurt: C. Egenolff, 1538), 16r. See also Erasmus Sarcerius, *In Ioannem evangelistam iusta scholia summa diligentia, ad perpetuae textus cohaerentiae filum* (Basel: B. Westheimer, 1540), 834. On Sarcerius's interpretation of Thomas, see Pflugk, "Die Geschichte vom ungläubigen Thomas," 212–13.

shows that without faith we are altogether blind, hardened, and nothing at all."[71] In his commentary from 1546, Cruciger observes that the doubt and weakness in all the apostles teach us to recognize that sin remains in those who have been reborn and to mourn that such darkness and weakness surround us.[72] Transforming the widely repeated claim from Gregory the Great that Thomas's actions (specifically, his touch) cured the unbelief of later generations, Lutheran exegetes emphasize the universal condition of disbelief and the persistence of doubt even among the faithful.

Lutheran commentators also engage the traditional concern with why and what Thomas doubted, but they elaborate more fully on Thomas's state of mind and extend these reflections to their readers and auditors. They acknowledge the traditional view that Thomas's doubt pertains to Christ's resurrection and portray him as willful and stubborn. Luther says he refused to believe and was "very firmly and rigidly stuck in unbelief," but he also underscores Thomas's weakness and fear, which all of the apostles share.[73] Thomas wants to believe but cannot. Luther's listeners, too, fail to hear God's voice in the words of the preacher: "we do not perceive this treasure, and are much coarser than Thomas, because we refuse to see this dear and precious treasure, God's own Word, which makes everything holy."[74] Bugenhagen makes a similar point in a sermon from 1525, but uses Christ's words in verse 29 to argue that those who receive the fruit of the resurrection through preaching and faith in the

71 Martin Luther, *Luther's Works*, 79 vols., ed. J. Pelikan, H. T. Lehman, C. B. Brown, and B. T. G. Mayes (St. Louis: Concordia, and Philadephia: Fortress, 1955—), 69: 426; hereafter abbreviated LW. The sermon was preached on April 4, 1540 and exists in notes by Georg Rörer in Martin Luther, *D. Martin Luthers Werke: Kritische Gesamtausgabe* (Weimar: H. Böhlau, 1883-2009), 49: 135–42; hereafter abbreviated WA. It also appeared in various published versions (cf. LW 77: 145–53); for details see introductory material by Christopher Boyd Brown in LW 69: 425–26; on Luther's sermons edited by Caspar Cruciger the elder, see the discussion by Benjamin T. G. Mayes in LW 77: xiii–xxiii. On Luther's interpretation of Thomas in general, see Pflugk, "Die Geschichte vom ungläubigen Thomas," 181–97.

72 Caspar Cruciger, *In evangelium Iohannis Apostoli enarratio Caspari Crucigeri, recens edita* (Strasbourg: Craton Mylius, 1546); published under Melanchthon's name in CR 15: 1–440; reference from CR 15: 431. Pflugk discusses this commentary, "Die Geschichte vom ungläubigen Thomas," 200–4. Most mistakenly treats this as Melanchthon's work (*Doubting Thomas*, 147–49). On Cruciger's authorship, see Timothy J. Wengert, "Caspar Cruciger (1504–1548): The Case of the Disappearing Reformer," *The Sixteenth Century Journal* 20, no. 3 (1989): 417–41.

73 LW 77: 150. Cf. Cyril, who also stressed the weakness of all the apostles, *Commentary on John*, 2: 689.

74 LW 69: 406; cf. 404.

Word are even greater than the apostles.[75] Sarcerius identifies Thomas's doubt as directed toward the gospel, since he is incredulous of the resurrection and does not believe Christ's promises or the words of the other disciples.[76] He is an example of those who do not want to believe the simple Word without external signs or who want to be led to faith by the judgment of reason and visible means and signs.[77] Sarcerius glosses Thomas's declaration, "I will not believe" (John 20:25) as "I will not be satisfied with the simple Word."[78] For these Lutheran exegetes, Thomas's failure to believe the resurrection represents a fundamental, universal, and sinful incredulity toward God's promise.

The traditional trend emphasizing and expanding the role of the divine plan and Christ's compassion is furthered in Lutheran explanations of how Thomas overcame his doubt and is likewise viewed from a Lutheran perspective on justification. In his earliest surviving treatment of the passage, Luther hardly discusses Thomas but rather sets up the entire scene with a lengthy discussion of why the way to God lies not through one's own works but in Christ's alien work. It is Christ's work alone that fulfills the law and overcomes sin, death, and the devil. Christ shows his hands and feet to the apostles and Thomas to prove this. Luther ends by stressing that this gift is grasped by faith, and that faith in Christ "comes through the preaching of the gospel," as Paul says in Romans 10:17.[79] As mentioned earlier, Brenz observes that God subjects all people to incredulity in order to have mercy on all; he adds that Christ connives with Thomas's disbelief similarly to the way that God connived with Joseph's brothers (Genesis 37) to a greater end, namely, the strengthening of our faith.[80] In other sermons, Luther repeatedly stresses Christ's gentle, friendly treatment of Thomas and all the apostles, whom he does not reproach but handles with great patience.[81] Sarcerius likewise emphasizes Christ's benevolence (*philanthropia*). Christ

75 Johann Bugenhagen, *Ungedruckte Predigten Johann Bugenhagens aus den Jahren 1524 bis 1529*, ed. Georg Buchwald, vol. 13 of Quellen und Darstellung aus der Geschichte der Reformationsjahrhunderts (Leipzig: M. Heinsius Nachfolger, 1910), 213.

76 Sarcerius, *Expositiones in evangelia festivalia*, 13v–15v; *In Ioannem evangelistam iusta scholia*, 834.

77 Sarcerius, *Expositiones in evangelia festivalia*, 16r; *In Ioannem evangelistam iusta scholia*, 834.

78 Sarcerius, *Expositiones in evangelia festivalia*, 16v; *In Ioannem evangelistam iusta scholia*, 835.

79 WA 17/2: 289–97.

80 Brenz, *In D. Iohannis evangelion* (1528), 345v. Brenz also echoes the earlier view that God knows how to turn bad things into good (346r).

81 For example, in a house postil from 1534 (LW 69: 404) and in a sermon from 1543 (WA 49: 273–74). Here there is an echo of Chrysostom's point that Christ came and showed his wounds for the sake of one soul, *Commentary on St. John*, 458.

doesn't reprehend Thomas but accommodates himself to his weakness, providing an example of how to deal with weak consciences.[82] Though doubt is culpable, humans are weak; hence, only God can cure it.

The heightening of the theme of Christ's compassion and condescension as the ultimate cause for Thomas's conversion results in a tension in Lutherans' attitudes toward visible signs and sensory evidence similar to that which we saw in Melanchthon. On the one hand, exegetes criticize Thomas's demand for sensory evidence or find other ways to downplay the haptic component. Luther comments in his 1534 house postil that it appears Thomas "wants to convert himself through the marks of the nails, which do not have any special power to convert anyone."[83] Elsewhere he says the demand is absurd; Thomas doesn't want to "believe with his eyes alone but will also feel and grope with his hands."[84] And in a particularly colorful passage from a 1543 sermon, Luther paraphrases Thomas's stubborn reply to the other disciples as "believe what you want, I won't believe it unless I put my finger into his wounds and my whole fist into his side; if that doesn't happen, I just won't believe."[85] Sarcerius characterizes Thomas's demand as proceeding from reason and (echoing Melanchthon's point) as seeking to judge spiritual realities by the judgment of reason: seeing and touching first and then believing.[86] Taking a different approach in a sermon from 1526, Bugenhagen allegorizes Christ's invitation to touch, saying that "finger" means the Holy Spirit in the believing heart, and Christ here invites doubting believers (and by extension, Thomas) to put this in his side, that is, to know the works that Christ has done out of love for them.[87]

On the other hand, interpreters frequently echo the traditional assertion that the entire episode occurred for our benefit, thereby opening themselves up for considering how the different senses work in Thomas's conversion and, indeed, for the faith of the others to whom Jesus showed his wounds. Hence they also give some surprisingly favorable assessments of external signs and even the haptic component. Bugenhagen comments that external signs lifted the apostles' faith; by showing his hands and feet, Jesus led them to believe.[88]

---

82 Sarcerius, *In Ioannem evangelistam iusta scholia*, 835. Weakness is also a major theme in Luther's sermons; see LW 77: 146–51.

83 LW 69: 404; WA 37: 380.

84 LW 77: 150; WA 21: 297; WA 49: 158.

85 WA 49: 273.

86 Sarcerius, *Expositiones in evangelia festivalia*, 16v; *In Ioannem evangelistam iusta scholia summa diligentia*, 834. In the *Expositiones*, Sarcerius admits that Thomas might have done this out of a good intention.

87 Bugenhagen, *Ungedruckte Predigten*, 324.

88 Bugenhagen, *Ungredruckte Predigten*, 213.

Luther acknowledges regarding Christ's concession to Thomas, "He grants him so freely not only to see him as the others but also to take hold of him and feel."[89] Others specify more precisely how Christ corrects Thomas's infirmity. Cruciger says that Christ offered himself for touching only *after* he had shown himself and healed Thomas's weakness; he indicates the method of healing by adding that the one who heard (*auditor*) was so strengthened and such great light was kindled in him that he made his profession.[90] Sarcerius, too, admits that Christ accommodated himself to Thomas's weakness but claims he used visible signs *simultaneously* with the Word to convert him. Christ permitted Thomas to put his fingers and hands into his side in order to lead him little by little to true faith.[91] Citing Augustine, Sarcerius extends this accommodation more broadly in his *Scholia*: "Therefore, since Christ led unbelieving Thomas to faith by the Word and signs, we are taught about God's usual way of dealing with us, according to which he makes use of both the Word and signs to lead us to faith."[92]

Despite these acknowledgments of the role of externals and touch in overcoming Thomas's doubt, Melanchthon's prioritizing of Christ's reply to Thomas in verse 29, "Have you believed because you have seen me? Blessed are those who have not seen and yet have come to believe" (NRSV) finds an echo in these Lutherans' final words on the question of the ground of certain faith. As for Melanchthon, such faith lies only in the Word of promise. After a long polemical excursus arguing against laying on of hands and the presence of miracles as proof of the Spirit and signs of the apostles' superiority in faith, Bugenhagen concludes his 1525 sermon by appealing to John 20:29, saying: "You have in this gospel the fruit of the resurrection, which is a treasure given to us through the preaching of the apostles and others."[93] Similarly, in his 1526 sermon, he designates this verse as a commendation to Thomas and the other disciples of a faith that does not rest on physical seeing but rather on an inner vision of the

89 LW 77: 151; WA 21: 297; WA 49: 159.

90 Cruciger, CR 15: 432.

91 Sarcerius, *Expositiones in evangelia festivalia*, 16v–17r.

92 Sarcerius, *In Ioannem evangelistam iusta scholia*, 835–36. See also Sarcerius, *Expositiones in evangelia festivalia*, 13v–14r, 17r. In the *Scholia*, Sarcerius comments that during his first appearance when Thomas was absent, Christ also led the other disciples to faith by the Word (his greeting of peace) and signs (showing his hands and side), and notes that it is important to pay attention to the end for which signs and sacraments are instituted. In this case, by showing his hands and side, Christ shows he wants to be known by the marks from the cross and that he thereby confirms the disciples and makes them more certain of the resurrection (829).

93 Bugenhagen, *Ungedruckte Predigten*, 218.

heart through the eyes of faith; we, he says, "do not touch Christ, but see him; we hear his voice and believe."[94]

Cruciger also stresses that this verse conveys a necessary and saving teaching, since anxious but pious minds want to know if they are calling upon the true God. The answer is not to be found in the uncertain view of deity he attributes to Xenophon and Plato, in an experience like that of Moses at the burning bush, in a monastic opinion that one must always be in doubt about the status of one's faith, or in a demand for visible signs that he attributes to the enthusiasts and Anabaptists. "We should not seek a visible appearance of God, nor should we doubt that we call upon God in the right way, but we call upon him truly and properly when the mind speaks to the God who reveals himself through the gift of the gospel and by sending his Son, our Lord Jesus Christ."[95] Even Sarcerius, who offers the most favorable assessment of externals accompanying the Word, condemns repeatedly any effort to put external means or signs before the Word or to rely on them apart from the simple Word. He sees Christ's words in verse 29 as a correction of Thomas's incredulity designed to teach that we should believe in the simple Word and not seek external signs in place of the certainty of the Word.[96]

In their engagements with Thomas's story, Lutheran interpreters repeatedly draw connections between the story and their readers and listeners. To be sure, the implications of the scriptural teaching for the faith of their contemporaries is a more or less explicit aim of all exegetes surveyed here, who see the episode as grounding faith that Christ is God and human and frequently make the point that Christ's resurrection is the proof and guarantee that we, too, will be raised. This is not surprising in light of John 20:31, which concludes the chapter.[97] However, Lutheran interpreters are more deliberate in universalizing Thomas's character and his doubt, stressing that all are doubters, rigidly stuck in incredulity, weak as far as trusting the Word of promise, and tempted to demand proof that conforms with fallen human reason. In addition, they not only present Thomas as an example for weak consciences to follow but,

94 Bugenhagen, *Ungedruckte Predigten*, 324–5. Earlier in this sermon, Bugenhagen points out that it is not enough to hear the outer word unless God brings it to life in the heart (323).

95 Cruciger, CR 15: 433.

96 Sarcerius, *In Ioannem evangelistam iusta scholia*, 837; cf. *Expositiones in evangelia festivalia*, 18v. In the *Expositiones*, Sarcerius says that Christ condemns all human senses, powers, and reason as far as their ability to grasp the things of God that can be known only by the Word.

97 "But these are written so that you may come to believe that Jesus is the Messiah, the Son of God, and that through believing you may have life in his name" (John 20:31, NRSV).

more importantly, through his encounter with Christ, they expand the focus from the content of Thomas's own faith to the subjective faith experience of those they address. Their goal is not, as for most of the exegetical tradition, to provide mainly a demonstration of the truth of the resurrection and Christ's two natures, but above all to convince their auditors and readers of the truth of the promise of mercy and that Christ is theirs.

Lutheran interpreters seek to affect their readers and listeners in this way by heightening the theme that Christ is to be not only known as the savior of the world but specifically embraced as one's personal savior. There are various ways in which they make this point. Brenz echoes but gives a new twist to the unusual interpretation of Thomas's confession found in Bruno of Segni, Ludolph of Saxony, Lefèvre, and Melanchthon's later postil. In his comments, Brenz observes "the entire emphasis in Thomas's confession lies on the word 'MY.' Whoever confesses that God is HIS OWN, denies everything belonging to himself and possesses all those things which are from God." Unlike Ludolph, Lefèvre, and Melanchthon, Brenz does not discuss this verse as a proof of Christ's divinity and humanity at all, but rather treats it only as a sign of Thomas's remarkable change of heart (which he compares to the apostle Paul) and an indication of how God works good things out of bad. Continuing by citing the opening phrase of Psalm 24 ("The earth is the Lord's and all that is in it," NRSV), he adds, "We are the Lord's and the Lord is ours. Hence all good things of God are ours, and this through faith in Christ Jesus."[98] In his 1525 sermon, Bugenhagen also does not treat this passage as a proof of Christ's two natures but rather as an indication that the Holy Spirit speaks through Thomas, who received the Spirit not when the other disciples did through insufflation, nor through the laying on of hands, but through the hearing of the Word.[99] He quickly extends this to his auditors: "Where the Word of God is in the heart, there the Holy Spirit is present; you have forgiveness of all sins, and not through the laying on of hands."[100]

98 Brenz, *In D. Iohannis evangelion* (1528), 346r. The pronouns "MEUS" and "SUUM" are printed in all capital letters in the original.

99 Recall that the notion that the Spirit spoke through Thomas when he made his profession appears also in Lefèvre (*Commentarii in evangelia*, 404r–404v); cf. also Melanchthon's later postil, where the Spirit's inner movement combined with Thomas's physical touching: "Therefore after Thomas recognizes the Lord (having heard his rebuke, 'do not be unbelieving, but believe' [verse 27]), he receives a new stirring of the heart [*novum motum*], since the Holy Spirit acts in him at the same time that he touches. For that reason, he cries out, 'my Lord and my God'" (CR 24: 759).

100 Bugenhagen, *Ungedruckte Predigten*, 218; cf. 217.

Other Lutherans hint at a more traditional interpretation of verse 28 as a proof of Christ's humanity and divinity but nevertheless underscore the theme of subjective appropriation of his saving benefits elsewhere in their comments, using first- and second-person forms of address. In the summary of the gospel reading prefacing his 1527 postil, Luther says that whoever recognizes Christ, as Thomas does, as God and Lord "does not fear either sin or death, neither the devil nor hell; in sum, he is safe from all anxiety, distress, and temptation, for he has one who is greater and more powerful than the one who is in the world."[101] Thus, when the law, the devil, and death come and threaten, Luther urges those afflicted to assert that Christ is theirs, saying: "I belong to that man; I am his, and he is mine; and where he stays, so I remain as well."[102] In a later sermon, Luther presents Thomas as being resurrected by Christ from the death of his unbelief and sin to faith. Completely changed by the power of Christ's resurrection, Thomas "believes it as certain and confesses that Christ, his Lord, is true God and man." Luther continues that the main point of this entire reading is that "we believe that the resurrection of Christ is ours and works in us."[103]

Sarcerius characterizes Thomas's exclamation as a confession of true faith in Christ and in his resurrection. He references the two natures, admitting in the *Expositiones* that this is one of the passages that proves that Christ is God. But in the remainder of his comments he focuses on what this accomplishes for salvation: "by the word 'Lord' Thomas confesses Christ was truly resurrected and made Lord over death, sin, and Satan. By the word 'God' Thomas confesses that Christ has been raised as God, to whom nothing is impossible."[104] At the end of his treatment of the chapter in the *Scholia*, moreover, Sarcerius glosses verse 31, "that Jesus is Christ, the son of God," more personally as "our savior, our intercessor, our ruler, and equally God with God the father."[105] Finally, Cruciger identifies Thomas's confession that Christ is God as the second of three *loci* in John 20 and gives it an unusual twist: the two terms, God and Lord, are joined together as in the prophets to distinguish the true God from the imaginary deities of the pagans.[106] Continuing this line of inquiry in his comments on the last part of verse 29, he stresses the necessity of instructing pious minds about

101 WA 17/2: 289.

102 WA 17/2: 293.

103 LW 77: 152; WA 49: 159.

104 Sarcerius, *Expositiones in evangelia festivalia*, 18r; cf. *In Ioannem evangelistam iusta scholia summa diligentia*, 836.

105 Sarcerius, *In Ioannem evangelistam iusta scholia*, 838; cf. *Expositiones in evangelia festivalia*, 19r.

106 Cruciger, CR 15: 432–33; cf. the similar point made with reference to the same passage (Ps. 20: 7) in Melanchthon's later postil (CR 24: 759–60).

how they know that they are calling upon the true God, and how this verse gives to a doubting soul a certainty that cannot be found outside the gospel: "Even if, moreover, it is difficult for us to assent to it, and great is the struggle of a heart debating whether the will of God expressed in the promise, 'come to me all you who are weary, and I will give you rest' [cf. Matt. 11:28] is also for you [*erga te quoque*], nevertheless, the mind ought to be strengthened by what has been said about faith: 'justified by faith, we have peace' (Rom. 5:[1]) and similar statements."[107]

These repeated efforts to shift the focus to Thomas's subjective experience of doubt and faith and to apply his example to the experience of those they address reveal Lutheran interpreters' overwhelming concern to assure weak and doubting souls of the truth and reliability of the divine promise of forgiveness. Herein lies the novelty in their reformation of doubt. Although they continue to affirm the importance of doctrine (e.g., Christ's divinity, humanity, and bodily resurrection) and the articles of faith, the problem they address in light of Thomas's story is a universal condition of incredulity not simply toward the truth of these doctrines but more importantly toward their personal relevance.

Luther's 1543 sermon provides a strikingly clear statement of this shift. After relating Thomas's great doubt and weakness and Christ's patient and compassionate handling of him and the other disciples in this episode and throughout the time he spent with them prior to his ascension, Luther remarks that this is the history that every Christian should know. However, he continues, this is only the *first* thing that they should know:

> In addition, we should also know why all this happened, why the dear Lord was resurrected, what necessity there was for our Lord God to do this. For it is not enough for us to know the history by itself, that he was raised—both the devil and the pope have this faith; they surely know this and also believe it ... But it is not enough for someone to know this alone; in addition, one has to have the faith according to which one knows why he suffered and why he was raised. As Saint Paul says to the Corinthians: he died for the sake of our sins and was raised for the sake of our justification. Whoever doesn't believe this as well doesn't believe anything at all. I have to apply the resurrection to myself, in my own person, and if I don't do that, then the other kind of faith is completely useless. I should

107 Cruciger, CR 15: 433.

> therefore say: our Lord Jesus Christ died for my sake; he was buried for my sake; and was, accordingly, for my sake raised from the dead.[108]

Luther spends the rest of the sermon—which runs to three more pages in the Weimarer Ausgabe—detailing how this subjective apprehension of Christ's benefits alone provides a sure refuge against the ongoing temptation to doubt brought about by the attacks of the devil, fear, sin, and the weakness of human nature.

Lutherans urge their auditors and readers not simply to learn from Thomas, but to realize their fundamental identity with him. To be sure, in the long history of interpretation traced above, the idea that the episode happened for the benefit of future generations and, moreover, was written (like the other signs in the Gospel of John) for them, was a traditional theme. Lutherans also draw some traditional lessons from the story of the doubting apostle, too; most notably, they find lessons for spiritual leaders on how to deal with weak consciences. Yet Lutheran readings aim at a more direct impact, more explicitly casting doubt as a persistent and universal problem. They view its object as not merely the fact of the resurrection and Christ's identity as God and human but more crucially as the reality of divine mercy and the experience of the promise. For these interpreters, it is hard to believe not just that Christ was raised but specifically that Christ was raised for me. Ultimately, they locate the sole ground for the certainty about this experience only in God, received through the promise of mercy. Again, this insight builds on a long tradition emphasizing divine compassion in this episode. However, Lutheran theological convictions about justification by faith and their interpretive program placing exegesis in service of proclaiming this gospel contributed to a reshaping of the image of the doubting apostle. So did the broader quest for certainty, with its drive toward immediacy, the appeal to experience, and the search for reliable knowledge that Schreiner has described as characteristic of the age. While some of these interests can be found in earlier and contemporary images of the doubting apostle, in Lutheran readings these concerns take unprecedented prominence.

108 WA 49: 274–75. Cf. Luther's similar observation in another sermon about Christ not leaving things with the mere history of the resurrection but instead bringing Thomas to faith in its benefits, raising him from his stubborn disbelief and sin (WA 49: 159; LW 77: 151).

4 Conclusion

Early sixteenth-century developments in the exegetical portrayals of the doubting apostle exemplify, in part, the emerging debates over the nature of religious doubt, the certainty of faith, and the role of empirical and sensory evidence in creating and sustaining subjective belief. While the novelty of Lutheran interpretations of doubting Thomas does not lie in an allegorizing or complete rejection of haptic experience and empirical evidence in overcoming doubt, Lutheran readings nevertheless reflect a distinctive reordering of the senses involved in this process. Despite its criticism of Thomas's audacious demand for confirmation from not one but two senses, the previous exegetical tradition was largely content to ring changes on Augustine's claim that seeing was the generic sense and, at times, to give the two senses of sight and touch a spiritualized interpretation. Through seeing with his physical eyes and perhaps touching Christ's human body with his hands, Thomas came to "see" and "touch" Christ's divine nature and attained and proclaimed faith concerning his full humanity and divinity. However, in the early modern period, Lefèvre and Erasmus added an emphasis on hearing and portrayed Thomas's coming to faith as involving sight, hearing, and touch. Whether or not they discussed the role of touch or vision in their treatments of Thomas, Lutheran interpreters, in contrast, prioritized the sense of hearing, subordinating the evidence from the other senses to the hearing of the Word as the only sure and certain ground of faith. In fact, they often refer to Romans 10:17 in their treatments of the pericope.

Nevertheless, it would be premature to draw a sharp confessional difference between Catholic and Lutheran understandings of incredulity, faith, and the bodily senses from these different emphases, at least in this early period. Instead, it is important to keep in mind the overlaps between the approaches of the two Catholic humanists and Lutheran reformers. Erasmus's concern for the divine promise as the ultimate object of Thomas's faith and Lefèvre's interest in divine agency and what God does for Thomas (above Thomas's confession of christological orthodoxy) share commonalities with Lutheran perspectives. Lutherans in turn acknowledge in various ways that God often uses externals, including haptic experience, alongside or in support of the preached Word to create and sustain faith. In the early decades in which the competing epistemological certainties traced by Schreiner were first emerging, these different approaches to the relationship of doubt and certainty were not seen by all as mutually exclusive.

One pronounced example of this fluidity can been seen in the fact that some key aspects of Lutheran exegesis of Thomas found an apparently uncontroversial afterlife in a commentary on John published by the French biblical scholar and Sorbonne product Claude Guilliaud.[109] Beginning in the mid-1530s, Guilliaud served as canon at Autun and as the theologian responsible for holding biblical lectures for the diocesan clergy. He amassed a large library that contained, among many volumes of patristic and humanistic writings, works by Protestant reformers. He wrote commentaries on Paul's epistles, the canonical letters, the Gospel of John, and the Gospel of Matthew that reflected his lectures. In these, he drew on patristic and more recent exegetical literature, often lifting passages wholesale from other authors. In his dedicatory epistle to his commentary on the Pauline letters (1542), Guilliaud described and justified this practice, noting that he often supplied the name of the author but at other times could not remember the source and so omitted this information.[110] In June 1545, however, this method got him into trouble with the theology faculty at the Sorbonne, which opened an inquiry into his commentaries on the Pauline and canonical epistles and placed them on the index of prohibited books. After two years, Guilliaud submitted revised versions, which were approved in June 1547 and published in 1548.[111] As Bernard Roussel has shown, in the commentary on Romans, Guilliaud drew heavily on the exegesis of Erasmus, the Parisian theologian Jean de Gaigny (d. 1549), and Martin Bucer (1491–1551).[112] It was likely the anonymous borrowings from Bucer and other "heretical" authors that raised the suspicions of theologians in Louvain, who notified their colleagues in Paris.[113]

---

109 Claude Guilliaud, *In sacrosanctum Iesu Christi evangelium secundum Ioannem enarrationes* (Paris: J. Roigny, 1548); hereafter cited as *Enarrationes*. On Guilliaud, see James K. Farge, *Biographical Register of Paris Doctors of Theology, 1500–1536* (Toronto: Pontifical Institute of Mediaeval Studies, 1980) 213–16.

110 Claude Guilliaud, *Collatio in omnes divi Pauli apostoli epistolas* (Paris: S. Gryphius, 1542), *3r. On Guilliaud's biblical work, see Bernard Roussel, "La formation biblique du clergé d'Autun entre 1540 et 1550: Bucer plagié, le chanoine Guilliaud censuré: Recherches nouvelles sur Claude Guilliaud (1493–1551), théologal d'Autun," in *Horizons européens de la Réforme en Alsace*, ed. M. de Kroon and M. Lienhard (Strasbourg: Istra, 1980), 321–29.

111 Roussel, "La formation biblique," 317; Farge, *Biographical Register*, 214–15.

112 Roussel, "La formation biblique," 323–29. See also Roussel, "Claude Guilliaud, un théologal pris en flagrant délit de dissidence (1542–1548)," in *Les dissidents du XVIe siècle entre l'humanisme et le catholicisme: Actes du colloque de Strasbourg (5–6 février 1982)*, ed. M. Lienhard (Baden-Baden: Éditions Valentin Koerner, 1983), 127–381; Roussel, "Recherche biblique et réforme religieuse, vingt ans après le groupe de Meaux: Claude Guilliaud, un chanoine théologal du diocèse d'Autun," in *Actes du colloque international Guilliaume Farel, Cahiers de la revue de théologie et de philosophie* 9, no. 1 (1983): 31–43.

113 James K. Farge, *Orthodoxy and Reform in Early Reformation France: The Faculty of Theology of Paris, 1500–1536* (Leiden: Brill, 1985), 249.

Guilliaud's *Enarrationes* on John had their origins in lectures and, according to Roussel, were drafted in written form between 1542 and 1544.[114] They were first published in 1548, after being approved by the Paris theology faculty. According to Farge, the commentary on John sailed through the review process just a month before Guilliaud won approval of his revised commentaries on Paul and the canonical epistles.[115] The work was reissued five times in the next eight years. In this commentary, Guilliaud continued his named and anonymous borrowings from patristic and more recent authors, especially from Cyril, Chrysostom, Theophylact, and Erasmus. However, no one seems to have noticed that the Lutheran interpreters Brenz and Sarcerius feature prominently if also anonymously in Guilliaud's comments on John 20:24–31.[116] The complexity of the early modern reformation of doubt can been seen in part in the way that appropriations from the Lutheran commentaries impact Guilliaud's Catholic portrayal of the doubting apostle.

Of all the works surveyed here, the form of Guilliaud's commentary is most like that of Sarcerius's *Scholia*, structured according to a line by line presentation of the biblical text, in Latin, with brief explanatory observations under each portion of the text. Whereas Sarcerius omits parts of the biblical text, Guilliaud's commentary reproduces the entire text of the passage and also has marginal summaries of the main point or question of each set of comments. For example, the marginal comment on "was not with them when Jesus came" (verse 24) notes that Thomas was absent when Christ breathed on the other disciples, but that the Spirit was also conferred upon him by Christ's design. The comments proper consist almost entirely of a passage explaining this point taken verbatim from Cyril of Alexandria. Although Guilliaud identifies Cyril, he does not indicate that the second sentence of his comments is taken directly from Sarcerius. It says that the evangelist implies Thomas would have believed if he had been present with the others.[117] This then leads into the

114 Roussel, "La formation biblique," 322.

115 Farge, *Biographical Register*, 215.

116 Guilliaud also seems to have borrowed a passage from a harmony of the passion and resurrection by Bugenhagen in his comments on verse 24; the issue raised is the number of the disciples at the time (why the evangelist says "one of the twelve" instead of "eleven"), which was addressed by a number of exegetes. Guilliaud's rendering with a reference to Paul and 1 Corinthians 15, however, follows Bugenhagen's wording closely; *Enarrationes*, 564; cf. Johannes Bugenhagen, *Annotationes ab ipso iam emissae, In Deuteronomium, In Samuelem prophetam, id est duos libros Regum: Ab eodem praeterea conciliata ex Evangelistis historia passi Christi et glorificati, cum annotationibus* (Basel: A. Petri, 1524), 447.

117 "Quasi dicat Euangelista, Si praesens fuisset Thomas, fortassis & cum aliis credidisset" (Guilliaud, *Enarrationes*, 564; Sarcerius, *Scholia*, 834). For the passage cited from Cyril, see *Commentary on John*, 2: 678–79.

question of whether or not he received the Spirit, since he was absent and did not believe. Guilliaud agrees with Cyril on this point.

Guilliaud's other seven or so borrowings from Sarcerius—all unattributed—have more significant implications for the themes of doubt and certainty. These appear in the comments on phrases from verses 25–27 and 29. Guilliaud cribs passages that criticize human reason for wanting to be convinced of the truth and certainty of the Word and to see and touch before believing, when it is rather the case that one ought to believe before seeing and touching.[118] He also borrows material stressing Christ's kindness in accommodating himself to Thomas's weakness and recommending this as an example of how to deal with weak consciences.[119] Although he does not take over Sarcerius's short explanation of "non credam" as "non ero simplici verbo contentus," he glosses Thomas's refusal by echoing a phrase about the simple Word from Sarcerius's comments on the first part of the same verse.[120] In his comments on verse 29, Guilliaud inserts two passages in which Sarcerius stresses the simple Word. To the first, Guilliaud adds a clarification that this refers to the gospel: "For the Lord wants us to believe in the simple Word, and not to seek external signs instead of the certainty of the Word, or the gospel."[121] Guilliaud uses the term "the simple Word" elsewhere in his comments, and even substitutes this phrase for "the

118 On Thomas's demand in John 20:25, Guilliaud rearranges points made by Sarcerius: "Haec enim continent periphrasim omnium rerum sensibus subiectarum, per quas humana ratio vult certificari de veritate & certitudine verbi antequam credat. Nam ratio primum vult videre, & palpare, postea credere, quum tamen credendum sit prius quam videas & palpes. Quare quae hoc loco Thomas dicit, sunt verba ipsissimae rationis & incredulitatis" (Guilliaud, *Enarrationes*, 565; cf. Sarcerius, *Scholia*, 834–35).

119 On the preface to Christ's return in John 20:26, Guilliaud revises some of the prose and expands Sarcerius's comments slightly: "Singularis est haec Christi philanthropia, qui neque Thomam incredulum reiicit, imo ne reprehendit quidem acriter, sed illius infirmitati per omnia se accommodat, ut illum lucretur ... [Guilliaud inserts some comments drawn from Chrysostom (not attributed) and Cyril (identified) and then returns to Sarcerius] ... Observa hoc loco Christi exemplum, quo docemur quomodo a nobis tractandae sint conscientiae infirmae, quibuscum patienter agendum est & aliquantisper tolerandum, donec aliquando nostra institutione perfectiores atque firmiores fiant" (Guilliaud, *Enarrationes*, 565; cf. Sarcerius, *Scholia*, 835). Guilliaud echoes Sarcerius's repetition of the former point at the opening of the comments on John 20:27: "Infirmitati Thomae Christus se accommodans, ut eum lucretur" (Guilliaud, *Enarrationes*, 566; cf. Sarcerius, *Scholia*, 836).

120 "Observa: signum pertinaciae est simplici verbo nolle credere, sed velle prius signa & res externas quibus certificeris, & subinde credas" (Guilliaud, *Enarrationes*, 565); "Pertinacia est seu obstinatio, non credere simplici verbo, sed expetere signa ac res externas, quibus certificeris de veritate verbi" (Sarcerius, *Scholia*, 834).

121 Guilliaud, *Enarrationes*, 567; the marginal gloss summarizes "credendum simplici verbi"; cf. "Et est usus huius correctionis, ut simplici verbo credamus, nec petamus externa signa pro certitudine verbi" (Sarcerius, *Scholia*, 837). For the second passage, see note 125 below.

divine promises" in an expanded borrowing from Erasmus in the comments on verse 27.[122]

Despite the emphasis on the simple Word, Guilliaud, like Sarcerius, sees external signs as an accommodation to human weakness. After the augmented passage from Erasmus, he adds a bridging sentence noting how difficult it is to believe the resurrection, since it surpasses the capacity of human reason. This he follows with a passage taken from Sarcerius's comments on the previous verse, describing the proper use of signs, which were instituted on account of human weakness to aid faith in the simple Word. He also includes a quotation that Sarcerius attributes to Augustine about fallen humanity's need for some kind of medium to see, know, and have faith in God.[123] Moreover, Guilliaud includes Sarcerius's brief gloss "signis externis certior factus" on the phrase "Because you have seen" (verse 29) at the start of his own comments on the passage, combining them with Erasmus's remarks about the involvement of three senses: "Since you have been made more certain by external signs, O Thomas, (for surely you saw me, heard me, and touched me), you persuaded yourself of my resurrection and believe that I live again, saying, 'my Lord and my God.'"[124] However, Guilliaud's stronger insistence on Thomas's touching and on faith received through the signs, along with his judgment that Christ affirms Thomas's confession with these words, can give the misleading impression that he places this faith gained through the assistance of signs on an equal par with faith in the Word. Ultimately, Guilliaud sees verse 29 proclaiming the superiority of faith satisfied with the simple Word, and he includes passages from Sarcerius and Brenz underscoring this point.[125] In his comments on verse 30, he clarifies that the purpose of signs and miracles is to invite and

122 "... & posthac noli aliis in rebus esse perinde incredulus, sed simplici verbo quanlibet tuis sensibus incredibile fuerit, crede" (Guilliaud, *Enarrationes*, 566); cf. "... & posthac noli aliis in rebus esse perinde incredulus, sed fidem habe promissis meis, quamlibet incredibilibus juxta commune hominum sensum" (Erasmus, LB 7: 645).

123 "Rursus adverte Dominum signis manu duxisse Thomam ad fidem, ut intelligamus signa propter nostram infirmitatem instituta esse, quae adeo magna est, imo maior est quam ut permittat nos simplici verbo credere, nisi signis etiam visibilibus adiuti fuerimus. Quare verissimum est quod scribit Augustinus, Homo ante peccatum videbat, Deum intelligebat, & illi fidebat; at post peccatum homo Deum capere non potest nisi medio aliquo adiutus" (Guilliaud, *Enarrationes*, 566; cf. Sarcerius, *Scholia*, 835). I have not been able to identify the source of the quotation from Augustine; it also appears in Lutheran catechetical writings by Sarcerius and Johann Spangenberg.

124 Guilliaud, *Enarrationes*, 567; cf. Sarcerius, *Scholia*, 837; Erasmus, LB 7: 645.

125 "... qui simplici verbo crediderint, neglecto interim rationis consilio, contempto sensuum applausu, posthabita etiam praesentia Christi in carne, & miraculis sepositis" (Guilliaud, *Enarrationes*, 567; cf. Sarcerius, *Scholia*, 837). "Credent enim Gentes meam resurrectionem, quam tamen oculis non viderunt. Quanto igitur minus viderunt & crediderunt,

confirm faith, to which he adds a brief passage from Brenz saying that the sacraments are the means for distributing Christ's good promises.[126]

Guilliaud's other borrowings from Brenz (also all unattributed) are clustered in his comments on Thomas's response to the other disciples (verse 25) and his profession of faith (verse 28). These passages allow Guilliaud to universalize Thomas's doubt and give a robust account of the meaning of his confession that includes virtually all the traditional claims about Christ's two natures but also the stronger emphasis on personal apprehension of Christ's saving benefits found in Lutheran exegesis. He opens his comments on Thomas's demand with Brenz's comparison between Thomas and Peter and his explanation for why the evangelist included this story. Though Guilliaud does not repeat Brenz's point about Thomas representing the voice of the flesh that is in all people, to Brenz's comment that this teaches us that the presumption of the flesh is empty, he inserts a clause emphasizing "our" untrustworthiness, presumption, self-flattery, and high estimate of our own abilities.[127] At the end of this passage, Guilliaud returns to Brenz, citing the observation that Thomas's incredulity advances our credulity. Following this with two ideas drawn from Sarcerius and Chrysostom about Thomas's demand for confirmation from the senses, Guilliaud concludes by citing Brenz's point that Christ connived with Thomas's incredulity in order to strengthen not just Thomas's own faith but also our own.[128]

---

tanto beatiores erunt" (Guilliaud, *Enarrationes*, 567; cf. Brenz, *In D. Iohannis evangelion* [1528], 346r).

126 Here Guilliaud revises and condenses considerably: "Usus enim signorum seu miraculorum, est ad fidem provocare, & illam confimare. Sacramentorum vero est, promissa Christi bona distribuere" (*Enarrationes*, 567–68). Brenz's original is more explicit about the priority of the Word and the difference between miracles and sacraments: "Miracula verbum confirmant, non fidem largiunter ... Alia autem est miraculorum, alia sacramentorum ratio. Nam, miracula verbi sigilla sunt. Sacramenta autem, sunt verbi instrumenta, quibus bona Christi promissa distribuuntur" (*In D. Iohannis evangelion* [1528], 346r).

127 "Quemadmodum Euangelistae multis verbis lapsum Petri descripserunt, non animo exprobrandi errati, sed ut doceremur quam vani sumus in pollicitationibus, & praesumptione quam de nobis induimus, dum nobis placemus, & nostras vires aliquid esse putamus: ita hoc loco Ioannes multis explicat Thomae incredulitatem, non libidine traducendi peccati: sed ut ostendat quam vanus sit genius carnis in Thoma adumbratus" (Guilliaud, *Enarrationes*, 565; cf. Brenz, *In D. Iohannis evangelion* [1528], 345v).

128 "Nostra enim credulitas in illius incredulitate promouet ... cui Christus eo conniuet ut fides non tam illius quam nostra stabilius firmaretur" (Guilliaud, *Enarrationes*, 565). In Brenz, these points are reversed: "Ita Christus conniuet ad incredulitatem Thomae, sed hoc iudicio, ut fides non tam illius, quam nostra stabilius firmaretur. Incredulitate enim Thomae, nostra credulitas promouet" (*In D. Iohannis evangelion* [1528], 345v).

Guilliaud's comments on Thomas's confession of faith in verse 28 stand as a remarkable conclusion to the exegetical trajectory represented in this survey. He echoes or quotes from a number of contemporary and traditional points, all unattributed with the exception of a single mention of Cyril. Though Guilliaud includes a robust statement of the dominant patristic and medieval view that Thomas professes here Christ's two natures, he frames these doctrinal points with attention to the effect on Thomas of the encounter with Christ that draws on Brenz, Erasmus, and Lefèvre and with concluding observations about the possessive pronoun "meus" taken from Brenz.

Guilliaud opens his comments on the wonderful change in Thomas with Brenz's claim that this transformation from incredulity to faith is beyond what anyone could imagine. He augments this point with a statement from Erasmus that though he was rather stubborn about believing, yet no one proclaimed more clearly than Thomas that Christ was God and man. A passage from Lefèvre follows to show that this change came about because Thomas was touched by divinity as he touched Christ's body, and thereby was fulfilled Christ's command to believe.[129]

In his ensuing account of the way that Thomas affirms Christ's two natures, Guilliaud echoes a number of traditional points. Thomas teaches Christ's two natures in one hypostasis. By calling him "Lord," Thomas indicates his human nature, the bodily resurrection, and that Christ shows himself to be Lord over sin, death, the devil, and hell. By calling him "God," Thomas proclaims his divine essence and that he is equally God and Lord. Guilliaud then supplies Augustine's statement that Thomas saw and touched the man and confessed God.[130] He concludes his collection of unattributed comments with an observation that this is one of the places in the New Testament ascribing to Christ the name of "God." The next passage, borrowed from and attributed to Cyril, makes the point that in the Greek the definite article is used to identify and distinguish Christ; this serves, like the other points in this section, to underscore the traditional focus on Christ's unique identity as savior.

129 "Quis unquam sua ratione & quanlibet ardua philosophia assequi potuisset, ex tam pertinaci incredulitate, tantam futuram fidem: & ex tam infideli & incredulo, factum esse fidelissimum: qui quo fuerat ad credendum difficilior, ita nemo clarius Christum Deum & hominem esse professus est. Tangendo, abundantius tactus est: nam tacto Domini corpore, tactus est divinitate, & impleta est pax qua Dominus domum ingressus, illos salutavit. Rursus impleta est iussio, qua dixerat, Noli esse incredulus, sed fidelis" (Guilliaud, *Enarrationes*, 566; Brenz, *In D. Iohannis evangelion* [1528], 345v; Erasmus, LB 7: 645; Lefèvre, *Commentarii in evangelia*, 404r).

130 Guilliaud, *Enarrationes*, 567. In his comments on verse 29 ("Because you have seen"), Guilliaud also reproduces the similar idea that Thomas saw one thing but touched another.

Like the Lutheran interpreters who also gave a traditional interpretation of Thomas's confession, Guilliaud also steers his discussion of this verse and of verse 31 to stress Thomas's personal embrace of Christ as savior and faith as subjective apprehension of Christ's benefits. Guilliaud's final observation on verse 28 returns to Brenz's exegesis and rearranges and expands his comments slightly. Having begun with Brenz's first sentence, he now skips to Brenz's comment about the possessive pronoun: "That exclamation 'my' reveals the extremely ardent emphasis of Thomas's confession. For the one who confesses from the heart (like Thomas) that God is his very own, denies everything belonging to himself and possesses those things which are God's: for he is in Christ, whom he puts on by a living faith, and Christ is in him." Guilliaud then turns back to the second sentence in Brenz's comments and addresses his readers directly:

> Consider again, when you see that from exceedingly great incredulity Thomas was made such an extraordinary confessor of the Christian proclamation, and that Paul, who in the beginning was an especially vicious persecutor of the church, became most powerfully bound to Christ and defender of the gospel, without doubt we ought to believe that these wonderful judgments of God are described here so that, giving attention to them, we might learn to know the singular and extraordinary goodness of God, who turns darkness into light and evil into good.[131]

The only part of Brenz's comments on verse 28 that Guilliaud does not reproduce is the allusion to Psalm 24 and the ensuing idea of a blessed exchange found in the last two sentences.[132] But this same notion is captured in Guilliaud's expansion to Brenz above: "for he is in Christ, whom he puts on by a living faith, and Christ is in him." An echo can be heard also in the citation from Sarcerius that he borrows in his comments on the end of verse 30. "The one who believes, confesses two natures in Christ and also the mystery of redemption and human salvation through him. He believes Christ is our savior, intercessor for us, our ruler, and equally God with God the father."[133]

Guilliaud's method in his commentary is clearly in continuity with the synthesizing medieval approaches, seeking to unpack the meaning of this curious episode by transmitting and embellishing the insights of past authorities.

131 Guilliaud, *Enarrationes*, 567; cf. Brenz, *In D. Iohannis evangelion* [1528], 345v–346r.

132 "Nos Domini sumus, & Dominus noster est. Proinde omnia Dei bona nostra sunt, ideoque; per fidem in Iesum Christum" (Brenz, *In D. Iohannis evangelion* [1528], 346r).

133 Guilliaud, *Enarrationes*, 568; Sarcerius, *Scholia*, 838.

However, his adoption of novel Lutheran perspectives, along with those of the biblical humanists and Catholic reformists Erasmus and Lefèvre, is striking when compared to contemporary Catholic treatments of the pericope. That, however, is a topic for another day.[134]

In comparison to some Lutheran exegetes, Guilliaud does not focus as much on doubt as a universal human failing. Though he presents it as a failure to rely on the simple Word of the gospel, he also denotes the object of Thomas's doubt as the fact of Christ's resurrection. Likewise, he gives more attention to the traditional christological doctrine of Christ's two natures. While he shows marked interest in addressing his readers' subjective experience of doubt and faith, he does not spend quite as much time drawing connections between Thomas's story and their situation. That may be related to genre, since Guilliaud's work is a commentary, whereas many of the Lutheran materials analyzed earlier were sermons. However, it should be remembered that Guilliaud's biblical lectures were directed, like those of Melanchthon and his Lutheran colleagues, for preachers in training, and thus can be considered as aids toward praxis. In fact, a sermon from Guilliaud on the reading for the Sunday after Easter exists and was published posthumously. Discussing there Christ's first appearance when Thomas was as yet absent, Guilliaud does connect Christ's commission of the disciples (John 20:21–23) to the situation of his clerical auditors. However, at the point that the reading turns to Thomas, the text simply states, "for the remainder, see the commentary on John."[135] Despite these differences, however, Guilliaud's positive reception of the Lutheran reformation of doubt in his reading of the incredulous apostle is unmistakable and stands as a compelling testament to the cross-confessional concern for doubt and quest for certainty in the early modern era.

---

134 Helmut Puff suggests that there is perhaps more overlap between Catholic and Protestant sermonizing on this passage in the way they pay attention to narrative detail and avoid "overt confessional agitation." Helmut Puff, "The Word," in *The Oxford Handbook of the Protestant Reformations*, ed. Ulinka Rublack (New York: Oxford University Press, 2017), 402. More detailed study of the theological accents and aims of Catholic interpreters is needed, however, to establish whether or not overlap extends to these elements.

135 Claude Guilliaud, *Homiliae quadragesimales*, ed. Maximilien Guilliaud (Paris: L'Huillier, 1568), 314; cf. the similar comment on John 20:23 (313).

CHAPTER 8

A Clearness Uneasily Observed: Leprosy, Perception, and Certitude in Calvin's *A Harmony of the Gospels Matthew, Mark, and Luke*

Mark M. Lambert

1 Introductory Remarks

> When Christ therefore sends the leper away to the priest, He shows that He had no other purpose than to heighten the glory of God. The showing was connected with the examination, and the gift was a symbol of thanksgiving ... For the Papists to make this a proof text of their own confession is most unperceptive.[1]

The great Reformation historian David Steinmetz diagnosed one of the key features of the era in his statement that the Bible was "in the fullest sense of the term, a sixteenth-century book."[2] The bucolic book, Steinmetz argued, "influenced European attitudes toward war and peace, the structure of civil government and the family, the process of human growth and development, theories of child-rearing and education, as well as attitudes toward economic relations and policies of taxation."[3] Few commentators exhibited as much command of this century-defining book as the Swiss reformer John Calvin. Indeed, almost as a nod to Steinmetz's catalogue, Calvin would rely upon the Biblical text in his articulation of numerous Genevan civic reforms, shifts in public policy, and

1 John Calvin, *A Harmony of the Gospels Matthew, Mark and Luke*, Calvin's Commentaries, vols. 1–3, trans. A. W. Morrison, eds. David W. Torrance and Thomas F. Torrance (Grand Rapids, MI: Wm. B. Eerdmans Publishing Company, 1972), I: 245. Cf. John Calvin, *Commentary on a Harmony of the Evangelists: Matthew, Mark, and Luke*, trans. William Pringle, 3 vols. (Edinburgh: Calvin Translation Society, 1845–46 [reprint Grand Rapids, MI: Baker Book House, 1984]), Volume I, 375. All selections will be from the Morrison translation. The title is a play upon Calvin's Luke 17:11–21 commentary: "Now Christ here used 'observation' to mean *a clearness easily observed*; as if He were denying that the Kingdom of God would be transcendent in obvious display," Calvin, *A Harmony of the Gospels Matthew, Mark and Luke*, II.134 (hereafter referred to as *Harmony of the Gospels*).

2 David C. Steinmetz, *Luther in Context* (Bloomington, IN: Indiana University Press, 1986), 44.

3 *Ibid.*, 44–5.

 | DOI:10.1163/9789004527843_009

most famously, his emphasis on the noetic Fall's consequences for the human rational faculties.

Though Calvin's post-Erasmian humanist context has been much acknowledged, particularly in his valuation of historical sources and philological precision as displayed in his biblical commentaries, Calvin's appreciation of *medical* knowledge has frequently been overlooked.[4] His theological writings on leprosy evince a clear exposure to authoritative medical texts. Given the Genevan's intellectual capaciousness, that he was well versed in contemporary medical discourse should hardly be surprising. But what is significant, I argue, is that Calvin's appeal to contemporary medical discourse pertaining to leprosy would shape his biblical commentary and theology in pivotal ways. As Susan Schreiner has reminded her students so many times: "What we do is try to find out what the questions of the author are and have the text ask the questions." Thus, in this essay I simply ask: why leprosy? Why, in Calvin's writings, is leprosy consistently yoked to discussions of auricular confession and the sacrament of penance? Why does the Swiss reformer identify leprosy's justificatory role here as so problematic?

In this essay, I focus on Calvin's interpretation of leprosy in his *Harmony of the Gospels Matthew, Mark, and Luke*, particularly his exegesis of Matthew chapter 8, with reference to his comments on the disease in the *Institutes of the Christian Religion*. I also prove Calvin as heir to a theological tradition in which auricular confession is construed via a medical idiom, and in which—largely by way of Gregory the Great—leprosy is triangulated with inner conditions and outer perception. A detailed analysis of Calvin's exegesis of leprosy reveals a clever grafting of medical knowledge onto the reformer's overriding preoccupation with questions of perception and certainty: issues that Calvin locates as fundamental to the Catholic tradition of auricular confession. In effect, Calvin

4 Only a smattering of sources address the status of medicine during the Reformation. These include Mary Lindemann, "Medicine and Healing," in *The Oxford Encyclopedia of the Reformation*, ed. Hans J. Hillerbrand (New York: Oxford University Press, 1996); idem, *Medicine and Society in Early Modern Europe*, 2nd ed. (Cambridge: Cambridge University Press, 2010); Charles Webster, ed., *Health, Medicine and Mortality in the Sixteenth Century* (Cambridge: Cambridge University Press, 1979); Ole Peter Grell and Andrew Cunningham, ed., *Medicine and the Reformation* (New York: Routledge, 1993); Gary Ferngren, "The Early Modern Period," in *Medicine and Religion: A Historical Introduction* (Baltimore, MD: The Johns Hopkins University Press, 2014), 136–64; and "The Early Modern Period," in *Essential Readings in Medicine and Religion*, ed. Gary Ferngren and Ekaterina Lomperis (Baltimore: The Johns Hopkins University Press, 2017), 188–220. Without question the best resource is now Lomperis, "Human Bodies in Pain as Spiritual Battlefields: Illness, Medicine, and Healing in Early Modern and Contemporary Christian Thought," (PhD diss., The University of Chicago, 2018).

appeals to the uncanny ability of leprosy to confound medical diagnosis and thereby undermine confidence in the human, i.e. priestly, capacity to "diagnose" sins and to more generally comment on the vagaries of visual perception.

2 John Calvin, Lucidly Brief Biblical Commentator

> It is a commentary I have worked out on a Harmony composed from the three Evangelists, with extreme fidelity and equal diligence ... So I have attempted, as far as my prowess allowed, to magnify the progress of Christ on His four-horse chariot, like one of His attendant heralds, and honest readers who have been helped by my efforts will not mind confessing that some success has met my endeavor. I compare the Gospel story quite deliberately to the *quadriga*, being set out as God willed by four witnesses.[5]

Published in Geneva in 1555 by Robert Estienne, John Calvin's *Harmony of the Gospels Matthew, Mark, and Luke* was the culmination of his New Testament commentaries. This was perhaps fitting because in the *Argumentum* to the *Commentary on the Gospel of John*, Calvin had claimed that one must begin reading the gospels with John in order to understand *why* Christ "was manifested," since John served "as a key to open the door into the understanding of the others."[6] In turning to the Synoptic Gospels, Calvin, in good humanist fashion, begins his undertaking with an appraisal of the word "Gospel," relying largely on Paul's definition in Romans 1:2–4 and concluding that the Gospel designation could justifiably be applied to the entire New Testament. He thus understands the Synoptic Gospels to complement John in significant ways. As to the overall structure of his commentary, he writes that: "there is no disagreement, first, that one can make no intelligent or apt comment on one of the three Evangelists without comparing the other two."[7] Consequently, Calvin treats the three authors simultaneously as forming one continuous narrative.

---

5 John Calvin, "Dedicatory Epistle," in *Harmony of the Gospels*, I.viii–ix.

6 Calvin, *Calvin's New Testament Commentaries*, 2nd edition, translated T. H. L. Parker, edited by D. W. Torrance and F. F. Torrance (Grand Rapids: Eerdmans, 1979), IV, 6.

7 Calvin, *Harmony of the Gospels*, I.xiii. Little attention has been devoted to this commentary with the lone full-length study being Dieter Schellong's *Calvins Auslegung der synoptischen Evangelien* (Munich: Chr. Kaiser Verlag, 1969). It can be noted that Calvin did not preach specifically on this material until the latter half of 1559 (and then through 1564), T. H. L. Parker, *Calvin's Preaching* (Louisville, KY: Westminster John Knox Press, 1992), 152.

Historian Darlene Flaming argues for two key circumstances of the writing of the commentary. The first is evidenced by the dedication of the commentary where Calvin praises the city of Frankfurt for its care of religious refugees from France and England, and though never mentioning him by name, alludes to the pernicious attempts of the Hamburg minister Joachim Westphal to eject those refugees from Frankfurt. The year prior, Westphal had published a treatise attacking Calvin's view of the Lord's Supper and Flaming sees that conflict especially pronounced in Calvin's extended—and impassioned—comments on Matthew 26:26.[8] Calvin's conflict with Michael Servetus is the other influence to which Flaming points, as evident especially in a passage on Luke 1:32. By contrast Calvin also has in mind two more positive, contemporary models: Andreas Osiander and Martin Bucer, both of whom produced their own gospel harmonies. Calvin mentions Osiander in the *Harmony* twice by name, likely in reference to the Lutheran pastor's *Evangelienharmonie* published in Nuremberg in 1537.[9] But Calvin is far more approving of Bucer's exegetical project, openly acknowledging his debt to the Strasbourg reformer.[10] In fact, Calvin praises him by name three times, though unlike Bucer, he avoids the extended theological discussions or *loci* of which Bucer was so fond.[11]

Throughout the *Harmony of the Gospels*, Calvin creatively melds his theological interests with his humanist training, particularly in his interpretation of language and rhetoric in the Synoptic gospels. For example, in his exegesis of Matthew 6:5–6, Calvin rejects the traditional allegorical reading of "enter into their closet," even as he cautions against interpreting the words literally. Instead, Calvin entreats his reader that Christ, "is speaking *comparatively*,

8 Darlene K. Flaming, "Calvin as commentator on the Synoptic Gospels," in *Calvin and the Bible*, ed. Donald K. McKim (Cambridge: Cambridge University Press, 2006), 133–4. Westphal's treatise, *Collectanea sententiarum d. Aurelii Augustini de coena Domini*, was published in Frankfurt in 1554 and dedicated to the city council there.

9 Passages on Matthew 2:16 and 20:29 respectively.

10 In his *Argumentum*, Calvin writes: "There is no question of my seeking the credit for the innovation—I freely confess (in the character of an honest man) that the method derives from imitation of others. I have particularly copied Bucer, that man of holy memory, outstanding doctor in the Church of God, whom I judge to have pursued a line of work in this field which is beyond reproach ... And should I at time dissent from him (as I have freely allowed myself to do as occasion demanded) he would be the last, if he were still alive on earth, to take it unkindly," Calvin, "The Theme of the Gospel of Jesus Christ," *Harmony of the Gospels*, 1.xiv. Bucer had published a commentary on the Synoptics in 1527, expanding that to all four gospels in 1530 followed by a revision in 1536.

11 See: *Comm. Matthew 2:23, Matthew 26:17, Luke 24:27*. A classic study is August Lang, *Der Evangelienkommentar Martin Butzers und die Grundzüge seiner Theologie*, Studien zur Geschichte der Theologie und der Kirche 11.2 (Leipzig, 1900, rpt. Aalen: Scientia Verl., 1972).

meaning that we should rather look for a corner, than go after a crowd of people so that they may see us at prayer."[12] This parsing of rhetorical layers is integral to how Calvin interprets the habitual use of parables in the Synoptic Gospels.[13] His interpretive principle accords with his more capacious focus on perception and our human struggle with blindness, a concern particularly relevant to his interpretation of leprosy. When interpreting a given parable, Calvin first succinctly states the thesis or central point; he then expands upon the parable's clear lesson while neither—and this is key for his treatment of leprosy—dismissing details outright nor belaboring over endless allegorical nuances (unlike the church fathers). Calvin's greater interpretative freedom vis-à-vis loci in the Synoptics explains his annoyance with Osiander, and permits him to more easily, and confidently, combine passages that are clear parallels.[14]

For understanding Reformation-era exegesis, there is no better place to start than the seminal scholarship of Steinmetz and Schreiner.[15] Their scholarship has undermined the illusion that Reformation exegesis was merely a prologue to the hermeneutical methods of modern critical exegesis and has shifted the

12 "Though some think the instance given is absurd, and attempt an allegorical explanation about the interior precinct of the heart, there is no need for such ingenuity ... So we must not press the words *Enter into thine inner chamber*, as though He told men to hide away, and say that we cannot pray aright unless without witness," Calvin, *Harmony of the Gospels*, I.202–3; emphasis mine. For more on Calvin's attention to lexicology and etymology see David L. Puckett, *John Calvin's Exegesis of the Old Testament*, Columbia Series in Reformed Theology (Louisville: Westminster John Knox Press, 1995), 56–66. Cf. Calvin's commentary on *Matthew 12:27, 39; Luke 17:7–10*.

13 "Although similitudes usually cast light on the matter in hand, yet if they consist of one continual metaphor they are enigmatic. Hence when Christ put forward this similitude, He wanted to wrap up in an allegory what He could have said more clearly and fully without a figure. But when the explanation has been given, the figurative word has more power and effect than the straightforward," Calvin, *Harmony of the Gospels*, II.63. Also: "It is always a settled principle that God's Word is not obscure save in so far as the world darkens it by its blindness," *ibid.*, II.64.

14 Cf. *Comm. Luke 24:36*. Richard Burnett, "John Calvin and the *Sensus Literalis*," *Scottish Journal of Theology* 57/1 (2004). Also see Calvin, *Harmony of the Gospels*, II.278; Flaming, "Calvin as commentator on the Synoptic Gospels," 140.

15 Steinmetz, in a pair of influential essays, really inaugurated this shift: David C. Steinmetz, "The Superiority of Pre-Critical Exegesis," *Theology Today* 37 (1980): 27–38; idem, "Theology and Exegesis: Ten Theses," in *Historie de l'exégèse au XVI*[e] *siècle*, Etudes de philology et d'histoire, 34 (Geneva: Librairie Droz, 1978): 382–4; Steinmetz followed these with: idem, *Luther in Context* (Bloomington: Indiana University Press, 1986); idem, *Calvin in Context* (Oxford: Oxford University Press, 1995); Susan Schreiner has also published voluminously on the sixteenth-century, but see especially *Where Shall Wisdom Be Found? Calvin's Exegesis of Job from Medieval and Modern Perspectives* (Chicago: University of Chicago Press, 1994) and *Are You Alone Wise? The Search for Certainty in the Early Modern Era* (New York: Oxford University Press, 2011), esp. 79–130.

burden towards seeing Luther and Calvin's biblical commentaries in *continuity* with their medieval forerunners.[16] Schreiner proves that Calvin's interpretation of Job, for example, is indebted to the earlier exegetical tradition, embodied best by Gregory the Great.[17] Pointing to Calvin's pervasive anxiety over sin's noetic consequences, she observes: "He started not from the issue of immediacy or of divine accessibility but from the unrestrained nature of the fallen mind. According to Calvin, the fallen mind 'wanders,' 'strays,' and veers off into 'labyrinths.' Only Scripture can keep the mind 'bridled' on the 'right path'."[18] Against the vagaries of naked spiritualism and the mind's propensity for idolatry, Calvin's quest for certainty found sanctuary in the comforting boundaries of the Word. Schreiner's position regarding the omnipresent concern for certitude in Calvin's thought will remain relevant throughout his discussions on confession and penance.

In 1539, Calvin published the second edition of his *Institutes of the Christian Religion* (a considerable expansion over the first edition), followed the next year by his now famous commentary on Romans. It is in this commentary (especially the Preface) that he defines his exegetical method, particularly by reference to the commentaries—and approaches—of Melanchthon and Bucer. Steinmetz summarizes:

> Calvin attempts to resolve the dilemma posed by the antithetical methods of Bucer and Melanchthon by commenting on each verse of a chapter (contra Melanchthon) and by making those comments as brief as the nature of the text will allow (contra Bucer). All lengthy discussions of theological topics are reserved for the pages of the *Institutes*, where they do not distract the reader from the immediate task of exegesis and can therefore serve as a kind of general introduction to the structure and meaning of Scripture as a whole. Calvin called his exegetical method "lucid brevity".[19]

---

16 Especially illustrative of this older paradigm is Hans Joachim Kraus, "Calvin's Exegetical Principles," *Interpretation* 31 (1977): 9–18.

17 See Schreiner, *Where Shall Wisdom Be Found?*, 116–18.

18 Schreiner, *Are You Alone Wise?*, 111. Pervasive verses in the contest over certitude were: Galatians 4:6, Romans 8:15–16, John 6:45, John 8:47, John 14:16–17, 26, and 1 Corinthians 2:15. Calvin memorably writes about certitude vis-à-vis Scripture in *Institutes* 1.6–9, esp. 1.9.2–3; 3.2.6 and 4.8–9. Also see his commentary on Luke 24:45 in *A Harmony of the Gospels*, III: 245.

19 Steinmetz, *Calvin in Context*, 13. Calvin outlines this reciprocal relationship in his *Institutes*' "Letter to the Reader". This resulted in a "hermeneutical circle" wherein the *Institutes* contributed the "architectonic structure of the Bible, the underlying plan of the whole, that placed the details in their proper context," Steinmetz, "John Calvin as an interpreter," 291.

Calvin was neither eager to embrace traditional allegorical readings of Scripture nor the classical dichotomy between spirit and letter. He instead championed the "natural" or "plain" sense of biblical passages. Still, Calvin's shift did not equate to, in Steinmetz's words, the "woodenly literal." Indeed, "perhaps it would therefore be more accurate to say that Calvin stood for a principled reduction of 'spiritual' readings of the text rather than a total and unconditional rejection of them."[20] Calvin also—significantly—was more apt to read the Old Testament and New Testament in *continuity* and less dialectically.

Calvin's consideration of leprosy epitomizes many of these principles and interpretive innovations. For example, in his *Commentary on the Last Four Books of Moses Arranged in the Form of a Harmony* (hereafter referred to as the *Mosaic Harmony*), we see how Calvin treats the issue at length, in recognition of the vast differences of interpretation regarding the meaning of leprosy. In fact, Calvin begins his exegesis of Deuteronomy 24 and Leviticus 13 by explaining: "Some are too eagerly devoted to allegories; some think that God, as a prudent Legislator, merely gave a commandment of a sanitary nature, in order that a contagious disease should not spread among the people."[21] He further explains: "This passage clearly shows that God, in desiring the lepers to be put out of the camp, *was not acting as a physician by any means*, and merely consulting the health of the people: but that by this external rite and ceremony He exercised them in the pursuit of purity."[22] True to his word, Calvin strives

---

"Lucid brevity" [*in perspicua brevitate*] comes from the preface of the Romans commentary. Regarding the relationship between the commentaries and *Institutes*, Richard Muller also neatly summarizes Calvin's method as: "the running exposition of the biblical text in commentary and sermon, coupled with the elicitation of theological *loci* from the text and the gathering of those *loci* together with the important dogmatic *disputations* of Calvin's time into the form of a basic instruction or *institutio* in theology," Richard A. Muller, *The Unaccommodated Calvin: Studies in the Foundation of a Theological Tradition* (New York: Oxford University Press, 2000), 29, 111–17. Also see Richard C. Gamble, "Brevitas et Facilitas: Toward an understanding of Calvin's Hermeneutic," *Westminster Theological Journal* 47 (1985): 1–17. Some scholars have referred to this structure of Calvin's theology as a *via media*: see Ford Lewis Battles, *Calculus Fidei: Some Ruminations on the Structure of the Theology of John Calvin* (Grand Rapids: Calvin Theological Seminary, 1978); and David Puckett, *John Calvin's Exegesis of the Old Testament*, 16. On "hermeneutical circles" in Calvin's exegesis, see R. Ward Holder, *John Calvin and the Grounding of Interpretation: Calvin's First Commentaries* (Leiden: Brill, 2006), 68–81.

20 David C. Steinmetz, "John Calvin as an interpreter of the Bible," in *Calvin and the Bible*, edited by Donald K. McKim (Cambridge: Cambridge University Press, 2006), 285.

21 John Calvin, *Commentaries on the Last Four Books of Moses Arranged in the Form of a Harmony*, vol. I–II, trans. Charles William Bingham (Grand Rapids: Baker House, 1984), II.11.

22 Calvin, *Mosaic Harmony*, II.12, emphasis mine.

for an exegetical balance between allegory and inappropriate medicalization. He makes a similar point in his commentary on Matthew 8: "For the Papists to make this a proof text of their own confession is most unperceptive." His argument raises two questions: why was leprosy linked with confession and why would medical accuracy problematize this "unperceptive" allegory?

3 Diagnosing the Ulcers of Sin: Leprosy's Exegetical Tradition

To further appreciate the many nuances of Calvin's interpretation of leprosy, one must be reminded of the resilience of illness as metaphor, and in particular the virulence with which leprosy has remained sutured to notions of moral opprobrium. In medieval theology, the association of sin with medical prognosis, and thereby disease, was seemingly inescapable. This is especially clear in the second half of Canon 21 of the Fourth Lateran Council (1215 CE):

> The priest should be discerning and prudent so that like a practiced doctor he can pour wine and oil on the wounds of the injured, diligently enquiring into the circumstances both of the sinner and of the sin, from which to choose intelligently what sort of advice he ought to give him and what sort of remedy to apply among the many available for healing the sick.[23]

Popularly referred to by its incipit, *Omnes utriusque sexus*, this canon obligated all Christians of the age of discretion to confess and receive the Eucharist at least once a year.[24] The canon likewise charged priests to approach the sacrament with the discernment of a skilled physician. But if Canon 21 pauses at the level of analogy between priest and physician, then Canon 22 makes the connection all the more explicit.[25] It is extraordinary that the Fourth

---

23 "Canon 21," in *Conciliorum oecumenicorum decreta*, ed. J. Alberigo et al. (Basel, Freiburg, Rome, 1972), 221.13–17; translated in *English Historical Documents, 1189–1327*, ed. H. Rothwell (London, 1975), 654–5.

24 "All the faithful of either sex, after they have reached the age of discernment, should individually confess all their sins in a faithful manner to their own priest at least once a year, and let them take care to do what they can to perform the penance imposed on them ... " Perhaps more importantly, this canon was codified in the *Decretales* of Gregory IX (5.38.12) ensuring its longevity.

25 "As sickness of the body may sometimes be the result of sin—as the Lord said to the sick man whom he had cured, *Go and sin no more, lest something worse befall you*—so we by this present decree order and strictly command physicians of the body, when they are called to the sick, to warn and persuade them first of all to call in physicians of the soul

Lateran Council's theology and theological language is crafted within a *medical* framework. The roots of this analogy are quite old, dating to the early Church Fathers and most notably Augustine's fondness of the *Christus medicus* motif. But despite the omnipresence of Augustine's influence, this analogy doesn't become commonplace until the thirteenth century.[26] Eventually, the doctrine of confession and sacrament of penance are characterized less by a singular Augustinian analogy and more a medical framework, which makes their connection to leprosy so pivotal.

Fully embracing the *medicus* analogy, Franciscan mystic David of Augsburg wrote, "No physician can fully recognize all the bodily diseases and afflictions, and since they are subtler than the body how much less can anyone fully distinguish all the spiritual sicknesses arising from human passions and temptations?"[27] Ironically, given the fondness for medical motifs, confessors' manuals and penitential literature increasingly scrutinized the medical profession.[28] Sins and malpractices specific to physicians and barber-surgeons were elucidated, with particular attention given to proper diagnosis before treatment. Writings concerning auricular confession—whether penitential

so that after their spiritual health has been seen to they may respond better to medicine for their bodies, for when the cause ceases so does the effect ... Moreover, since the soul is much more precious than the body, we forbid any physician, under pain of anathema, to prescribe anything for the bodily health of a sick person that may endanger his soul," Norman P. Tanner, *Decrees of the Ecumenical Councils* (Washington, DC: Georgetown University Press, 1990), 245–46.

26 See R. Arbesmann, "The Concept of 'Christus medicus' in St. Augustine," *Traditio* 10 (1954): 1–28; John T. McNeill argues, "The penitent was regarded as one morally diseased and ill, and his treatment is, in the Penitentials, repeatedly, even habitually, referred to as the task of the moral physician," in "Medicine for Sin as Prescribed in the Penitentials," *Church History* 1 (1932), 14; also see Nicole Bériou, "La confession dans les écrits théologiques et pastoraux du XIIIe siècle: médication de l'âme ou demarche judiciaire?" *L'Aveu*, 261–82.

27 David von Augsburg, *De exterioris et interioris hominis compositione secundum triplicem statum incipientium, proficientium et perfectorum libri tres* (Quarachhi, 1899), 180. Referenced in Murray, "Counseling in Medieval Confession," 69–70. The classic study remains Henry Charles Lea, *The History of Auricular Confession and Indulgences in the Latin Church*, 3 vols. (Philadelphia: Lea Brothers and Co., 1896). Also see John Bossy, "The Social History of Confession in the Age of the Reformation," *Transactions of the Royal Historical Society* 25 (1975): 21–38. Confessors' *summae* and manuals begin to proliferate, especially after those composed by Alain de Lille circa 1200 CE, *Liber poenitentialis*, ed. J. Longère, 2 vols. AMN 17–18 (1965); the genre takes on new importance with the rise of the mendicant orders.

28 See Darrel W. Amundsen, "Casuistry and Professional Obligations: The Regulation of Physicians by the Court of Conscience in the Late Middle Ages," in *Medicine, Society, and Faith in the Ancient and Medieval Worlds* (Baltimore: The Johns Hopkins University Press, 1996): 248–288.

literature, confessors' manuals, or even Lateran canons—were saturated with an anxiety about properly diagnosing or perceiving sins. One can sympathize with the "attractiveness" of leprosy for these authors and theologians: if only sins were as nakedly visible!

With respect to the exegetical tradition, few works of early Christianity were more cited and revered than Gregory the Great's lengthy commentary on the book of Job, the *Moralia in Job*. Gregory's meandering *Moralia* has nevertheless provided us with one of the sharpest interpretations of leprosy: "For in leprosy both a portion of the skin is brought to a bright hue, and a portion remains of a healthy color. Lepers therefore are a figure of heretics, for in that they blend evil with good, they cover the complexion of health with spots."[29] The leprous metaphor is utilized in service of Gregory's prevailing reading of Job's friends who represent heretics guilty of wrongly condemning Job for his adversities.[30] The metaphor also helps Gregory with an interpretative problem faced by many commentators of how to rescue the moral wisdom embedded in the speeches of Job's friends but remain faithful to the eventual divine reproof at the culmination of the text. Job's saintly forbearance and ambiguous skin afflictions caused his cult to thrive during the Middle Ages and endeared him to victims of the plague, pox, and even leprosy.[31]

29 Gregory the Great, *Morals on the Book of Job*, Vol. 1, Book v, xi, 28. I have selected from *Moralia in Job: Morals on the Book of Job by Saint Gregory the Great*, 3 vols. (Ex Fontibus Company, 2012). For the critical edition see St. Gregory the Great, *Moralia in Iob*, ed. Marcus Adriaen, *CCSL*, vols. 143, 143A, 143B (1979–85); also see the new edition: Gregory the Great, *Moral Reflections on the Book of Job*, 4 vols., trans. Brian Kerns (Collegeville, MN: Cistercian Publications, 2014–17). In this passage, Gregory also directly alludes to the cleansing of the ten lepers in the Gospel of Luke. See the important study Jean Gribomont, "Le texte biblique de Grégoire," in *Grégoire le Grand*, ed. Jacques Fontaine, Robert Gillet, and Stan Pellistrandi, Colloques internationaux du Centre National de la Recherche Scientifique, Chantilly, 15–19 September 1982 (Paris: CNRS, 1986): 467–75.

30 "Let us now search out how their words agree with heretics; for some of the opinions which they hold are very right, but in the midst of these they fall away to corrupt notions; for heretics have this especial peculiarity, that they mix good and evil, that so they may easily delude the sense of the hearer," Gregory the Great, *Morals on the Book of Job*, Vol. 1, Book v. xi, 28. Gregory later reproves the friends for their perceptual limits: "They know not how to enquire deeply into the secret judgments of God, and humbly to investigate that which they cannot understand," 23.17.30.

31 See L. L. Besserman, *The Legend of Job in the Middle Ages* (Cambridge: Harvard University Press, 1979), esp. 1–89; S. Terrien, *The Iconography of Job through the Centuries: Artists as Biblical Interpreters* (University Park, PA: Pennsylvania State University Press, 1996), 35–6, 99–102; and Christine M. Boeckl, *Images of Leprosy: Disease, Religion, and Politics in European Art*, Early Modern Studies 7 (Kirksville, MO: Truman State University Press, 2011), 25–6, 75–7.

While Gregory uniquely applies leprosy as a metaphor to the Joban text, the allegorizing of leprosy is not new; it owes its origin to Augustine. In a homily on Luke 17:11–19, Augustine explains: "Lepers, we may not absurdly suppose, are the types of those who have not the knowledge of the true faith, but show forth various teachings of error ... like the body of one stricken with leprosy, wherein various foul colors appear in different places along with the true color of the skin."[32] Augustine and Gregory were far from alone in this project of allegorizing leprosy. In parallel fashion, leprosy has historically been deemed symptomatic of more specific sins. The cleansing of Naaman, the leprous Syrian commander, in the Jordan River, found in 2 Kings 5, grew to signify the conquest of original sin. Hugh of St. Victor, the influential 12th-century theologian, considered the immersions of Naaman in terms of the "seven-fold leprosy of human pride," which he contrasted with the "seven-fold humility of Christ."[33]

Calvin was intimately conversant with Gregory's writings and there are obvious resonances between Gregory's interpretation of leprosy and Calvin's, especially in a shared focus on the issue of perception.[34] According to Schreiner, there are two hermeneutical assumptions that inform Gregory's entire exegesis of Job: "His metaphysical presupposition that reality is hierarchical, and his assumption that the perception of the true nature of reality is gained only by an inward ascent made possible through suffering."[35] In fact, Gregory's assertion that "Wisdom lies not on the surface of things but lies hidden in the unseen," can operate as a heuristic key for the entire voluminous commentary.[36] For the papal exegete, this perceptual and hierarchical approach to scripture is

32 Augustine, *On Gospel Questions*, Book 11, Chapter XL.

33 Hugh of St. Victor, *Opera Omnia, PL*, clxxvii, *Miscellanea*, lib. III, cols 639–40. Curiously, Hugh conflates the Naaman narrative with those of Miriam and King Uzziah, who are stricken with leprosy as a punishment for prideful disobedience (Numbers 12 and 2 Chronicles 26:16–23 respectively).

34 Indeed, in the 1559 *Institutes*, Calvin cites from Gregory's *Dialogue*, letters, and homilies well over fifty times, exceeded only by references to Augustine. Calvin also cites Gregory 30 times outside of the *Institutes*. See Anthony N. S. Lane, *John Calvin: Student of the Church Fathers* (Edinburgh: T&T Clark, 1991), 58, 62 n. 45. Unfortunately, Calvin's love for Gregory has not been reflected in the secondary literature in comparison to Calvin's well-documented appeal to Augustine. Lester Little writes: "While Augustine was Calvin's main patristic inspiration in matters of church dogma, Gregory held a similar position with regard to church polity," Lester K. Little, "Calvin's Appreciation of Gregory the Great," *Harvard Theological Review* 56, no. 2 (April 1963): 146. Interestingly, the first edition of the *Institutes* from 1536 contains merely a single reference to Gregory, and it's a rather oblique one. All of the key Gregory references appear first in the 1543 edition—the first edition following Calvin's return from Strassburg.

35 Schreiner, *Where Shall Wisdom Be Found?*, 23.

36 Gregory the Great, *Moralia*, v.v.8.

coupled to a medicinal sense of suffering that can clarify one's perception of themselves and their reality: Job is thus a textbook for how suffering elevates one's perception.[37] In this context, leprosy is entangled with concerns about ambiguous surfaces both literal and figurative.

Gregory proposes humanity as a microcosm with the potential for bridging the divide between sensible, mutable materiality and rational, immutable spirituality: "how this whole universe consists of things visible and invisible, how He created man, so to say, gathering together in a small compass another world, yet a world of reason; how constituting this world of soul and flesh, He mixed the breath and the clay by an unsearchable disposal of His Might."[38] Gregory's theological anthropology betrays his Galenic humoral assumptions: he identifies humanity as bodily constituted by four humoral qualities—hot, cold, dry, moist—which are complemented by three spiritual qualities.[39] He even admits that these humors can be affected by climate, diet, and habit and consequently, determine individual temperament or propensity for particular sins.[40] Gregory's concern with perception and "looking beyond" the surface is eloquently expressed in a passage that prefigures the theology of the Fourth Lateran Council: "For since He is our inward Physician, He first made known the corruptions of our wound, and afterwards pointed out the remedies for obtaining health."[41]

---

37 "[Gregory] analyzes suffering in terms of interiority and then proceeds to use the sanative nature of affliction as a hermeneutical construct. In Gregory's spirituality, suffering and the hierarchical view of reality are intimately connected. Suffering turns the soul inward so that it can ascend toward God. The connection of interiority, suffering, and ascent reflects the parallel between Gregory's exegetical method and his hierarchical view of reality: Both suffering and exegesis lead to an interior ascent," Schreiner, *Where Shall Wisdom Be Found?* 27.

38 Gregory the Great, *Morals on the Book of Job*, 6.15.18.

39 "But man, who consists of soul and body, consists of seven qualities. For he flourishes in three spiritually and in four bodily. For in the love of God he is excited in three qualities spiritually, when it is said to him by the Law; *Thou shalt love the Lord thy God with all they mind, and with all thy soul, and with all thy strength.* [Matthew 22:37] But he consists of four qualities bodily; because, namely, he is composed of hot and cold, of moist and dry matter," Gregory the Great, *Morals on the Book of Job*, 35.16.42. Cf. *Morals on the Book of Job*, 26.17.28 and 7.28.35. Also see Carole Straw, "Gregory's Moral Theology: Divine Providence and Human Responsibility," in *A Companion to Gregory the Great*, eds. Bronwen Neil and Matthew Dal Santo (Leiden: Brill, 2013), 183.

40 See *Morals on the Book of Job*, 3.22.45 and 29.22.45.

41 Gregory the Great, *Morals on the Book of Job*, 35.8.11.

Calvin was clearly familiar with the *Moralia* as well as Gregory's *Homilies on the Gospels*.[42] Moreover, Calvin's exegesis of passages pertaining to leprosy are responses to a broader tradition wherein confession and the "diagnosis" of sins were expressed in medical idioms. Figurative language aside, how was leprosy understood and treated medically?

4 John Calvin and Medical Knowledge

> But, as to the various kinds of leprosy, I confess that I am not a physician, so as to discuss them accurately, and I purposely abstain from close inquiry about them, because I am persuaded that the disease here treated of affected the Israelites in an extraordinary manner, which we are now unacquainted with; for what do we now know of a leprous house?[43]

In many ways, John Calvin embodies the ideals of Renaissance humanism.[44] He mastered Latin, Greek, and Hebrew, possessed a deep background in law through his studies at Orléans and Bourges, studied philosophy at the Collège de Montaigu, and even published a commentary on Seneca's *De Clementia*.[45] Flaming identifies in the *Harmony of the Gospels* two references to Cicero and

---

42 In Calvin's later works, Johannes van Oort has highlighted a noticeable decline in Calvin's citations of Gregory—a trend that correlates to a distinct increase in Bernard of Clairvaux citations. The interpretation of leprosy is a clear exception to that trend, which I suggest owes to Calvin's admiration of Gregory's perceptual focus and employ of medical idioms. See Johannes van Oort, "John Calvin and the Church Fathers," in *The Reception of the Church Fathers in the West: From the Carolingians to the Maurists, Vol. 2*, ed. Irena Backus (Leiden: Brill, 1997), 661–700.

43 Calvin, *Mosaic Harmony*, 11.13.

44 David Steinmetz asserts: "There is no reason to dispute the thesis that Calvin, like many of the early Protestant reformers, found the intellectual agenda of the humanists congenial and embraced many of their methods and goals," "The Scholastic Calvin," in *Calvin in Context*, 247; also see Quirinus Breen, *John Calvin: A Study in French Humanism*, 2nd edition (North Haven, CT: Archon Books, 1968). Muller calls for a consideration of both Calvin's context and the humanistic conversations to which he was privy, especially arguing for a greater engagement between Calvin and Melanchthonian humanism. See Muller, *The Unaccommodated Calvin*, 13–14, 40, 178–9, 185.

45 Battles described Calvin's Seneca commentary as "the apprenticeship of a consummate Scriptural exegete," see *Calvin's Commentary on Seneca's De Clementia*, trans. and ed. Ford Lewis Battles and André Malan Hugo, Renaissance Text Series (Leiden: Brill, 1969), 87. Barbara Pitkin also points to Calvin's commentary on Seneca's *De Clementia* and, of course, the shaping of ecclesiastical and civic law in Geneva. Barbara Pitkin, "Calvin's Mosaic Harmony: Biblical Exegesis and Early Modern Legal History," *The Sixteenth Century Journal* 41, no. 2 (Summer 2010): 457–8.

Horace each, a quotation from Ovid, and a reference to Plutarch's *Lives*.[46] Although he was arguably aware of Peter Lombard's *Sentences* and the *Glossa ordinaria*, as demonstrated above, Calvin's exegetical efforts relied more heavily on the unglossed Greek and Hebrew texts of the Bible.[47] His *Harmony of the Gospels* relies upon his personal translation of Greek New Testament passages, even if he references—and contextualizes his translation with—the Erasmus and Vulgate translations.[48] Calvin's aptitude for language is masterly demonstrated in the *Mosaic Harmony* with his commentary on Leviticus 13:2:

> This, then, must be observed in the first place, that the Greek and Latin word *lepra*, and the Hebrew צרעת, *tzaragnath*, extend further than to the incurable disease, which medical men call *elephantiasis*, both on account of the hardness of the skin, and also its mottled color; not, however, that there is an entire agreement between the thickness of the man's skin and that of an elephant, but because this disease produces insensibility of the skin. This the Greeks call Ψώρα, and if it be not a kind of leprosy, it is nearly allied to it. Thus we see that there was a distinction between the *scab* and leprosy.[49]

Calvin exercises tremendous exegetical caution in carefully identifying and distinguishing between the terminological variants that the Vulgate had simply collapsed into *lepra*. Indeed, he discloses his humanist pedigree in the attention he devotes to leprosy *as a disease* and his desire for accurate medical knowledge about it.

But what was the status of medical knowledge about leprosy in early modernity? In accordance with the authority and model in Leviticus 13, priests had historically been responsible for initiating and conducting such medical examinations of those suspected of having leprosy. However, beginning in the thirteenth century, medical practitioners (and especially learned physicians) began to supersede them in this role. After the fourteenth century,

46 *Comm. Luke* 2:11 and *Comm. Matthew* 22:2; *Comm. Luke* 16:14 and *Comm. Matthew* 23:29; *Comm. Luke* 8:52; and *Comm. Mark* 10:21 respectively; see Flaming, "The Synoptic Gospels," 135, n.21. Additionally, Plato is twice referenced, as are the Stoics: *Comm. Matthew* 19:5; *Comm. Matthew* 5:2 and 5:10 respectively.

47 Still, Steinmetz is quick to clarify that "Calvin's Hebrew and Greek Bible was formally but not materially unglossed. His library, if not the margins of his Hebrew and Greek text, was filled with the work of glossators, ancient and modern," "The Scholastic Calvin," 254.

48 Flaming identifies six passages where Calvin explicitly references Erasmus's translation: *Comm. Luke* 1:1, 7:37, 11:41, 19:9 and *Comm. Matthew* 10:17, 10:24. "The Synoptic Gospels," 144, n.71.

49 Calvin, *Mosaic Harmony*, 11.13.

examinations became formalized by the swearing of oaths invoking the just—and omniscient—God and frequently required the examinee to swear the oath while touching a crucifix, gospels, or the like. According to medical historian Luke Demaitre, the rapid spread of oaths "signaled growing apprehensions about deception. The challenge of deception by hiding symptoms or, in a remarkable inversion, simulating them suggested that 'truth' was legally ambivalent."[50] While leprosy historically served as a suggestive metaphor for heresy (insofar as its skin lesions purportedly revealed a corrupt, inner condition), the disease was actually quite notoriously difficult to diagnose. In fact, medieval and early modern medical treatises attempt to delineate mechanisms to better perceive patients' internal states and circumvent potentially deceptive surfaces.

The protocol and structure of this *iudicium leprosorum* betrayed an anxious attempt at diagnostic thoroughness. These visitations frequently involved up to seven examiners, including physicians, surgeons, and barbers, and on occasion, individuals who were already diagnosed with leprosy. Demaitre notes that, "in numerous certificates [of diagnosis], examiners vowed that they had looked, 'in detail' (*exquisite, umbständlich*), at 'every single part of the body, from the sole of the feet to the top of the head'—this sequence, customary in certificates."[51] Given the polyvalence and semiological deceptiveness of skin lesions, physicians employed various blood tests, urine analysis, probing for limb anesthesia, as well as reference to a host of diagnostic checklists of potential signs.[52] In fact, uroscopy was an especially ubiquitous means for "seeing" beneath the skin, with the jordan (or urine flask) serving as the iconographical

---

50 Luke Demaitre, *Leprosy in Premodern Medicine: A Malady of the Whole Body* (Baltimore: The Johns Hopkins University Press, 2007), 52. Contrary to the popular narrative of people with leprosy as the most despised of outcasts, Demaitre documents several examples of individuals counterfeiting a diagnosis of leprosy. Efforts to counterfeit the "clapper," the traditional mark of the leprous beggar's charitable privilege, signal that the enterprise could be quite lucrative and thus attractive to many. Due to a sudden swell in mendicants in the Habsburg regions, in 1531 Charles v limited the collecting of alms to those with leprosy alone. In 1547, following a sudden, inexplicable surge in the number of "leprous" beggars, the emperor decreed that every leprous individual was required to carry their certificate of examination and diagnosis on their person at all times. See Demaitre, 52–59.

51 Demaitre, *Leprosy in Premodern Medicine*, 200. He later notes: "This disease forced medical teachers and practitioners, more consistently than most other diseases, to choose between personal and professional response, between the authority of doctrine and the persuasiveness of appearances, and between a tightened or widened scope of symptoms," 226–7.

52 Demaitre has illustrated that many of the prescribed blood tests, which were often designed to probe for abnormal levels of coagulation, were both based upon clinical experimentation and could even successfully identify Hansen's disease; Demaitre, "The

emblem of the medieval physician—similar to its modern counterpart, the stethoscope. Medical examiners entangled in the mechanisms of the *iudicium* were neither treating nor ministering to a patient so much as solemnly pronouncing the very public fate of an examinee. "The ultimate impetus for applying a broad spectrum of criteria to the diagnosis of leprosy—broader than for any other disease—came from social pressures on the diagnosticians. Medical examiners were expected to deliver a decisive report ... [I]n addition to applying privileged knowledge, they issued judicial verdicts."[53] The similarities between the medical procedures of the *iudicium* and the diagnostic authority of the Levitical priests are unmistakable. Regardless, the medical history of the medieval era and early modernity point to a rapid accumulation of diagnostic criteria in an effort to identify what was widely recognized as a particularly complex and elusive disease.

That John Calvin was interested in the field of medicine should hardly be surprising given that his own health was notoriously precarious. The reformer possessed a frail constitution and was continuously sick. In a 1564 letter to Montpellier physicians, he confessed to be suffering from gout, kidney stones, ulcerated hemorrhoids, chronic indigestion, *and* quartan fever.[54] Yet despite God's benevolent providence, Calvin expects believers to act with prudence and due responsibility: "we are not at all hindered by God's eternal decrees either from looking ahead for ourselves or from putting all our affairs in order ... for he who has set the limits to our life has at the same time entrusted to us its care; he has provided means and helps to preserve it."[55] Chief among such means are the various remedies available through the art of medicine—means with which God "clothes" God's providence.[56] In fact, Calvin strongly

---

Description and Diagnosis of Leprosy by Fourteenth-Century Physicians," *Bulletin of the History of Medicine*, lix (1985): 327–44.

53 Demaitre, *Leprosy in Premodern Medicine*, 234. The reliance upon a broad spectrum of criteria was also undoubtedly connected to the increasing propensity of patients to sue practitioners over negligence and incorrect diagnoses, often resulting in heavy damages. See Carole Rawcliffe, "The Profits of Practice: The Wealth and Status of Medical Men in Later Medieval England," *Social History of Medicine*, i (1988): 61–78.

54 Steinmetz, *Calvin in Context*, 19. On Calvin's medical history see John Wilkinson, *The Medical History of the Reformers: Martin Luther, John Calvin, and John Knox* (Edinburgh: Handsel Press LTD, 2001). Through a careful review of Calvin's correspondence and early biographies, Wilkinson attempts to construct a medical profile of the reformer. He also concludes that Calvin suffered from (and died from) pulmonary tuberculosis.

55 John Calvin, *Institutes of the Christian Religion*, ed. John T. McNeill, trans. Ford Lewis Battles (Louisville: Westminster John Knox Press, 2006) Book 1, chapter XVII:4, 216. Cf. Calvin, *Institutes*, Book 1, chapter XVII:3, 215; and *Harmony of the Gospels*, I.307.

56 "For this reason, God pleased to hide all future events from us, in order that we should resist them as doubtful, and not cease to oppose them with ready remedies, until they

implies that to ignore or neglect such remedies is tantamount to sin, not to mention appalling foolishness. The illuminating benefits of the art of medicine, entrusted though they are to the corrupted minds of fallen humankind, are nonetheless a gift of the Spirit of God.[57]

Calvin not only approves of "the art and practice of medicine," but he also deems this knowledge compatible with theology. Calvin's writings are consistently buoyed by medical idioms and references, such as his remarks on the lancet and cautery in his commentary on Isaiah 4:4.[58] Aside from his myriad remarks on leprosy, Calvin's most protracted medical analysis appears in his commentary on 2 Timothy 2:17, "*And their word will eat as doth a gangrene.*" He claims: "Benedictus Textor, the physician, has drawn my attention to the fact that Erasmus has translated this passage badly, for he has confused two different diseases and made them one, speaking of cancer instead of gangrene. But Galen in many passages and especially in the definitions of his book *On*

---

are either overcome or pass beyond all care. I have therefore already remarked that God's providence does not always meet us in its naked form, but God in a sense clothes it with the means employed," *Institutes* 1.17.4. The second sentence of this passage is an addition of the 1559 edition of the *Institutes*. But many of his comments on medicine were present from the 1539 edition.

57 "If we regard the Spirit of God as the sole fountain of truth, we shall neither reject the truth itself, nor despise it wherever it shall appear, unless we wish to dishonor the Spirit of God. For by holding the gifts of the Spirit in slight esteem, we contemn and reproach the Spirit himself. What then ... Shall we say that they are insane who developed medicine, devoting their labor to our benefit?" Calvin, *Institutes*, 2.2.15, 273–4. Calvin's argument in these passages is strongly indebted, I suggest, to Bonaventure's masterwork, *On the Reduction of the Arts to Theology*. Lomperis outlines "Calvin's soteriological pedagogy of disease was two-sided: by helping individuals develop a proper theological perspective, it simultaneously trained them in pious living ... It also trained individuals in piety, thus strengthening their perseverance in faith which was essential dimension of true justification," in "Human Bodies in Pain as Spiritual Battlefields," 201.

The noted humanist reformer, Philip Melanchthon also championed anatomy, read Vesalius's paradigm-shattering work, and was reputed to have attended dissections as the University of Wittenberg. See Jonathan Sawday, *The Body Emblazoned: Dissection and the Human Body in Renaissance Culture* (New York: Routledge, 1995), 111–19; and Vivian Nutton, "Wittenberg Anatomy," in *Medicine and the Reformation*, ed. Ole Peter Grell and Andrew Cunningham (New York: Routledge, 1993).

58 "When abounding iniquity is not punished, we become corrupted along with others; and therefore it is necessary that God should earnestly warn us, and, like a physician, apply physic, and the lancet, and sometimes proceed to burning," Calvin, *Commentary on the Book of the Prophet Isaiah*, trans. William Pringle (Grand Rapids: Baker Book House, 1984 reprint) vol. 1, 156. Also see Michael Stolberg, "Metaphors and Images of Cancer in Early Modern Europe," *Bulletin of the History of Medicine* 88, no. 1 (2014): 48–74.

Unnatural Swellings distinguishes the one from the other."[59] What follows is an extended—particularly given his emphasis on "lucid brevity"—parsing of medical authorities and the etymological nuances between *cancer* and *gangrene*. Much as he does with leprosy, Calvin insists that medical precision is a vital crutch to a theological argument.

But an important question remains: was leprosy present in Geneva during Calvin's residency there and would he have encountered it? The short answer is *yes*. According to medical historian Léon Gautier: "Until 1536, there are only two diseases on which official acts and especially the Council registers bring us information, that's it, leprosy and plague."[60] Further references indicate the presence of two houses for the care of those with leprosy with notarial evidence, indicating that the house at Chêne still housed three individuals with the disease in 1554 and two in 1556.[61] Significantly, the Council registers contain multiple references to physicians commissioned to examine suspected leprous individuals, including the occurrence of such an examination on 20 March 1565.[62] Given Calvin's prominent role in the civic minutiae of

---

59 Calvin, *The Second Epistle of Paul the Apostle to the Corinthians and the Epistles to Timothy, Titus, and Philemon*, trans. T. A. Smail, *Calvin's New Testament Commentaries*, eds. David W. Torrance and Thomas F. Torrance (Grand Rapids: Eerdmans, 1972), 314. The only extended analysis of this passage I've found is Lindsay J. Starkey, "Gangrene or Cancer? Sixteenth-Century Medical Texts and the Decay of the Body of the Church in Jean Calvin's Exegesis of 2 Timothy 2:17," *Renaissance and Reformation* 39, no. 3 (Summer 2016): 111–32. Benedictus Textor, or Benoit Tixier (d. 1560), was Calvin's personal physician in Geneva. Textor was an accomplished physician who in the 1550s had published a plague treatise, *De la Maniere de Preserver de la Pestilence*, as well *De Cancri Natura et Curatione* (which would explain his interest in Erasmus's translation error). Calvin dedicated his commentary on II Thessalonians to Textor, expressing his immense gratitude for the physician's aid with his wife's illnesses. One also gets the impression that the two learned men frequently discussed theological issues; see Davis A. Young, *John Calvin and the Natural World* (New York: University Press of America, 2007) 147; Machiel A. van den Berg, *Friends of Calvin*, trans. Reinder Bruinsma (Grand Rapids: Eerdmans, 2009), 134–43.

60 Léon Gautier, *La medicine à Genève jusqu'à la fin du XVIII siècle*, Mémoires et documents publiés par la Société d'histoire et d'archéologie de Genève, 2d ser., 10 (Geneva: J. Jullien, Georg, Libraires-Editeurs, 1906), 75. Gautier notes that leprosy was incredibly recurrent around Geneva up until the mid-14th century, but less than a century later it was exceptionally rare. He discovered references to two brothers diagnosed with the disease in 1596, Jean and Antoine Tournier of Bourdigny, with no references after that (101).

61 Gautier, *La medicine à Genève jusqu'à la fin du XVIII siècle*, 99. References from 1536 indicate that the admission numbers were much higher at that point. Gautier writes: "Ces deux établissements étaient l'un à Carouge, l'autre à Chêne. La maladière de Carouge occupait l'emplacement ou le voisinage immediate de l'ancien cimetière de cette ville," 78. See 82–96 for his analysis of reform documents related to these two institutions.

62 "Suspects depuis plusieurs années et déjà examinés à plusieurs reprises par des homes de l'art qui n'avaient pu arriver à des conclusions formelles, Vachat et Bonnevie furent tous

Genevan life, there is little question that the reformer would have been aware of these institutions and the concomitant examinations of those with leprosy. However, Calvin does not consider leprosy to be a just cause of divorce—contrary to common practice at the time.[63] But in the *Mosaic Harmony*, not only does Calvin distinguish between *lepra* and *elephantiasis*, but he also ventures a further distinction in his commentary on Leviticus 14:34: "another sort of leprosy is here treated of, as to which we may not unreasonably rejoice that it is now unknown to us."[64] He refers to the presence of leprosy on the walls of the Israelites' homes, and correctly notes that "true" leprosy or Hansen's disease does not occur outside of a human host.[65] In both respects, his medical assertion is precisely correct. Calvin is creatively folding accurate, contemporary medical terminology and knowledge about leprosy into his exegetical writings.

5 The Role of Leprosy in Calvin's Exegesis and Theology

Before his discussion of Leviticus 13 and 14 in his *Mosaic Harmony*, Calvin most thoroughly considered the subject of leprosy in his *Harmony of the Gospels*, especially a joint commentary on the assemblage of Matthew 8:1–4, Mark 1:40–45, and Luke 5:12–16. The trio of passages report that Christ, after preaching on the mountain, healed an individual with leprosy by means of his word and the touch of his hand. Calvin immediately situates his interpretation within a largely medical framework:

> Although we recognize that leprosy was a different kind of disease to *elephantiasis*, it is agreed that it is difficult to cure. If it has persisted for a long time, there were only rare instances of anyone recovering. Even if we

deux déclarés ladres confirmés, après nouvel examen médical, le 20 mars 1565. Le Conseil leur ordonna en conséquence de se séparer des gens sains et de ne hanter personne," *ibid.*, 100.

63 "They want leprosy to be a just cause for divorce because not only the husband but also the children may be infected. But for my part, while advising a godly man not to come in contact with his wife if she is a leper, I do not permit him to divorce her," Calvin, *Harmony of the Gospels*, II.246; of note is the fact that Calvin views leprosy as contagious and not hereditary. Cf. John Witte, Jr., "The Marital Covenant in John Calvin's Geneva," *Political Theology* 19, no. 4 (2018), 290–1.

64 Calvin, *Mosaic Harmony*, II.27.

65 "It was a sad sight to behold the leprosy invading the human body; but there was something portentous to perceive it affecting their houses also, and driving out the owners and their families; for if they wittingly and voluntarily remained there, the contagion spread to themselves and all their furniture," *Mosaic Harmony*, II.27.

> allow that physicians might have given some assistance from the knowledge of their craft, it is quite evident that there was nothing of a human order in this miracle.[66]

Calvin not only consistently demonstrates his awareness of the distinction between λέπρα and ἐλεφαντίασις but he also points to the disease's obstinacy in the face of treatment, thereby accenting the miraculous nature of the cure. Significantly, he acknowledges the medical reality of the disease, denying that the entire episode is merely an exercise in metonymy. He adopts a similar approach in his comments on Matthew 4:18–25.[67] Calvin appears especially moved by Christ's decision to touch the sick individual despite the fact that "in the Law, the touch of the leper was contagious." Though his word alone would have been sufficient to heal the leprous subject, the act of touch was a profound gesture of divine compassion, and as construed by Calvin, symbolic of the incarnation.[68] Finally, Calvin counters the sacramental basis of auricular confession and penance in this passage, specifically the command: "show thyself to the priest."

The above passages are complemented in the *Harmony of the Gospels* by Calvin's commentary on Luke 17:11–21, the famous case of the ten "lepers". Calvin signals an initial distinction between the passages, noting that Luke's report on the ten "lepers" principally concerns the "disgusting and incredible ingratitude of the Jewish people."[69] Again, Calvin marshals his own interpretation of the passage to undermine the practice of auricular confession. Interestingly, he also uses this episode about leprosy and its cure to interrogate the Catholic insistence upon the easily observable nature of the kingdom of

66 Calvin, *Harmony of the Gospels*, I.243.

67 "*Lunatici* is the term given to those in whom the force of the disease increases or declines according to the phases of the moon, for instance, those who suffer from epilepsy, and the like. We know that diseases of that sort are not curable by the means of nature. When Matthew says that Christ healed all disease, you must understand sickness of every kind. For it is certain that not all were freed from their illnesses, but that there was no sort of disease which, offered to Him, He would not cure," Calvin, *Harmony of the Gospels*, I.159.

68 "There is such purity in Christ he absorbs all uncleanness and pollution, He does not contaminate Himself by touching the leper, nor does He transgress the Law. For in assuming our flesh, He has granted us more than the touch of His hand, He has brought Himself into one and the same body with us (*in unum idemque corpus nobiscum coaluit*), that we should be the flesh of his flesh. He does not only stretch out His arm to us, but He comes down from heaven, even to the very depths; yet catches no stain thereby, but stays whole, clears all our dirt away, and pours upon us His own holiness," Calvin, *Harmony of the Gospels*, I.244.

69 Calvin, *Harmony of the Gospels*, II.131. Cf. the interpretation of these passages in Lomperis, "Human Bodies in Pain as Spiritual Battlefields," 192–6.

God: "Now Christ here used 'observation' to mean a clearness easily observed; as if He were denying that the Kingdom of God would be transcendent in obvious display. He means that they are quite wrong who look with their physical eyes for the Kingdom of God, since it is in no way physical or earthly but the inward and spiritual renewing of the soul."[70] He ventures a similar point in his commentary on Luke 16:19–31, the parable of Lazarus and Dives (the rich man). Curiously, he never mentions leprosy with respect to the story, despite the graphic description of the destitute Lazarus's open sores resulting in a vast exegetical tradition that considered the beggar to be leprous. But Calvin does contrast Lazarus's loathsome visage with the imperceptible beauty of his inner soul: "In [Lazarus] God's graciousness was so hidden, and he was so oppressed by the ugliness of the cross and insults that fleshly understanding could grasp nothing beyond the curse."[71] I suggest that Calvin's wording here is meant to recall that of the "suffering servant" in Isaiah 53:4—who in the Vulgate is depicted as leprous!

True to his theological method, Calvin argues against the legitimacy of auricular confession and the sacrament of penance (including the discussion of confession and satisfaction), in both the *Institutes* and in his commentary on the *Harmony of the Gospels*. And what is the thematic filament linking both arguments? Leprosy. After first summarizing the "scholastic" position (and revealing that his primary concern is one about certitude), in *Institutes* III. 4, Calvin initiates his refutation of the scholastic/papist argument by focusing on leprosy.[72] Knowing how complicated leprosy can be to medically diagnose, Calvin reasons that given the priesthood's paucity of medical knowledge, the

70 Calvin, *Harmony of the Gospels*, II.134.

71 Calvin, *Harmony of the Gospels*, II.117. Lepromatous leprosy, the most serious form of the disease, is infamous for causing ulcerated nodules. Though Calvin here merely focuses on the ulcers, the long tradition associated with this parable understood Lazarus (through a conflation with Lazarus of Bethany and "Simon the leper") as a leprosy sufferer.

72 Schreiner's observation about Calvin's obsession with certitude is entirely correct since his position on the Scholastic doctrine of penance is that "unless this knowledge remains clear and sure, the conscience can have no rest at all, no peace with God, no assurance or security; but it continuously trembles, wavers, tosses, is tormented and vexed, shakes, hates, and flees the sight of God. But if forgiveness of sins depends upon these conditions which they attach to it, nothing is more miserable or deplorable for us," Calvin, *Institutes*, 3.4.2. He again summarizes the Roman position in 3.4.15 and makes his position most clear in 3.4.22. He explicitly addresses the question of certitude in 3.4.18 and 21. Calvin addresses the allegorical arguments vis-à-vis leprosy at length in 3.4.4, followed by a discussion of the unbinding of Lazarus (the patron saint of people with leprosy!) in 3.4.5. Both the "leprosy" and Lazarus passages primarily originate from the 1536 edition, aside from a few additions in 1539 and references to Chrysostom from the 1559 edition. Indeed, both passages read as rough sketches of his later arguments in his Biblical commentaries.

mandate of priestly examination could not possibly rest upon medical grounds. He acknowledges that in time, physicians would be better suited for examining potential symptoms of leprosy and that the restriction of this injunction to the sons of Aaron was meant to signal the solemnity of such an examination.[73]

As demonstrated by his record in Geneva, Calvin obviously conceded a need to "purify" the Church by means of exile or excommunication (and sometimes execution). However, his goal in his exegetical discourse on the priestly examination is to undercut the confessor-certainty of priests by emphasizing the diagnostic *un*certainty inherent in leprosy. He observes that the Levitical command to sequester a suspected infected person for seven days was actually a concession against a rash judgment. This is ultimately due to the diagnostic intractability of the disease.[74] But what troubled Calvin even more were the ramifications of such diagnostic uncertainty with respect to confession and absolution:

> Thus, according to them, forgiveness depends upon the judgment of the priest, and unless he wisely discerns who deserve pardon, his whole action is null and void. In a word, the power of which they speak is a jurisdiction connected with examination, to which pardon and absolution are confined. On this point one finds no firm ground. Indeed, there is a bottomless pit. For where confession is not complete, the hope of pardon is also impaired.[75]

According to his understanding of the "scholastic" position on penance and confession, absolution is entirely contingent upon precision in examination: that alone fills Calvin with considerable anxiety. But this priestly prerogative is in turn based upon an allegorical interpretation of leprosy examinations in the Bible. Calvin knows that the medical diagnosis of leprosy is extremely fraught and thus, he directs his exegetical polemic at the weakest part of the priestly argument: the foundation. In other words, Calvin is relying upon his *medical* knowledge of leprosy to bolster a *theological* argument.

---

73 See Calvin, *Mosaic Harmony*, 1.15. In this passage, Calvin alludes to the medieval and early modern mechanism of examination for those suspected of suffering from leprosy.

74 "Assuredly no medical skill could declare on the seventh day a leprosy to be incurable ... unless God should in some special manner discover the uncleanness, and guide the eyes of the priests by His Spirit. What we translate 'shall pronounce him clean, or unclean,' is in Hebrew, 'shall clean, or unclean him;' thus the dignity of the judgment is more fully established, as though it had proceeded from God Himself," Calvin, *Mosaic Harmony*, 1.16.

75 Calvin, *Institutes*, 3.4.22.

With respect to the healing of the leprosy patient in Matthew 8, Calvin emphasizes Christ's obedience to the ceremonies of the law with his command that the cleansed subject should show himself to the priest. Calvin argues, "As the ceremonies of the Law were not yet abolished, Christ did not wish them scorned or overlooked ... When Christ therefore sends the leper away to the priest, He shows that He had no other purpose than to heighten the glory of God. The showing was connected with the examination, and the gift was a symbol of thanksgiving."[76] Christ's instructions would further make the miracle manifest before the priests and give the former "leper" an occasion to acknowledge God's power and benevolence in healing him. But, Calvin decries, "For the Papists to make this a proof text of their own confession is most unperceptive. They would make *leprosy an allegory for sin*, and the priests, appointed by the Pope, those who recognize the leprosy of the spirit."[77] Although Calvin acknowledges that *technically* the priests were given this legal authority over examining leprosy, Christ now claims that authority. As he describes it, Christ alone "may diagnose that spiritual leprosy," and the priests no longer have the jurisdiction "to give a verdict upon leprosy" ("De discerner entre ladrerie et ladrerie").[78]

As he did earlier in his *Harmony of the Gospels*, Calvin takes advantage of the account of the ten leprosy sufferers to once again critique the practice of auricular confession:

> But the Papists foolishly build their auricular confession on this. I grant that Christ sent the lepers to the priests; but it was not to vomit up their sins into the priests' ears, but rather that they might offer a sacrifice as the Law laid down. Nor were they sent to cleanse themselves, in the way that confession brings cleansing to the Papists, but to show the priests that they were already clean.[79]

---

76 Calvin, *Harmony of the Gospels*, I.245. Cf. "Why then does Christ send lepers to the priests? That the priests may not charge him with breaking the law, which bade that one cured of leprosy be shown to the priest, and atoned for by offering sacrifice. He bids cleansed lepers do what the law enjoins ... Truly, this miracle was to be a proof for them. They had declared them lepers; now they declare them cured," Calvin, *Institutes*, 3.4.4.

77 *Ibid.* "Doivent avoir le jugement et la cognoissance de la ladrerie spirtuelle." Emphasis mine.

78 *Ibid.*, 246. Cf. "All priestly offices have been transferred to Christ and are fulfilled and completed in him. The whole right and honor of the priesthood has therefore been transferred to him," *Institutes*, 3.4.4.

79 Calvin, *Harmony of the Gospels*, II.132. Cf. *Institutes*, 3.4.19 where Calvin employs the same phrase: "but heap up sins upon sins until they vomit all of them up at once."

I suspect the reference to "vomiting out their sins" is a clever quip upon medieval and early modern medicine's frequent use of purgatives to expel corrupt humors—a common treatment for leprosy. In this passage, much as in the Matthew 8 episode, the priests were intended to be witnesses to the miraculous healing performed by Christ with respect to the ten leprous individuals. Of course, Calvin, with no shortage of critical gloating, points out that only *one* of the cleansed individuals returns to Christ following their "confession."[80]

Calvin further undercuts the medical analogy by arguing that although Leviticus appoints the office of cleansing to the priest, the honor of the cure (forgiving of sins) belongs to God alone. Note the effectiveness of Calvin's efforts to rhetorically quarantine the allegorizing of leprosy ("they would make leprosy an allegory for sin") since if one commits to such an interpretation, Christ alone "may diagnose that spiritual leprosy" and the papal position on auricular confession is undermined. But to appeal to leprosy as a medical reality likewise undermines the papal claim, given the disease's infamous tendency to confound diagnostic certainty. Calvin had drafted a similar argument in the *Institutes*:

> They therefore take refuge in allegories: it was laid down by the Mosaic law that priests should distinguish between stages of leprosy. Sin is spiritual leprosy; it is the duty of priests to pronounce concerning this. Before I answer, I ask in passing why, if this passage makes them judges of spiritual leprosy, do they assume cognizance of natural and carnal leprosy? As if this reasoning were not to mock Scripture: the law entrusts the recognition of leprosy to the Levitical priests, let us take this over for ourselves; sin is spiritual leprosy, let us also be judicial examiners of sin![81]

With no shortage of wit, Calvin exposes how deceptively sanitized such a purely allegorical argument is since to address "natural and carnal leprosy" hopelessly complicates the Papist position.

---

80 "They are twice foolish for not reckoning what an evil stain of bad repute they cast on their confession—that they have done well when out of the whole band of those who went to the priests only a tenth returned to Christ and all the rest impiously kept away from Him. They cannot use this as a pretext for their confession without it rebounding on them that none returned from the priests to give glory to God," Calvin, *Harmony of the Gospels*, II.132.

81 Calvin, *Institutes*, 3.4.4.

Of course, lurking behind all of his writings on leprosy is Calvin's theological predilection for issues of perspective and perception.[82] Schreiner has written at length on the omnipresence of the problem of perception in Calvin's sermons on the book of Job, complemented by his "understanding of providence as a dialectic between revelation and concealment."[83] This focus is why 1 Corinthians 13:12 repeatedly operates as a hermeneutical key throughout the sermons *and* why nature occupies such a pivotal revelatory role. Schreiner points out that, "The juxtaposition between nature and history inherent in the text of Job becomes a hermeneutical strategy by which Calvin can emphasize the dialectic between the visible and the hidden, the knowable and the inscrutable."[84] He firmly believed that our knowledge of God the Redeemer and our knowledge of God the Creator resulted in a mutually supportive, harmonious whole. Our senses help facilitate this knowledge of God, as outlined in Calvin's famous quote: "The world is rightly called the mirror of divinity. Believers, to whom God has given eyes to see, discern the sparks of his glory as it were shining out in every individual creature. The world was founded for this purpose, that it might be the theater of divine glory."[85] This is why, I think, one can imagine Calvin poring over the medical texts: if the human body is counted a microcosm of creation, then medicine is a means for refining one's theological palate to better savor this delicacy of nature.[86] More pressingly, if

82 See his commentary on 2 Corinthians 4:17, where Calvin plays upon the furtive ambiguity of outward decay, (i.e., physical affliction) masking inner spiritual vigor, John Calvin, *Commentary on 2 Corinthians*, trans. William Pringle (Grand Rapids: Baker, 1989), 212.

83 Schreiner, *Where Shall Wisdom Be Found?*, 122. Calvin's perspective on Job are extremely relevant since he preached his famous series of sermons on the biblical book from February 1554 to March 1555, thereby overlapping with his *Harmony of the Gospels*.

84 "The revelation visible in nature must be distinguished from the ambiguity characteristic of history. Although God governs both realms, providence is not equally discernible in both spheres," *Ibid.*, 138.

85 John Calvin, "Commentary on Hebrews," *Calvin's New Testament Commentaries*, ed. David W. Torrance and Thomas F. Torrance (Grand Rapids: Eerdmans, 1959–72), vol. 12, 160. Cf. Calvin, *Institutes* 1.14.21. For a summary of the debate in Calvin literature about the role of creation as a viable source for knowledge of God, see Schreiner, *Where Shall Wisdom Be Found?*, 246, n. 94. Schreiner's *The Theater of His Glory: Nature & The Natural Order in the Thought of John Calvin* (Durham, NC: Labyrinth, 1991) and *Where Shall Wisdom Be Found?* are now the most authoritative interpretations of Calvin on this point. Schreiner argues: "To Calvin's mind, all Job had to do was 'open his eyes' and look at these visible works of God; he would have seen there the testimonies of the infinite power and wisdom of God who created and still controls the cosmos. The creation, Calvin says, pleads the Lord's case. God imprints his glory on the mute creation and rejects those who refuse to contemplate him in his works," *Where Shall Wisdom Be Found?*, 142.

86 In an uncanny echo of Gregory the Great, Daniela Bohde argues that early modern anatomists and their accompanying illustrators assumed that "the truth always lies within, in

Calvin attributes such little perceptual acuity to Job, then he will certainly be pessimistic regarding the "diagnostic" capabilities of the priesthood!

Immediately following this section on leprosy in the *Institutes*, the Swiss reformer disputes the prevailing allegorical interpretation of the "unbinding" of Lazarus.[87] In his *Commentary on the Gospel According to John*, Calvin more thoroughly critiques this appeal to the raising of Lazarus to support auricular confession: "The Papists act an excessively ridiculous part, by endeavoring to draw auricular confession from this passage. They say, 'Christ, after having restored Lazarus to life, commanded his disciples to loose him; and therefore it is not enough for us to be reconciled to God, unless the Church also pardons our sins'."[88] With his exegesis of this passage, Calvin makes no mention of leprosy, though, much as with the parable of Lazarus and Dives, there was a vast exegetical tradition (complemented by the cult of saints) which associated Lazarus of Bethany with leprosy. I think it is no accident that his interpretation of Lazarus directly follows that of leprosy.[89]

Moreover, littered throughout this relatively brief chapter in the *Institutes* are numerous medical motifs and idioms. For example, Calvin writes: "since it is the Lord who forgives, forgets, and wipes out, sins, let us confess our sins to him in order to obtain pardon. He is the physician; therefore, let us lay bare our wounds to him."[90] He even maligns priests as pernicious barber-surgeons: "there these cruel butchers, to relieve the wounds that they had inflicted,

---

the interior, hidden by a surface sheath, which one has to penetrate," Daniela Bohde, "Skin and the Search for the Interior: The Representation of Flaying in the Art and Anatomy of the Cinquecentro," in *Bodily Extremities: Preoccupations with the Human Body in Early Modern Culture*, ed. Florike Egmond and Robert Zijnenberg (Burlington, VT: Ashgate, 2003), 19–20. While I cannot prove that Calvin had knowledge of anatomy or ever observed a dissection, clearly this anatomical hermeneutic was one that he shared.

87 "They derive a second argument from the same source, that is from an allegory—as if allegories were of great value in confirming any dogma!" *Ibid.*, 3.4.5. The traditional argument was focused on John 11:44 and Jesus' command to his disciples to unbind the risen Lazarus and let him go.

88 John Calvin, *Commentary on the Gospel According to John*, trans. William Pringle (Edinburgh: Calvin Translation Society, 1843–48; Grand Rapids, MI: Baker Book House Company, 1984 reprint) vol. 1, 447.

89 See Carole Rawcliffe, *Leprosy in Medieval England* (Rochester, NY: Boydell Press, 2006).

90 Calvin, *Institutes*, 3.4.9. Regarding general confession in a congregation, he adds: "for when they are members of a feeble and diseased body they ought not to boast of health. Nay, they cannot but contract some contagion and also bear some part of the guilt," *ibid.*, 3.4.11. The second part of that passage originates in the 1559 edition, and he adds in the 1543 version: "Therefore, every time we are afflicted either by pestilence or war, or barrenness, or any other sort of calamity, if it is our duty to take refuge in mourning, fasting, and other signs of our guilt, we must least of all neglect this very confession upon which all the rest depends," *ibid.*

applied certain remedies, asserting that each man should do what lay in his power ... [O]ther medicines that alleviated this sort of pain were applied ... but all these things cannot cover the wound, and are less an alleviation of the evil than poisons disguised with honey."[91] Obviously familiar with the medicalized idiosyncrasies of the penitential tradition, Calvin's polemical incisions have subverted these same tropes and although *Christus medicus* remains, the priesthood has been charged with medical malpractice.

Calvin's interpretation of leprosy in his commentary on the harmony of the Gospels reveals a series of significant points. First and most obviously, auricular confession and the sacrament of penance are habitually linked to the subject of leprosy largely owing to the priestly jurisdiction established in Leviticus. Thus, to reinterpret leprosy as presented in the aforementioned passages necessarily bears upon the scriptural authority for auricular confession. Second, although Calvin certainly recognizes the symbolic generativity of leprosy, he is nevertheless insistent that the passages in question refer to a legitimate medical reality—one with which he is clearly familiar. As a consequence, there is a qualitative difference between, for example, how Calvin exegetes the episode of the ten leprosy sufferers and how Augustine reads the same passage. Third, Calvin's reliance upon medical knowledge about leprosy is most consequential insofar as he capitalizes upon how notoriously difficult the disease is to diagnose. The medical uncertainties associated with leprosy undermine the diagnostic credibility of the priests and thereby call into question the very foundation upon which the "Papists" base auricular confession. Finally, this exegetical focus upon the outward examination of leprosy permits the Swiss reformer yet another opportunity to comment on matters of perception and visual deceptiveness.

6 Conclusion

In this essay, I have analyzed John Calvin's deployment of contemporary medical knowledge pertaining to leprosy in order to shape his biblical commentary and theology in pivotal ways. With a focus on his *Harmony of the Gospels Matthew, Mark, and Luke* and the *Institutes of the Christian Religion*, I have demonstrated how the Swiss reformer uses a focus on leprosy to problematize issues of perception and, more pressingly, the Catholic tradition of auricular confession and the sacrament of penance. Calvin habitually appeals to leprosy's infamous ability to thwart accurate medical diagnosis as a means to

91 *Ibid.* 3.4.17.

undermine confidence in the human (i.e., priestly) capacity to "diagnose" sins and to more generally comment on the vagaries of visual perception.

But what does this add to our understanding of Calvin? Calvin's exegetical treatment of leprosy not only validates his overwhelmingly preoccupation with issues of certainty and perception but also reemphasizes his theological indebtedness to Gregory the Great. Moreover, as further testimony to his intellectual capaciousness, in his writings on leprosy Calvin evinces a precision in terminology and a facility with medical theory that far surpasses a prosaic awareness of the disease.

CHAPTER 9

Not without Scripture: William Perkins, the Light of Nature, and Proofs of the Existence of God

Richard A. Muller

1 William Perkins, the Early Orthodox Context, and the Proofs

William Perkins (1558–1602) has been rightly recognized in recent scholarship as a major formulator, together with Richard Hooker, of an English Reformed theology in defense of the confessionality and catholicity of the Church of England and, equally, of a form of early Reformed orthodoxy in dialogue with the thought of Reformed theologians in Europe.[1] His theology reflects the complex needs of a generation of Protestant theologians who faced confessional, institutional, apologetic, and polemical issues not addressed in detail by earlier Reformed formulators and codifiers.[2] Among these issues, the relation of general to special revelation and of natural theology to Christian belief came into increased focus for reasons both polemical and institutional. The presence of early Deist and Epicurean arguments against traditional Christian assumptions concerning God gave rise to an emphasis in apologetics on evidences and proofs of the existence of God not seen among the Reformers.[3] In

1 See W. B. Patterson, *William Perkins and the Making of a Protestant England* (Oxford: Oxford University Press, 2014); idem, "Richard Hooker and William Perkins: Elizabethan Adversaries or Allies?" in W. Bradford Littlejohn and Scott N. Kindred-Barnes, eds., *Richard Hooker and Reformed Orthodoxy*, pp. 61–71; idem, "William Perkins as Apologist for the Church of England," in *Journal of Ecclesiastical History*, 57/2 (2006), pp. 252–269; also Ian Breward, "The Life and Theology of William Perkins, 1558–1602" (Ph.D. dissertation, University of Manchester, 1963); and Rosemary A. Sisson, "William Perkins, Apologist for the Elizabethan Church of England," in *Modern Language Review*, 47/4 (1952), pp. 495–502; also note, Richard A. Muller, *Grace and Freedom: William Perkins and the Early Modern Reformed Understanding of Free Choice and Divine Grace* (New York: Oxford University Press, 2020).

2 See Richard A. Muller, *Post-Reformation Reformed Dogmatics: The Rise and Development of Reformed Orthodoxy, ca. 1520 to ca. 1725*, 4 vols. (Grand Rapids: Baker, 2003), I, pp. 60–72, 270–284; Willem J. van Asselt, "The Fundamental Meaning of Theology: Archetypal and Ectypal Theology in Seventeenth-Century Reformed Thought," in *Westminster Theological Journal*, 64 (2002), pp. 319–335.

3 See John Platt, *Reformed Thought and Scholasticism: The Arguments for the Existence of God in Dutch Theology, 1575–1650* (Leiden: Brill, 1982). On the issue of "Deism"—contrary to the statements of earlier scholarship, there was worry over Deists and Deism in between Viret's

 | DOI:10.1163/9789004527843_010

what follows, I propose to examine Perkins' approach to the proofs of God's existence, a topic largely neglected in studies of his thought,[4] and to identify its place in the early orthodox development of Reformed thought.

Arguably, Perkins stands in the broad line of Reformed development, holding two sources of the knowledge of God, the light of nature and the light of Scripture, but also evidences a deeply practical concern for the inward person and the ways in which knowledge of God can either be distorted by sin or become a support of piety. It is this latter concern that gives his extended proofs their particular character and that presses the basic epistemological question of how God may be known into the further questions of how that knowing operates in the context of disbelief, doubt, hypocrisy, and distortion, all brought on by the sinfulness of human nature. These early orthodox developments are illustrated, in Perkins' own time, by the apologetic work of writers like Georges Pacard and Philippe Du Plessis-Mornay,[5] as also by the presence of definitions of theology, natural and supernatural, and of proofs in the more systematic positive theological treatises of the era.[6] So also in Perkins' time was

comments in 1564 and the controversies of the late seventeenth century: see Richard A. Muller, "Was it Really Viral? Natural Theology in the Early Modern Reformed Tradition," in Maria-Cristina Pitassi and Daniela Solfaroli Camillocci eds., *Crossing Traditions: Essays on Reformation and Intellectual History in Honour of Irena Backus* (Leiden: E. J. Brill, 2017), pp. 507–531, here p. 518.

4 Note the discussion in John R. Tufft, "William Perkins, 1558–1602: his Thought and Activity" (Ph.D. dissertation, University of Edinburgh, 1951), pp. 101–104. Perkins' arguments are noted in Wallace W. Marshall, "Puritanism and Natural Theology" (Ph.D. dissertation, Boston College, 2007). John Platt, *Reformed Thought and Scholasticism: The Arguments for the Existence of God in Dutch Theology, 1575–1650* (Leiden: Brill, 1982), unfortunately only looks at the Dutch contemporaries of Perkins and a few continental predecessors like Ursinus and Bastingius.

5 Georges Pacard, *Theologie naturelle, ou recueil contenant plusieurs argumens, raisons, et demonstrations prinses de la nature, lesquelles est prouvé manifestement qu'il y a un seul Dieu, qui par sa providence gouverne cest univers, que le monde e esté creé, que l'ame humaine est immortelle, & que l'Escriture saincte est celeste, & Divine, contre les Epicuriens & Atheistes* (La Rochelle: P. Haultin, 1579; Niort: René Troismailles, 1606); Philippe Du Plessis-Mornay, *De veritate religionis Christianae liber; adversus atheos, Epicureos, ethnicos, Iudaeos, Mahumedistas, & caeteros infideles* (Antwerp: Christopher Plantin, 1583), in translation, *A Vvoorke Concerning the Trewnesse of the Christian Religion, Written in French: Against Atheists, Epicures, Paynims, Iewes, Mahumetists, and Other Infidels*, trans. Sir Philip Sidney and Arthur Golding (London: John Charlewood and George Robinson, 1587), hereinafter cited as *Trewnesse*. On Pacard, see Muller, "Was it Really Viral?", pp. 518–521; on Mornay, see Olivier Fatio, "La vérité menacée: L'apologétique de Philippe Duplessis-Mornay," in *Bulletin de la Société de l'Histoire du Protestantisme Français*, 144 (1998), pp. 253–264.

6 Cf. Franciscus Junius, *Loci nonnulli theologici: de theologia, sacris scripturis, Deo ac creatione* (Heidelberg: Commelianus, 1612), I.iii (pp. 9–13); Gulielmus Bucanus, *Institutions of the*

there a concerted effort to develop a framework for academic theological discourse by Reformed thinkers at various universities and academies, notably at Leiden under the tutelage of Franciscus Junius, whose *De theologia vera* argued the nature and shape of the discipline of theology and influences several generations of Reformed theologians.[7] Perkins' role at Cambridge, quite different from the large-scale definitional and systematic impact of Junius' work, certainly served both in detail and scope to place Cambridge among those Protestant universities at the forefront of theological formulation in his time.[8]

Although Perkins did not write a full "body of divinity" or "commonplaces of theology," taken together his major works contain all or nearly all the topics of a theological system. Three works in particular—the *Armilla Aurea* or *Golden Chaine, An Exposition of the Symbole of Creed of the Apostles*, and *The Whole Treatise of the Cases of Conscience*—offer presentations of large portions of the body of divinity, albeit from very different perspectives. The first of these works presents Christian doctrine specifically as related to the "causes of salvation and damnation";[9] the second, as it expands on the framework of the creed; and the third, as it relates to the inward life of the Christian and provides "comfort to the consciences of those that [are] distressed."[10] Definitions of theology, comment on the "light of nature" or reason, and presentations of evidences or proofs of the existence of God are found in two of these works, namely the *Golden Chaine* and the *Cases of Conscience*. The *Exposition of the*

Christian Religion, framed out of God's Word, trans. R. Hill (London: George Swindon, 1606), i (pp. 1–2).

7 Franciscus Junius, *De theologia vera, ortu, natura, formis, partibus, et modo illius, libellus:, quo omnes Christiani, de sua dignitate, et theologi de gravitate sui ministerii secundum Deum admonentur* (Leiden: Plantin, 1594).

8 Cf. Patterson, *William Perkins*, p. 62.

9 William Perkins, *Armilla Aurea, id est, theologiae descriptio mirandam seriem causarum & salutis & damnationis juxta verbum Dei proponens* (Cambridge: John Legat, 1590); idem, *A Golden Chaine, or the Description of Theologie Containing the Order of the Causes of Saluation and Damnation, According to Gods Word. A view whereof, is to be seene in the table annexed. Written in Latine, and translated by R. H. Hereunto is adioyned the order vvhich M. Theodore Beza vsed in comforting afflicted consciences* (Cambridge: Iohn Legate, 1592).

10 William Perkins, *The Whole Treatise of the Cases of Conscience Distinguished into Three Bookes: the first whereof is revised and corrected in sundrie places, and the other two annexed. Taught and deliuered by M. W. Perkins in his holy-day lectures, carefully examined by his owne briefes, and now published together for the common good, by T. Pickering Bachelour of Diuinitie. Whereunto is adioyned a twofold table: one of the heads and number of the questions propounded and resolued; another of the principall texts of Scripture vvhich are either explaned, or vindicated from corrupt interpretation.* (Cambridge: Iohn Legat, 1606), fol. A2r. Hereinafter cited as *Conscience*.

Symbole, beginning as it does with "faith," offers only the confession that God exists and no proofs. Perkins also offers proofs of the existence of God in his early catechism, the *Foundation of Christian Religion*.[11]

Perkins' delineation of the proofs is not altogether original. He does not reference his sources, but his arguments reflect both ancient philosophical and medieval scholastic materials. Among his immediate predecessors in the Reformed tradition, Perkins drew on paradigms of proofs that can be found in a work of sacred theology like Ursinus' lectures on the Heidelberg Catechism as well as those found in apologetic treatises like those of George Pacard and Philippe du Plessis Mornay. As will be demonstrated in the following, Perkins' proofs belie the claims of the older scholarship that the presence of proofs of the existence of God in post-Reformation Protestant theology represents the intrusion of an incipient rationalism. What is of particular interest in Perkins' use of the proofs is the way he deploys the arguments, how he amalgamates logical and rhetorical argumentation, and how he deploys the proofs in the service of piety within the context of Christian belief, doubt, and temptation.

2 Preliminaries: The Order of Argument and Sources of the Knowledge of God

Perkins assumed a traditional balance of general and special revelation as known via nature and Scripture and he argued that the existence of God is both "evident" and demonstrable, adjusting his arguments to the varied genres of his writings. He offered two short proofs in his *Foundation*.[12] In the *Golden Chaine*, after presenting Scripture as providing "a doctrin sufficient to live well" and defining theology as "the science of living blessedly for ever," he inserted "evidences" for the existence of God.[13] Perkins reserved his extended series of proofs of the existence of God for his late-in-life lectures on the conscience, published posthumously as the *Cases of Conscience*.[14] There, although they

11 William Perkins, *The Foundation of Christian Religion Gathered into Sixe Principles. And it Is to Bee Learned of Ignorant People, That They May Be Fit to Hear Sermons with Profit, and to Receiue the Lords Supper with Comfort* (London: Thomas Orwin, for Iohn Porter, 1590). N.B., later editions included in Perkins' *Works* are much abbreviated.

12 Perkins, *Foundation*, sig. A6r–v.

13 Perkins, *Golden Chaine*, i (p. 1).

14 Given that the proofs are found in the second book of the treatise, they are not found in the 1604 edition of William Perkins, *The First Part of the Cases of Conscience Wherein Specially, Three Maine Questions Concerning Man, Simply Considered in Himselfe, Are Propounded and Resolued, According to the Word of God. Taught and deliuered, by M. William Perkins in his Holy-day lectures, by himselfe revised before his death, and now published for the benefit*

are placed prior to the chapter on Scripture, these theological *loci* of God and Scripture are found in the second book of the treatise, after Perkins has argued the "subjection and power of conscience" in relation to goodness and sinfulness: in other words, even here the proofs do not serve as a presupposition for Christian theology.[15] The locations of Perkins' proofs already point toward once conclusion concerning their place in his thought: contrary to what has often been claimed about proofs of the existence of God and their place in Reformed theology, Perkins' exposition reveals a significant relationship between reason, the proofs, and the inner life and piety of Christians.

In his *Foundation*, Perkins indicated that there are two sources of persuasion that God exists, the testimony of Scripture and "plaine reason."[16] The arguments from reason offered in the *Foundation* presume the agreement of truths of reason with truths of Scripture: the rational arguments are accompanied by marginal citations of biblical texts, indicating Perkins' assumption that basic rational truths are confirmed by divine revelation. His initial proof is based on the "wonderfull frame of the world," second proof rests on the pangs of the sinful conscience.[17]

The argumentation in Perkins' *Golden Chaine*, added in the second editions of the Latin and English, is quite brief in relation to the subsequent density of argumentation on the causes of salvation and damnation. In his first chapter, Perkins first notes that "the bodie of Scripture, is a doctrin sufficient to live well" and that the principal form of knowledge comprehended in Scripture is theology, defined as "the science of living blessedly for ever" and distinguished into two parts, concerning first God and then God's works.[18] Unlike the other two works in which Perkins offers proofs, his *Golden Chaine* provides no further definition of sources of the knowledge of God—in other words, there is no reference to natural knowledge or the light of nature, and therefore no preparation for his recourse to a list of non-biblical evidences for the existence of God at the very beginning of the second chapter of his *Golden Chaine*. Arguably, Perkins' intention here, as in his two other approaches to proofs is "not ... to

---

of the Church (Cambridge: Iohn Legat, 1604). On the publication of Perkins' work on conscience, see Patterson, *William Perkins*, pp. 102–103.

15 Perkins, *Conscience*, 1.i (on degrees of goodness), ii (on the nature of sinfulness), iii (on the subjection and power of conscience).

16 Perkins, *Foundation*, sig. A4r.

17 Perkins, *Foundation*, sig. A6r–v.

18 William Perkins, *A Golden Chaine, or the Description of Theologie Containing the Order of the Causes of Salvation and Damnation, According to Gods Word. A view whereof, is to be seene in the table annexed. Written in Latine, and translated by R. H. Hereunto is adioyned the order vvhich M. Theodore Beza vsed in comforting afflicted consciences* (Cambridge: Iohn Legate, 1592), i (p. 1).

dispute the question, whether there be a God or no," but simply to note, for the sake of the believer, that the existence of God ought to be plain to all and not to be doubted.

Perkins' most fully developed discussion of method as well as presentation of the doctrine of the knowledge of God and the proofs occurs in his *Cases of Conscience*. There he notes that in his first section, he presented conscience in relation to "Man simply considered" whereas in the second division of the subject he examines "Questions concerning Man, as he stands in relation."[19] Of the two relations, to God and to other human beings, the "relation to God … as a Christian" is first in order; next, consideration of the Scriptures, and after that the issue of religion, "or the worship that is due to God" and the time of worship.[20] The order of these chapters also reflects the order of Perkins' proofs, first from nature, second from Scripture, and third looking toward final glory and rest in God.

3 In the Background of Perkins' Proofs: The Forms of Atheism

Perkins understood the problem of atheism as not only or even primarily to be a matter of formal argumentation against the existence of God, but as a matter of sinful imagination and temptation yielding not explicit denials of the existence of God but rather irreligious and immoral behavior, idolatry, and other false belief.[21] In this understanding of atheism, Perkins stood on common ground with his contemporaries.[22]

---

19 Perkins, *Conscience*, II.i (p. 201).

20 Perkins, *Conscience*, II.i (pp. 201–202).

21 Note George T. Buckley, *Atheism in the English Renaissance* (New York: Russell and Russell, 1965); Michael Hunter, "The Problem of 'Atheism' in Early Modern England," in *Transactions of the Royal Historical Society*, Fifth Series, 35, (1985), pp. 135–157; David Berman, "The Repressive Denials of Atheism in Britain in the Seventeenth and Eighteenth Centuries," in *Proceedings of the Royal Irish Academy. Section C* (1982), pp. 211–245; also Leif Dixon, "William Perkins, 'Atheisme,' and the Crises of England's Long Reformation," in *Journal of British Studies*, 50/4 (2011), pp. 790–812, who misses entirely the definitions offered by Perkins and mistakenly assumes (p. 795) that "anti-atheist writings suffered from an obvious conceptual confusion over what 'atheism' was" and (p. 798) that in various writings of the era the term "atheism" was "used as a descriptor of something else."

22 Cf. Henry Smith, *Gods Arrowe Against Atheists* (London: Iohn Danter, 1593; London: Thomas Parker, 1604); and John Dove, *A Confutation of Atheisme* (London: Edward Allde for Henry Rockett, 1605); and note Marshall, "Puritanism and Natural Theology," pp. 11, 31–39.

In his *Treatise of Mans Imaginations*, Perkins devoted an entire chapter to the problem "Of mans naturall thoughts concerning God" and the ways in which human imagination devises atheistic conceptions.[23] When Scripture speaks of "the imaginations of mans heart," it indicates "the *understanding faculty* of the soule, whereby man useth reason: which *S. Paul* cals (Eph. 4:23) *the spirit of the minde*."[24] The problem of the human imagination is that after the fall, the natural faculty "is practised by evill thoughts."[25] Here, as in his proofs of the existence of God, the epistemological issue addressed by Perkins is not merely how human beings know, but how the mind, specifically the faculty of framing inward images or concepts and afterward the faculty of adjudicating good and evil, operate with what is known and how the ways of knowing relate to sin and salvation. The problem of the knowledge of God will begin with the imagination and lead directly to the conscience.

To the point—with which he agreed—that there is a knowledge of the existence of God "ingrafted" in the "nature" of all human beings, Perkins responded,

> We must know that these two thoughts, *There is a God*, and *there is no God* may be, & are both in one & the same heart: the same man, that by the light of nature thinketh there is a God, may by that corruption and darknesse of minde that came by *Adams* fall, thinke there is no God: for two contraries being not in highest degree, may be in one and the same subject: as light & darknesse in the same house: heate and cold in the same body.[26]

The atheist with whom Perkins is concerned, then, is not a speculative thinker who mounts metaphysical arguments against the existence of God, but an inwardly conflicted person who has some sensibility of truth but who also, in some way, denies it. Such denial of the existence of God is the first of four "capitall evil thoughts" identified by Perkins. This denial arises in two ways. First, the human imagination, left to itself and not enlightened by the Word

23 William Perkins, *A Treatise of Mans Imaginations. Shewing, His Naturall Evil Thoughts. His Want of Good Thoughts: The Way to Reforme Them*, iii, in *The Whole Works of … Mr. William Perkins*, 3 vols. (London: John Legatt, 1631), II, pp. 459, col. 1–467, col. 1.

24 Perkins, *Treatise of Mans Imaginations*, iii (p. 458, col. 1); cf. Francis Holyoke, *A Dictionarie Declaring the Etymologies, the Originall and Derivation of All Words Used in Any Latine Authors, with the Reason of Their Derivations and Appellations* (London: Felix Kingston, 1640), s.v. "Imaginatio," defined as a "conceiving in the mind"; and Henry Cockeram, *The English Dictionarie: or, an Interpreter of Hard English Words* (London: for Edmund Weaver, 1623), s.v. "Imaginarie," defined as "that which is conceived in the minde."

25 Perkins, *Treatise of Mans Imaginations*, iii (p. 458, col. 2).

26 Perkins, *Treatise of Mans Imaginations*, iii (p. 459, col. 2).

of God, turns God into an idol, whether by robbing God of his omnipresence by attempting to hide sins from him, or by denying providence and divine justice, as if God neither provides for his creatures nor punishes sin. Second, the unenlightened imagination will replace the true God with a false God, "an idol of [one's] own braine," by placing "felicity" in pleasure, gluttony, or riches.[27]

The inward thought that there is no God results in two kinds of outward atheism: atheism in practice and atheism in judgment. Atheism "in practice" as distinct from a philosophical or metaphysical atheism, is the sin of denying God, not theoretically, but in actions, life, and conversation,[28] characteristic of those who, in Henry Smith's words, "for more libertie of sinning, would strive against the being of a God."[29] Atheism in judgment appears in three forms or "degrees": first, when people "hold, and accordingly worship the true God, Creator of heaven and earth, but yet so, as they conceive of, and worship him otherwise that he hath revealed himselfe in his word."[30] The least of these degrees is exemplified by the Turk, who worships the Creator, but acknowledges Jesus only to be a great prophet and who conceived of "God out of the Trinity" and as a result "worshippeth nothing but an Idoll."[31] The second degree of atheism in judgment is the outright worship of idols, exemplified by the worship of heavenly bodies. The third and highest degree of atheism in judgment and the most despicable form of atheism is the absolute denial of the existence of God.[32]

There are, moreover, three more "capitall" or "damnable" evil thoughts. The second, then, is to think of the Word of God, in particular, the gospel, as foolishness: this kind of thought is characteristic of the natural man who, as the Apostle states, "perceiveth not the things of the Spirit of God" (1 Cor. 2:14).[33] The third "wicked imagination" is that worship is in vain—a thought that, Perkins comments, is not always in the mind but enters on occasion, especially on the occasion of being called to service.[34] A fourth and final atheistic or evil thought is "a thought of distrust" that God has no regard for the person, will not help him, and will not be merciful. This thought had its beginnings in

27 Perkins, *Treatise of Mans Imaginations*, iii (p. 460, col. 1).

28 Perkins, *Treatise of Mans Imaginations*, iii (p. 460, col. 2); cf. Dove, *Confutation*, pp. 3–4; Mornay, *Trewnesse*, pp. 10–11.

29 Smith, *Gods Arrow* (1604), p. 1.

30 Perkins, *Treatise of Mans Imaginations*, iii (p. 460, col. 2).

31 Perkins, *Treatise of Mans Imaginations*, iii (p. 460, col. 2–461, col. 1); cf. Smith, *Gods Arrow*, p. 48; Dove, *Confutation*, p. 1.

32 Perkins, *Treatise of Mans Imaginations*, iii (p. 461, col. 2).

33 Perkins, *Treatise of Mans Imaginations*, iii (p. 462, col. 2), citing the text from the Geneva Bible.

34 Perkins, *Treatise of Mans Imaginations*, iii (p. 465, col. 1–2).

the temptation leading to the fall of Adam and Eve, when Eve looked at the forbidden fruit and doubted what God had said concerning it. Perkins adds further examples, of Moses, David, and the children of Israel, commenting that in time of "peace & ease," people develop "presumptuous thoughts" that, when peace and ease are past, "give place" to "thoughts of distrust ... in their roome and stead."[35]

The purpose of lining out at some length the several kinds of atheism is not, as in the apologetic writings of the era, to refute them in a series of arguments against atheism itself. Rather, Perkins' purpose, looking directly toward his work on the conscience, is to lead his readers to the examination of their own inward thoughts in order to identify dangers. He notes that most people will claim that they have never doubted the existence of God—but also that they may "easily deceive [themselves] herein, for a man cannot alwayes discerne what be the thoughts of his own heart."[36] The problem faced by the person seeking to examine himself is that there are "two kindes of cogitation, or as one may say, reasons," the first of which relates simply to the function of the mind or intellect in knowing or thinking something. The second is "a reflexe cogitation or reason," by which a person judges or examines the fact that he knows or thinks about something. This is the function of conscience.[37]

The conscience, as Perkins defines it elsewhere, is an intellective function that judges good and evil after the fact and that can accuse the will—as distinct from the practical intellect which adjudges the good or evil of an object prior to the act of will.[38] Here too, he indicates a problem: since the fall, the conscience itself is corrupted by original sin and can fail to do its proper work. A person may have evil thoughts that are not recognized as such by the conscience.[39] Still, Perkins appeals to the conscience and to the heart commenting that "wee must bee admonished to use all good meanes whereby we may ... finde out this and such like abominations that be in us."[40] Prayer and the hearing of the Word can be means by which the Spirit of God enables a person to "reject his owne naturall reason, and stoppe up the eyes of his naturall minde" and "be made wise unto salvation."[41]

---

35 Perkins, *Treatise of Mans Imaginations*, iii (p. 466, col. 1–2).

36 Perkins, *Treatise of Mans Imaginations*, iii (p. 461, col. 2).

37 Perkins, *Treatise of Mans Imaginations*, iii (p. 461, col. 2–462, col. 1).

38 William Perkins, *A Discourse of Conscience. Wherein is Set Downe the Nature, Properties, and Differences Thereof: as Also the Way to Get and Keepe a Good Conscience*, in *Works*, I, p. 517, col. 1.

39 Perkins, *Treatise of Mans Imaginations*, iii (p. 462, col. 1).

40 Perkins, *Treatise of Mans Imaginations*, iii (p. 462, col. 2; cf. p. 463, col. 2; 465, col. 1–2).

41 Perkins, *Treatise of Mans Imaginations*, iii (p. 464, col. 1).

4 Perkins' Early Proofs of the Existence of God

From the earliest to the last, all of Perkins' proofs are situated in the context of his expositions of Christian doctrine and all, at least in part, address the inward person, specifically the conscience. There is, accordingly, little concern for what might be called traditional apologetics; rather, the concern is for the cultivation of right belief in the heart and mind. Perkins' *Foundation of Christian Religion* begins with a series of six "principles" that become the basis for further "exposition" in the body of the document. The first principle, presented as an answer to the question, "What doost thou beleeve concerning God?" reads, "There is one God creator and governour of all things, distinguished into the Father, the Sonne, and the holy Ghost."[42] The exposition of this first principle asks what can be considered to be more fundamental questions, echoing initially an anonymous catechism of the previous decade and presaging the Westminster catechisms by asking "What is God?"[43] Perkins answers that God is a "spirit, or spirituall substance, most wise, most holie, eternall, infinite" and then asks "How do you perswade yourself that there is such a God" and responds "Besides the testimonie of the Scriptures, plaine reason will shew it."[44]

This second question marks a distinctive departure from the usual catechetical approach. Of the predecessor English catechisms, none that I have seen offers proofs of the existence of God. Perkins had, however, some precedent for presenting proofs of the existence of God in a catechetical exposition, notably in the printing of Ursinus' exposition of the Heidelberg Catechism published in 1589, the year before Perkins' published his *Foundation*.[45] It may be

42 Perkins, *Foundation*, fol. A4r.

43 Perkins, *Foundation*, fol. A6r; cf. Anonymous, *Certaine short questions and answeres very profitable and necessary for yong children, and such as are desirous to be instructed in the principles of the Christian fayth* (London: Robert Waldegraue for Thomas Man, 1582), fol. Aii recto.

44 Perkins, *Foundation*, fol. A6r.

45 Zacharias Ursinus, *The Summe of Christian Religion: Delivered by Zacharias Vrsinus in His Lectures Vpon the Catechisme ... Translated into English by Henry Parry, out of the last and best Latine editions, together with some supplie of wants out of his Discourses of Divinity* (Oxford: Ioseph Barnes, 1589). This edition, as indicated in its subtitle, was considerably augmented beyond the earlier editions, whether in Latin and English, that had been published in England, and this particular section, "Of God," belongs to the augmentation. The editorial strata of Ursinus' exposition have been studied by T. D. Smid, "Bibliographische Opmerkingen over de Explicationes Catecheticae van Zacharias Ursinus," in *Gereformeerd Theologisch Tijdschrift*, 41 (1940), pp. 228–243. Note the extended analysis of Ursinus' proofs in Platt, *Reformed Thought and Scholasticism*, pp. 49–56. Ursinus' influence on Perkins is indicated at length in Muller, *Grace and Freedom*.

impossible to determine whether Perkins consulted this printing of Ursinus' exposition, but his catechetical argument does reflect two of the five "reasons" offered in Ursinus' exposition.

The first reason to be persuaded of the existence of God rests on the workmanship of the world. Perkins' marginal references to Romans 1:20 and Acts 14:17 underline his assumption that the testimonies of reason are not without biblical parallel. Contemplation of the framework or workmanship of the world yields the immediate conclusion that such a world could neither make itself or be made by any of the creatures in it and that "the maker of it must needes bee God."[46] This conclusion is similar to what a person would draw if, coming into a strange country, he saw "faire and sumptuous buildings" but noticed no living creatures other than birds and beasts: he would conclude that people had once been there. Perkins would repeat this argument in his later *Cases of Conscience*. Ursinus' first argument also rests on the creation, but is more focused on the order of things than on their workmanship:

> Now order is instituted, but of a wise and understanding nature. In nature there is order. Therefore, there is a superior mind of intelligent power, which instituteth & maintaineth the same.[47]

Perkins' second ground for belief in God is the conscience, again, an argument that would reappear in Perkins' later works. When person commits a major crime—murder, adultery, blasphemy, fornication—and manages to hide his offence from other people, he still often experiences a profound fear in his conscience "and feeles the verie flashings of hel fire: which is a strong reason, to shew that there is a God, before whose judgement seate he must answere."[48] Like Ursinus, Perkins cites Romans 2:15. Although Ursinus argued the point more objectively than Perkins, writing of the "terrors of conscience which are stroken into the minds of the wicked after they have sinned," that point toward the existence of a judge who can be no other than God,[49] his exposition may have provided Perkins with the precedent for including proofs of God in a catechetical exposition. Perkins' brief statements of proof have, however, a more experiential accent—among other things, not only noting terrors of conscience, but identifying them as the result of sins concealed from other

46 Perkins, *Foundation*, fol. A6r–v; similarly, Dove, *Confutation*, p. 19.

47 Ursinus, *Summe*, p. 278.

48 Perkins, *Foundation*, fol. A6v.

49 Ursinus, *Summe*, p. 279.

human beings the memory of which brings fear of hell fire and the judgment seat of God.[50]

The *Golden Chaine*, as one might expect, takes a different approach to the proofs than Perkins' catechism, although two of the catechetical arguments are reflected in those presented in the *Golden Chaine*, namely the proofs based on the natural order (numbers 1 and 6) and on conscience (number 4). Perkins here identifies eight grounds of proof:

> That there is a God, it is evident; 1. by the course of nature: 2. by the nature of the soule of man: 3. by the distinction of things honest and dishonest: 4. by the terrour of conscience: 5. by the regiment of civill societies: 6. the order of all causes having ever recourse to some former beginning: 7. the determination of all things to their several ends: 8. the consent of all men well in their wits.[51]

There is no elaboration of evidences. What may be noted, however, is that Perkins' more elaborate list echoes the proofs in Ursinus' catechetical exposition, with their mixture of rhetorical and demonstrative argumentation. Ursinus first noted the order of nature, paralleling Perkins' first evidence. Next Ursinus offered two arguments, one on the "nature & excellencie of mans mind" and another on the ability of the mind to distinguish "honest things & dishonest," closely resembling Perkins' second and third evidences.[52] Ursinus' fourth proof rests on the universal existence of religion and the consent of all human beings to the proposition that God exists, which is the point of Perkins' eighth evidence. Ursinus' final proof, as already noted, is concerned with the terrors of conscience, reflected in Perkins' fourth evidence.[53] Although, moreover, all of these arguments are *a posteriori*, it is striking that none are offered in a strictly demonstrative manner and that there is little resemblance to the "five ways" offered by Aquinas in the *Summa theologiae*: the closest resemblance is to Aquinas' fifth way, the argument from the governance of the world.

In a subsequent passage in the *Golden Chaine*, Perkins also indicates the epistemological basis for his brief set of evidences. The evidences are not merely matters of rational argument to be set forth in formal demonstrations for the sake of convincing an atheist or a doubter. Rather, as argued in much of

50 Perkins, *Foundation*, fol. A6v.
51 Perkins, *Golden Chaine*, ii (p. 2).
52 Ursinus, *Summe*, p. 278.
53 Ursinus, *Summe*, p. 279; note that conscience, in relation to universal consent is Smith's initial argument, *Gods Arrow*, pp. 2–3.

the older classical and Western philosophical tradition, they are "notions"—*koine ennoiai* or *notiones communes*—embedded in the mind as remnants of the image of God. Specifically, all human beings have some recognition "that there is a God, and that the same God punisheth transgressions: that there is an everlasting life: that we must reverence our superiours, and not harme our neighbours."[54] Beyond this, the "remnant of God's image" is also evident in the conscience,[55] a point that Perkins will connect with the proofs in his later work. The evidences of God's existence, therefore, operate in the inward life in the most basic patterns of knowing and in the operations of conscience on the doubting mind and heart.

5 Proofs for the Conscience—Extended Argumentation

When Perkins returned to the proofs of the existence of God in his last lectures, he presented a far more elaborate model than found in this two early works and he spoke directly to the issue of the troubled conscience. What had previously occupied barely two pages in the original of Perkins' *Foundation* and only a short paragraph in the *Golden Chaine*, extends to nearly sixteen pages in Perkins' *Cases of Conscience*. In addition, whereas the *Golden Chaine* had only offered a series of *a posteriori* evidences or rhetorical points and the *Foundation* presented two evidences, one *a posteriori*, the other rhetorical from conscience, each related to scriptural texts, the *Cases of Conscience* presents three distinct groups of proofs: five *a posteriori* arguments from "the light of nature," each with rhetorical associations and issues related to the conscience, three arguments from "the light of grace", and a final argument based on "the light of glorie."[56] From a purely formal perspective it is of interest that Perkins cites Scripture not in the set of proofs based on Scripture where the biblical basis would have been obvious to his readers, but in the first and third sets.

Perkins' citation of Scripture in connection with proofs from the light of nature in his *Foundation* and his *Cases of Conscience* relates to the genre of both works. Reformed works of apologetics like Pacard's *Théologie Naturelle*, Mornay's *Trewnesse*, or Dove's *Confutation* offer logical or rhetorical arguments and, when sources are cited, the sources are from the ancient philosophical tradition. Thomas Morton's *Treatise of the Nature of God* presents a primarily philosophical argument, designed to provide a more firm knowledge of God to

54 Perkins, *Golden Chaine*, xii (p. 12, col. 1); cf. Ursinus, *Summe*, p. 358.
55 Perkins, *Golden Chaine*, xii (p. 13, col. 1).
56 Perkins, *Conscience*, II.ii (pp. 202–218).

one who already believes the fundamental points of Christianity. Morton offers an occasional reference to passages of Scripture.[57] More frequent references to Scripture in proofs, particularly in arguments from the order of nature or from conscience, are found in the sacred theologies of the era, like Ursinus' *Summe*, Bucanus' *Institutions*, and Polanus' *Syntagma theologiae*, where the proofs are located after the prolegomena and the *locus de Scriptura*.[58] Reformed writers include references to Scripture in the proofs when they are stated in the context of belief—on the assumption that Scripture itself contains statements concerning the existence of God as revealed in the natural order and that Scripture serves to confirm the rational arguments.

The proofs in Perkins' *Cases of Conscience* are placed into the context of general belief, setting his work apart from a purely apologetic genre. The *Cases of Conscience* also share with the doctrinal theologies of the day not only the proofs, but also chapters or *loci* on Scripture, religion, and the sacraments—all designed, however, from the perspective of addressing the conscience and leading it toward assurance of salvation in the exercise of piety. Indeed, Perkins explicitly excludes the typical apologetic function of the proofs, identifies atheists as "traytors to God," worthy of death, and indicates that is it not his purpose to dispute the question of whether or not there is a God.[59] The problem of philosophical or metaphysical atheism, then, had little interest for Perkins. Rather, his focus was on an aspect of practical atheism, namely inward denials of God by those who outwardly accept that God indeed exists: the intention of his proofs, mirroring the concerns expressed in the *Treatise of Mans Imaginations*, is to address the dangerous "inward corruption of the soule" that leads the human heart and conscience to deny both God and divine providence.[60]

The first series of proofs, taken from nature "proove that there is a God"; the second set, taken from Scripture "beget faith" and generate belief that there is a God; the third pair of proofs, from the "light of Glorie" promise "a full and perfect knowledge of the Godhead."[61] This threefold light represents three "degrees of knowledge" by which the mind is enlightened concerning the truth

57 Thomas Morton of Berwick, *A Treatise of the Nature of God* (London: Tho. Creed for Robert Dexter, 1599).

58 Ursinus, *Summe*, pp. 279–281; Gulielmus Bucanus, *Institutions of the Christian Religion, framed out of God's Word*, trans. R. Hill (London: George Swindon, 1606), i (pp. 1–2); Amandus Polanus, *Syntagma theologiae christianae* (Hanau: Wechel, 1609), II.iv (col. 262–263).

59 Perkins, *Conscience*, I.ii (pp. 202–203); Perkins was hardly alone in the era in his view that atheists ought to be executed or, at least, exiled: note, Pierre du Moulin, *A Treatise of the Knowledge of God*, trans. Robert Codrington (London: A. M., 1634), p. 17; Dove, *Confutation*, pp. 16–17; and cf. Marshall, "Puritanism and Natural Theology," p. 45.

60 Perkins, *Conscience*, I.ii (p. 203).

61 Perkins, *Conscience*, II.ii (pp. 204, 216, 218).

of God both for "this present life, and for that which is to come."[62] Perkins argues further that there is a God-given purpose and order in the three lights of revelation. Their purpose taken together is to enlighten the human mind by "degrees of knowledge" to receive "direction in the truth of the Godhead."[63] This purpose is achieved in the order:

> the light of nature serves to give a beginning and preparation to this knowledge: the light of grace ministers the ground, and gives further proofe and evidence: and the light of glory, yeelds perfection of assurance, making that perfectly and fully knowne, which by the former degrees was but weakly and imperfectly comprehended.[64]

Perkins begins his exposition of individual proofs by indicating that consideration of the light of nature ought to be of spiritual profit even to a person established in faith. In this initial section Perkins borrows from apologetic models like those of Pacard and Mornay, both in selection of topics and in argumentative content. The proofs from the light of nature, divide into five distinct topical groups. First, a proper knowledge of the existence of God against atheistic inclinations can be drawn from the framework of the world and from the datum of creation itself, as indicated by the Apostle Paul: the "eternall power and Godhead are knowne by the Creation of the world" (Rom. 1:20).[65] Perkins here focuses on the problem of the eternity of the world, posing an argument for creation *ex nihilo* against a view of the eternity of the world as tantamount to pantheism: those who hold that the world had no beginning will be pressed to conclude that the world is God, inasmuch as they assume that all things "have their being of themselves without a beginning" and "a substance of it selfe" that has no beginning can only be properly identified as God.[66] This, in Perkins' paradigm, would be a version of "atheism in judgment." He does not mount an argument against pantheism, presumably because he views its own logic as a *reductio ad absurdum*, nor does he identify the "Atheist" in question, but merely goes on to a denial of the eternity of the world. If there were no beginning, then, logically, there would be no ending—but in the world

62 Perkins, *Conscience*, II.ii (pp. 203–204).
63 Perkins, *Conscience*, II.ii (p. 203).
64 Perkins, *Conscience*, II.ii (p. 204).
65 Perkins, *Conscience*, II.ii (pp. 204–208); cf. Pacard, *Théologie Naturelle*, I.iv.
66 Perkins, *Conscience*, II.ii (p. 205).

things are mutable and corruptible, and therefore have an ending. It they have an ending, they must have had a beginning.[67]

Given, then that the world had a beginning, there are two possible explanations: either the world made itself or it was made from nothing. Both of these explanations are, however, absurd: if one claims that the world made itself, "then the world was before it was"; if one claims it came from nothing, "nothing brings forth nothing: and that which is nothing in it selfe, cannot bring forth something."[68] It must therefore be acknowledge as true "that the was some substance eternall and Almightie that framed this goodly *Creature* the World, besides it selfe."[69]

Perkins does not leave the argument in the abstract—he offers an adaptation of a rhetorical argument presented by the Stoic, Chrysippus, in Cicero's *De natura deorum*.[70] If a person walking in a forest comes upon "goodly faire buildings" in addition to herbs, trees, birds, and beasts, but sees no people, he will "reason to himselfe" that the buildings did not exist from eternity and that they were not built by the flora and fauna of the forest: he will conclude that some person built them. Even so, contemplation of the world yields the recognition that the world did not make itself and that it was not made by any of the creatures in it, but by a "most wise, most cunning, and everlasting" creator, "and that is God."[71]

Perkins' second argument reflects both Pacard and Mornay, but adds a distinctly religious appeal. It rests on "the frame of the world" and the order of creatures in their "foure sorts and kindes": there are inanimate, "bare" substances that lack life, sense, and reason, like the sun, moon, and stars; there is a second kind of creature that has substance and life, but no sense or reason,

---

67 Perkins, *Conscience*, II.ii (p. 205). Perkins may well have been aware of the London publication of major works of Giordano Bruno, *De la causa, principio, et uno* (Venetia [London]: [J. Charlewood], 1584); and *De l'infinito vniuerso et mondi* (Venetia [London]: [J. Charlewood], 1584) Perkins may also have known of Bruno's ill-received public lecture at Oxford in 1583: on which, see Ernan McMullin, "Giordano Bruno at Oxford," in *Isis*, 77/1 (1986), pp. 85–94. On Bruno's understanding of the infinity and eternity of the world and the relation of God as *Natura naturans* to the world as *natura naturata*, see J. Lewis McIntyre, *Giordano Bruno* (London: Macmillan, 1903), pp. 180–188, 196–197; and Dorothea Singer, *Giordano Bruno: His Life and Thought* (New York: Schuman, 1950); also Paul-Henri Michel, *The Cosmology of Giordano Bruno* (Ithaca: Cornell University Press, 1973).

68 Perkins, *Conscience*, II.ii (p. 205).

69 Perkins, *Conscience*, II.ii (pp. 205–206).

70 Cicero, *De natura deorum libri tres*, commentary by G. F. Schoemann, ed. Austin Stickney (Boston: Ginn & Heath, 1881), II.vi (pp. 83–84).

71 Perkins, *Conscience*, II.ii (p. 206).

like plants, trees, and herbs; there is a third kind that has substance, life, and sense, plus a power of self-motion, but that nonetheless lack reason, like fish and land animals; and there are creatures that have substance, life, sense, and reason, namely human beings.[72] There is, then, an ascending series of degrees in the created order. Moreover, the lower forms of creatures serve the higher—with the "creature that hath most giftes" being served by all. Perkins does not take the standard route of the argument and simply infer the necessity a divine being capable not only of creating but also of ordering and framing the whole of creation. Rather he draws a religious conclusion: it is fitting that this highest creature, the human being, "have something to honour and serve," specifically "a substance uncreate, most holy, most wise, eternall, infinite, and this is God."[73]

A second series of arguments "drawn from the light of nature" references the "preservation and government" of the created order. These arguments, as indicated in Acts 14:17 are "touched by the Holy Ghost."[74] Of interest here is that Perkins takes arguments from the cycles of reproduction that led Aristotelians to argue the eternity of the world,[75] but which now—having set aside the notion of an eternal world—simply argue the existence of a divine power undergirding finite life and ongoing being. Perkins notes that food, in itself "void of life," serves to nourish and maintain life; garments that are in themselves "void of heate" preserve the heat of the body even in extreme cold. Similarly, neither rain, nor earth, nor sun have power in themselves to bring forth plants in their incredible variety. Such "vertue" or "power" in objects can only arise from "a divine and heavenly power, above, and beside the power of these creatures."[76] Further the way in which a "bird brings forth the egge" and "the egge againe brings forth the bird" or, similarly, a worm weaves itself a cocoon and from the cocoon a fly emerges—and that these processes go on "from yeare to yeare" also bespeaks a wonderful power beyond the capabilities of creatures.[77]

---

72 Perkins, *Conscience*, II.ii (pp. 206–207); cf. Pacard, *Théologie Naturelle*, I.v (pp. 95–96); Mornay, *Trewnesse*, p. 3.

73 Perkins, *Conscience*, II.ii (p. 207).

74 Perkins, *Conscience*, II.ii (p. 208).

75 Note, e.g., Siger of Brabant, *Question on the Eternity of the World*, in *St. Thomas Aquinas, Siger of Brabant, St. Bonaventure: On the Eternity of the World*, trans. with an intro. by Cyril Vollert, Lottie Kendierski and Paul Byrne (Milwaukee: Marquette University Press, 1964), pp. 85–87.

76 Perkins, *Conscience*, II.ii (pp. 208–209); cf. Pacard, *Théologie Naturelle*, I.v (pp. 95–96); Mornay, *Trewnesse*, pp. 4, 6.

77 Perkins, *Conscience*, II.ii (pp. 209–210).

Third, there are arguments, also grounded in "the light of nature" that "are taken from the soule of man."[78] The soul is endowed with an understanding or rational faculty that has engrafted in it "from the beginning certaine principles."[79] These principles, which stand apart from any individual soul must have a cause beyond the self—namely a wise God. Similarly, the soul is endowed with a conscience that has the capacity to testify concerning truth and to confirm the truth judgments. An atheist has no suitable explanation of why and to what or whom the conscience bears record or of why the conscience instills a fear of punishment for sins committed in secret. Indeed, the conscience "will accuse [the sinner], terrifie him, cite him before god, and give him no rest." The only suitable explanation is that there is a God who knows the testimony and punishes sins.[80] Here too, in the case of a proof from conscience, Perkins reflects a rhetorical argument based on the fears of the emperor Caligula that had been used, notably, by Calvin, Pacard, and Mornay.[81]

Fourth, proofs also are drawn from the "ground of principle written in every mans heart in the world, none excepted, that there is a God."[82] The argument, ultimately taken from Cicero, has parallels in numerous Reformed theologians of the early modern era, including Calvin, Pacard, and Mornay.[83] Pagans worship idols, thereby acknowledging the existence of divine power. Even so, Laban, who worshiped false gods was nevertheless bound by the oath he made with Jacob, given his recognition of the existence of "a Godhead ... that knowes the truth" and abhors lies.[84] It is also common among all peoples to say that "it raines, it thunders, it snowes, it hailes," rather than "nature or heaven raines or thunders"—tacitly acknowledging a divine power that causes the rain and the thunder.[85] As a final point, Perkins adds that, although various persons have denied the existence of God, none has ever published a discourse proving that there is no God.[86]

---

78 Perkins, *Conscience*, II.ii (pp. 210–212); cf. Pacard, *Théologie Naturelle*, I.v (pp. 95–105).

79 Perkins, *Conscience*, II.ii (pp. 210–211); so also Ursinus, *Summe*, pp. 278–279.

80 Perkins, *Conscience*, II.ii (pp. 211–212); cf. Pacard, *Théologie Naturelle*, I.ii (p. 67); note Ursinus, *Summe*, pp. 279–280.

81 Cf. Suetonius, *Lives of the Caesars*, IV.li, in *Suetonius*, 2 vols., trans. John Carew Rolfe, revised ed. (Cambridge: Harvard University Press, 1951), pp. 482–483; and note the argument in Calvin, *Institutes*, I.iii.2; Pacard, *Théologie Naturelle*, I.ii (p. 65); and Mornay, *Trewnesse*, p. 11. Ursinus does not reference Caligula.

82 Perkins, *Conscience*, II.ii (pp. 212–214).

83 Cf. Cicero, *De natura deorum*, I.xvii; Calvin, *Institutes*, I.iii.1; Pacard, *Théologie Naturelle*, I.ii (pp. 58–59); Mornay, *Trewnesse*, p. 10.

84 Perkins, *Conscience*, II.ii (p. 213).

85 Perkins, *Conscience*, II.ii (p. 213); cf. Pacard, *Théologie Naturelle*, I.ii (p. 57).

86 Perkins, *Conscience*, II.ii (p. 214).

Perkins' fifth series of arguments returns to the issue of a hierarchy of creatures broached previously in his second series of arguments.[87] Here, however, Perkins argues the interdependence of causes in the hierarchy, yielding the conclusion drawn "by all Philosophers" that there must be a "cause of all causes ... caused by none," upon which all of the lower causes, namely, the creatures depend and "to whome all creatures doe tend, as to their ende."[88] Finally, to those who fail to be fully convinced by any of these proofs, given that they have never seen God, Perkins responds rhetorically. Doubters believe in the wind and the air and have never seen either—they also are content concerning knowledge of their own faces, which they have seen only in a "glasse" or mirror: "Why then may not this content thy heart, and resolve thee of the Godhead, in what thou seest him in the glasse of the creatures?"[89]

Perkins concludes his proofs with two sections—one dealing with the "light of grace," the other with the "light of glorie."[90] Despite their brevity, their identification as "sections" places them on a par with the preceding, far lengthier, section on proofs resting on the "light of nature." Like other early modern Reformed, Perkins identifies an initial kind of proof by the light of grace "in the writings of the Prophets and Apostles" as consisting in "expresse testimonies."[91] In addition to testimonies, there are prophecies and miracles, the former demonstrating that there is a knowledge that lies beyond human comprehension, explicable only on the assumption of the existence of God; the latter revealing a power beyond all natural causes, in fact an omnipotent power "which is the author of nature itself," namely, God.[92] Proofs by the light of glory comprise Perkins' final and briefest category: whereas human beings in the present life can have only an imperfect knowledge of God—as provided either by the light of nature or "spectacles of his creatures" and by the light of grace or "glasse of the word and Sacraments"—after death, in the presence of God, the "imperfection and weakness" of human understanding will be removed, God will be seen clearly, and the ultimate answer given to the question of the existence of God.[93]

87 Perkins, *Conscience*, II.ii (pp. 214–216).
88 Perkins, *Conscience*, II.ii (p. 215).
89 Perkins, *Conscience*, II.ii (p. 215).
90 Perkins, *Conscience*, II.ii (pp. 216–218).
91 Perkins, *Conscience*, II.ii (p. 216); cf. Muller, *Post-Reformation Reformed Dogmatics*, III, pp. 184–185.
92 Perkins, *Conscience*, II.ii (p. 217).
93 Perkins, *Conscience*, II.ii (p. 218).

6 Observations and Conclusions

Perkins' proofs were not constructed either as an apologetic directed toward metaphysical atheists or as a rationalistic foundation for sacred theology, nor were they framed as demonstrations after the manner of Thomas Aquinas. Although they reflect aspects of Aquinas' so-called five ways, they are closer in structure and content of argument to the proofs offered by other early modern Reformed writers like Ursinus, Pacard, and Mornay. Perkins' proofs, moreover, as distinct from Pacard's and Mornay's, are situated in the interpretive context of belief in which Scripture supplies the ultimate norm of theology. They are consistently directed toward believers, and they are addressed either to a weakened faith or to the conscience: their purpose, like the corrective and normative functions of the law, was pedagogical, not prolegomenal.

Both in their earliest formulation and in the extended treatment of the *Cases of Conscience*, Perkins' proofs were directed toward the inward life of doubt and belief. If only one of his proofs was *from conscience*, arguably, all of his proofs were directed *to the conscience*. Specifically, these proofs are all matters of testimony and judgment, addressed to the faculty that assesses the truth of testimonies and judgments.

The extended structure of Perkins' argument, moving from nature, to grace, to glory and indicating a perfection by degrees toward assurance, mirrors the states of humanity in the order of salvation, where among the regenerate there remains a conflict of nature and grace, with grace necessary to overcome the remaining sinfulness of human nature, and glory having by grace fully restored human nature.

Perkins' approach to the proofs evidences a recognition, characteristic of much older Reformed theology, that not only do Scripture and reason agree on fundamental truths about God and creation but that the two sources of knowledge of God are not utterly separate. Just as faith is a virtue of rational, not irrational, creatures, so does the biblical revelation not only overlap with the rationally accessible revelation in nature, it also includes the truths concerning God and creation that are known to reason. If, then, Perkins' proofs draw on natural theology, it is a Christian natural theology—perhaps as suggested by Pierre Viret[94]—that operates epistemologically in relation to faith and piety, and not without Scripture.

94 Cf. Muller, "Was it Really Viral," pp. 512–514.

CHAPTER 10

The Suffering and Death of Christ as Epistemological Framework in Reformation-Era Lutheran Teaching: Martin Luther, Veit Dietrich, and Cyriacus Spangenberg

Vincent Evener

Scholarship on confessionalization and ecclesial and social discipline in the Reformation era has focused on the formal mechanisms employed by ecclesial and temporal authorities to enforce doctrinal and moral conformity.[1] Significant questions remain, however, concerning how and how much processes of confessionalization and discipline were advanced through preaching and devotional literature, including sermons, catechisms, and prayer and hymn books.[2] Scholars have pointed out that clergy did not simply pursue the agendas of temporal authorities but sometimes criticized the latter; and they have identified a range of goals in the relevant literature. In an overview of Lutheran preaching in the age of confessionalization (defined in this instance as *c.*1550–*c.*1675), Mary Jane Haemig and Robert Kolb describe an overriding intention to mediate God's Word to the congregation; pastors wanted to inspire repentance, proclaim forgiveness (creating faith in Christ according to

1 For overviews, see Ute Lotz-Heumann, "Imposing Church and Social Discipline," in *The Cambridge History of Christianity Volume 6: Reform and Expansion 1500–1660*, ed. R. Po-Chia Hsia (Cambridge 2007); R. Po-Chia Hsia, *Social Discipline in the Reformation: Central Europe 1550–1750* (London 1989); Thomas A. Brady, Jr., "Confessionalization: The Career of a Concept," in *Confessionalization in Europe, 1550–1700*, ed. John M. Headley, Hans J. Hillerbrand, and Anthony J. Papalas (Burlington 2004): 1–20.

2 Often cited is Bodo Nischan's argument that later-sixteenth century preachers turned their efforts from finding to defending truth; see "Demarcating Boundaries: Lutheran Pericopic Sermons in the Age of Confessionalization," ARG 88 [1997]: 199–216; here 201. John M. Frymire, *The Primacy of the Postils: Catholics, Protestants, and the Dissemination of Ideas in Early Modern Germany* (Leiden 2009), has amply demonstrated the significance of postils to the confessional and disciplinary goals of Catholics and Lutherans. Susan C. Karant-Nunn, *The Reformation of Feeling: Shaping the Religious Emotions in Early Modern Germany* (Oxford 2010) describes how clergy sought to discipline emotions, seeing this work as part of larger processes of confessionalization and social discipline. For a helpful overview of mechanisms of discipline and education, Carlos M. N. Eire, *Reformations: The Early Modern World, 1450–1650* (New Haven 2016), 586–617.

 | DOI:10.1163/9789004527843_011

the Lutheran understanding of *fides ex auditu*), console in the face of suffering and temptation, shape the daily life of faith, and prepare hearers to face death with hope of eternal life.[3] Ronald K. Rittgers has argued that flourishing clerical and lay practices of verbal consolation provide a counterweight to scholars' recent preoccupation with discipline;[4] consolation was as much a goal of the clergy as discipline.[5]

The present essay takes a different approach toward correcting the view of clergy and their pedagogical production as mere instruments of the state by examining how the laity were taught to engage in discernment and self-discipline; rather than examining discipline narrowly as an effort to control the unwilling, I am seeking to understand how clergy sought to persuade and equip through pedagogy.[6] However much temporal authorities may have been content with subjects who toed the line in life and landed in hell after death, clergy who took the time to construct and publish sermons and devotional literature seldom were. My focus will be on a series of sermons on the passion included in Luther's *House Postils* beginning in 1545.[7] Veit Dietrich was the author of all but one of these sermons, which he published initially as a separate devotional work; Dietrich, who compiled the *House Postils*, inserted his passion sermons without identifying himself as their author, and they circulated as Luther's work.[8] The *House Postils* were by far the most widely disseminated

---

3 Mary Jane Haemig and Robert Kolb, "Preaching in Lutheran Pulpits in the Age of Confessionalization," in *Lutheran Ecclesiastical Culture, 1550–1675*, ed. Robert Kolb (Leiden 2008), 117–58; here, esp. 118, 121–23, 148–54; Haemig and Kolb cite a range of scholarship, including scholarship reflecting an emphasis on discipline and corrective scholarship.

4 Ronald K. Rittgers, "The Age of Reform as an Age of Consolation," *Church History* 86 no. 3 (September 2017): 607–42.

5 Ronald K. Rittgers, *The Reformation of Suffering: Pastoral Theology and Lay Piety in Late Medieval and Early Modern Germany* (Oxford 2012). The point is stated on p. 8; the evidence is provided in Chapters 7–8, pp. 163–217.

6 I intend neither to assert the innocence of the disciplinary endeavor nor to dismiss it as de facto inappropriate; discipline broadly defined to include education is a core human endeavor. For more on my views, see Vincent Evener, "The Future of Reformation Studies," *Church History and Religious Culture* 97, nos. 3–4 (December 2017): 310–21.

7 The first edition of the *House Postils* was published in 1544 without the passion sermons; I consult the 1545 edition, *Haußpostil D. Martin Luthers ... Mit fleiß von newem corrigirt vnd gemeret mit XIII. Predigen von der Passio oder histori des leide[n]s Christi* (Nu[e]rmberg 1545), VD 16 ZV 10044, abbreviated as LHP.

8 The authorship of the sermons was debated in modern scholarship; WA 60: 319–21 issued a firm rejection of arguments for Luther's authorship, with one exception: Dietrich adapted Luther's Good Friday sermon from April 3, 1534, which was already included in the first 1544 edition of the *House Postils*, to serve as Sermon 11 in his devotional book; he then used the version from his devotional book, integrated within his other sermons, in the 1545 *House Postils*. Dietrich's devotional book is *Passio oder histori vom leiden Christi Jesu vnsers Heylands*

preaching manual among Lutheran clergy of the later sixteenth and seventeenth centuries: according to John M. Frymire, there were 84 editions of the *House Postils* printed between 1544 and 1609, meaning there were over 100,000 copies in circulation.[9] The short sermons were suitable not only for the time-crunched pastor, but also for devotional use, including preparation for hearing sermons. The sermons specifically on the passion helped shaped a distinctly rich Lutheran tradition of preaching and devotion around Christ's suffering and death.[10] Reformation-era Lutheran clergy produced many books on the passion, frequently compiled from sermons, for use in preaching, devotion, or both.[11] Robert Kolb has argued that these Lutheran books were shaped fundamentally by the dialectic of Law and Gospel.[12] Here, I delineate a broader range of strategies for teaching discernment and self-discipline evident in Dietrich's passion sermons; Dietrich himself followed vectors established in Luther's earlier works, as described below, while placing particular weight on practices of visual meditation and recollection. In the final section of this essay, I compare Dietrich's strategies to those of a later author, Cyriacus Spangengberg. Spangenberg's *Passio*, first published in 1557, offers one example of how the emerging Lutheran tradition could be transformed to meet new challenges and contexts.[13] Scholarship has yet to illuminate the diverse development of the Lutheran tradition.

(Nu[e]rmberg 1545), VD 16 D 1598. My primary concern here is not with reconstructing Luther's or Dietrich's "authentic" voice, but with the nature of the instruction on discernment and self-discipline delivered to the people through Luther's *House Postils*, which shaped preaching and devotion.

9 John M. Frymire, "Works: Sermons and Postils," in *The Oxford Encyclopedia of Martin Luther*, ed. Paul Hinlicky and Derek Neslon, 3 vols. (Oxford 2017), 3:561–89.

10 Johann Anselm Steiger, "Bemerkungen zur Geschichte der lutherischen Passionstheologie und Gerhards Stellung in ihr," in Johann Gerhard, *Erklährung der Historien des Leidens vnnd Sterbens vnsers Herrn Christi Jesu nach den vier Evangelisten* (Stuttgart-Bad Cannstatt 2002), 487–505; here, 495, has shown that the *House Postils* were particularly important for Johann Gerhard as he compiled his *Eklahrung*.

11 For an overview, see Robert Kolb, "Passionsmeditation: Luthers und Melanchthons Schüler predigen und beten die Passion," in *Humanismus und Wittenberger Reformation*, ed. Michael Beyer and Günther Wartenberg (Leipzig 1996): 267–93; Martin Elze, "Das Verständnis der Passion Jesu im ausgehenden Mittelalter und bei Luther," in *Geist und Geschichte der Reformation*, ed. Heinz Liebing and Klaus Scholder (Berlin 1966): 127–51.

12 Kolb, "Passionsmeditation," 268–73, 277–83, 293; Kolb discusses too the influence of methodological and exegetical strategies promulgated by Philip Melanchthon and Caspar Cruciger.

13 After the 1557 printing by Georg Rhau (VD 16 S 7649), a revised version with four new sermons treating the entire passion was printed in Eisleben in 1564 (VD16 S 7650/VD16 S 7702) and again in 1570 (VD16 S 7651/ VD16 S 7703)—both the Eisleben editions were printed by Urban Gaubisch. I use the 1564 edition, *Passio. Vom Leiden vnd sterben vnsers*

This volume is dedicated to my *Doktormutter*, Susan Schreiner, and her work is profoundly relevant here. Schreiner's *Are You Alone Wise?* demonstrates that early modern religious thought was shaped by a pervasive yearning for certitude of doctrine and salvation and a corresponding fear of vulnerability to deception.[14] Here, we will see that preaching and devotional literature aimed to instill appropriate certitude, to caution against false certitudes—both Dietrich and Spangenberg warn of false *Sicherheit* or *Vermessenheit*, which they define differently—and to equip Christians with the capacity to discern their world and their own religious experiences. Luther himself no less than the Spanish mystics had been concerned with discernment of the spirits;[15] Lutheran preaching and devotional literature in turn attended deeply to inner thoughts and motives, as well as to outward historical realities, in order to teach discernment to laity who were to find their intimacy with God through faith and in daily vocation.[16]

1 Discernment and Self-Discipline in the Dietrich-Luther Sermons on the *Passion*

Dietrich's passion cycle used clearly discernible strategies to equip Christians for daily discernment and self-discipline, all of which required Christians to take the passion story as their epistemological framework for assessing themselves and the world. I will list seven strategies here. First, the cycle not only enjoined the memorization and recollection of the passion story, but encouraged Christians to treat the story as a "painting" that could be deciphered by spiritual seeing—this required faith and right instruction—and then used as a lens for examining one's own experiences, thoughts, feelings, and context. This image of the crucifixion was to be recalled especially in trials, whenever conscience or the devil assailed with images of sin, death, and hell. The inward visualization of the passion took over the function of an outward relic or

HErrn Heilands vnd Seligmachers Jesu Christi etliche scho[e]ne vnd nu[e]tzliche Predigten, which will be abbreviated CSP.

14 Susan E. Schreiner, *Are You Alone Wise? The Search for Certainty in the Early Modern Era* (Oxford 2011), 258–59, 261–62.

15 For Schreiner's treatment of Luther and the Spanish mystics around the theme of discernment of spirits, see ibid., 271–85 (Ignatius of Loyola), 291–320 (Luther and Theresa of Avila).

16 For an overview of the vast scholarship on Luther and mysticism, see Ronald K. Rittgers, "Martin Luther," in *Protestants and Mysticism in Reformation Europe*, ed. Ronald K. Rittgers and Vincent Evener (Leiden 2019): 34–55; my own views on conceptualizing the Protestant reception of mysticism are outlined in the Epilogue to this volume, 429–39.

icon.[17] Second, Dietrich drew extensive parallels between New Testament Jews and "papists," aiming to equip Christians to avoid both supposed Jewishness in themselves and the threatening secret Judaism of intra-Christian enemies; in so doing, he continued strategies found in Luther's *Wartburg postil* (1522) and in Johannes Bugenhagen's harmony and commentary on the passion, which was seminal for the Lutheran passion tradition.[18]

Within this framework, Dietrich used Judas and the Jews, on the one hand, and the counterexamples of Peter and Simon the Cyrenean, on the other, to offer a searching examination of both the dynamics of sin and the causes of rejection of the Gospel. Here, a third strategy for teaching discernment and self-discipline involved terrifying believers by presenting frivolous consent to sin as a reckless plunge into the abyss: like Judas, one might stumble into deep, unforeseen offense and despair of mercy. In a fourth move, Jews and papists were related and equated in the obstinate rejection of truth; in so doing, Dietrich like Luther wanted to warn evangelicals about the pride that shut human ears to clear proclamation. They also wanted to vindicate the Gospel. The fault lay with the hearer not the doctrine, lest papist rejection unsettle evangelical confidence.[19] Here, we see that confessional division demanded not simply doctrinal clarity, but pastoral response.

Fifth, with resonance to the mystical tradition, possibly mediated through Luther, Dietrich sought to inculcate humility in terms of self-accusation for sin and willing surrender to God's will in suffering. At the same time, sixth,

---

17 The encouragement of visual imagination and recollection is especially prevalent in Luther's 1519 *Ein Sermon von der Bereitung zum Sterben*, WA 2: 685–97; LW 42:99–115, completed several months after Luther outlined his perspective on passion mediation in *Ein Sermon von der Betrachtung des heiligen Leidens Christi*, WA 2: 136–42; LW 42:7–14. The centrality that Dietrich wanted to give the practice as a way of finding consolation and courage in suffering is evident in the dedicatory epistle to his separate *Passio*, A5r–7v; focusing on 2 Cor. 4:18, this epistle teaches that Christians must look beyond suffering that is seen and felt to find the invisible—a gracious God through Christ and the promise of eternal life. Paradoxically, the invisible is manifest in the spoken Word and especially the crucified Word; Christ's passion is thus a "mirror" of consolation for those who look rightly, but if the image falls from view, "discontent, impatience, and finally doubt" set in. While presenting his sermons as Luther's, Dietrich did not include his explanatory epistle; thus, readers encountered the sermons' exhortations to visual recollection without the preparatory instruction and framework.

18 For analysis of these two works, see Vincent Evener, "'Our Jews': Anti-Judaism and the Formation of Reformation-Era Christians," *Journal of Religion* 99, no. 4 (October 2019): 403–31.

19 See ibid., and Vincent Evener, "Jewishness as an Explanation for Rejection of the Word: Caspar Güttel's Reception of Martin Luther's Anti-Judaism," *Church History and Religious Culture* 95 (2015): 203–221.

advice on visual scriptural recollection and on prayer sought to teach evangelicals not to allow despair to penetrate too deeply into their hearts. The self was to be understood as a battleground between God and Satan, in which faith inspired by the Spirit and the temptation to sin and despair stirred by the devil warred for possession of the innermost citadel. The most important form of self-discipline—alongside the humble recognition of one's sinfulness—was hearing and clinging to the promise of forgiveness for the faithful repentant. Discernment required, seventh, applying the theology of the cross as a lens for understanding and responding to all experiences and to distinguish true and false crosses. The faithful were to be marked by courage in suffering. To view the world and one's own experiences through the theology of the cross allowed one to endure patiently and courageously amid trials.

Each of these strategies was employed as the biblical narrative allowed or inspired. In the ensuing analysis, accordingly, I will employ subheadings that recall these strategies, but I will not treat each strategy in order. Indeed, the strategies delineated here are richly interconnected—they could have been distinguished and enumerated differently—and I have numbered them primarily to highlight how consistently and intentionally Dietrich aims to remake perception, thought, and feeling. My analysis below thus loosely follows the progression of the sermons themselves, showing how Dietrich intertwined his strategies in order to use the biblical stories to teach discernment and self-discipline. I do not claim to have uncovered every relevant strategy; equally, I do not deny the centrality of the Law-Gospel dialectic emphasized by Kolb, but I seek to understand more of what Dietrich wanted to accomplish and how he instilled that dialectic itself as an epistemological framework and as a depiction of subjective experience.

1.1 *Visual Memorization and Recollection*

Dietrich's sermons on the passion are preceded in the postil collection by a short preface and a longer sermon on Romans 6 that promises to explain the "use of Christ's suffering."[20] The latter argues that the purpose of preaching on the passion is to teach people why Christ suffered and how they ought to benefit from and use his suffering. Readers are offered a series of "sermons" gathered from scripture on these key points: the intention was to encourage memorization of consoling passages that could then be recalled in tribulation.[21] More

20 These materials are found in 1544 editions and do not belong to the group of sermons introduced by Dietrich in 1545.

21 LHP, 119r–122v [Forward]. The sermons are numbered; relevant numbers will be placed in brackets.

striking, however, is the encouragement of visual recollection introduced by Dietrich the ensuing sermons.

Dietrich's sermon on Christ's anguished prayer in Gethsemane works to fashion thought and emotion. He implicitly applies Luther's teaching that Christ must be received as a sacrament—as "consolation against sin and bad conscience"—before he is regarded as an example of right disposition and action, particularly in suffering. He teaches, further, that Christ suffered the full weight of every human sin and of divine wrath over this sum of wickedness.[22] It is the unfathomable depth of Christ's suffering that compels the faithful to always think and speak of it, Dietrich says. Christ's supra-human *Todesangst* is a mirror or "painting of sin," necessary because human nature is "blinded and ruined," both unable to recognize the depth of the human plight or the severity of divine wrath and hardened in this disposition by the devil and the world. Dietrich reminds his audience that even God's Son, "eternal justice" itself along with the sinless humanity of Christ, trembled before God's wrath. Dietrich's examples of sinning include moral lapses like greed, usury, un-discipline, adultery, and whoring—all sins of "bad desire."[23] Following the terror, however, the image of Christ's anguish can become consolation: human beings cannot avoid being overcome by flesh and the devil, and Satan seeks to bring Christians into "open offense"—as in Peter's denial of Christ—in order to "paint" an image of sin for the sinner. Against this demonic picture, the Christian may "fix this image of the Mount of Olives before [himself or herself]" and speak words of encouragement to the heart. "Do not let sadness capture your heart," Dietrich teaches, "but say, 'It is enough that my Lord Jesus has thus sorrowed and feared.'"[24]

1.2 *Securing the Heart from Despair while Adopting a Stance of Humility*

Christ's prayer in Gethsemane is offered as an example of how to pray in "anxiety, tribulation, and distress (*angst, anfechtung, vnd not*)." Dietrich warns first and foremost against any indulgence of despair: sorrow for sin is necessary, but one must not permit "distress" to penetrate the heart too deeply, to the extent that prayer seems futile. An undisciplined response to anxiety regarding salvation or to any suffering threatened the central goal of Lutheran teaching,

22 LHP, 123b–124a [Sermon 1]. On the theme of divine wrath in Lutheran passion devotion, see Johann Anselm Steiger, "Zorn Gottes, Leiden Christi und die Affekte der Passionsbetrachtung bei Luther und im Luthertum des 17. Jahrhunderts," in Johann Anselm Steiger, ed., *Passion, Affekt und Leidenschaft in der Frühen Neuzeit*, 2 Vols. (Wiesbaden 2005), 1: 179–201.

23 LHP, 124r–125r[1].

24 LHP, 125r–v[1].

namely faith understood as trust in God's promise of mercy. Dietrich thus used the theology of the cross to counter what he saw as the assumption of fallen nature that God must be hostile and mean evil when God allows suffering to come upon people. Christians must understand themselves as adopted children of God, and they like Christ can and must pray with "heart and trust" that God is benevolent and means them well even when they suffer. Without such "confidence," there can be "no true prayer."[25]

All the same, the sermon on Gethsemane ends with an exhortation to humble submission to God's will that reminds of late-medieval mysticism:[26] "place yourself in God's will," Dietrich exhorts, "even if he wants to leave you longer in such distress—such that you would bear and suffer it patiently, as you see Christ do that here." Dietrich counsels submission, come what may in temporal needs, while teaching that Christians can pray with certainty that God wants to "preserve us in his Word, make us holy, and forgive sins and give the Holy Spirit and eternal life. He wills that all human beings shall be saved." Thus, *resignatio ad infernum* is not advised even as a meditative exercise. Also rejected is the idea that God predestines unto damnation. One ought to yield to God's will in temporal suffering because God may intend it to "be useful or good for your salvation (*seligkeit*) or God's honor." Dietrich describes payer as the "best medicine (*artzney*)" against *Anfechtung* and the attendant danger of despair. The disciples slept as Christ' prayed because they had fallen into despair, yet God rescued them, and Christians may hope in the same.[27]

1.3 *Watching Out for Presumption, Listening to Preaching and the Promise*

Dietrich commends humility and even self-humbling (made possible by faith) not only in terms of submission to the divine will in the face of suffering but also and more often in terms of avoiding presumption in one's faith life. Throughout the sermons, he uses the terms "vermessen sein," "vermessenheit," "sicher sein," and "sicherheit."[28] Dietrich points out that Peter himself came "easily into such a great fall, even though he previously counted body and life as little for Christ's sake." Peter's story also teaches Christians to seek grace with

---

25 LHP, 126r–v[1]; see also the discussion of Peter's sorrow, LHP, 140r–v[5].

26 See Note 16 *Supra*, and Vincent Evener, *"Enemies of the Cross": Suffering, Truth, and Mysticism in the Early Reformation* (New York: Oxford University Press, 2021).

27 LHP, 126v–127v[1]. For Spangenberg, the disciples' sleeping evidenced their *Vermessenheit*; CSP, U1r.

28 See e.g. LHP, 129r[2] (on Judas), 138r–139r[5] (on Peter), 155v–156r[9], 171v[13]. On *Sicherheit* in sinning as an abuse of evangelical teaching for which that right teaching must not be blamed, see LHP, 127v–128v[2].

humility after a fall.[29] Dietrich devotes significant attention to the stories of Peter and Judas to illustrate the dynamics of sin and warn his audience accordingly. He insists, first, that Judas sinned "willingly and with forethought," while Peter was caught off guard, falling from "foolishness or weakness"; second, that Judas had despised many prior warnings from Christ about his indulgence of sin; third, that Judas' greater sin brought greater torment of conscience; and fourth, that Judas despised the promise of forgiveness that Peter learned well and clung to. Dietrich thus discourages a light-hearted attitude toward moral transgression, and he encourages attentiveness to preaching![30] As an apostle, Dietrich explains, Judas proclaimed "repentance and forgiveness of sin in the name of Jesus," baptized, exorcised, and performed other miracles; but he regarded himself as a good apostle and thought little of stealing from the common purse. Thus, he opened himself to the devil's influence and was enticed into a fall so great that he despaired of rescue.[31] The question was one of vulnerability: would the person be open to Christ or the devil, the Word or lies? A telling line from Sermon 12, which allegorizes the notion of Christ as the final Easter Lamb, says that Christ cannot be consumed either by the undisciplined or the works-righteous: "Whoever wants to enjoy his things cannot be undisciplined (*rohloss*), smug (*sicher*), and godless like our Epicureans, who want to be good Christians even when they do whatever they desire." But Christ also cannot be consumed by those who "do not keep doctrine (*lehr*) pure and falsify the teaching of faith with human teaching and commands, as the pope does."[32]

1.4 *Judas and the Jews as an Image of the Catholic Enemy*

Judas was for Luther as for much of the prior Christian tradition the paragon of Jewish perfidy, and Dietrich followed this assumption in using Judas and the Jews not only to show the dynamics of sin—to warn of *Sicherheit* as a slippery slope into the abyss of sin and despair—but also to depict the Catholic enemy. In the passion cycle, Jew-Papist associations served primarily to provide assurance that papist obstinacy did not undermine claims about the clarity and effectiveness of evangelical teachings.[33] Why had hearing not produced faith,

29 LHP, 138r[5]; on humility as necessary to repentance, 140v[5].

30 LHP, 139v–140r[5]. He also contrasts Paul's "unknowing" persecution of Christ and the faithful to that of the high priests and the Pharisees. Later, he argues that Christ's prayer, "Father forgive them," excludes those who know their evil and refuse to repent, "wie vnsere Junckherren die Papisten," LHP, 164r[11]. On Sermon 11, see Note 8 *supra*.

31 LHP, 128r–129v[2].

32 LHP, 168v[12].

33 For a study of Jew-Papist associations in the *Wartburg Postil* (1522) and Bugenhagen's Passion harmony, see Evener, "Our Jews."

if right preaching conveyed the Spirit? Thus, Dietrich offers the story of Judas' betrayal of Jesus as a "comfort and warning" in the face of the kindred betrayal of papal clergy. A marginal annotation reads, "Bapst ist auch ein Judas." The church must always suffer the betrayal of clergy: the pope has the "Judas purse around his neck," and he "betrays and sells the Gospel." The pope treats the Gospel as the "Jews treated the Lord Christ before Caiaphas and Pilate"; like Judas coming to seize Christ with a mob of "servants of the high priests and authorities (*Obersten*)," the pope gathers a mob of "monks, priests, and universities (*Hohenschule*[*n*])" in order to "persecute the Gospel and damn it as the worst heresy." Pilate serves here as an image of worldly authority that persecutes at the behest of Rome.[34] Dietrich warns the faithful not to take the apparent prosperity of the papal clergy and monks as evidence of divine favor; their eternal judgment is coming, and their consciences already afflict them.[35]

Like Luther, Dietrich links papist and Jew by genealogy and type. In the fourth sermon of the cycle, he says the Gospels' depiction of the "judicial process" before the Caiaphas was intended primarily to steel the faithful to face the same—to be falsely accused and handed over by spiritual authorities to temporal authorities. Dietrich uses theses passages to console and commend patience to the persecuted, and he warns against taking offense and losing heart at the seeming triumph of the other side.[36] "Everyone" regarded the high priests and elders as "pious holy people" on account of their office and status, Dietrich says; now "the pope, bishops, monks, and priests" enjoy such false regard. Dietrich cautions, "Don't look here at the office, otherwise you will be deceived; look there at how they act toward Christ, what kind of heart and will they bring to him ... then you will be able to judge." The high priests revealed

34 LHP, 129v–130r[2]. In the sixth sermon, Dietrich describes—again with explicit parallel to his own day—how the high priests manufactured charges of *Aufruhr* against Christ because they knew Pilate cared little for religious matters; see LHP, 141v–142r[6]. For further connections between New Testament characters and sixteenth century conflicts, see LHP, 144r[6], 146v–148r[7], 149r–152r[8]. Dietrich maligns as Jew-like both clerical enemies and the mob of Catholics, while depicting rulers as guilty primarily of pursuing worldly interests and opening themselves to deception by the clergy. Johannes Bugenhagen took the same approach in his harmony on the Passion—see Evener, "Our Jews," 427–28—and this approach remained significant in the Lutheran tradition (including with Spangenberg; see below) as a way to censure, excuse, and persuade rulers.

35 LHP, 130r[2].

36 LHP, 135v–136r[4]. The twin lesson of *Geduld* and *Trost* is repeated at the conclusion of this sermon: LHP, 137v–138r[4]. John 15:20 ("Der knecht sol es nicht besser haben den sein Herr") is cited at LHP, 136r[4], then again in later sermons: 142r–v[6], 150v[8].

their heart in their inability to "tolerate" Christ. Likewise, the Roman clergy show themselves as "Judas-Children."[37]

Dietrich compares the judicial process against Christ and the processes used in his own day against evangelicals: the first "injustice (*unbilligkeyt*)," he asserts, is that both the high priests and papists set themselves up as accusers and judges; the second is the use of "lies and false witnesses." Dietrich fashions a series of pointed questions accusing Christ of keeping company with the wicked, of novel teaching, and of disregard for learning and authority: "Are you alone learned? Are we all fools?" In Dietrich's exegesis, the servant who strikes Christ for responding impudently to the high priests finds his successor in *Pfaffenknechten* and "blatherers" like Johann Cochlaeus and Georg Witzel—a one-time Lutheran whose defection was a sore spot.[38]

1.5 *The Passion as a Painting of Self and Other*

The use of Jewish characters from the New Testament to depict forms of papist hostility to evangelicals and the use of Judas to depict the descent into sin that evangelicals themselves had to fear continued in the sixth sermon, "How Christ is handed over to Pilate and Judas hangs himself." The New Testament story is presented as a source of visual reflection.[39] At the outset, Dietrich says it "paints a fine image" of the "beginning and source" of persecution, namely in the offense of the prideful at the Word.[40] He later says that the "terrifying example" of Judas is "diligently depicted (*fu*[*e*]*rgemalet*) so that we recognize there, as in a painting, the very manner and nature of sin and protect ourselves against it." Dietrich writes, "For this is the first color, with which one should paint sin, if one truly and genuinely paints it, that it seems a minor, insignificant, harmless thing. One doesn't worry about God's wrath." Sin is welcomed as a cuddly kitten, which sleeps and lets itself be stroked, but then awakes as a "ferocious" animal. One cannot protect against this sin except through God's special help. After the fall comes the assaults of conscience, inflamed by the devil, who ruined Judas and seeks to ruin all Christians. Dietrich laments that no one sees the end in the beginning—but he commends reflection on Judas to just that end. The image of Judas hanging unmasks sin, which "colors and adorns itself, and puts on a beautiful young mask (*Schembart*) so that one sees

---

37 LHP, 136r[4].

38 LHP, 136v–137r.

39 A later sermon makes use of Simon carrying Christ's cross as an image of the church's necessary suffering: LHP, 152v–153r[9].

40 LHP, 141v[6].

nothing ugly in it. Whoever could remove the mask right away, and wash away the makeup with a caustic lye, would flee from sin as from the devil."[41]

For those who have fallen into sin, however, the terrifying image of Judas needs to be rejected in favor of the image of mercy: Judas committed suicide because he allowed Satan to paint before him an image of damnation that occluded his view of mercy. He was unprepared for the trial because he "despised the Word and listened without diligence." "When sin awakes, preaches to you and troubles you, you must defend and preserve yourself with the Holy Gospel, which paints (*mallet*) Christ for you in this way, namely, that he suffered and paid for the sin of all the world. It paints God the almighty creator and Father thus, that he does not desire the death of the sinner … [but that] the sinner turn and live." Verbal and visual memory were to work together here, Dietrich advised: "Don't go to bed or get up before you have spoken a beautiful saying—or two, three, or four—to your heart [about God's forgiveness]." Dietrich recommended specific passages, commending their daily use as the "true soul medicine (*seel artzney*) that Judas lacks."[42]

1.6 *Willful Error*

Throughout the passion sermons, Dietrich reflects Luther's preoccupation with the will's role in religious error: if Luther and his followers had re-discovered the self-evident meaning of scripture, if the proclamation of that meaning effected faith in hearers, and if double predestination was unacceptable as an explanation for failure to hear in a way that produced faith, then blame had to be lodged in the sinners who heard the message but heard it not. While Pilate (like other temporal rulers) foolishly expected a divine reward for spilling innocent blood, Dietrich teaches, "the Jews" were "even more frivolous," for they called a curse upon themselves and their descendants. That curse came within 40 years and has lasted 1,500, Dietrich declares, yet the Jews remain "embittered" against the redeemer. Willfully deceived, they "delight in lies and error, they seek diligently to obscure scripture for themselves, and they cannot come to a right understanding."[43] It is important to note that Dietrich makes no attempt to blame rabbis for the distortion of scripture but speaks of Jews *en masse*. They are guilty in his view not of pure ignorance and error, but of stubborn refusal to accept truth that, on some level, they cannot deny. Here, Dietrich wanted again both to warn evangelicals about the dynamics of sin and

41 LHP, 142v–144r[6].
42 LHP, 144v–145r[6].
43 LHP, 151v[8].

despair and to explain an enemy whose very existence threatened to undermine evangelical certitude.[44]

In the final sermon of the cycle, there is a searching examination of the concept of willed error, as Dietrich describes the high priests' efforts to deny the resurrection: they have the tomb guarded because they have heard and understood Christ's promise of resurrection. Subsequently, they cannot deny what the guards have seen, but they buy the guards' silence rather than seeking forgiveness. All the while Christ's word is a "burning fire and gnawing worm in their hearts," and they "know in their hearts that Christ ... has raised from the dead"; but "possessed by more than one devil," they "adorn and comfort themselves with knowing lies." The papists continue this attitude, and like the high priests before them, they only "drive people to the truth" because their lies are coarse and obvious.[45]

Sermon 11, which stemmed from Luther himself,[46] teaches that Christ is the true priest who offers his own "body and blood" while praying for those who kill him, who were indeed "only servants and attendants (*knecht vnd diener*) of our sins." Christ's priesthood is contrary to appearances and worldly expectations, but Christ teaches it clearly in his words.[47] Thus, Luther polemicizes against Catholic clergy for claiming that "we ourselves should be priests, offer ourselves, and obtain eternal life through our own works," while they curse evangelicals for regarding Christ as "the one true priest." Their sin is not simple ignorance, he charges, but a malicious rejection of loud and clear truth. They are (as Isaiah depicts) "blind with seeing eyes"; they have "open ears" but do not hear, "a stubborn heart without understanding." Their disposition can only be explained as a curse of peculiar "blindness," for they too "hear and see" Christ who announces himself the true sacrifice and mediator between God and sinners.[48] For his own audience, Luther enjoins an exercise of seeing with the heart rather than the eyes; incorporated within Dietrich's cycle, Luther's words here underlined that the use of scripture as a painting of truth required spiritual vision, the eyes of faith rather than fallen reason and desire:

44 LHP, 152r[8]: The sermon explains that Pilate's line was destroyed for his role in the crucifixion, just as the Jews were punished. Thus, this story serves as a warning to princes and consolation to evangelicals, who ought not be troubled by the delay in God's vengeance against sixteenth-century persecutors.

45 LHP, 173r–174v[12].

46 See Note 8 *supra*.

47 See Note 17 *supra*.

48 LHP, 162v–163r[11].

> Therefore, let us open our hearts and see our priest Christ in his true adornment (*schmuck*). Beneath your eyes you will find no adornment in him, for how shamefully, miserably and wretchedly he hangs there. But see him in your heart; there you will find such a jewel and treasure—for which you will never again be able to thank him enough. First of all he is adorned with great, heartfelt obedience to his father … The second jewel is the great love he has for us … Outwardly one doesn't see such adornment, but inwardly one sees him just as his Word sufficiently testifies.[49]

1.7 *The Theology of the Cross, Courage in Suffering*

Throughout, the passion cycle invokes the idea that God's favor is received under contraries.[50] The theology of the cross served to encourage yielded acceptance of suffering and to provide a consoling epistemological framework to an afflicted body of Christians. According to Dietrich, the "true preacher or Christian" knows both that Christ is a king and that his kingdom is not of this world; "in this world he does nothing more than testify to the truth." Christian subjects must be like their king, who looked like "a poor beggar" and a "miserable, wretched person" before even a lesser ruler like Pilate. While Herod seeks and enjoys every earthly desire and the esteem of the world, Christ's kingdom consists of "giving the Holy Spirit, forgiveness of sins, and eternal life. This kingdom begins here on earth, but only in Word and faith; outside of Word and faith there is suffering and dying on earth, just as our king himself suffered and died."[51] Dietrich admonishes, "Whoever knows the way (*art*) of this king and his kingdom surrenders himself willingly (*gibt sich willig*) under the cross," knowing that the servant must suffer like the master and that temporal suffering will give way to eternal "joy and majesty." Thus, the Christian is "courageous even in the midst of trial and tribulation," whereas those who do not know

---

49 LHP, 163r–v[11].

50 Sermons 10 (Dietrich) and 11 (Luther), LHP, 156r–165v, deal extensively with the need to judge not by appearances but by the Word; both served Dietrich's insistence on visual recollection: one was to see the world through the image of scripture as the only way to avoid deceit. Sermon 11 teaches that Christ is truly highest priest and king, although in his torment he appears to be neither. The literature on Luther's "theology of the cross" is vast; one helpful article is Robert Kolb, "Luther's Theology of the Cross Fifteen Years after Heidelberg: Lectures on the Psalms of Ascent," *Journal of Ecclesiastical History* 60, no. 1 (January 2010), 69–85. See too Susan Schreiner's discussion of "appearances and reality" in Luther: *Are You Alone Wise?*, 323–32.

51 LHP, 150r–v[8]. Such advice sought to avert an undisciplined response of despair in the face of suffering; see also LHP, 152v–153r[9]. Luther lists an array of sufferings at the top of 153r.

the manner of Christ and his kingdom—who do not see through the theology of the cross—can only "be sorrowful, complain, murmur, be impatient, and finally completely despair." These ignorant ones regard Christ as an earthly king and thus interpret deprivation of "body and life and goods" as an indication of divine wrath. Dietrich makes use of the story of the two criminals crucified at Christ's side, explaining that one saw a failed temporal king, while the other understood the true nature of Christ the king and his kingdom.[52]

1.8 *Distinguishing the Christians' Cross from Sinners' Deserved Suffering, Seeing the Self as Cosmic Battleground*

The association of suffering with the truth was never a simple matter[53]—the wicked also suffered and sometimes with apparent patience. The ninth sermon accordingly used the image of Simon of Cyrene to elucidate a distinction between the cross of Christians and the mere suffering of the wicked, which is always (Dietrich says) a "well-deserved punishment." In the early years of the Reformation, Luther had sought to unmask the pride behind the suffering of papists and radicals, insisting that his opponents' suffering was self-chosen or embraced as an occasion to earn merit before God and the esteem of others.[54] These concerns remain evident in the present sermon, which directs polemic against monks, nuns, and Anabaptists while using Simon to teach both that the true cross is not self-chosen and that only Christ's cross wins salvation.[55] That said, Dietrich focuses primarily on morally undisciplined evangelicals, mentioning specifically both thieves and married people whose sexual transgressions bring "poverty of goods, shame, syphilis [literally, French disease] and all misfortune." These sinners are not victims of inevitable weakness but people unwilling to be directed to a better course. Thus, says Dietrich, "not all suffering is and is called a cross," but only underserved suffering "for the sake of the lord Christ, his Word, and confession." Indeed, true Christians "must know themselves as poor sinners" who deserve far more suffering than God sends them. When endured with such humility, their suffering is not primarily punishment but a "true, holy cross" and a divine help to salvation. The holy ones are persecuted by the devil and the world not because they are sinners, but on account of their faith in the Word, their desire to follow God's will, and their eagerness to convert others. Satan afflicts their bodies with sickness and their

52 LHP, 150v–151r[8].

53 See Evener, "*Enemies of the Cross*," esp. 6–7.

54 Ibid.

55 LHP, 154v[9].

consciences with "sorrow, melancholy, terror, and the like," and he also lays hold of their temporal goods, as in the case of Job.[56]

Consistent with the goal of teaching believers not to let sorrow oppress their hearts, Dietrich uses the story of Simon to console the faithful and encourage prayer grounded in "hope of rescue and help"; hope entices to prayer, he says, whereas the memory that one is a sinner makes one "cold and lazy" with respect to prayer. Fear grips the heart and keeps one from turning to God. Thus, the prayer of the sufferer should contain an admission of guilt but also a request for God's help and vengeance against the evil one. Dietrich provides the words for such a prayer, promising they will make the heart "cheerful (*munter*) ... consoled (*gestrost*) and courageous (*wacher*)."[57]

2 Dietrich's Luther and Spangenberg

Comparison of the Dietrich-Luther sermons to Spangenberg's can illustrate some of the significant continuities and variations that were possible within the frameworks established by Luther and developed by Dietrich. A striking discontinuity between Spangenberg and the Dietrich cycle is that Spangenberg does not commend visual recollection of the passion; he does, however, describe the passion as a "library" containing all necessary books for the Christian[58]—thus, he continued to hold up the passion as an epistemological framework for assessing one's own religious experiences and encountering the world. In prefatory materials, Spangenberg outlines the purpose of preaching and contemplating the passion—one must know why Christ suffered and died, what the benefits are, and how those benefits are received. Christ bears the "pain, death, punishment and hell" sinners have deserved, and sinners receive this gift by faith; from faith comes consolation in trials, the ability to submit to God's will in humility, the work of imitation, and gratitude. Consistent with the dialectic of Law and Gospel, one must know that one's own sins caused the crucifixion—along with God's mercy and the Jews' wickedness, Spangenberg explains—and one must be terrified that divine wrath

---

56 LHP, 153r–154r[9]. The caveat that the suffering of the faithful is not "primarily (*vornehmlich*)" punishment for sin preserves an understanding of suffering as benevolent punishment intended to spur repentance; Dietrich reminds his audience that "God is also accustomed to punish his own on account of sin."

57 LHP, 154r–v[9].

58 CSP, B7v–8r.

did not spare even God's Son. This Law prepares one to trust that Christ has taken on sin and that sinners become pleasing to God through faith.[59]

In teaching Christians to use the passion as a library, Spangenberg employs extensive allegory, perhaps reflecting the study of medieval commentators like Ludolphus of Saxony, even though Spangenberg's allegories consistently convey evangelical doctrine. Thus, within his overarching perspective on scripture as a clear instruction book for understanding oneself and one's world, Spangenberg does commend an exercise of searching for the ever deeper meaning of particular images, figures, or stories—including those surrounding the anointing of Jesus's feet by Mary,[60] the ass and the foal ridden by Jesus on Palm Sunday,[61] Christ's triumphal procession into Jerusalem,[62] Christ's hunger and the fig tree that Christ curses,[63] Caiaphas' torn clothing and Christ's undivided garment,[64] the women who follow Christ to Calvary weeping,[65] and much more.[66]

All that said, as Spangenberg's exegesis reaches the passion itself—he spends a great deal of time on preliminary events—the alignment of contemporary opponents with Judas, the high priests, and the Jews in general appears as a pervasive strategy. Whereas Dietrich used Judas as an image of both reckless evangelical sinners and papist clergy who betrayed Christ for financial gain, Spangenberg found in Judas primarily the image of false *evangelical* clergy who betrayed the church for financial or professional gain or to avoid persecution. Spangenberg's *Passio* bitterly attacks those who were willing to compromise with the emperor following the Lutheran loss in the Schmalkald War—they are "evangelical hypocrites," "eigennu[e]tzige Mundchristen," "vergleichern der Religion."[67] Spangenberg aligns Roman clergy primarily with the high priests,

---

59 CSP, A2r–7v, B1r–C3v (the dedicatory epistle and first sermon, both exegeting Isaiah 53: 4–6).

60 CSP, 6r–v.

61 CSP, F8v–G1r.

62 CSP, G2r–3v.

63 CSP, H4r–5r.

64 CSP, Bb1r, Gg5r–v (here also allegorizing the lots cast for the garment).

65 CSP, Ff6v; according to Spangenberg they signify improper contemplation of the passion that rouses one to hatred of the Jews rather than recognition of one's own guilt; here, Spangenberg was dependent on Luther's 1519 sermon, *Ein Sermon von der Betrachtung des heiligen Leidens Christi* (see Note 17 supra). See further Ff 7r–v.

66 For further examples, see CSP L6v, N8r–O1v, Ff5r–6r, Gg2r, Hh4v, Jj1r, Kk1v–3r, Kk4v, Kk6v, Kk7r.

67 CSP, K7r, L2r, L3v, T3r–v; X2v; X2v–3v, Z4v, Bb4v. The discussion of Judas' kiss describes how Judas as a false follower gave Christ over to his "worst enemies, the Jews," just as "false

sometimes also with the scribes, the Pharisees, or the Jews more generally.[68] The Jew-Papists are the open enemies to whom the Judas-evangelicals betray true teaching and true believers. As for Luther and Dietrich, the Jew-Papist connection for Spangenberg explains rejection of the Word and the persecution of evangelical faithful. Spangenberg offers a sophisticated discussion of "willed ignorance," in one instance appealing to legal terminology to argue that even if the Jews were genuinely ignorant of Christ's messianic and divine identity, they were obligated to learn it from scripture and the prophets just as a citizen is obligated to know the law (*Stadtrecht*).[69] More often, Spangenberg like Luther and Dietrich presents a complicated image of simultaneous knowing and not knowing.[70]

evangelical hypocrites" commend true religion "to the papists as its public enemies." X5v–6v. Like Dietrich, Spangenberg faults Judas for assuming that his sin exceeded God's mercy; but he quickly dismisses Judas' regret as the "gallows sorrow" of one who sinned against his own conscience, the Gospel, and right teachers and hearers. He turns this into a warning against those who supported the Interim. Cc2v–3r; see also Cc5r, Cc6r. In the final sermon of his work, Spangenberg teaches that the Jews wanted to conceal their responsibility for Christ's death by pushing that responsibility on others (Ll8r), just like those "secret enemies and traitors of the Gospel still today" (Mm1v).

68 CSP, E4r–v, G7r–v, H5r, I2v–3r, X3v–4r, Y8v–Z1v, Aa6v–7r, Aa8r–v, CC4v–5v, Gg4r–5v (here, Spanengberg aligns persecutors of truth past and present; such references do not necessarily separate Interimists and Adiaphorists from Catholics), Kk7v, Mm2v–4v. In the final section cited here, blanket references to Jews and papists are prominent, and one marginal note refers to the *Blutdurst der Papisten*, who want to see the land run with Lutheran blood up to the knees. Throughout Spangenberg's work, the papists' manipulation of temporal authorities to persecute the evangelical faithful is presented as identical to the high priests' interaction with Pilate; Pilate himself serves as a positive and then negative example to instruct contemporary rulers. See esp. Cc6r–Ee8v, as well as Aa2v–4v, Cc2r. Spangenberg sees the common mob ("gemeine Po[e]bel") of both his own day and the New Testament narratives as gripped by temporal interests and the desire to please human beings; thus, they are easily driven to act "without reason and understanding against the truth." See Bb3r, Ee3r–v.

69 CSP, Gg3r–v, which also claims that some Jews knew outright what they were doing.

70 Like Luther, Bugenhagen, and Dietrich, Spangenberg teaches that God punished the Jews' willed ignorance with inability to see, and he uses this point to warn evangelicals; see CSP Ff8r, Kk1v, Kk4r, Mm1v, Mm3v. In the first of these citations, one reads, "What the Lord Christ now threatens for the stubborn Jews [is] not only temporal punishments but also spiritual anguish, grief, blindness, doubt and stubbornness. That is also threatened for all those who capriciously and knowingly attack the truth and pious Christians." Rhetoric against Jews can be especially strong in the final sermon, which is partly dependent on Johannes Spangenberg's *Die historia Vom Leiden vnd sterben vnsers HERRn Jhesu Christi. Sampt dem XXII. vnd LXiiii. psalm Dauid* ... (Magdeburg 1543), VD 16 S 7836; the elder Spangenberg doesn't draw connections between papists and Jews, however. Cyriacus

The treatment of Caiaphas is illuminating. Spangenberg argues that Caiaphas "should have known" from scripture and from Christ's miracles that he "was the true messiah and God's Son," but the high priest was "deceived" by "self-interest" and "took offense that Christ did not appear as a worldly king." He was "partly convinced in his own conscience, but he nevertheless followed reason and outward appearance more than God's Word." Spangenberg adds, "That is also the hindrance still today, as a result of which the most powerful and wise people on earth cannot come to true knowledge of Christ and his Word."[71]

Fearing a repetition of the military defeat and readiness to compromise that followed the Schmalkald War, Spangenberg identifies *Sicherheit* or *Vermessenheit* in the face of anticipated but not present persecution as the chief spiritual danger for his hearers and readers.[72] Less frequently, he warns of *Vermessenheit* with respect to a broader range of trials.[73] Spangenberg teaches believers to rely on faith in the Word rather than reason and sense perception[74]—yet he refuses to attribute the failure of compromisers to misjudgment rather than fear and self-interest. Dietrich's worry about frivolous sinning finds little reception here, even though the terminology of *Sicherheit* or *Vermessenheit* remains continuous. That said, both Dietrich and Spangenberg were united in seeking to inculcate an attitude of courageous confession in the

---

depicts the punishment of the godless as a chief consolation for the faithful, part of the *Trostlehre* of David (a figure of Christ) in Psalm 64; see Ll4v, MM2v.

71 CSP, Aa6v.

72 See CSP, L6r–v, T1v–2v, T3v, T7v–8r, U8v–X2r (here Spangenberg also complains about evangelicals' indulgence in frivolous pleasures while the church throughout the world suffers persecution), X3r–v, Y2r–v, Z3v–4v, Z6r–v, Z7v. Some of these references do not necessarily pertain only to persecution, although that is the primary form of suffering described as Spangenberg relates the text to his context. Spangenberg admonishes Christians not to rely on their own powers, to pray to God for preservation in trials—he can call this stance *Demut* (T2v, Y2v, Z4v)—and to have confident faith that no persecution or other suffering comes upon the faithful except with God's permission (see esp. X1v).

73 See e.g. CSP, D2r–6r, T4v, T6r–v (citing Bernard of Clairvaux). Spangenberg interprets John 14 as a *Trostpredigt* for manifold trials (M2r–3r, M6v, N3r–v), and he warns that Christians must judge by faith in the Word not reason and sense perception (M4v, M5v, N1r). Spangenberg discusses Christ's promise of the Holy Spirit here at length, M7r–N2r.

74 See preceding citation.

face of persecution[75] and patient submission to God's will in all suffering—evangelical *Gelassenheit*, enabled by faith.[76]

3 Conclusion

This brief summary of Spangenberg's expansive book serves only to illustrate the variation that could emerge in strategies for teaching discernment and self-discipline in the Lutheran passion tradition, within which Dietrich's sermons under Luther's name occupied a central place. My primary goal in this essay has been to show that equipping believers for discernment and self-discipline was indeed a central goal of this preaching and devotional literature, and that sophisticated strategies were used to encourage the internalization of doctrine, epistemological framework, and habits of discipline. The passion was offered as hermeneutical key to scripture—to the Law and the Gospel—on the one hand, and as lens for viewing one's own experiences and contexts on the other. Dietrich's sermons commended a strategy of visual memorization and recollection, whereas Spangenberg commended allegorizing scriptural passages along evangelical lines. Both Dietrich and Spangenberg drew extensive connections between New Testament and sixteenth-century figures, including to depict the face of sin and willful ignorance. For both authors, Christ was the model for facing trials and persecution, while the existence and thriving of the enemy—for Spangenberg, this included the papist and the Interimist or Adiaphorist enemy—was a pastoral crisis in light of the conviction that scripture was clear and right teaching was a vehicle for the Holy Spirit. Before all else, Spangenberg wanted to avert future betrayal.

The aspirations and anxieties that Susan Schreiner has shown to be pervasive in early modern religion—the yearning for certitude of doctrine and

75 Spangenberg attacks the temptation to *Stillschweigen* at CSP, G3r–v, X4v, Z2r, Z3r, Z4v, Z6r, Aa7v, Dd3v, Hh6r, and Hh8r. Spangenberg treads carefully in explaining passages where Christ refused to answer accusation: silence might sometimes be appropriate, but never silence that amounted to denial of truth. See Aa5r–6v, Dd4r. The figure of Joseph of Arimathea causes Spangenberg to caution against despising "secret disciples," even as Joseph's request for Christ's body serves Spangenberg's more frequent demand for open testimony: Kk5r–v.

76 CSP, G4r–5r, T7r, T8r–U1r, U2r, X1v, Y7v, Z2v–3r, Bb2r–3r, Gg2v, Hh4v, Hh8v. On the perception that God imposes the cross and suffering more on the pious than the wicked, see Ff8r–Gg1r. Spangenberg briefly states the positive ends of God's discipline for God's children, and he reminds that the wicked will ultimately be damned. For critique of self-chosen crosses, Gg1v.

salvation; the fear of deceptive inner experiences and outward appearances[77]—shaped the passion devotion commended to believers by Dietrich and Spangenberg. The believer was to be assured of forgiveness and of belonging to the true church, despite God's very real wrath over sin and God's seeming favor for the Roman party with its history, pomp, wealth, and political sway. The passion was offered as a painting (Dietrich) or a library (Spangenberg) to give believers a new epistemological framework—a new way of perceiving and analyzing, of feeling and acting, in response to the world and their own experiences. Yet the resulting life involved constant denial of desire and of reason—fallen reason which justifies the claims of pleasure, comfort, and self-direction. Until eternity dawned, the believer could only live in hope and trust that things were not as they seemed. The need to construct this self, both confident and divided against itself and the world of appearances, helps to explain why Luther, Dietrich, and Spangenberg gave the passion—with its paradoxical display of triumph underneath apparent humiliation and defeat—such a central role in their lay pedagogical and devotional work.

77 See Schreiner, *"Are You Alone Wise?"* 262f.

PART 3

Into Modernity

CHAPTER 11

Visions and Prophets in Seventeenth-Century Lutheran Germany: The Case of Jacob Fabricius

Jonathan Strom

In recent years, prophecy has become a topic of interest for scholars who have wrestled with the impact of the Protestant Reformation and the changes in the confessional culture, particularly Lutheranism.[1] This concern for prophecy and how it both challenged and undergirded the authority of theologians and the ordained clergy intersects with one of the central themes of Susan Schreiner's work on authority and certainty in the early modern era.[2] The seventeenth century proved to be a decisive period among Lutherans, especially those in Germany, for the ways in which prophecy shaped debates around authority, especially clerical authority, in the church. One episode, on which I will focus below, looks at debates around prophets and visions within Lutheran Orthodoxy in the first half of the seventeenth century. Although little known in the historiography, the debate between Jacob Fabricius, Superintendent in Stettin, and Jacob Stolterfoth, pastor in Lübeck, helped determine the boundaries of debate around legitimate lay prophecy.[3] Indeed, Fabricius' more expansive view, found some initial favor, but eventually lost out among those Pietists later in the seventeenth who remained within the confessional Lutheran church, making such lay prophecy almost exclusively the province

---

1 See for instance, G. Sujin Pak, *The Reformation of Prophecy: Early Modern Interpretations of the Prophet and Old Testament Prophecy*. (New York: Oxford University Press, 2018); Jürgen Beyer, *Lay prophets in Lutheran Europe* (*c. 1550–1700*), (Leiden: Brill, 2017). Leigh Penman, *Hope and Heresy: The Problem of Chiliasm in Lutheran Confessional Culture, 1570–1630*, (Dordrecht: Springer Netherlands, 2019); Lionel Laborie, Ariel Hessayon, eds., *Early Modern Prophecies in Transnational, National and Regional contexts*, 3 vols. (Leiden: Brill, 2021).

2 Susan Schreiner, *Are You Alone Wise? The Search for Certainty in the Early Modern Era*. (Oxford: Oxford University Press, 2011).

3 On the lack of discussion in the historigraphy, see the comment by Hans Schneider, "Hochmann von Hochenau and Inspirationism. A Newly Discovered Letter." *Brethren Life and Thought* 25 (1980), 213–214. See also my earlier article: Jonathan Strom, "Jacob Fabricius, Friedrich Breckling und die Debatte um Visionen und neue Offenbarungen," in: *Der radikale Pietismus. Perspektiven der Forschung*, ed. Wolfgang Breul, Marcus Meier, und Lothar Vogel (Vandenhoeck & Ruprecht: Göttingen, 2010) as well as more recently, Kofler, *Prophetie*, 176–281.

 | DOI:10.1163/9789004527843_012

of radical Pietists and other dissenters. Fabricius's openness underscores the diverse streams of Lutheran thought at the beginning of the seventeenth century that had not yet coalesced into rigid lines that it came to represent later.

Prophecy could encompass a range of meanings in early modern Protestantism that ranged from unfolding scripture's full meaning to new revelations and visions that could predict or foretell the future.[4] The renewed emphasis on biblical authority during the Reformation made it inevitable that Old Testament models of prophecy would take on new relevance even as Luther and others struggled to contain more radical models of prophecy. The Zwickau prophets or Thomas Müntzer challenged the authority of more mainstream reformers like Martin Luther, who in turn sought to marginalize the radicals even as they continued to embrace an understanding of prophecy closely bound to the interpretation of the Word of God and linked to exemplars in the Old Testament. Both David Steinmetz and G. Sujin Pak have described a kind of "domestication" of prophecy over the course of the sixteenth century in which biblical models of prophecy that originally animated lay interpretation of scriptures and the priesthood of all believers were harnessed to support the authority of the new Protestant clergy.[5] This tendency towards a consolidation of clerical authority is part of broader trends in confessionalized culture of the sixteenth-century Protestantism and especially Lutheranism where dynamic and sometimes destabilizing elements of the early Reformation, such as the common priesthood or the priesthood of all believers, were increasingly marginalized in confessional forms of Protestantism.[6]

Despite the domestication of biblical prophecy, radical prophets still arose that challenged confessional authorities at the end of the sixteenth century and early seventeenth century, particularly as tied to apocalyptic expectations and millenarian calculations.[7] But as Jürgen Beyer and Susanne Kofler have demonstrated lay prophecy did not entirely disappear within confessional

4 An excellent historical overview is in Pak, *Reformation of Prophecy*, pp. 3–28.

5 Pak, *Reformation of Prophecy*, p. 333, and David Steinmetz, "The Domestication of Prophecy in the Early Reformation," in: *The Word Leaps the Gap: Essays on Scripture and Theology in Honor of Richard B. Hays*, ed. J. Ross Wagner, et al. (Grand Rapids: Eerdmans, 2008), 532–542.

6 On, for instance, the marginalization of the priesthood of all believers and its partial recovery in the seventeenth century, see Jonathan Strom, "The Common Priesthood and the Pietist Challenge for Ministry and Laity," in *The Pietist Impulse in Christianity*, edited Christian T. Collins Winn et al.

7 See for instance, Robin Bruce Barnes, *Prophecy and Gnosis, Apocalypticism in the Wake of the Lutheran Reformation*, (Stanford: Stanford University Press, 1988); Leigh T. I. Penman, *Hope and Heresy: The Problem of Chiliasm in Lutheran Confessional Culture, 1570–1630*, (Dordrecht: Springer Netherlands, 2019).

Lutheranism.[8] These cases of lay prophecy that included visions and auditory revelations were distinct from the form of the biblical prophecy described by Pak, and they were often challenging to civil and ecclesial authorities in practice but often not fraught in terms of doctrine. On one level they show how the supernatural imbued everyday life for many Christians, Protestants included, but on another they also signal a plurality of Lutheran confessional cultures in the seventeenth century in which questions of new revelation and even the nature of the biblical canon were not as decisively resolved as sometimes assumed.[9]

During the turmoil in the early Thirty Years War in which loyalties were often strained amid shifting alliances and even betrayals among fellow religionists, a debate within confessional Lutheranism in Germany arose that illustrated the lack of resolution on questions of prophecy and authority. The issue for us is not really about radical prophets who fundamentally challenged the authority of the Lutheran church, such as Johann Ludwig Gifftheil who modeled himself on the warrior-angel of Michael in Daniel 12 and stormed the pulpit in 1634 in Tübingen with a drawn sword proclaiming the imminent judgment of God.[10] Nor is it about a case of delusional prophecy in Königsberg in 1636, when Johann Adam Adelgreiff claimed to have received a vision of seven angels who revealed to him that he was to represent corporeally the person of God the father on earth. After refusing to recant before the clergy under the threat of torture and execution, he was executed for blasphemy and his remains burned.[11] Even moderate proponents of visions, as we will see below, recognized these as *Schwärmer* (enthusiasts) or mentally unstable. Rather the

8 Beyer, *Lay Prophets*; Koffler, *Prophetie.*

9 Thomas Kaufmann has criticized the notion of a uniform confessional Lutheranism. See Thomas Kaufmann, "What is Lutheran Confessional Culture?" in: *Religion as an Agent of Change: Crusades—Reformation—Pietism*, ed. Per Ingesman, (Leiden: Brill, 2016).

10 On Gifftheil, see F. Fritze, "Friedrich Gifftheil" *Blätter für württembergische Kirchengeschichte* 40 (1940): 90–105, as well as Gottfried Arnold, *Unpartheyische Kirchen- und Ketzer-historie: vom Anfang des Neuen Testaments bis auf das Jahr Christi 1688.* Parts 3 & 4 (Frankfurt/Main, 1729), pp. 100–102. On Gifftheil's later involvement in millenarian movements in Britain, see Kenneth Gibson, "Apocalyptic and Millenarian Prophecy in Early Stuart Europe. Philip Ziegler, Ludwig Friedrich Gifftheil and the Fifth Monarchy," in *Prophecy: The Power of Inspired Language in History, 1300–2000*, ed. Bertrand Traithe and Tim Thornton Thrupp 1997. Beyer, it is worth noting, does not include Gifftheil as a Lutheran lay prophet because he "deliberately left the Lutheran church." Beyer, *Lay Prophets*, p. 12.

11 Arnold describes the case of Adelgreiff, *Unpartheyische Kirchen- und Ketzer-historie*, pp. 50–51.

question was whether within forms of confessional Lutheranism, lay prophecy and new revelation could be accepted at all.

In 1629, Jacob Fabricius, the Lutheran court preacher in Stettin, published a number of tracts that contained the visions and ecstatic experiences of a number of Protestant women. The late 1620s were years of heightened eschatological expectations for Protestants in Germany. Inflation, crop failure, and most of all the ongoing war colored attitudes in Germany. Christian IV of Denmark had been decisively defeated by the Imperial forces under Wallenstein. The German Protestant princes were themselves deeply fractured, Catholic forces seemed to be in the ascendant, and the Edict of Restitution issued by the Emperor demanded the return of all church property secularized after the Reformation. The mood of Protestants was dark and pessimistic about its future.[12]

The court preacher Jacob Fabricius was clearly fascinated with ecstatic visions. Firsthand, he encountered a local woman, Benigna König, whose visions at court in Stettin had become a sensation, and he published them in a pamphlet with a dedication to the Pomeranian duke and duchess.[13] Later that year, he gathered the visions from König, Christina Poniatovia, the daughter of a Bohemian pastor, whose visions Comenius would later repeatedly publish, and Margaretha Heidewetter from Cottbus, and published them as *Göttliches Wunderbuch* or *Divine Miracle Book* to provide, as the foreword described it, comforting examples of faith amid the trials of the ongoing war but also to chastise the faithless Protestants und urge them to turn away from what he saw as their "apostasy" and repent.[14] Fabricius, however, was no religious radical, and he was one of many Lutheran clergy to intensify their calls for repentance in the midst of the Thirty Years War. He had studied at the Lutheran universities of Rostock and Greifswald, receiving his his doctorate from the latter, and

12 On this, see Hartmut Lehmann. *Das Zeitalter des Absolutismus: Gottesgnadentum und Kriegsnot.* (Stuttgart: Kohlhammer, 1980), pp. 110–112 and 124–27. See also Barnes, *Prophecy and Gnosis,* pp. 249–256.

13 Jacob Fabricius, *Historischer Bericht oder Erzehlung Der Christlichen Sprüche und Schrifftmeßigen Wort/ Welche Benigna Königs/ Ein Gottsehliges Mägdlein/ im Fürstlichen Alten Stettinschen Frawen Zimmer/ bey ihren gehabten Neun unterschiedlichen Entzückungen/ in gegenwart vieler Personen/ mit gantz lauter Stimme/ geredet hat.* Alten Stettin, 1629. Koffler discusses further editions in 1629 and gives in-depth analysis. Koffler, 119–165.

14 *Göttliches Wunder-Buch. Darinnen auffgezeichnet und geschrieben stehen, I. Himlische Offenbahrungen und Gesichte, einer gottfürchtigen Jungfrawen auß Böhmen, vom Zustand der Christlichen Kirchen ... II. Propheceyungen, Klagreden, und ernstliche Bußvermahnungenm eines frommen Christlichen Mägdleins zu Cottbus in NiederLausitz. III. Christliche Sprüche, und schrifftmäßige geistreiche Reden/ einer gottsehligen Jungfrawen, im Fürstlichen Frawenzimmer zu Stettin in Pommern,* s.l. 1629. A second edition appeared in 1630. Fabricius' editorship is likely but not entirely certain.

he was the court preacher for Duke Bogislav XIV in Stettin.[15] What was unusual about Fabricius was his explicit approval of visions and lay prophecy in calling Protestants to account during this period. As a proponent of lay visions, Fabricius is representative of an ambivalence within the Lutheran tradition on the nature of revelation and exclusivity of scripture. The visions of laymen and women, even when doctrinally unobjectionable, could nevertheless constitute a challenge to clerical authority in the seventeenth century.

Fabricius was one of the leading churchmen of North Germany, and when Gustavus Adolphus landed in Pomerania in 1630 he chose Fabricius to be Superintendent of his military chaplains and his personal confessor. Fabricius traveled with the Swedish forces, and remained close to the king. When Gustavus Adolphus was killed at the battle of Lützen, according to legend it was Fabricius who rallied the retreating troops by singing a Lutheran hymn and helped prevent a complete rout.[16] He returned to Stettin in 1632 where he continued to grapple with the question of visions and ecstatic experiences.

The Baltic cities and North Germany were rife with visionaries and prophets during the 1620s and 1630s. Some of these were benign and not cause of great concern. For instance, Jürgen Beyer has described the visions of a layman in Lübeck, whose descriptions of apparitions urging the city to repair its relationship with an abandoned graveyard were not strongly contested by the city's clergy, even if they expressed skepticism about their validity.[17] Others presented greater challenges to the authority of the clergy like the example of Gifftheil cited above. Stettin, the major Pomeranian port city, saw more than its share of prophetic visionaries during the 1630s, and, Jakob Fabricius, who had since become General Superintendent in Pomerania after his campaigns with Gustav Adolph, continued his interest in them. In the mid-1630s, he took

15 On his biography, see Friedrich Wagnitz, Jacob Fabricius (1593–1654) Herzoglicher und Königlicher Hofprediger im Dreißigjährigen Kriege in: *Persönlichenkeiten aus der pommerschen Herzogszeit, Teil 2*, (Kiel, 2003), 28–51, und Berthold Kitzig, *Gustav Adolf, Jacobus Fabricius und Michael Altenburg, die drei Urheber des Liedes Verzage nicht, du Häuflein Klein!* Göttingen, 1935. See also briefly, Kofler, p. 227.

16 See the story recounted in Russell Frank Weigley, *The Age of Battles:The Quest for Decisive Warfare from Breitenfeld to Waterloo*, (Bloomington: Indiana University Press, 2004), pp. 33–34 as well as other accounts such as Richard Brzezinski, *Lützen 1632: Climax of the Thirty Years War*, (Westport: Praeger, 2005), p. 74.

17 Jürgen Beyer expands on this case in detail, Beyer, *Lay Prophets*, pp. 133–154. He sees lay prophecy in cases like this as providing an opportunity to speak out on matters of common concern rather than as criticism of the clergy or church. See also Jürgen Beyer, "A Lübeck Prophet in Local and Lutheran Context." In *Popular religion in Germany and Central Europe, 1400–1800*, edited by Bob Scribner and Trevor Johnson, 166–182. London: Macmillan, 1996.

up correspondence with Johann Warner (also Werner), a well-traveled peasant from Meissen and visionary.[18] Warner began having visions in 1629 in which he predicted that the Swedish king would save Protestant Germany. Many of his other visions were highly critical of Lutherans, who in Warner's words had "whored with Babel" through their actions during the war.[19] His critical visions and accompanying calls to repentance intensified after the Peace of Prague in 1635, when in the eyes of Warner, many Lutherans theologians encouraged the Protestant princes to accept unfavorable terms of the treaty and acquiesce to Imperial demands. He was highly popular among the strongest Imperial critics, especially the Swedish forces, and for a time he traveled with entourage of Swedish field marshal Johan Banér.[20]

According to Fabricius's opponents, Fabricius initiated contact with Warner when he was travelling with the Swedish troops and in fact sent him a number of queries about passages in scripture that appeared obscure.[21] Many of his colleagues were appalled that the Superintendent showed such interest in the visions of this peasant prophet, though they were not entirely surprised given his pervious interest and publications. Arriving in Stettin on Banér's recommendation, he was received warmly by Fabricius who took him up into his household. Fabricius was fascinated with Warner and examined him closely on the basis of his Lutheran faith. While there were some questions about the Warner's understanding of justification and repentance, Fabricius judged him to be a "good pious Christian and modest man, who had nothing to do with the Weigelians or other enthusiasts or erring spirits."[22] Fabricius even introduced Warner to his colleagues who regarded him warily. Fabricius helped prepare Warner's visions for publication that then appeared in the spring of

18 Many of the documents to this interaction and the subsequent controversy are found in: Caspar Heinrich Starck, *Lubeca Lutherano-Evangelica, das ist, der Kayserlichen, Freyen und des Heil. Römischen Reichs Hanse- und Handel-Stadt Lübeck Kirchen-Historie*, Hamburg, 1724, pp. 1014ff, here p. 1015. The originals along with other documents not found in Starck are in the archives in Lübeck: Archiv der Hansastadt Lübeck (AHL). AHL, Geistliches Ministerium 6.0–1, Tomus IV, 732ff.

19 Arnold, *Unpartheyische Kirchen- und Ketzer-historie*, p. 234. Barnes gives a short account of Warner's prophecy and noted that many orthodox Lutherans applauded his political prophecy. Barnes, *Prophecy*, pp. 253–254.

20 Ibid., and Johannes Micrälius, "Des Johannes Micrälius eigenhändige Fortsetzung seiner Bücher vom alten Pommerlande, enthaltend die Geschichten des Jahres 1638," *Baltische Studien* 3 (1835), p. 147. Mircrälius was Fabricius's brother-in-law. Kofler, *Prophetie*, p. 231. Beyer is especially strong on Warner's relationship to the Swedish forces. Beyer, *Lay Prophets*, pp. 172–183.

21 Starck, *Lubeca Lutherano-Evangelica*, p. 1015.

22 Micrälius, "Eigenhändige Fortsetzung," p. 147.

1638. These chronicled the origins of his visions from 1629 through his most recent, and contained at the end a vigorous defense of his Lutheran orthodoxy and a strong denial that he was in any way an enthusiast.[23] Warner's visions and especially their publication initiated a new round of controversy in the city. Some clergy accused him of being an "*Irrgeist*," an "erring spirit," and were especially irritated that Fabricius not only stood by him and defended Warner in a sermon but actively aided him in the publication of the tract.[24] In fact, several suspected that Fabricius was responsible for much of the text since they doubted a peasant could have the Biblical knowledge to write the document.[25]

The clerical opponents of Fabricius—a majority of the Stettin clerical council (*Geistliches Ministerium*)—received no support from the Swedish authorities in Stettin, who tacitly or perhaps not so tacitly supported Fabricius and reproved the clergy who brought the controversy into the pulpits. Seeking theological condemnation, the clergy in Stettin turned to the Lübeck clerical council. The clergy in Lübeck had been in the forefront in the 1630s in their criticisms of spiritualists and visionaries. On behalf of the clerical councils in Lüneburg, Hamburg, and Lübeck, Superintendent Nicolaus Hunnius composed a tract, *Extensive Account of the New Prophets* in 1634 that was particularly aimed at the distribution of mystical literature and was aimed at Paul Felgenhauer and other spiritualists rather than visionaries like Warner.[26] But that same year, Jacob Stolterfoth, pastor at the Marienkirche wrote a booklet against visions *Consideratio Visionum, Or Scriptural Consideration, How One Should Today Treat Visions* that appeared in at least three editions in 1630s.[27]

In the hopes that they would find support against of Fabricius's position many of the Stettin clergy appealed to the Lübeck Ministerium to offer

23 *Johan Warners Auß Bockendorff/ im Lande Meissen bürtig/ selbst eigene Beschreibung etzlicher Visionen, Welche ihm sind von Gott/ wegen des Zustandes der Lutherischen Kirchen und ihrer Widerwertigen/ innerhalb Neun Jahren/ gezeiget worden* (n.p., 1638).

24 Micrälius, "Eigenhändige Fortsetzung," p. 148.

25 Starck, *Lubeca Lutherano-Evangelica*, p. 1015.

26 Nikolaus Hunnius, *Außführlicher Bericht Von Der Newen Propheten/* (*die sich Erleuchtete/ Gottesgelehrte/ und Theosophos nennen*) *Religion/ Lehr unnd Glauben/ damit der Satan die Kirche Gottes auffs newe zu verunruhigen sich unterstehet*, (Lübeck: 1634). On the background, Wolf-Dieter Hauschild, *Kirchengeschichte Lübecks: Christentum und Bürgertum in neun Jahrhunderten*, (Schmidt-Römhild: Lübeck, 1981) p. 302. See also Theodor Schulze, "Das Ministeirum Tripoliltanum (1535–1712)", *Lübeckische Blätter* (1896), 400–401.

27 Jacob Stolterfoth: *Consideratio Visionum: Oder Schrifftmessiges Bedencken, Was von Gesichtern heutiges Tages zu halten sey / Aus Liebe der Warheit, unnd den Einfältigen zur Nachrichtung* (Lübeck, 1634). An additional edition followed in 1634 and another with a slightly different title in 1636. Briefly on Stolterfoth's arguments, see Beyer, *Lay Prophets*, pp. 194–196.

a judgment of Warner's visions and Fabricius's "irresponsible" actions. They explicitly cited Stolterfoth's book and darkly hinted that one of Fabricius' allies, the rector of the *Stadtschule* was preparing a refutation of Stolterfoth. Beyond an explicit reproof of Fabricius, the clergy sought approval that they could openly preach against the visions and visionaries in the pulpit.[28]

While clearly sympathetic, the Lübeck clergy did not go as far as the Stettin clergy wanted. They wrote that they hoped the Superintendent would consult with his colleagues. They were openly skeptical of Warner's visions, but because they found no particular theological errors, they were hesitant to condemn them publicly and urged the clergy in Stettin to reach agreement with the Superintendent on the matter rather than allow their differences to become public.[29] Superintendent Hunnius wrote Fabricius and admonished him to be careful of such visions and remain "with God's written Word as the infallible guide of the whole of Christianity." Hunnius urged him to consult with his colleagues before publishing anything further on visions and to reach a consensus with them on the matter to avoid further controversy in the "Christian congregation of Stettin."[30] The Lübeck clergy acted hastily, however, by responding without first getting additional information from Fabricius.

Their intervention in fact drew an angry response from Fabricius who denied any wrongdoing and accused his Stettin colleagues of misrepresenting the situation and questioning his orthodoxy. He defended Warner, "the pious peasant, who hadn't offended one single person to this day with his language or his life" and sent Hunnius documents showing how he had sought the opinions of his colleagues in the matter.[31] In fact, the one-sided account of the Stettin clergy put Hunnius and the Lübeck Clerical council in a difficult position, and while they still considered Warner's visions highly suspect, they refused to say that the visions were necessarily inspired from the devil, as the opponents of Fabricius had hoped they would in light of their pronouncements against prophecy in earlier publications. Further, the Lübeck clergy now admonished the Stettin clergy to reach a brotherly agreement with the Superintendent rather than publicly debate the issue.[32]

The controversy in Stettin in the 1630s surrounding Warner left Fabricius in perhaps a stronger position. But the Warner case was not the only instance of

28 Starck, *Lubeca Lutherano-Evangelica*, p. 1017.
29 Starck, *Lubeca Lutherano-Evangelica*, p. 1020.
30 Starck, *Lubeca Lutherano-Evangelica*, p. 1022. The letter from Hunnius to Fabricius was dated 4 June 1638.
31 Starck, *Lubeca Lutherano-Evangelica*, p 1025.
32 Letter of Lübeck Ministerium to the Stettin 6 July 1638. Starck, *Lubeca Lutherano-Evangelica*, pp. 1031–33.

visions and visionaries at that time. A second case of a visionary in 1638 is also instructive for Fabricius' position regarding visionaries.

Gottfried Friedeborn was the son of a prominent family in Stettin and had a university education. However, as a tutor in Danzig, Friedeborn claimed that it had been revealed to him that he was the male child named in Revelation 12:5 that was to rule the world with an iron rod. Seeing himself as a greater prophet than Luther himself, Friedeborn claimed to be a divine instrument of the imminent judgment, which God intended soon to visit upon Germany. His family connections—his uncle was one of the city's burgomasters—insured that he was discreetly sent back to Stettin. Back in his home town, his visions only intensified. Fabricius's opponents argued that the toleration of visionaries such as Warner had encouraged more visionaries in the city like Friedeborn, who apparently tried to ingratiate himself with the Superintendent and complained bitterly about the clergy.[33] But Fabricius and his allies dealt with Friedeborn in a much different manner than with Warner.

From the start they considered Friedeborn's visions heterodox and considered him, accurately or not, influenced by "Weigelian books."[34] Fabricius sought to disabuse Friedeborn of his position, but according one account, Friedeborn turned on him and attacked him "with completely dishonorable words."[35] Friedeborn was imprisoned and the clergy continued to work "to win him" to their point of view. He was released for a time but responded again with his violent prophecies. For instance, in a letter to the city syndic, Friedeborn declared that he was one of the four eternal sons of God and called himself "the arch-high priest and viceroy of the eternal realm and king of the entire world, prince of peace of all damned creatures."[36] As proof of his visions, he prophesied that an earthquake would topple the tower of the town's largest church on Pentecost.

Unlike Adelgreiff in Königsberg—with whom Friedeborn explicitly identified himself—he was not treated in Stettin by Fabricius and others as a blasphemer or as a legitimate visionary but rather as a mentally-ill young man. At one point, Fabricius and others in Stettin suggested that he be sent to Hamburg to a work house so that he could be brought "ad sanam mentem."[37] Over several

33 See the letter of Christian Gross to Hunnius date 23 May, 1638. Starck, *Lubeca Lutherano-Evangelica*, p. 1018.

34 Micrälius, "Eigenhändige Fortsetzung," 159.

35 Micrälius, "Eigenhändige Fortsetzung," 160.

36 A copy of the letter is found in the Archiv der Franckeschen Stiftungen (D 121:68) and is reprinted in Theodor Wotschke, "Gottfried Friedeborn ein Glaubenszeuge?" *Blätter für Kirchengeschichte Pommerns* IX, (1932), pp. 22–26.

37 Micrälius, "Eigenhändige Fortsetzung," p. 160.

years, Friedeborn persisted in his prophecies and resisted the efforts of the clergy to dissuade him from them. Eventually, however, he was released and having relinquished his prophetic activities later became the pastor in a small rural parish in Holstein.[38]

It is important to recognize that Fabricius clearly distinguished between visionaries such as König or Warner, whom he considered pious and orthodox, and heterodox or mentally-ill individuals like Friedeborn. Amid growing questions about the validity of visions in the early 1640s, Fabricius composed a treatise on visions in 1641 and published it the next year. *Probatio Visionum, The Examination of Visions*, was remarkably free of polemics and reflects his experiences in Stettin with visionaries like Warner and Friedeborn.[39] The problem that Fabricius sets out in this tract is how Christians can distinguish properly the true divine visions from the deceptions and temptations of the devil. Citing a series of Bible verses—foremost among them the passages from Joel 2 that your sons and daughters shall prophesy and 1 Thessalonians 5:20–21 "Do not despise the words of prophets, but test everything; hold fast to what is good" (NRSV) as well as Christian authorities from Chrysostom to Luther, Fabricius argued for the continuing possibility of visions and revelation in his own time. He was particularly critical of those who rejected visions and prophecy out of hand and categorically dismissed them as the work of the devil or the foolish fantasies of enthusiasts.[40]

In developing his criteria, Fabricius laid out a series of marks by which one could judge the validity of visions. The most important of these marks, was the conformity of the vision or revelation to scripture and the confessions of the Lutheran church. He argued that just as theologians accepted or rejected the Church fathers' views based on their orthodoxy, so must one also approach the question of visions.[41] The second mark of true visions was the truth or validity of the visions themselves and particularly the fulfillment of their predictions. Since God cannot lie, divine revelations, Fabricius argued, but must needs come true. Fabricius acknowledged that some visionaries also performed

38 On Friedeborn's later life and involvement with radical dissenters: Jonathan Strom, "Gottfried Friedeborn: Prophezeihung und Kritik eines Geistlichen im 17. Jahrhundert" in: *Geistliche Lebenswelten. Zur Sozial- und Mentalitätsgeschichte der Geistlichen in Spätmittelalter und Früher Neuzeit*, ed. Manfred Jakubowski-Tiessen, (Neumünster: Wachholtz, 2005).

39 Jacob Fabricius, *Probatio Visionum: Das ist: Christliches, in Gottes Wort ... wolgegründetes Bedencken Von Gesichtern, Deren etliche können Göttliche Offenbarungen, etliche aber Teufflische Verführungen seyn.* (Nürnberg, 1642).

40 Fabricius, *Probatio*, B1r.

41 Fabricius, *Probatio*, B1r.

miracles, but while this might be a further confirmation of the visions' validity, he did not consider it an essential mark. He laid special emphasis on the character of the visionary and his or her piety. He was careful to note, however, that the individual's status in the world or learnedness had nothing to do with the visions' truth. In fact, he noted, that God often used the meanest and most despised of the world for his purposes.[42] Consequently piety and humility before God and humanity became central marks of the true visionary. He was particularly careful not to require visionaries to be knowledgeable in all theological matters. Another important mark for Fabricius was that while divine visions might initially case disquiet or fear, eventually a truly divine vision would comfort and refresh the heart of the visionary rather than induce horror or fear.[43] Fabricius laid particular weight of the visionary's character and emphasized that he or she must be of sound mind, and he excluded those who might be considered mad or raving.[44] In general, Fabricius set a very high bar for visions with his specific criteria and especially doctrinal orthodoxy.

After establishing criteria for divine revelations, Fabricius turned to the nature of the revelations themselves. Visions could occur in a number of different modes. In some cases, the visionary become an instrument of God and hears audible speech or sees with the eyes a divine image; often, the two modes are combined. The visions can also occur internally in which the Spirit speaks directly to the heart. Any of these visions, can occur in the three states, Fabricius noted, during sleep, when one is awake, and also—and here particularly importantly—during an ecstatic experience when the senses become blind and deaf to the external world.[45] The content of visions themselves may come as simple expressions of divine mysteries in words that all understand; they may also be expressed in terms of parables whose immediate meaning is less apparent; or they may contain actual prophesies of future things that are to come.[46]

Having laid out the criteria and a morphology of visions and prophecy, Fabricius invoked history. He detailed century by century examples of visions and prophecies that have occurred in Christianity, including, for instance, medieval mystics such as Hildegard of Bingen, Mechthild of Magdeburg, and Joachim of Fiore though predictably Fabricius sought to put them in an anti-papal context. He followed this with a summary of authorities who had

42 Fabricius, *Probatio*, 50.
43 Fabricius, *Probatio*, 60.
44 Fabricius, *Probatio*, 65.
45 Fabricius, *Probatio*, 91.
46 Fabricius, *Probatio*, 108–109.

supported divine visions and then concluded with responses to the most common objections to visions.

The *Probatio Visionum* was first published in Nürnberg and clearly had the support of Johannes Saubert, one of the leading Lutheran theologians of South Germany.[47] Its popularity and approval in Nürnberg was indicated by a further edition of the book the following year.[48] Not all Lutheran theologians were pleased with Fabricius's book, and the theological faculty in Wittenberg raised concerns in a letter and opinion, although they did not publish them until nearly twenty years later.[49] While the Wittenberg theologians kept their criticisms from wide circulation, a strong and polemical response to Fabricius appeared in 1645 penned by the Lübeck pastor Jacob Stolterfoth. In the 1630s, the Lübeck clerical ministerium had become one of the leading voices against the new prophets and visionaries.[50] Superintendent Hunnius had since died, but Stolterfoth, who had published his tract against contemporary visions in the early 1630s, now took the lead in attacking Fabricius.[51]

Stolterfoth's response to Fabricius disputed the central thesis of the *Probatio* that it was possible to distinguish divinely inspired visions from those of the devil. Where Fabricius's tone was measured and moderate, Stolterfoth's was aggressive and biting, reprising older arguments from the sixteenth century on the discernment of spirits.[52] While he did not name Fabricius directly in the appendix, there was little doubt about the target of his polemics. In places, Stolterfoth sought to distort Fabricius's argument. He accused him of

---

47 Saubert wrote an epigram for Fabricius's *Probatio*. See also, Kofler, *Prophetie*, p. 269, who also notes the support of Johann Valentin Andreä for Fabricius's *Probatio*. Among orthodox Lutherans, Saubert took a moderate position with regard to religious radicals. See Richard van Dülmen, "Orthodoxie und Kirchenreform. Der Nürnberger Prediger Johannes Saubert (1592–1646)" *Zeitschrift für Bayerische Landesgeschichte* 33 (1970), 636–786, here 730–33.

48 Jacob Fabricius, *Probatio Visionum: Das ist: Christliches, in Gottes Wort … wolgegründetes Bedencken Von Gesichtern, Deren etliche können Göttliche Offenbarungen, etliche aber Teufflische Verführungen seyn*: 2nd ed., Nürnberg: Wolffgang Endter, 1643.

49 See the critical appraisal and their letter to Fabricius dated 14 April 1645: *Consilia Theologica Witebergensia, Das ist, Wittenbergische Geistliche Rathschläge Deß theuren Mannes Gottes, D. Martini Lutheri, seiner Collegen, und treuen Nachfolger, von dem heiligen Reformations-Anfang, biß auff jetzige Zeit*, Frankfurt, 1664, S. 804–817.

50 See Theodor Schulze, "Die Anfänge des Pietismus in Lübeck." *Mittheilung des Vereins für Lübeckische Geschichte und Alterthumskunde* 10 (1902): 72–73.

51 Stolterfoth republished his earlier *Consideratio Visionum* of 1634 and then added an appendix that was double the length of the original text. Jacob Stolterfoth, *Consideratio Visionum Apologetica, Das ist schrifftmässiges Bedencken, Was von Geischtern heutiges Tages zu halten sey*. (Lübeck, 1645).

52 See, for instance, the discussion in Schreiner, *Are you Alone Wise*, chapter 6.

favoring heterodox visionaries who rejected Lutheran doctrine, a position Fabricius explicitly rejected. He further argued that Fabricius had turned prophecy and visions into a mark of the true church, and consequently made visions necessary.

This is not the place to to review all of Stolterfoth's charges, but behind these exaggerations and to a certain extent distortions of Fabricus' position, there were a number of fundamental differences that divided them and, I would argue, divided Lutheran orthodoxy in the first half of the 17th century. First, Stolterfoth argued that visions and prophecies had ended once and for all during apostolic times.[53] Stolterfoth challenged the interpretation of the key biblical passages that were central to Fabricius's argument. Joel 2:28, the most frequently cited passage in support of visionaries, was understood by Stolterfoth to have been fulfilled during apostolic times.[54] The key passage from 1 Thessalonians 5 "Do not quench the Spirit. Do not despise the words of prophets, but test everything; hold fast to what is good; abstain from every form of evil," was interpreted by Stolterfoth to refer only to testing church doctrine and not an endorsement of visions.[55] Against these, Stolterfoth posed passages from the Bible that one should not seek to know the future.[56] While Stolterfoth does not deny prophecy and visions in the Bible, these are things that he sees to be irrevocably past.

Second, Stolterfoth saw canonical scripture as so complete that it required no further elaboration in the form of visions or prophecy. With the completion of the New Testament, God had resolved not to give any further revelations. Stolterfoth noted that since God did not promise or pledge in his written Word that we should receive visions in these last times, we have no need of them. Continuing in this line of logic, Stolterfoth argued, "The special commands that come to human beings through visions, must either agree with God's word or not. Should they agree with God's word, they are superfluous. But if they do not agree with God's word, they are entirely in vain."[57] Stolterfoth's argument is essentially one of the complete sufficiency of scripture, and he contended that contemporary visions inevitably degrade the authority of scripture.[58] On this point, he and Fabricius indeed did have a fundamental disagreement.[59] And in fact, Fabricius' frequent citations from the apocryphal book of Sirach, did seem

53 Stolterfoth, *Consideratio Visionum Apologetica*, pp. 26, 43.
54 Ibid., p. 148.
55 Ibid., p. 267.
56 Ibid., p. 61.
57 Ibid., p. 59.
58 Ibid., p. 59.
59 Fabricius, *Probatio* p. 169.

to suggest in more ways than one that his understanding of scripture was more capacious than Stolterfoth's.[60]

A third point of disagreement was on the issue of lay and clerical authority. Although Stolterfoth did not argue that scripture was immediately clear or obvious, nevertheless it was the sole prerogative of the clergy to interpret scripture to the public. One of the great dangers that visionaries presented was its challenge to clerical authority. Stolterfoth was quite explicit that they threatened to bring the ordained office of ministry into disrepute by what he saw as their competing claims, and he argued that tolerating visionaries would denigrate the office of ministry.[61] In fact, Stolterfoth sought to tie Biblical prophecy as closely as possible to the ordained office of ministry by repeatedly identifying the prophets of the Old Testament with the office of the ordained preacher.[62] Stolterfoth argued that lay challenge to clerical authority was only possible if the ordained ministers were derelict in their duty.[63] In contrast, Fabricius saw the visionaries as an important check on the ministry. Implicitly he recognized their religious experience as an authority that did not trump scripture, but added to it. By granting visions and prophecies an important role, even if they were not essential, Fabricius validated religious experience—including that of the laity—with the Lutheran church. The fact that Stolterfoth could accept certain extraordinary natural phenomena such as comet appearances and other heavenly lights as divine signs, interpreted of course by the clergy, but not visions underscores his distrust of lay religious experience.

The publication of Stolterfoth's vituperative tract set off a round of polemical exchanges on all sides, which continued into the early 1650s.[64] In his final tract

60 Ibid., pp. 2, 25.

61 Stolterfoth, *Consideratio Visionum Apologetica* pp. 66, 398.

62 Ibid, p. 221.

63 Ibid., 140.

64 Against Stolterfoth, Fabricius and a fellow pastor from Pomerania responded: Jacob Fabricius, *Invicta Visionum Probatio: Das ist: Wollbefästigte Wiederlegung der nichtigen Scheingründe, mit welchen ein Streitsüchtiger Sophist mein hiebevor gedrucktes Büchlein von Prüfung der Gesichter ... mit nichten überwunden hat.* Stettin: 1646 and Samuel Plasterus, *Kurtze Endeckung und Hintertreibung des Irrthumbs / welchen M. JACOBUS STOLTERFOTH, Preidger zu Lübeck / in seiner Consideratione Visionum Apologetica, hat ausgesprenget / In Drey Capittel abgetheilet / und Christliebenden Hertzen / zum guten Nachdencken / für Augen gestellet* (Stettin: Georg Goetsche.1646). Stolterfoth responded with: *Kurtze Antwordt auff die newlich außgesprengte Chartec, darinnen einer, der sich Samuelem Plasterum, Pastorem zu Wartenberg nennet, mich ... eines sonderlichen Irrthumbs überführen wollen* (Lübeck: 1646) and: *Nothwendige höchstabgedrungene Warheit und Ehrenrettung wieder die sehr hefftige Schrifft, so D. Jacobus Fabricius ... unter folg. Titul: invicta visionum probatio, Das ist Wolbefästigte Wiederlegung ... mit nichten überwunden hat: unlängst ans Liecht gegeben, darin er mein vor diesem heraus gegebens Schrifftmässiges Bedencken ... gantz und gar zu*

on the topic, Fabricius distilled their differences into two main points of contention: whether God-given visions could have occurred after the time of the Apostles and whether one is forced to reject all possible visions without properly discerning their truth according to the scripture. The controversy, however, resulted in no real resolution on the fundamental differences described above, and at times the debate devolved into *ad hominem* attacks on their opponents. To a certain extent, the urgency surrounding the question of vision and prophecy had declined in the late 1640s as the final phase of the Thirty Years War came to an end and the prominence of lay prophets receded. After the mid 1640s, the number of prophets and visionaries in Germany declined, something that the Lübeck clerical council had predicted in the 1630s when they in part attributed the appearance of such prophets to the ongoing war.[65] As Johannes Wallmann also explains it, a kind of eschatological weariness had begun to set in at the end of the war.[66] And after Fabricius' death in 1654, the debate receded from memory though did not entirely disappear.

Conclusion

Jacob Fabricius articulated a moderate position on visions and lay prophecy that he judged was compatible with Lutheran confessions and orthodox doctrine as well as fully grounded in scripture. Though we might be tempted to see Fabricius as an anomaly within Lutheran orthodoxy in the first half of the seventeenth century, he represented one stream of Lutheran confessional culture that took continued to take the possibility of divinely given visions seriously. His case indicates how unresolved questions of the sixteenth century persisted well into the seventeenth on questions of prophecy, biblical interpretation, and clerical and lay authority. His approach was relatively sober-minded and limited. He did not believe that prophets could challenge established Lutheran doctrine or scripture, and he sought on the basis of his criteria to discern true

ruiniren ... vergeblich bemühet. Lübeck: 1647. Both Fabricius and Plasterus responded with further tracts and a additional defender of Fabricius was drawn into the fray: Joachim Brockwedel, whose *Abgedrungene Vertheidigung des Büchleins, genand Considerationis Stolterfothianae consideratio / Welche, zur Bestätigung desselbigen unwiedersprächlicher Warheit herfürgiebet, und dem unbefugten Wiedersprechen M. Jacobi Stolterfoths* (Alten Stettin, 1650), which is as far as I know the last tract in this exchange. Others were drawn into the debate as well, see Kofler, *Prophetie*, 246, and Beyer, *Lay Prophets*, pp. 199–200.

65 Letter of Lübeck Ministeirum to Stettin Ministerium, 4. Juni 1638 Starck, 1019.

66 Johannes Wallmann, *Philipp Jakob Spener und die Anfänge des Pietismus. Vol. 42, Beiträge zur historischen Theologie.* 2nd ed. Tübingen: J. C. B. Mohr (Paul Siebeck), 1983, 328.

prophets from those were enthusiasts (*Schwärmer*) or mentally deranged such as Gottfied Friedeborn. Jürgen Beyer sees the debate that evolved around Fabricius, visions, and prophecy as primarily political in nature driven by their views on Swedish intervention in Germany during the Thirty Years War rather than predominately theological concerns.[67] Politics mattered to be sure, but Susanne Kofler's emphasis on the theological arguments is less reductive and grants that fundamental issues were at stake in the controversy, including the sufficiency of scripture, lay authority, and the possibility of separating the true from false spirits.[68] Fabricius may have overplayed the depth of support among his fellow Lutheran theologians for his positions, but without question he represented a significant, if minority position, garnering the support of several prominent theologians such as Johannes Saubert.

In the second half of the seventeenth century, Lutheran orthodoxy moved increasingly in the direction of verbal inspiration of scripture and more rigid exegesis that tended to exclude the discernment of spirits, which could in certain instances authorize lay prophecy. Instead it tied prophecy as such almost exclusively to the office of ministry and the ordained clergy, a move akin to the domestication of prophecy at the end of the sixteenth century.[69] In this sense, it was much more the arguments of Stolterfoth rather than Fabricius that prevailed among the Lutheran orthodox theologians such as Abraham Calov and Johannes Quenstedt in the second half of the century.

One might expect that with the rise of the reform impulses of the Pietist movement and a new emphasis on the Spirit and lay involvement that arguments for prophecy and visions like those articulated by Fabricius would again win favor, especially with its renewed emphasis on the common priesthood or priesthood of all believers that Lutheran orthodoxy had marginalized.[70] Indeed, there was an explosion of lay prophecy at the high point of the Pietist controversies in the late 1680s and early 1690s. New prophets arose including the "inspired maids" of Halberstadt, Quedlingburg, and Erfurt whose ecstatic visions, calls for repentance, and even stigmata-like manifestations riveted Protestant Germany.[71] One of the most prominent of these visionaries was Rosamunde Julianne von der Asseburg, whose specific visions and

67 Beyer, *Lay Prophets*, pp. 199–200.

68 Beyer, Lay *Prophets*, pp. 199–200; Kofler, *Prophetie*, pp. 246–257.

69 In overview, Heinrich Schmid, *The Doctrinal Theology of the Evangelical Lutheran Church*, (Philadelphia, 1899), pp. 45–50 and pp. 340–342.

70 For this shift see Strom, "The Common Priesthood."

71 Mori is especially good on these developmennts, see Ryoko Mori, *Begeisterung und Ernüchterung in christlicher Vollkommenheit: Pietistische Selbst- und Weltwahrnehmungen im ausgehenden 17. Jahrhundert*, (Halle: Verlag der Franckeschen Stiftungen, 2004),

auditory revelations were hailed by some Pietists as direct revelations from Christ. Championed by the radical Pietist couple, Johann Wilhelm Petersen and Johanna Eleonora Petersen, Asseburg's visions gained wide interest, coming to the attention of those far beyond the Pietist circles, including Leibniz.[72] In defending Asseburg, Petersen cited Fabricius expressly.[73] Other theologians with Pietist sympathies referred back to Fabricius as demonstrating the divine nature of visions and new revelation. Barthold Meyer, Superintendent in Wolfenbüttel, who eventually lost his position because of his explicit support for visions and prophets, consulted Fabricius in the midst of the controversies.[74] Johann Winckler, a prominent Hamburg churchman, also referred back to Fabricius's arguments in his qualified defense of Petersen.[75]

Yet, while some prominent Pietists such as August Hermann Francke were initially fascinated by lay prophets and the possibility of visions in the early 1690s, those Pietists who remained within the confessional Lutheran church such as Francke, increasingly distanced themselves from any sort of lay visions and prophecy, even under the limited conditions carefully sketched by Fabricius. Rather than emphasize lay prophecy and possible visions that had a high potential for disruption, these church Pietists tended to focus on personal conversion as the epitome of lay religious experience, experiences that lent themselves much more to shaping and control by the Pietist clergy. And, like their orthodox counterparts, they appropriated the prophetic role almost exclusively to the office of ministry and the ordained clergy and moved in an increasingly Biblicist direction.[76]

---

pp. 103–248. and Ruth Albrecht, *Begeisterte Mägde: Träume, Visionen und Offenbarungen von Frauen des frühen Pietismus* (Leipzig: Evangelische Verlagsanstalt, 2018).

72 Albrecht published a number of Asseburg's revelations from manuscript sources. Ruth Albrecht, *Begeisterte Mägde*, pp. 34–40. On the controversy surrounding Asseburg, see Mori, *Begeisterung und Ernüchterung*, pp. 103–119. Daniel J. Cook, "Leibniz on 'Prophets', Prophecy, and Revelation," *Religious Studies* 45 (2009), p. 284.

73 Albrecht, *Begeisterte Mägde*, p. 61.

74 Martin Brecht et al., *Der Pietismus vom siebzehnten bis zum frühen achtzehnten Jahrhundert*, Geschichte des Pietismus vol. 1, (Göttingen: Vandenhoeck & Ruprecht 1993) p. 361. On Meyer's use of Fabricius's book, see Mechhild Raabe, *Leser und Lektüre im 17. Jahrhundert. Die Ausleihbücher der Herzog August Bibliothek Wolfenbüttel 1664–1713*, München 1998, S. 205.

75 Albrecht, *Begeisterte Mägde*, p. 133.

76 On the role of conversion experiences in Pietism, see Jonathan Strom, *German Pietism and the Problem of the Conversion* (University Park: Penn State Press, 2018). Johann Baptist Crophius, a former Lutheran and ardent Pietist become Catholic priest, wrote a remarkable early account of Pietism in the 1690s and noted of early Pietists: "in part they are Biblicists; in part they are visionaries." Johann Baptista Crophius, *Wahrhafft und Gründlicher Bericht Von der unter den Lutheranern neuentstandenen Sect, welche der*

Where prophecy and visions grabbed hold in Pietism was among the radical Pietists who moved beyond the boundaries of the confessional churches. Some formed new associations such as the Communities of True Inspiration and built their movement on the ongoing nature of ecstatic prophecy. Others remained unattached prophets and preachers such as Ernst Christian Hochmann von Hohenau.[77] The radical Pietist production of the *Berleburg Bible* (1726–1742), a highly commented multi-volume work, particularly emphasized the full prophetic potential of the Joel 2 passage and as Albrecht notes, held on to the hope that such prophecy is not finished "but continues on and can be actualized at any time."[78]

In some respects, the radical Pietists were the inheritors of Fabricius' openness to lay prophecy and visions, but unlike Fabricius, these radical Pietists were no longer tethered to the confessional doctrines of the Lutheran or Reformed churches nor were they bounded by the scriptural text as he had advocated. The guardrails that Fabricius had carefully constructed to promote the proper discernment of spirits and distinguish true visions from those inspired by the devil or mental instability fell away among the radicals. At the same time, among eighteenth-century confessional Lutherans, including ardent church Pietists, lay prophecy and visions could find little room even within the carefully circumscribed limits that Fabricius had established, effectively ending this confessional approach to discerning spirits in the modern era.

Pietismus oder die Pietisterey Insgemein genennt wird (Vienna, 1700), §23. After the early 1690s church Pietists moved much more strongly to the biblicist side of the equation.

77 On these, for instance, see Hans Schneider, *German Radical Pietism*, trans. By Gerald MacDonald (Lanham: Scarecrow Press, 2007), pp. 90–95, 118–124.

78 Albrecht, *Begeisterte Mägde*, p. 208.

CHAPTER 12

"Much More for Use in This Present Age": Augustine Baker and Life-Writing at Cambrai Abbey, 1624–1633

Karen E. Park

The English Benedictine community of Our Lady of Consolation Abbey at Cambrai, France, was a place where, during the mid-17th century, life writing by and about women was both practiced and encouraged. The best known of the *lives* composed there is undoubtedly *The Lady Falkland Her Life*, a biography of Elizabeth Tanfield Cary, also known as the Lady Falkland—an Early Modern English recusant writer and playwright who was the mother of four early members of the abbey at Cambrai. In this chapter, I argue that the *Life* should not be read as if it followed a medieval or pre-Reformation model of exemplary life writing or hagiography, but instead as part of a program of deliberately realistic, non-hagiographic "modern" life writing which was both encouraged and modeled by the community's influential spiritual director and confessor, Dom Augustine Baker. Baker was quiet, reclusive, and strongly attracted to the English mystical tradition. He spent his religious life as a Benedictine priest without a community of other monks, since he was a "tabler," a member of an order without who paid for his board when lodging in various homes or religious communities. Between 1624 and 1633, he lived with the newly founded community of English Benedictine nuns at Cambrai, serving as their confessor, spiritual advisor, and literary mentor. And he was deeply inspired by their piety and intelligence. It was a remarkably reciprocal relationship in many ways.

Like his namesake the Bishop of Hippo, Augustine Baker believed in the spiritual importance of life writing. Not only did he write his own life story several times; he also wrote lives of some of the nuns for whom he served as confessor and spiritual advisor. Under his explicit guidance and with his encouragement, these nuns also engaged in life writing themselves. While Augustine Baker did not possess the literary gifts of his namesake, a flaw he readily admitted,[1] he had very clear ideas about the purpose of life writing. He

1 "I desire pardon not onlie for my tediousness in expressmentes (which is a defect in my writings that I cannot amende) but also for my iterations in divers places of one and the self same thing, which might sometimes happen through error of memorie, as not remembering that

 | DOI:10.1163/9789004527843_013

conveyed these to the women of Cambrai, who used life writing both as part of their personal spiritual development and for mutual edification.

1 Our Lady of Consolation Abbey: Daughters of English Catholicism in France

The Abbey of Our Lady of Consolation was founded in 1623 with the substantial dowry provided by Cresacre More (1572–1649) for his daughter Helen, who was the great-granddaughter of Thomas More. The More family was not the only famous Catholic family affiliated with Our Lady of Consolation. Four daughters of the English playwright Elizabeth Tanfield Cary, the Lady Falkland, also joined the community within the first decade of its founding. Both the Lady Falkland and Helen More (who took the name Gertrude in religious life) became the subjects of lengthy biographies written at the Abbey during the 1630s and 1640s. Gertrude's *Life* was written by Augustine Baker, and Elizabeth Cary's was written collaboratively by her daughters, the nuns. These documents, which both come out of the same community, are striking for many reasons, not least because of their similar orientation towards their subjects. Rather than following many hagiographic commonplaces, both *lives* are honest and critical regarding their subjects' human weaknesses and failings. Neither is concerned with the miraculous or supernatural, but rather with the workings of everyday life, and the ways in which God's grace can transform ordinary people into exemplars of the faith.

This straightforward and unadorned approach is in some ways surprising, given Baker's own profoundly mystical leanings. And of course, mystical writing was on the ascendant in Catholic Europe during the years of Baker's life, which overlapped with such visionaries as Teresa of Avila (1515–82), John of the Cross (1542–91), Francis de Sales (1567–1622) and Vincent de Paul (*c*.1581–1660). Yet despite Baker's encouragement of the nuns in the mystical and contemplative life, his approach to spirituality was decidedly down to earth. Mystical contemplation of the Divine nature could, he and the nuns agreed, take place in the here and now, among people who were extraordinary but also flawed in ways both human and familiar.[2]

I had allreadie written it" *Father Baker's Autobiography* as published in Catholic Record Society *Memorials of Father Augustine Baker and Other Documents of the English Benedictines*, Justin McCann and Hugh Donnelly, eds. Published by the Catholic Record Society, London, 1933, 10.

2 Margaret Truran describes a copy of *Sancta Sophia* inscribed "This Booke belongs to the Library of our Bl. Ladys of Comfort Cambray." At the back of the book, upside-down on the

The Lady Falkland, Her Life is the better known of the two documents. In recent decades, the *Life* has begun to receive the attention it deserves as an important literary work rather than merely a set of biographical clues useful primarily as background information on Elizabeth Cary's own remarkable literary productions. Interest in the biography among scholars of Early Modern women's literature has been significant, which is not surprising given that Cary is believed to be the first Englishwoman to write an original play and publish it under her own name, *The Tragedie of Miriam,* (1613) as well works of history, biography, and devotional literature. The *Life* provides remarkable details about Cary's character, propensities, and seminal episodes from her childhood, adolescence, and adult life.

Elizabeth Cary was the only child of a well-known lawyer and landowner, Laurence Tanfield, and his wife, Elizabeth. She was precocious and her father loved to talk over his difficult cases with her, including those having to do with people accused of witchcraft. On one occasion, according to the *Life*, she proved that an accused "witch" was nothing more than a simple-minded and confused old woman by getting her to confess to bewitching someone who had died many years before her birth.

Elizabeth Cary showed an early interest in theology and read Calvin's *Institutes* by the age of 12. She disagreed with it so vehemently and argued against it so forcefully that her father declared "This Girle Hath a Spirit Averse from Calvin!" Her mother, who was less pleased by her daughter's intellectual pursuits than her father was, forbid her to read except at appointed hours. So young Elizabeth bribed the servants to give her candles and was "in debt to them more than 100lbs by her 12th year." Her parents deemed her far too learned and intelligent to find a husband (as a child she studied French, Spanish, Italian, Latin, Hebrew, and Transylvanian), so a less articulate girl had to be hired to conduct the correspondence between Miss Tanfield and the husband her parents found for her. He was Henry Cary, the Lord Falkland, and they were sure that her quick wit would turn him off immediately.

Although the marriage between Elizabeth and her husband produced "11 children born alive," it was an unhappy one. Henry was an up-and-comer in the court of King James. He was a soldier and an administrator, not drawn to theology or literature, and particularly intolerant of Catholicism. In fact, he

page is written in a 17th century hand "3 drames of Sena ... powder of rhubarb." Evidently, the book on contemplation was well used, even brought into the kitchen where it was used in a pinch for a grocery list. Truran, Margaret. "'The Present Author Hath Bin Driven to This': What Needs Was Father Baker Trying to Meet?" In *That Mysterious Man: Essays on Augustine Baker, 1575–1641*, edited by Michael Woodward, Vol. 15. Analecta Cartusiana 119. Salzburg: University of Salzburg, 2001, 7–8.

had been assigned to enforce anti-Catholic laws in Ireland for a time. While the family was away in Ireland, Elizabeth, who had long been attracted to Catholicism, nurtured her faith. Upon their return to England, Henry was soon called away again, and while he was abroad Elizabeth began keeping company with a group of highly intellectual Benedictine priests. Through reading the theological and hagiographical works they gave her, and after suffering the death of her beloved eldest daughter who was killed in a horse-riding accident, she converted to Catholicism—publicly and against her husband's will.

This humiliated Henry Cary and jeopardized his career goals. He was incensed. He took the very unusual step of officially leaving his wife (though he did not divorce her) and he took all 11 of the children with him. She was left destitute, with only one maid (who had converted with her) for company. With no children, no money, and no friends, she could scarcely find food at times. She had to petition the King's Privy Council for maintenance, further humiliating her husband in the eyes of his colleagues at court.

The *Life* ends with a relating of its own genesis. Elizabeth was denied custody of her children even after the death of her estranged husband, who ensured that his Catholic wife would never get her hands on them by entrusting the younger children to his eldest son Lucius—himself an ardent Protestant. Eventually, Elizabeth arranged to kidnap her six youngest children from the care of their brother and smuggle them to France, where all four of the girls entered the Convent at Cambrai and both boys became Benedictine priests.[3]

Mary Beth Long has situated this work within the post-medieval hagiographical tradition, noting the changes in depictions of saintly women after the Reformation. Long shows how, in its overall plot and structure, *The Lady Falkland Her Life* conforms to earlier hagiographic models. For example, Elizabeth Cary was a precocious child, her adulthood marked by challenges from villainous "unbelievers" who tried to keep her from her chosen path—Catholicism—and who punished her for her piety.[4] While the overall structure does fit into the typical exemplary hagiographic account in many ways, what is

3 The *Life* is a collaborative document, written primarily by one of Cary's daughters, most probably Lucy Cary, but edited and commented upon by several of her siblings. Since the manuscript was written there have been four published versions of it. These are by Catholic historians Richard Simpson (1857), Lady Georgianna Fullerton (1883), and scholars Barry Weller and Margaret Ferguson (1994) and Heather Wolfe (2001). Weller and Ferguson's student-friendly version pairs it with *Tragedie of Mariam* thereby encouraging its use as a supplement to the play. Wolfe's version retains the marginalia and is accompanied by an extensive handwriting analysis. Most scholarship today, including this essay, relies upon Wolfe's version.

4 Long, Mary Beth "The Life as Vita: Reading *The Lady Falkland Her Life as Hagiography*" *English Literary Renaissance* 38, no2 (2008), 309.

truly distinctive about *The Lady Falkland Her Life* is how it *doesn't* conform—namely, with the inclusion of many personal anecdotes that show Elizabeth Cary's deep personal flaws.

According to the *Life*, she was a poor housekeeper and money manager, she took no care with her appearance, and she neglected the duties of her large household. If, as Long claims, post-Reformation female hagiography underwent a significant change, situating female sanctity within the domestic rather than the public sphere, we are left wondering why this exemplary woman was so bad at managing her domestic life.[5] The answer to this question lies in the particular culture of life writing at the convent. As Long puts it, "The *Life* then, is a story about a woman who wrote women saints' lives, by women who read them in a setting that cherished them."[6] But because of the spiritual direction of Augustine Baker, the sisters did not merely cherish hagiography. They also engaged in a particular form of critical or realistic life writing, one modeled by Baker himself.

2 Dom Augustine Baker, OSB (1575–1641) and the Literary Culture of the Abbey

Augustine Baker composed *The Life and Death of Dame Gertrude More* in 1635, two years after More's death of smallpox at age 27. As both confessor and spiritual teacher of the fledgling group of nuns at Cambrai, Baker was himself a prolific writer, penning what has been estimated as well over a million words, many of them during the nine years he spent at Cambrai. Baker had strong mystical and contemplative leanings and is best remembered for his works *Sancta Sophia* (1657) and the *Secretum* (his commentary on the classic of English mysticism *The Cloud of Unknowing*). His vast output of writing fell broadly into two categories: antiquarian research on pre-dissolution Benedictine monasteries, which was published as *Apostalatus Benedictinorum in Anglia* (Douay, 1626) and mystical/spiritual writings that were edited by Fr. Serenus Cressy and published as *Sancta Sophia*.

Baker was chosen by the Benedictine congregation to shepherd the flock of nuns at Cambrai after they rejected the first priest appointed to the position because of his rigid and formulaic Ignatian approach to prayer. No fan of Ignatian spirituality himself, Baker claimed that had Dame Gertrude only had the Spiritual Exercises to sustain her prayer life "she would have both lived and

5 *Ibid.*
6 *Ibid.*

died most miserablie."[7] The nuns at Cambrai were strongly and deeply committed to the contemplative life. They remained extremely loyal to Baker, supporting him when he faced charges of illuminism and anti-authoritarianism and referring to him in convent documents as "the venerable Father Baker" and "our spiritual father," even long after his departure from the community.

There is much about Baker that was unusual, and his writings often reflected controversial or unorthodox positions. For example, he did not believe that the contemplative life was open only to professed religious. He wrote that lay people, even the unlearned and uneducated, could have a perfect contemplative life out in the world, and that it was not by necessity inferior to the religious life in any way. Because of his egalitarian attitude regarding the potential of all people to achieve holiness, he tended to hold women in high esteem.[8] He was also generally distrustful of the mechanical, regimented style of prayer proscribed by the Council of Trent. In fact, given his own post-Tridentine, strongly Ignatian context, Baker's ultimate reliance on God alone for spiritual guidance is particularly striking. In *Sancta Sophia*, for example, he argues that all teachers and all institutions are subordinate to the internal directions and inspirations of God's Holy Spirit. It is these beliefs which led to suspicions of illuminism and anti-authoritarianism.

While Baker was a mystic (having at least once attained what he felt to be perfect union with the divine), he also had a practical side and was deeply concerned with the ordinary workings and everyday operations of proper spiritual formation in the contemplative life. It was to this end that he encouraged the nuns at Cambrai to both read and write other exemplary lives. Baker composed biographies not only of Dame Gertrude but also of another nun, Dame Margaret Gascoigne, as well as Margaret's brother Francis Gascoigne, an Abbey benefactor. Baker was the subject of no less than three contemporary biographies written by his followers (Leander Pritchard, Peter Salvin, and

---

7 Wekking, *Augustine Baker O. S. B. The Life and Death of Dame Gertrude More Edited from All the Known Manuscripts*, 3.

8 For example, one of his instructional treatises to the nuns includes this statement: "No man is easily able to persuade you that a thing is no sin which indeed is a sin, so clearly doth naturall light discern it ... I say that though the understanding of those of your sex be not so judicious and perfect in other matters as is that of men, yet in this point of discerning evill, where really it is so by the law of nature, in matters that concern yourselves, having in you any good desires towards God, I esteem you not inferior, if not superior, even to learned men." From Augustine Baker's treatise *Secure Stay* as quoted in Rodrigues, Teresa, "That Mysterious Man?" in *"Stand Up to Godwards": Essays in Mystical and Monastic Theology in Honour of the Reverend John Clark on His Sixty-Fifth Birthday*, 123–55. Analecta Cartusiana 204. Salzburg: University of Salzburg Press, 2002, 129.

Serenus Cressy). He also composed an autobiography, which he included as part of *The Secretum*.

Baker was often inclined to explain and defend his intentions as a writer, and he did so with regard to the practice of life writing. In his introduction to Dame Gertrude's *Life*, he makes his purpose in writing the document very clear. He writes:

> In our present age (we have heard of readde) of miraculous fastings, abstinences, watchings, and other corporall and externall doings, rapts, and Extasies, vision and apparitions, and revelations, and other supernaturall and extraordinarie operations true or supposed. None of thes greate matters, or such things (the vereties yet whereof oft times are verie uncertain) shall the Reader finde in this present relation; but some other things more imitable by others, and more tending to edification of soules, and much more for use in this present age.[9]

In this passage, Baker reveals that he has a specific purpose in mind for life writing. He intends to deliberately avoid medieval hagiographical commonplaces in order to present a life story that is more realistic and less fantastic, and therefore more imitable by others and more edifying. He is aware that his project represents a departure from the norm and that what he is doing is new and timely—or, as he puts it, "more for use in this present age." He warns his readers that should they expect to find visions, apparitions, miracles, or other supernatural or extraordinary events in Gertrude's life story, they will be disappointed.

Baker's attitude toward "supernatural and extraordinary operations" is in line with many of the Protestant reformers, who since the earliest days of the Reformation had seen supernatural events as evidence not of sanctity but of the presence of the diabolical. William Tyndale argued this point with Dame Gertrude's great-grandfather Thomas More when he claimed that the miracles of the saints in the medieval church were nothing more than the fulfillment of the prophecy of Paul that "The Antichrist shall not only come with lying signs and disguised with falsehood, but also with lying miracles and wonders" (2 Thess. 2:9). New ways of telling the stories of Christian men and women had to be developed, with John Foxe's *Book of Martyrs* being the earliest and most significant attempt to rewrite the literature of sainthood in a Protestant mode.

9 Wekking, *Augustine Baker O. S. B. The Life and Death of Dame Gertrude More Edited from All the Known Manuscripts*, 2.

So Augustine Baker's de-emphasis on the miraculous was not new. It had been the project of the magisterial reformers to divorce sanctity from the supernatural for at least a century before Baker began to write religious biography, and the growth of Anabaptism in England only solidified this position. As a Catholic and a Benedictine, Baker would not have seen miracles as evidence of the demonic, yet in life-writing, "supernatural and extraordinary operations" were still problematic for him because he viewed them as a distraction from authentic religious and contemplative life. Baker's project was therefore not to describe what was extraordinary about Gertrude More but what was ordinary, so that his readers (the nuns) could be edified and inspired by the knowledge that they could also find grace, fulfillment, and even perfection in God. Regarding miracles and extraordinary occurrences common in other exemplary lives, Baker complains that:

> (these saints lives) are of that nature, that we cannot to do not much turne them to edification or other good, but either to curiositie, or ells to a mere wondring, or at the most, to the extolling of the holie person towards or by whome the things were acted, without farther relation of the same to anie true good or benefit of the soule.[10]

The acts of reading and writing the exemplary lives of others were prominent features of life at Our Lady of Consolation. As members of a Benedictine community, the sisters would have participated in the *lectio divina*. They would have read and listened to saints' lives and martyrologies, their own writings and those of other nuns, and various other spiritual works as part of their formation in religious life. We know that Baker left detailed instructions and reading lists for the nuns and that these were meticulously copied and preserved, both at Our Lady of Consolation and later at its daughter house, Our Lady of Good Hope in Paris. These catalogues represent an incredibly wide range of material from every era of the Church's history and reflect clearly on the importance Baker placed on reading and its relationship to the spiritual and contemplative life. A treatise Baker composed for the nuns at Our Lady of Consolation entitled "Concerning the Librarie of this Howse" makes explicit the spiritual value he placed on books and reading. Baker writes:

> ... (and) good bookes are a necessarie food for your soules; for by them you are (as by the voice of God) incited to devotion, and nourished in it, and greatlie holpen and directed in your spirituall course. And therefore

10 Wekking, 2.

> they are of farre more worth and more to be regarded then is transitory pellf of money or other temporal goodds, that neither have spirit, nor do cause spirit, but most commonly are a cause ... to hinder and oppress the spirit.[11]

Lucy Cary's time at Our Lady of Consolation did not overlap with Baker's tenure there: he left in 1633, and she arrived in 1638. But the Cary sisters would have read and heard, perhaps many times, not only the lives of the saints and the Holy Scriptures, but also the lives of several of their deceased fellow sisters, whose experiences were intended to inspire and edify the nuns. Although the Cary sisters most likely never met either Augustine Baker or Gertrude More, their lingering presence would have been palpably real during the sisters' years at the Abbey. In fact, an English Catholic who visited Our Lady of Consolation in 1646, just about the time that *The Lady Falkland Her Life* was composed, indicated that he was visiting in order to "spend a day or two to visit thos truly Religious Nuns of St. Benedicts Order, whom Reverend Father Baker's directions and Mother Gertrude Moor's Piety had so admirably distinguisht from many other Monasteries of that Order."[12] Lucy Cary seems to have heeded Baker's warnings as she composed the life of her mother, the Lady Falkland, a text whose realistic and even critical tone is often striking.

3 *The Lady Falkland, Her Life* and *The Life and Death of Gertrude More*

As we turn to a close comparison of *The Lady Falkland Her Life* and *The Life and Death of Dame Gertrude More*, it will become clear that Lucy Cary did not force the story of her mother's life into a hagiographic paradigm. Nor did she include so many unflattering details about her mother in order to distance herself from her or her memory. She was instead participating in the deliberate creation of a post-Reformation literary style, one which downplayed hagiographical commonplaces in an attempt to make the work more useful and spiritually edifying. A context in which biographies were read and written for the purpose of spiritual edification made Lucy's composition of *The Lady Falkland Her Life* possible. The text was written while Lucy was part of a convent community

11 From MS H9 at Colwich Abbey, Staffordshire as quoted in Cramer "Librarie of this Howse", 108.

12 As quoted in Wolfe, "Reading Bells and Loose Papers: Reading and Writing Practices of the English Benedictine Nuns in Cambrai and Paris," 153.

that used biography as a form of communication and inspiration, and *The Lady Falkland Her Life* was composed with the expectation that it too would be of spiritual value to the community.

Baker's composition of the life of Dame Gertrude self-consciously and deliberately avoids hagiographical representations of her. There is nothing miraculous about her life or her death, though there is much to be admired and emulated. Baker did not intend to awe Gertrude's fellow sisters—to have done so might have discouraged them from seeking the same path as she. Rather, Baker wanted them to know that they too were capable of great holiness and sanctity as long as they remained "well-minded." The miraculous and supernatural are not part of the narrative of Dame Gertrude's life, and they are missing from *The Lady Falkland Her Life* as well. Lucy Cary, in following the example set by Baker, chose a forthright and realistic tone in writing about her mother. She did not make her into an example of shining perfection, but wrote about her very human flaws as well as her ability to transcend them and achieve a measure of sanctity despite them.

There are some striking similarities and parallels between the character of Gertrude More as she is presented by Baker and the character of Elizabeth Cary as she is presented by Lucy Cary. Both, for example, are described as having terrific fluctuations of mood and temperament. Of Gertrude, Baker writes that:

> ... she seemed to have in her 4. or 5. repugnant or contrarie qualities or conditions; whereof one was, that she was verie meerrie, and yet verie much subject to great sadnesses. Another that she was of a timorous or scrupulous conscience, and yet of much couradge, and boldness, or hardinesse. A thirde that she had a great propension to extroversion, and yet a great propension to Introversion ... so that I maie saie, that none was more timorous in conscience as to some respects,; and yet as to some other none freer or bolder: None more meeririe and cheerfull, and yet none more subject to sadness, or more easile cast into it.[13]

This description of Gertrude More as labile and flighty is reminiscent of Elizabeth Cary's characterization in *The Lady Falkland Her Life*. Lucy Cary describes her mother as highly prone to moodiness and inconsistency. One example among many must suffice, as when Lucy writes:

> She always seemed scarce able to doe smale things, but greate ones by the grace of God she sometimes did; in little matters she seemed somewhat

13 Wekking, 25.

> subject to herself, in those of more importance she could and did command herself; she could be passionate in extremity for the least (even childish thinges,) but in more great, has many times shewed much constancy and patience.[14]

Elizabeth Cary's emotional instability went beyond moodiness and into true mental illness. During several of her pregnancies, she became so depressed "in so deepe melancholy" that she was unable to eat or drink for 14 days (except a little beer with toast).

After this experience, the story of which is partially crossed out by the author(s) or a later editor, Elizabeth Cary mostly overcame her sadness. Or did she? It is clear in the following passage that depression was an ongoing struggle for her.

> From this time she seemed so farre to haue ourcome all sadness, that she was scarce euer subjet to it on any occasion (but only once) but always looked on the best side of every thinge, and what good euery accident brought with it; her greatest signe of sadness (after) was sleeping, which she was sued to say she could doe when she would, and then had most will to, when she had occasion to haue sadd thoughts waking; which she much saught to avoid, and it seemed could (for the most part) doe it, when she gaue herself to it.[15]

Throughout *The Lady Falkland Her Life*, Cary's daughters maintain a remarkably critical stance towards their mother. The reader learns that with regard to Elizabeth's projects and plans she was "better att contriving than executing,"[16] that she "always much esteemed and loved order (when she remembered there was such a thinge),"[17] and that "what she sayd could not always be stood to."[18] We also learn that Elizabeth was always in debt, was frequently rash and unpredictable, and could not be relied upon to keep her word. She did not manage her finances properly and did not always take care of her obligations. Yet she was obedient to God's call, even when it led to abandonment by her husband due to her recusancy.

14 Wolfe, *Elizabeth Cary Lady Falkland Life and Letters*, 144.

15 *Ibid*, 118.

16 *Ibid*, 118.

17 *Ibid*, 144.

18 *Ibid*, 215.

Gertrude More's short life as a sister was also full of sadness. She did not want to become a nun but entered the convent out of obedience to her father. Her outgoing and extroverted disposition was poorly suited to life in the convent. Baker writes:

> She hath divers times told me that she came to Religion much against her will and in a maner forced by him, whome she had not power to resist, by reason of the great affection she bore unto him. It seemes to me, that he did see some tokens of signes in her of God Allmighties grace and did hope for great good effects to comme thereof that he should so farre presume and build upon her for a foundation, that he would not be dnied by her, when as yet she herself was so unwilling and farre from it.[19]

Like Elizabeth Cary, Gertrude More was the brilliant daughter of a doting but controlling father. While Cary was forced into an unhappy marriage, More was forced into the convent, where she, like Cary, struggled with depression and despair.

> And though she (Gertrude) seemed, at least after he had long and much sollicied her, to be willing when she sawe there was no remedie, yet she greeved inwardly, and retiring and withdraweng herself in solitarines would sitte weepeing and lamenting for it ... And when her friends and those of the House did observe an allteration in her, as that she did grow more retired and solitarie, they esteemed it to be mere devotion and nothine ells, and that she had ben praieng, when she was greeving privately to herself.[20]

These states of mind were considered sinful, not merely signs of a troubled spirit.

The approach to life writing that took place at Our Lady of Consolation meant that neither Lucy Cary nor Augustine Baker needed to portray their subjects as saintly in order for them to be held up as exemplars for the community. To have elevated them through traditional hagiographic devices, leaving out undesirable and even sinful behavior, would have been in opposition to the literary traditions of the community, and would have undermined the biographies' spiritual worth. The purpose of life writing at Our Lady of Consolation Abbey was to create spiritual resources that would serve the real women of

19 Wekking, 328.
20 *Ibid.*

the community who continued to struggle with their calling and their lives in the convent. Lucy Cary and Augustine Baker deliberately presented the Lady Falkland and Dame Gertrude as devotional subjects who could be emulated and understood—women who were ordinary both in their sinfulness and in their spiritual potential, and whose goodness and strength were therefore available to all.

CHAPTER 13

Evidence of Things Unseen: John Wesley's Hermeneutics of Conscience

William Schweiker

It is a singular honor and joy for me to be able to contribute to this Festschrift in honor of Professor Susan Schreiner, colleague, friend, and confidant of many years. Not only do I treasure her wit, as so many do, but also her constant concern for those persons excluded from view, unacknowledged, and often without care. Knowing the Calvinistic bent of Susan's mind, I nevertheless think that her ongoing support of others bespeaks a deeply settled Methodist tenor of heart and life. And since I share with Schreiner the legacy of Methodism and John Wesley at its origins, it is about Wesley that I have decided to write. Yet no matter the topic chosen, the following pages have been written with lasting affection for Susan.

1 Introduction

> This is the religion we long to see established in the world,
> a religion of love and joy and peace, having its seat in the heart,
> in the inmost soul, but ever showing itself by its fruits.

It is widely known that John Wesley is not considered an A-list theologian. He wrote no systematic theology, was suspicious of any religion of the mind that lacked heartfelt vitality, and believed that persuasion, not demonstration, was the task assigned to someone commissioned to preach the Gospel. Wesley spoke of his focus as "practical divinity," and he is, as such, usually lauded as an evangelist and organizer. While no doubt true, I think those judgments are still a bit off the mark, and I hold that judgment for reasons other than denominational loyalty. The test for any theology, whether philosophical, dogmatic, or ethical, should be the truth it sheds on life before God and the actual orientation it gives to the conduct of peoples' lives. Accordingly, the focus of this essay is on the theological and ethical trajectory of John Wesley's thought.

With Wesley, I share the Protestant reticence about speculative forms of theology that claim with great certainty to know the being and inner-workings of

 | DOI:10.1163/9789004527843_014

the Godhead. What, or who, makes life worth living must be, for any thoughtful person, the most basic question of human life. And human beings seem to be those kinds of creatures who want to flourish, to conduct their lives more or less freely, find their lives in some way complete, and to know some measure of happiness, however conceived. By answering those questions, Wesley makes an important, if not final, contribution to Christian thought as well as Christian life. And he does so, I want to show, by engaging and interpreting scripture in and through ancient and modern strands of thought about the human good.

How then to proceed? Given my aim to show the possible contribution of Wesley to current Christian thought and life, my engagement with the *Discourses on the Sermon on the Mount* (1746) will be a reconstruction of its basic claims in relation to other positions in the history of thought.[1] That is, it is not possible in one essay, or even one book, to clarify the complexity of Wesley's work in the *Discourses*. I also make no claim to being a historian of Wesley's work or to having scoured his archived papers, hymns, sermons, and writings in order to answer historical questions *per se*, say, the possibility of various periodizations of his thought. My task, rather, is to provide a historically informed constructive thinking with and beyond Wesley's work. At the center of the inquiry is the question of the relation between self-understanding and a sense or intuition of the norm(s) that should guide a life that might unify a desire for happiness with a sense of rightness or justice.[2]

While constructive, my approach in what follows opens some complex issues in understanding Wesley and his possible contribution to current thought. These issues hover around what was called after eighteenth-century thinkers "moral sense theory," or, more broadly, "ethical intuitionism," and what I am calling a hermeneutics of conscience for reasons to be explained later. I begin,

---

1 Dates in parentheses are those of the original publication of works. In Wesley's case, this date does not necessarily correspond to the date in which a sermon or discourse was given, nor how many times it was given. That is certainly the case with the *Discourses on the Sermon on the Mount*, the contents of which were written and delivered over a period of years. Likewise, there are different dates given by Albert Outler and Timothy Smith. Where there are differences, I have followed Smith insofar as this is the one used to structure a comprehensive chronology by The Wesley Center of Northwest Nazarene University, which has the most complete holding of Wesley material now available in the USA.

2 Readers of this volume know that we are not subjecting the thinkers explored to the standards of contemporary biblical criticism, theology, or philosophy. To do that would be to commit the sin of "presentism," reading the past by our standards, that Professor Schreiner has rightly and vigorously combatted her entire career. I take Wesley as he presents himself and hope to show what, if anything, we can learn for the purposes of current thought and life. That will require a good deal of interpretive labor, a task and method I will explain in due course.

then, not with the *Discourses*, but by clarifying my focus on Wesley's thought in terms of the problem of the human good; I will then turn to moral sense, before explaining what I take to be his use of scripture in order to awaken and perfect conscience. I hope to show that Wesley develops a religious and moral hermeneutic with its own distinctive insights. That last step in the argument will also be to see if any of Wesley's argument can be salvaged for our time.

It should be noted that my line of argument accords with Wesley's own method of thinking. While he called himself "a man of one Book," in fact he engaged, in good "Anglican" fashion, the tradition of Christian thought, reasoned reflection, and, in his own twist, experience.[3] I am, then, deploying these multiple resources in order to get at and to articulate the experience Wesley sought to illuminate and proclaim, that is, the fusion of happiness and holiness in Christian life in this world and, he believed, the next. Given this line of argument, we move in this essay towards scripture rather than begin with it since we must have in hand the presuppositions of Wesley's account of human existence and the Christian life in order to understand his use and interpretation of the scripture from which he claimed to derive his position.

2 The Human Good

Wesley's specific contribution to theological reflection with and through scripture is, I hope to show, at the intersection of perception, sensibility, and conduct, that is, how, with the help of scripture, one's perception and sense of the divine reality is reflexively related to one's self-understanding as a moral agent. What can and must motivate one's conduct? It is to have, as he constantly puts it, the mind that was "in Christ." However, this account of human action is not an end in itself, and for a simple reason. No matter how one analyzes the dynamics of human action (intention, desire, will, decision, etc.), one must also provide some criteria for good human action, and, likewise, what motives are in fact consistent with that good.

Wesley is distinctive not just because he looks to the character of human action and its perfection, as Catholic and Orthodox thinkers have always done, but because he outlines the Christian life through an interpretation of the Sermon on the Mount rather than, say, the Decalogue (John Calvin), Pauline

3 I am aware that there are debates about when in the course of the English Reformation it is right to use the term "Anglican" about Carolinian Divines. With Wesley, this is beside the point insofar as he always saw himself as an Anglican, and merely added to Thomas Cranmer's sources of theology his conception of experience.

thought (Luther), or natural law and the virtues (Aquinas). Wesley takes his cue for the Christian life from Christ's "teaching us the true way to life everlasting; the royal way which leads to the kingdom; and the only true way—for there is none besides ... "[4] And he was clear that this teaching is for everyone, even "all generations to come." In a word, the norm for the Christian life is a depiction of a way of life, rather than a conception of the highest good or an account of the laws of God. Better put, Christ's pedagogy, for Wesley, provides an account of the relation between the highest good and the law of love in the Christian life.[5] In so conceiving his task, Wesley outlines a conception of the human good and the idea of human nature it presupposes.

Wesley argued, no doubt surprisingly to those who see him as a dour evangelist, that while Christ taught the royal way to heaven, he also sought to establish in this world "a religion of love and joy and peace," as noted above. Christianity is about earthly and heavenly happiness as well as personal and social holiness. As put in his sermon "On the Wedding Garment" (1790), God is love and "cries aloud, Be holy, and be happy; happy in this world and happy in the world to come."[6] It is the connection between happiness and holiness that is the specific focus of Wesley's idea of the human good, although it must be admitted that in our age happiness and "holiness" rarely traffic together and their relations to human motivation are often denied. I return to this problem much later in these reflections.

In one respect, the link between happiness and holiness is unremarkable for those who know Wesley's thought and activism. Yet in ways rarely noted, it connects him with strands of thought usually separated by wide rifts. These connections also traverse the Sermons and *Discourses*.

On the one hand, to champion "happiness," that is, the ancient aim of life as well-being and well-doing (*eudaimonia*) in this world and the next, binds Wesley to strands of Catholic, Christian Humanist, and Aristotelian ethics. It also warrants his insistence on some measure of human freedom, presupposing prevenient grace, which he found both in scripture and in human experience. We are not, despite Luther's claims against Erasmus in *The Bondage*

---

4 John Wesley, *Sermons on Several Occasions,* First Series (London: Epworth Press, 1975); Sermon 16, Discourse on the Sermon on the Mount, 1, 186. Henceforth I refer to these texts as the Discourses and, when needed, note their number and the sermon number in the Forty-Four Standard Sermons.

5 He has several sermons on the topic of Law, see, ibid., Sermons 29–31.

6 *John Wesley's Sermons: An Anthology*, eds. A. Outler and R. P. Heitzenrater (Nashville: Abingdon Press, 1991), 564–565.

of the Will, simply clay pots on the potter's wheel.[7] Later in his life, as is well known, Wesley took up the name "Arminian," with its emphasis on freedom and God's sovereignty, even though that is not precisely his position. In fact, Wesley stands in the grand tradition of Christian theology that emphasizes human freedom and responsibility but without denying that the freedom to respond to and cooperate with God is grounded in grace.[8] Finite, fragile, and sinful we are, but Wesley was sure that the genuine love of God and neighbor required as a condition of their possibility that we freely do so. What is love not freely given? It is, obviously, not love but mere obedience; it is not a heart zealous for what is good but too easily grudgingly duty-bound.

On the other hand, Wesley's emphasis on holiness and perfect love linked his thought to the ancient fathers of the church as well as Pietists and Puritans interested in "heart religion" or, as Jonathan Edwards put it, holy affections.[9] Whether or not holiness can be fully attained in this life, and Wesley was a bit ambiguous on the point, it signals that for him human beings are aspiring creatures, and not simply for happiness. There is an aspiration to perfection, to the righteousness of God and completion in life, that resides in the human heart and, while distorted by sin, is not eradicated by sin. Wesley linked the claim of righteousness in human existence to "conscience." He wrote in "On Conscience" (1788):

> What is conscience, in the Christian sense? It is that faculty of the soul which, by the assistance of the grace of God, sees at one and the same time,
> (1) Our own tempers and lives,—the real nature and quality of our thoughts, words, and actions; (2) The rule whereby we are to be directed; and,
> (3) The agreement or disagreement therewith.[10]

---

7 *Luther and Erasmus: Free Will and Salvation*. The Library of Christian Classics: Ichthus Edition. Rupp, E. Gordon; Marlow, A. N.; Watson, Philip S.; and Drewery, B. trans. and eds. (Philadelphia: Westminster Press, 1969).

8 For a discussion of the theological issues involved, see Don Thorsen, *Calvin vs Wesley: Bringing Belief in Line with Practice* (Nashville, TN: Abingdon Press, 2013). The point, philosophically stated, is that Wesley was a compatibilist about human freedom. That is, a measure of human freedom is compatible with God's sovereignty. This is worked out, on my reading, through Wesley's understanding of types of grace and particularly prevenient grace.

9 Jonathan Edwards, *The Nature of True Virtue* 1755 (Eugene, OR: Wifp and Stock Publishers, 2003).

10 John Wesley, "On Conscience" http:Wesley.nnu.edu/john-wesley/the sermons-of-john-wesley-1872-edition/sermon-105-on-conscience. Accessed December 21, 2019. This site,

Conscience is knowing oneself with (*con-scientia*) the moral law. It links the perception of one's dispositions, desires, and conduct to knowledge of God's rule for life, the law of love, and the extent to which life and rule cohere. This idea of conscience, we will note below, is Wesley's account of moral sense.

Before exploring the moral sense, it must be noted that basic to Wesley's conception of the human good as the unity of happiness and holiness is a conception of the human being. In his sermon on Romans 4:5, "Justification by Faith" (1739), Wesley writes that in paradise Adam (or humanity) was "By the free, unmerited love of God, … holy and happy: he knew, loved, and enjoyed God, which is, in substance, life everlasting."[11] But of course, humanity did fall in disobedience to God. And what was the consequence?

> His (Adam's) soul died, was separated from God; separated from whom the soul has no more life than the body has when separated from the soul. His body, likewise, became corruptible and mortal, so that death then took hold of this also.[12]

Like most of the Christian tradition, human beings, for Wesley, are composite creatures, body and soul. The soul derives its life from God and the body from the soul. In the state of sin, he insists, along with some Eastern Fathers, the issue is not so much guilt, although it includes that as well, but it is much more death, death everlasting he says.

This understanding of our humanity and our plight means several things of importance. Unlike Platonized forms of Christian thought, the soul is not the *form* of the body that, as eternal, must escape the body to know the Good or God. With Aristotle, whom he studied in school, and Thomas Aquinas, Wesley agrees that the human is a unity of body and soul.[13] But for Wesley this means not simply, as Aristotle thought, that the distinctive function of human beings was reason. That is, the informed being that we are is not a distinctly rational being, where reason is the form of the body. For Wesley, what is distinctive about human beings is that we are vivified, made alive, by love. And this love,

---

The Wesley Center of Northwest Nazarene University, has the most complete holding of Wesley material now available.

11 *Sermons on Several Occasions*, Sermon 5, 50.

12 Ibid., 51 (my addition).

13 On Aquinas and Aristotle, see Denys Turner, *Thomas Aquinas: A Portrait* (New Haven, CT: Yale University Press, 2013). Turner, rightly I think, sees Aquinas as a naturalist both in his epistemology and axiology. I draw connections between Wesley and Aquinas since they are obviously in his texts but also bespeak the Anglican attempt at a middle way between Aquinas and Calvin.

different than in Platonic thought, is in biblical fashion for God *and* neighbor; our social nature cannot be eradicated in the human good and it is not, as with Aristotle, a step on the way to contemplation. Our highest good is to be alive in love. It is to be vivified in union with divine love. That means, with respect to redemption, that God must not only *impute* righteousness to us, as Luther held, but also *impart* it to us as well. In the Sermon "Justification by Faith" we also read: "The one (justification) implies, what God does *for us* through his Son; the other (sanctification), what he works *in us* by his Holy Spirit."[14]

Wesley's account means that the human good is about becoming and being alive in God and others, and this is regeneration. It is being restored to the created state wherein Adam was alive in love with the living God and so happy and holy. The Christian life is becoming alive and is the "true way" to life, whereas a life of sin is the working of death in human existence, a life contra-love, that is, Christianly seen, death itself.[15] Sanctification, if we use the dogmatic terms, is at the core of Wesley's account of redemption and the moral life. That fact finds exegetical expression in Wesley's choice of the Sermon on the Mount as the picture of the whole of the Christian religion.

If this is indeed the case for the Christian religion, and Wesley clearly holds that it is, then the question of the human good must mean the unity of happiness and holiness in this life and the next. It is not that the highest good is a supernatural perfection of the natural good (as Aquinas held), nor that the highest good is discontinuous with our embodied condition (as Platonists would have it); rather, it is the *perfection* of our created nature, possible as beings alive through love in this life and completed in the next. As Charles Wesley put it in one of his greatest hymns, "Love Divine, All Loves Excelling":

Finish then thy new creation,
Pure and spotless let us be;
Let us see thy great salvation,
Perfectly restored in thee;
Changed from glory into glory,
Till in heaven we take our place,
Till we cast our crowns before thee,
Lost in wonder, love and praise.[16]

---

14 Ibid., 52 (my additions and emphasis).

15 It would help here, if time allowed, to explore forms of death: physical, social, spiritual, and the ways one can be alive (say) physically and yet spiritually dead; spiritually alive and yet physically dying. On this see William Schweiker, *Dust That Breathes: Christian Faith and the New Humanisms* (Oxford: Wiley-Blackwell, 2010).

16 Charles Wesley, "Love Divine, All Loves Excelling" in *The United Methodist Hymnal* (Nashville, TN: Cokesbury, 1989), #384.

However, given this account of the human highest good, consistent with claims about the meaning of being human, we confront a problem. It is what Immanuel Kant, Wesley's contemporary, called the "moral antinomy." What does this mean?

3 The Problem of the Highest Good

As we have seen, Wesley conceived of the highest human good as the unity in love of happiness and holiness. In his Sermon "The Way to the Kingdom" (1742), Wesley writes: "But true religion, or a heart right toward God and man, implies happiness as well as holiness. For it is not only 'righteousness,' but also peace and joy in the Holy Ghost."[17] Peace and joy, which cannot be lost, are, he says, "a divine taste, of the powers of the world to come." Holiness is a love of humankind, doing good to all one can, and refraining from harm and evil. It is to be zealous for good works, he says. The unity of happiness and holiness "joined in one, are sometimes styled, in the inspired writings, 'the Kingdom of God' … and sometimes 'the Kingdom of Heaven.'"[18] The highest good, and so assurance of God's mercy, banishes fear in life: the fear of torment, of evil, of God's wrath, and even fear of death. The Kingdom within vivifies a profound courage and confidence or assurance of peace and joy. This unity is God reigning in the soul, as it was for Adam before the fall, and a sense of heaven or everlasting life. So, the highest good is the unity in love of righteousness, peace, and joy animating the life of the believer and moving them to be zealous for good works. It is to be alive in the God of love.

The idea that the human highest good is the unity of happiness and holiness is a claim about both human "nature" and, for Wesley, the Christian life. This idea also situates him within the history of thought. Consider some exemplary thinkers if we are to understand the problem involved in this conception of the highest human good.[19] Reference, if not explicit citation, to these positions can

17 Wesley, *Sermons on Several Occasions*, Sermon 7, 77.

18 Ibid., 78.

19 I leave aside here positions which Wesley and most Christian theologians would reject outright, such as ancient hedonists (Epicurus), modern materialists (Hobbes), and, in Wesley's time, those who see human sin in terms only of social structures (Rousseau) or deny God as source and end of the moral life (Hume). From Wesley's perspective, and others I note, these positions simply do not have a complex enough account of human existence to make sense of the human highest good. Against them, sometimes cited and sometimes not, Wesley engaged in dispute and refutation, or what was called in his time "controversial divinity."

be found in Wesley's Sermons and *Discourses* for those schooled in the history of theology and philosophy.

Some moralists (again, Aristotle, e.g.) grant that for an action to be virtuous it must be a mean between excess and deficiency, done at the right time, in the right way, and for the right reason.[20] Aristotle can even claim that human happiness is action in accordance with virtue, seemingly binding happiness with moral rectitude. But the activity that most nearly meets that demand in human existence is, for him, contemplation, since, as noted above, the distinctive function of human beings is the capacity to reason. A human action is a rational action. This also means for Aristotelian ethics that happiness can be lost due to luck, fate, bad circumstances of birth, or whatever can adversely befall human life. The link between happiness and virtue is contingent and vulnerable to forces beyond one's control. Not so for Wesley, or, interestingly, the Stoics, so important for Christian natural law thought.[21]

In contrast to Aristotle, ancient Stoics, like Marcus Aurelius, argued that virtue and virtue alone is the highest good.[22] If we are clear about what, in fact, is in our control, namely, the rectitude of our lives, and what is not in our control, then no ill can trouble us. The Stoics collapsed happiness into virtue or duty, an analogue to Wesley's holiness, so that, come what may, the Stoic sage flourishes even if in pain, wrongly punished, or facing the loss of loved ones. The Stoic seeks self-sufficiency through a virtuous life freed from the cares of normal human attachments. While Aristotle thought that a person in the throes of pain or loss could hardly be called "happy," and thus that *eudaimonia* is vulnerable to loss by the most virtuous of people, not so the Stoics. Nothing can rob the Stoic of *eudaimonia* other than the agent himself (and it is always a "him"). The rectitude of the agent is vulnerable only to the agent's own dispositions, intentions, and conduct. Viciousness is always self-betrayal and self-harm. For Wesley, the highest good also cannot be lost since it is God reigning in the soul. But the unity of happiness and holiness cannot be, as for the Stoic, the reduction of one to the other, happiness to virtue. What is more, Wesley would

---

20 Aristotle, *Nicomachean Ethics*, trans. T. H. Irwin (Indianapolis: Hackett Publishing Company, 1999), Introduction.

21 Here again Wesley has much in common with Thomas Aquinas, although charting his own way. See Ralph McInerny, *Ethica Thomistica: The Moral Philosophy of Thomas Aquinas*, Revised Edition (Washington, DC: Catholic University of America Press, 1997). Like Thomas, Wesley is acutely aware that human happiness is the well-being of body *and* soul since we are composite beings.

22 Marcus Aurelius, *Meditations*, trans. M. Hammond (New York, NY: Penguin Classics, 2006).

find the admonition to *apathia* to be the antithesis of a life zealous in love and service for others.

If the ancient debate about the unity of happiness and virtue, or holiness, focused in good measure on the problem of human vulnerability and weakness, the early modern debate turned on freedom and continued into the Enlightenment and thus Wesley's own lifetime. The question of freedom versus God's sovereign determination of all things, and so predestination as well, was at the heart of dogmatic debates during Wesley's ministry. The debate dogged him throughout his ministry, especially as advanced by strident Calvinists. For our purposes, the question of freedom is important for the moral life. Without some measure of freedom—and the debate is over the measure and meaning of freedom—the moral life makes little sense, and responsibility becomes null and void. That was, in fact, Wesley's worry about predestinarian thought; he thought that it would lead to antinomianism or quietism since human choices would have no ultimate consequence.

One final historical example can be cited on the unity of the highest good in order to grasp the distinctive direction of Wesley's thought. Immanuel Kant argued in his *Critique of Practical Reason* (1788)—published, one should note, the same year as Wesley's "On Conscience"—that the idea of the highest good is, in his terms, a *synthetic a priori*.[23] That is, the unity of happiness (however an agent sees this) and virtue (conformity to duty) is a *fact of reason*, that is, a unity in one idea prior to any experience of it.[24] We can and do think of the unity of happiness and duty as a fact, but it is a *rational fact* not embodied in the world. The wicked too often flourish while the innocent wrongly suffer. Yet the *idea* of the unity of happiness and virtue, the highest good, is a postulate of practical reason. Its warrant, on my reading, is so that we can, in hope, stave off despair at the human condition. After all, "what can I hope for?" is, according to Kant, the founding question of religion. If justice and peace are not genuine human possibilities within the scope of time then what becomes of our moral striving and our moral convictions?

For Kant, morality is about making oneself *worthy* of happiness rather than seeking happiness itself. Given that, duty (or respect for the moral law) must play a central role in orienting human life, while the idea of the highest good is placed beyond the terrors of present history. In fact, Kant held that practical

23 Immanuel Kant, *Critique of Practical Reason*, trans. A. Reath, Cambridge Texts in the History of Philosophy (Cambridge: Cambridge University Press, 1997).

24 Kant is a "liberal" thinker insofar as he thinks there is no way to adjudicate what people believe happiness to be and, further, that people should be free to pursue whatever ends they want as long as it does not violate the moral law. Wesley's relation to liberalism so defined would be an interesting topic to explore, but it is beyond the scope of this essay.

reason demands that we postulate the ideas of immortality and God in order to insure the time needed to be moral enough to merit happiness, as well as an all knowing and powerful Judge to reward and punish and thus to insure the highest good. Kant argued, in his critical works, that he sought to limit reason in order to make room for faith.[25] But Kant's rational moral faith is rather distant from Wesley's heartfelt, reasoned religion. What is more, insofar as God's Spirit works in believers in this life, it would be wrongheaded and morally dangerous, for Wesley, to leave the matter of the highest good to rational postulates or to believe that human freedom does not rely on divine empowerment. Morality warrants, for Kant, a rational conviction to act *as if* one's commands are commands of God, which is how he defines religion. For Wesley, the capacity to live a righteous life is dependent on God. Kant proposed an ethical theology; Wesley gives us a theological ethics.[26]

4 The Moral Sense and Forms of Divinity

I have tried to set forth in brief compass Wesley's idea of the human good and the highest good as well as to contrast it, when possible, with other prominent positions in the history of Western moral thought. This reconstruction of Wesley's position has been culled from Sermons and the *Discourses*. What has been left unexplored is how he imagined that human beings could ever perceive the unity of happiness and holiness, and so the reality of God ruling in the soul, the kingdom of God within, or the mind that was in Christ. That is, admittedly, a complicated problem, and it is one that many Christian thinkers dodge or assign to mystery and mysticism.

Insofar as we cannot get inside another person's soul, as it were, how, then, could any account of God's working in the self prove itself? On this point, Wesley, like Luther before him, insisted that genuine faith must become immediately active in love of neighbor. One's conduct is, in some respects, a manifestation and appearance of one's ruling tempers and so of the disposition of one's soul. As Wesley put it: "By salvation I mean, not barely (according to the vulgar notion) deliverance from hell, or going to heaven, but a present deliverance from sin, a restoration of the soul to its primitive health."[27] Randy Maddox

25 This is stated in the B-Preface to the *Critique of Pure Reason* (1787).

26 I have compared Kant and Wesley for constructive purposes in other contexts. See William Schweiker, "God and the Human God" in *God and the Moral Life*, eds. M. Renaud and J. Daniel (New York: Routledge, 2018).

27 John Wesley, *Farther Appeal to Men of Reason and Religion, Pt.* 1, 1.3, *Works*, 11:106.

explains this best when he writes, "Both John and Charles placed sanctification at the center of soteriology, valuing justification as the doorway into this larger focus." They called their Methodist followers to "holiness of heart and life" nurtured in the full range of the "means of grace."[28]

On my reading, Wesley's account of a right disposition toward God and others, and so Christ reigning in the heart, takes several interrelated forms. First, one must awaken to one's spiritual condition, to know oneself. "This is," he writes, "the first repentance, previous to faith, even conviction, or self-knowledge."[29] This awakening, a Christian enlightenment (we might say), is grounded in God's prevenient grace as the condition for faith and conviction, that is, to the freedom and power to accept God's saving grace or not. Yet faith is not, as some hold, mere assent to scripture or Church teaching; it is not "notional belief." It is, second, evidence of things unseen and confidence in what is hoped for. It is the capacity to discern that the known universe was made by God and, therefore, reality is not reducible to the empirical condition of reality (cf. Hebrews 11:1–3). That is not a denial of Wesley's adoption of John Locke's epistemology. Quite the contrary is the case, actually. For Wesley, self-knowledge is not a matter of introspection (Descartes), but, rather, is the reflection on actions, experiences of the world, others, and scripture through which one interprets and tries to understand the tenor of one's life. This is why, later, I will speak of Wesley's hermeneutics. Knowledge is a matter of experience; *a priori* or innate ideas simply do not exist. But unlike Locke, and in concert with his near contemporary Jonathan Edwards in the New World, we also have a *moral sense*, that is, a non-inferential intuition, an inward perception of the agreement or disagreement between the revealed will of God and one's heart and life.[30] That is the meaning of conscience, or moral sense, for Wesley.

Thus, by the grace of God human beings are endowed with a moral sense and thereby in the condition of sin able to be awakened to life by God's grace. As he notes, it is "by faith that the eye of the mind is opened, to see the light of the glorious love of God, and as long as it is fixed thereon, on God in Christ, reconciling the World unto Himself, we are more and more filled with the love of God and man ... "[31] So, third, saving faith is the assurance of God's grace for oneself, an adopted child of God, and Christ's love shed in the heart as a

---

28 Randy Maddox, "The Theology of John and Charles Wesley" in *T&T Clark Companion to Methodism*, 20–35. Edited by Charles Yrigoyen, Jr. (New York: T&T Clark, 2010).

29 Wesley, *Sermons on Several Occasions*, Sermon 7, "The Way to the Kingdom," 79.

30 See ibid., Sermon 11, "The Witness of Our Own Spirit."

31 Ibid., Sermon 23, *Discourse on the Sermon on the Mount*, 7, 307.

principle of life and action. It is, as noted above, to be made alive in love; it is to have the energy or vitality of one's life in love of God and neighbor.

On this point, Wesley's thought in the Sermons and *Discourses* shows traces of Cambridge Platonism, especially, scholars tell us, of John Norris. There is an ideal world transcendent of empirical reality and grasped, for Norris, rationally. Yet Wesley seems, in terms of the debates of his time, to straddle the rationalist (Norris) and empiricist (Locke) divide. He wants to hold that we have perceptual knowledge of God but knowledge not reducible to the five empirical senses or rational ideas. His account has been called "perceptible inspiration."[32] For the purposes of this inquiry, that conception of inspiration poses the question of Wesley's account of conscience. It is, we must say, a kind of sixth sense. He writes:

> [W]e may understand by conscience, a faculty or power, implanted by God in every soul that comes into the world, or perceiving what is right or wrong in his own heart or life, in his tempers, thoughts, words, and action.[33]

Conscience is the capacity to know oneself with knowing the Word of God insofar as scripture enjoins or forbids an action, rather than being self-legislating as in Kant's ethics. More profoundly, it is the perception and judgment of whether or not the love of God and neighbor is the acting temper of one's life and conduct. And this judgment discloses the extent of one's being alive, of one's freedom from the bonds of sin and death, and thereby, as argued above, the extent of righteousness, joy, and peace in one's life. The good conscience is a perception in one's own life of the unity of happiness and holiness in this world and the next. The troubled conscience is a testimony to one's bondage to sin and death.

The question then becomes, where does this account of conscience fit in Wesley's overall theology, and how, if at all, might it relate to the *Discourses*? On the first point Randy Maddox has helpfully noted:

> Eighteenth century English authors typically identified three genres of theology: 1) practical divinity, focused on nurturing and forming believers; 2) doctrinal or speculative divinity, concerned with articulation and defense of specific doctrines as normative; and 3) controversial

32 See Joseph W. Cunningham, *Wesley's Pneumatology: Perceptible Inspiration* (Ashgate, 2014).

33 Wesley, *Sermons on Several Occasions*, Sermon 11, "The Witness of our Own Spirit," 125.

> divinity, devoted to criticizing on rational, historical, or scriptural grounds the beliefs and practices of rival groups.[34]

While Wesley practiced all three of these genres of theological reflection even in the *Discourses*, there is little doubt that the majority of his work is rightly called, as noted before, practical divinity. How then does that relate to conscience?

We have seen that Wesley set forth an account of Christian life and happiness as the fruit of the faith that justifies sinners. This differs from some other reformers. John Calvin understood conscience to be a *sensus divinitatis* but one seriously distorted by sin. Because of sin, God has graciously condescended to republish the natural law in the Decalogue. Unsurprisingly, then, Calvin focuses his account of the Christian life, culminating in self-sacrifice, on the revealed Law. Luther, for his part, wrote commentaries with a Pauline bent, but his concern was with the terrified and saved conscience or how one stands before a righteous God.

Wesley is distinctive in exploring the Sermon on the Mount as the key to the Christian life. In fact, in the first Discourse, he wrote that Christ's purpose was to give "a general view of the whole" of this religion ...

> to lay down at once the whole plan of His religion; to give us a full prospect of Christianity; to describe at large the nature of that holiness without which no man shall see the Lord ... Above all, with what amazing love does the Son of God here reveal His Father's will to man![35]

Wesley's treatment of the *Discourses on the Sermon on the Mount* are, we must say, a combination of practical, doctrinal, and controversial divinity even as their backbone is thoroughly practical. What is more, each of the thirteen *Discourses* on the Sermon, published together in 1748, can, in fact, stand on its own and was written as such. Wesley organizes the Sermon around three themes, as he tells us: 1) the sum of true religion, 2) rules touching on right intention for outward actions, and 3) the hindrances of this religion. True to his overall teaching, the Sermon, on his account, demonstrates that while true religion abides in the human heart, it must also be social and active in the

---

34 Randy Maddox, op. cit.

35 Wesley, *Sermons on Several Occasions*, Sermon 16, Discourse 1, 188–189. On the idea of the vision of God as the highest good see Kenneth Kirk, *The Vision of God* (New York: Harper and Row, 1931).

world. Personal and social holiness always travel together, and they also travel with genuine human happiness. The Sermon is a guide to the way to heaven, a description or pedagogy of the Christian life.

By excavating in the Sermons and *Discourses* the connections between Wesley's theology and other thinkers, ancient and modern, we have already traversed, in brief, the three themes he used to organize the *Discourses on the Sermon on the Mount*. How is that so? First, true religion, as we have seen, is the kingdom of God reigning in the inner self that is evidence of the unity of happiness and holiness in this life and the next. Righteousness, peace, and joy are the hallmarks of holy living. Second, this is the regeneration, the new birth, of the self to the created condition of human beings. Such inward religion also governs and animates the purity of one's intentions; the good conscience is the judgment about one's own life by the rule of God. It is to be awake in the love of God and others and thus, as a religious affection, evidence of things unseen, the ideal reality of God's being and doing. And we have also seen, third, some of the hindrances of religion ranging from the denial of God's mercy to conceptual problems in previous thinkers.

Importantly, Wesley sees these three principle branches of true religion, as he puts it, spanning the Sermon on the Mount: Chapter five in Matthew's Gospel discourse is on true religion; Chapter six of the Gospel "are rules for that right intention which we are to preserve in all our outward actions … "; and, third, Chapter seven of Matthew examines hindrances of religion.[36] Insofar as there are thirteen *Discourses* which examine in minute details the three branches of religion, it is, as noted before, impossible to enter into their specifics in this essay. However, without exploring each of the *Discourses* in detail, we do have something of the gist, the force of Wesley's thinking.

Now, the question of this inquiry returns in full force ever mindful of the problem of presentism, that is, the temptation simply to loop Wesley into and judge him by our contemporary outlook. What, we must ask, can we make, if anything, of Wesley's thought for our times? How might we answer that question and so conclude our inquiry?

5 A Hermeneutics of Conscience

In the history of Christian thought there have been many texts written not simply to expound Christian doctrine, but, much more, to grant the reader the possibility of self-examination and also, it is hoped, growth in faith. One thinks, for

36 Ibid., Sermon 16, Discourse 1, 189–190.

instance, of St. Augustine's *De Doctrina Christiana* or his *Enchiridion*.[37] There is also Bonaventure's *Itinerarium Mentis ad Deum*, Luther's catechisms, Edward's *Religious Affections*, Schleiermacher's *Speeches*, Kierkegaard's *Sickness unto Death*, *Fear and Trembling*, and *For Self-Examination*. During Wesley's time, Puritan divines and others, like William Law, also sought to provide means for self-examination and even a therapy for the sinful soul. In this respect, Wesley's practicing practical divinity by means of interpreting the Sermon on the Mount might be distinctive in terms of the scripture chosen, but its overall task is long-standing and spans the whole of the Christian tradition. We obviously cannot examine these various kinds of practical divinity, to borrow Wesley's term, but we can, I judge, see that the *Discourses* are a kind of hermeneutics of conscience. What does that mean?

Hermeneutics is the art of interpretation aimed at understanding. The object of interpretation is anything that makes some claim to meaning and yet is ambiguous, difficult to understand, for various reasons, and thus must be interpreted. But what is being interpreted in the *Discourses*? Obviously, Matthew's account of the Sermon on the Mount, but if the task is practical divinity, then what actually is being interpreted is the reader's own life. And true to his principle of the centrality of scripture, the text must interpret us, as it were. This means, again, that self-understanding is not reached through pure introspection, but through interpretation, especially of scripture, in which the self understands itself as constituted by relation to God and to others, whether loving or not. The *Discourses* aim to enable the stages of faith from the initial awakening to one's spiritual condition, through the perception and evidence of things unseen, reaching saving faith and the realities and hindrances of actual life. By interpreting us through the text, Wesley enacts in his interpretation the priority of God's grace revealed in scripture to a free response to or denial of that grace. In other words, it is to enable one's moving on to perfection and thus the unity of happiness and holiness in life.

In *A Plain Account of Christian Perfection*, he writes regarding perfection:

> In one view, it is purity of intention, dedicating all the life to God. It is giving God all our heart; it is one desire and design ruling all our tempers. It is the devoting, not a part, but all our soul, body,

37 For an invaluable recent engagement with Augustine's thought see *Augustine Our Contemporary: Examining the Self in Past and Present*, eds. W. Otten and S. Schreiner (Notre Dame, IN: University of Notre Dame Press, 2018). My own contribution to that volume, "The Saint and the Humanities," pp. 249–266, is germane to the present inquiry insofar as I am taking Wesley's designation of the Sermon on the Mount and his own practical divinity as a kind of pedagogy of life.

> and substance to God. In other view, it is all the mind that was in Christ, enabling us to walk as Christ walked. It is the circumcision of the heart from all filthiness, all inward as well as outward pollution. It is a renewal of the heart in the whole image of God, the full likeness of Him that created it. In yet another, it is the loving of God with all our heart, and our neighbors as ourselves.[38]

For Wesley, perfection is another name for holiness, that is, the complete love of God and love of the neighbor as one's self. There are stages of the Christian life, a going on to perfection, as he puts it in the sermon "Christian Perfection" (1739). God's action and presence in a believer's heart does not contravene one's own freedom; it restores and vivifies human freedom. It is oriented towards the restoration of one's created nature, towards the renewal of the image of God in the person. Insofar as that is the case, then the highest good is not contrary to finite existence, but, rather, the transformation of human existence into the proper embodiment of its loves. This is "heart religion," "true, scriptural, experimental religion," and the "way to heaven" as he puts it. Importantly, the highest good is not delayed until heaven nor is heaven a denial of our humanity. For Wesley, conscience is our inner perception of the agreement of intention, disposition, and act, made open to understanding through interpreting scripture and experience. We can conclude that the *Discourses*, as teaching about Christ's teaching, aim to educate conscience about the right rule of life, to vivify it to be zealous for good works, and, finally, to enable the unity of righteousness, joy, and peace to thus free us from outward sin and willfully so. God's grace is sufficient for such a life.

On reaching this point, one might despair of the usefulness of Wesley's hermeneutic of conscience for our time, and for at least three reasons. First, in the realm of the so-called first and second worlds, one would be hard-pressed to hold that most people conceive of their happiness in terms of joy and peace. The human conceptions of happiness seem almost infinite in number and kind. To be sure, people do seek peace and joy (however understood), but these do not seem bound to peoples' awareness of their spiritual condition. Happiness seems, in late-modern societies, beyond the reach of morality or religion. Second, it is even more difficult in morally diverse societies to think that one could conceptualize a single righteousness or to imagine that human beings hunger and thirst for righteousness. To be sure, there are global movements for social justice across a range of topics (sexual, environmental,

38 Wesley, *A Plain Account of Christian Perfection* 1766 (Kansas City, Mo.: Beacon Hill Press, 1966), sec. 27.

economic, political, etc.). Yet these movements too often disconnect the quest for social justice from the demand of personal holiness. The idea is that social mechanisms (courts, tribunals, commissions, NGOs, etc.) can rectify social injustice, whatever the moral condition of people happens to be. Justice does not depend on virtue and is at best a prelude to social peace. That means, third, that Wesley's conception of the human highest good is utterly foreign, maybe naïve or dangerous, to most people. It would seem to be an imposition rather than an interpretation and pedagogy of freedom embodied, textually, in Jesus Christ's teachings.

What then of Wesley's hermeneutic of conscience? Certainly many theologians in our time have taken up the banners of dogmatic and controversial divinity to address secularism and religious diversity. But that hardly seems Wesley's way. At issue is the kind of question we deem the matter of conscience to be. If it is a purely conceptual question, then his account is clearly psychologically outdated (conscience is hardly a "faculty" of the soul, if it exists at all). If it is a textual question, then we enter into the endless debates of biblical scholars about the meaning of the Sermon on the Mount.[39] Then again, were we to construe the question historically, there is clearly much more work to be done than what I have been able to do in this essay, and especially work to save Wesley from pious but shallow interpretations. Yet none of these ways of construing the question nor other forms of "divinity" get at Wesley's own aim; that seems, on my account, to be the heart of his reader/hearer.

In our time of moral diversity, rampant consumerism, social activism and despair, maybe what is needed is to confront a text so foreign to us that it might awaken us to our plight however one might freely respond to that plight. In "Awake, Thou That Sleepest" (1742), the only sermon by Charles Wesley in the Standard Forty-Four Sermons that was preached at Oxford while he was yet a student, Charles notes,

> By sleep is signified the natural state of man: that deep sleep of the soul, in to which the sin of Adam hath cast all who spring from his loins: that supineness, indolence, and stupidity, that insensibility of his real condition, wherein every man comes into the world, and continues till the voice of God awakens him.[40]

39 For the most brilliant contemporary interpretation see Hans-Dieter Betz, *Sermon on the Mount*. Hermeneia (Minneapolis, MN: Fortress Press, 1995).

40 Wesley, *Sermons on Several Occasions*, Sermon 3, 1.

A theological hermeneutic of conscience for our time must assume that most people are asleep to matters divine and can only struggle to awaken us to our moral and mortal condition. And should that happen and be perceived by the inner self in the light of righteousness, peace, and joy, then maybe it will be heard as the voice of God. One will know that is the case, if it then ignites a journey towards a life of love lived here and now and hopefully in some world beyond. Nothing less is the task of practical divinity today.

CHAPTER 14

The Bible and Evangelical Christianity in Fascist Italy: The Vatican and Polemical and Physical Violence

Kevin Madigan

Major Characters

Borgongini-Duca, Francesco (1884–1954)
Nuncio to the Kingdom of Italy. He would spearhead the anti-Protestant campaign after Tacchi-Venturi.

Buffarini Guidi, Guido (1895–1945)
Undersecretary for Internal Affairs during the time period covered here. He collaborated with Borgongini-Duca and issued a decree in 1935 that criminalized Pentecostal Christianity.

Pacelli, Eugenio (1876–1958)
Secretary of State during the pontificate of Pius XI, whom he succeeded as Pope Pius XII in 1939.

Pope Pius Xi (Achille Ratti) (1857–1939)
The Pope during most of the fascist period, one quite alarmed by "the Protestant invasion" and distressed at what he took to be governmental nonchalance, or ineffectiveness, in suppressing it.

Pizzardo, Giuseppe (1877–1970)
Secretary of Ecclesiastical Affairs under Pacelli, often corresponding with Borgongini about anti-Protestant stratagems and communicating to him directives from Pacelli

Tacchi Venturi, Pietro, S.J. (1861–1956)
Very powerful Jesuit intermediary between Pope Pius XI and Mussolini, with whom he met more than 100 times from 1923–1939, to whom he conveyed the Pope's requests and reactions.

 DOI:10.1163/9789004527843_015

In a catechetical-style vademecum on Protestantism written in the 1930s, the author, a powerful prelate in Rome, poses a question and supplies the response:

> Q. What do Protestants believe?
> A. Whatever they wish.

The foundation for promiscuous, indeed boundless creed-making was, the author went on, the injuction in Protestant "sects" (*setti*—for Protestants groups were never dignified in Italy with the noun *chiese*, or churches, of which there was of course just One) to read the Bible for oneself and to interpret divine revelation in a non- or anti-hierarchical environment. The principle of interpreting without authoritative magisterial guidance, he argues, is the "foundation of every democratic error, from liberalism to socialism and anarchy."[1]

The author of this document was Eugenio Pacelli, then Secretary of State at the Vatican, and the future Pope Pius XII (1939–1958). These comments were part of a document that went out from the Vatican under the name of his boss, Pope Pius XI (1922–1939). Entitled "The Pope's Circular," the document reflected critical Roman Catholic views on the sufficiency of scripture that, as Susan Schreiner has taught us so well, hearkened back to the sixteenth century. But this document was written in the twentieth century in a very particular context: the attempt on the part of British and American Protestant missionaries, during the fascist period in Italy (ca. 1922–1943), to convert Italian Catholics to evangelical Christianity and away (as they saw it) from priesthood, popery, and paganism. That attempt elicited from many Italian clerics a slew of polemical literature and from the Vatican a campaign of suppression, whose contours are now clear, thanks to documents only recently made available at the Vatican archives.[2] In this article, both a small intellectual and social history of the Bible in fascist Italy, I try to show how polemical reaction to evangelical views on the Bible and its interpretation reflected and led, on the social level, to physical violence done (usually by clerics) to Protestant readers and vendors of the Bible in the fascist period.

1 "The Pope's Circular" (ASV, AESI 795/395, ff. 3–58 [n.d.]); quote may be found at f. 52.

2 This article is taken from various parts of my recent book *The Popes against the Protestants: The Vatican and Evangelical Christianity in Fascist Italy* (Yale: 2021). Based largely on the Vatican and Jesuit archives, it documents the Vatican's campaign against proselytizing evangelical Protestants during the fascist period.

1 "The Protestant Danger": A Brief History

Almost immediately after the end of the Great War, a campaign of evangelical Christian proselytizing, suspended by the European conflict, resumed in Italy. From the point of view of Catholic polemicists, it was dangerously metastasizing across the peninsula. By the late 1920s, it was possible and indeed common for Catholic writers in Italy to compose alarmed pamphlets on the "Protestant phenomenon," or, more typically, "the Protestant danger" (*il pericolo protestante*), and even more ominously, "the Protestant Conquest of Italy."[3] Each of these was the title of at least one published polemical pamphlet or private, often highly-sensitive ecclesiastical report—and widely-understood shorthand for an ordeal by which many European Catholics, even before the pontificate of Pope Pius XI (1922–39), were deeply exasperated, or panicked.[4] (Some Catholic polemicists feared that the Anglo-Saxon effort at Protestantization portended an American imperial and cultural conquest.)[5] In 1919 a writer for CC claimed that the number of converts in Italy had doubled since the war began just five years earlier, and he expressed fear that this number would only increase as travel became easier and more common, as converts returned from America to Italy,[6] and as well-financed organizations from the Anglo-Saxon countries made Protestantism seem attractive.[7] That fear was not utterly irrational. As historian John Pollard has observed, "in the 1920s and 1930s, Italians returning from America would bring with them the seeds of the first serious Protestant dissent in Italy in modern times, nuclei of Baptists, Jehovah's

---

3 See, e.g., Giordani, 1931; P. Tacchi Venturi (written under pseudonym "Veritas") 1927; and Cardinal C. Dalmazio Minoretti (Archbishop of Genoa), *Il Pericolo Protestante* (Genoa: Buona Stampa, 1935). May be found in AESI pos. 795 fasc. 397, f. 30.

4 And Canadian Catholics as well. See the Jesuit polemic *La Y.M.C.A. aux États-Unis, au Canada: l'antidote*, by Édouard Lecompte, S.J. (1856–1929) (Montréal: L'Oeuvre des tracts, 1920). The YMCA was regarded, not wrongly, as the principal institutional structure for international Protestant proselytizing and was present in many of the major cities of Italy. It was also the subject of many scores of polemical pamphlets and of secret reports to ecclesiastical authorities, which listed cities and addresses where YMCAs were present.

5 As did Fr. Pietro Tacchi Venturi, the powerful Jesuit intermediary between Pope Pius XI and Mussolini, whose writing on the issue (again entitled *Il Pericolo Protestante*) I discuss below.

6 Many Italians converted to evangelical Christianity while resident in the United States. Called *americani*, many, upon their return, were avid proselytizers, as the quote from Pollard, below, suggests. The demographic claim here was chronologically wrong. In fact, the number of Protestants in Italy doubled in the decade or so before the War.

7 See CC 70/2 (1919): 231–33; and Pollard 2014, p. 116 for brief discussion. The numbers from the Jesuit writers at CC must, of course, be taken with caution. See also Giordani 1931, pp. 9–10 for statistics, equally to be taken with critical care. See Crivelli 1934 for a typical introduction to Protestant "sects," intended expressly for the education of Catholic parish priests.

Witness [*sic*], Pentecostal and Seventh-Day Adventist organisations, especially in the south."[8] We might add, in addition, that the presence of Wesleyans, above all American Methodists, was intensely irritating to Vatican officials.

In response, Catholic writers launched a vigorous and widespread polemical offensive. Contemplating this offensive, Pollard has observed, quite justly, that "Roman ecclesiastical anti-Protestantism was as virulent as anti-Judaism" would come to be.[9] While of course the former was never lethal, it nonetheless superseded the latter in cultural space and gravity, verbal and sometimes physical ferocity, and duration (for many clerics, if not for Il Duce). It lasted from ca. 1920–38. In the archives of the Vatican Nunciature to Italy, we find a letter from Secretary of State Eugenio Pacelli to the nuncio, Borgongini-Duca, warning him of "Protestant propaganda" in meridional Italy. The date? March 25, 1938, or about eight months before the promulgation of the notorious "Racial Laws" and roughly four months before the publication of the "Racial Manifesto."[10] As we shall see, it was no accident that campaigns against "foreigners," Protestants and Jews above all, overlapped, especially after 1935. Exasperation with the presence and aggressive proselytizing of the Protestants was especially pronounced in the wake of the "Conciliation" (*Conciliazione*) of 1929.[11] Occasionally, frustration and anger with the stubbornness of the "problem" of Protestant propaganda, the startling refusal or slowness of the government to recognize it as a problem, and the indolence of diocesan clergy, even bishops, boiled over. Protestants had long been represented as "heretics," but as the *ventennio* wore on, they could be symbolized in the rhetoric of the end-times. In 1937, for example, one cleric, frustrated with the impotence of local ordinaries, angrily asked, recurring to the apocalyptic rhetoric associated

---

8 Pollard 2008, p. 54.

9 Pollard 2005, p. 211.

10 Pacelli to Borgongini-Duca (ASV, ANI b. 49, fasc. 2, f. 360 [25 March 1938]). The letter was motivated by a missive received by Pacelli, sent 16 March 1938, from Giovanni Costantini (1880–1956), Bishop of Luni (1929–1956). The Questor of Spezia had notified the ordinary that the Secretary of the Evangelical [Baptist] Mission for Spezia, Secretary of Evangelical Mission for Puglia and Naples, had visited evangelical communities in Naples, Barletta, Bari, Taranto, Altamura, Matera, Castelnuovo and other minor centers and had been "triumphantly received"—this despite has having expressed "offensive opinions regarding the current economic state of the Regime"—which caused the Questura of Spezia to intervene and spy on him. Pacelli suggests that Borgongini be in touch with the appropriate governmental officials, advice the nuncio hardly needed in 1938, by which time he had collaborated with Buffarini, Undersecretary of State, in the suppression of Pentecostal communities in all of Italy.

11 I.e., the solution to the "Roman Question" in the Lateran Pacts, ratified by the Holy See and the Kingdom of Italy, by which the Vatican was created and agreements were reached concerning relations between, and prerogatives of, church and state.

with the recent arrival of evangelical missionaries in Italy, why they could not summon the energy to fight "the antichrists of our day?"[12] Many Catholics, incensed by Protestant presence, proselytizing and propaganda, hoped that agreement between church and state would herald the establishment (in the eyes of some, the restoration) of a Catholic confessional state.[13]

Protestant presence and proselytizing was intimately associated with the process of Italian unification (the Risorgimento) in the late nineteenth century and the liberal political regime it ushered in and sustained until the outbreak of war in 1914. Through much of the nineteenth century, the geographical area that would become the Kingdom of Italy (1861) was, demographically speaking, almost entirely Roman Catholic. The only ancient religious minority was Jewish. Since the early modern period, Protestants on the peninsula were represented almost exclusively by the Waldensian church, concentrated in the valleys of the Western Piedmont. In many ways, this community, which had been severely persecuted in the sixteenth and seventeenth centuries, had been ghettoized and then self-segregated as a sectarian community with only modest influence on Italian culture.

Freedoms given in the liberal legislation passed in 1861 enabled evangelical communities from Italy, Britain and the United States to establish communities and to launch campaigns of conversion throughout what was now national territory. In general, these communities remained small throughout the nineteenth century. In the pre-war years of the twentieth century, the number of Italian Protestants doubled. Likely because of a new emphasis on social justice among proselytes, large numbers of lower-class Italians converted. They were concentrated in the provinces of Southern Italy and Sicily. Some of these communities had been touched by the incipient spread of socialism in Italy. Even more significant was the impact of *americani* returning to Italy. Many of those established evangelical communities in the towns in meridional Italy from which so many had emigrated.

The dramatic political changes occurring in the wake of the First World War, above all the emergence of fascism, swept away the liberal order in which Italian Protestantism had emerged, was encouraged and had, if modestly,

12 "Osservazioni" in "Circa la relazioni degli Ordini sul proselitismo protestante" (ASV, SCC, SC b. 1 fasc 1936 [1 August 1936]).

13 The most recent book on the campaign, the first to take advantage of the archives available at the Vatican since 2006, gives the name "Il 'pericolo protestante'" to its title (Zanini, 2019). Just released, this book was, regrettably, unavailable when I completed this article in the Autumn of 2019. I was able, however, to have many conversations with the author over the Fall 2019 academic term, when Zanini was in residence at Harvard University. This is perhaps the first book not written by an Italian with strong confessional interests.

grown. In Catholic regions of Europe, the defeat of the Central Powers and the collapse of the Austro-Hungarian empire caused anxiety over the growth of Anglo-American political power. The growth of British influence in the Middle East and of American missionizing in the Caribbean and South America caused Catholic powers to raise the alarm. In Italy, the Conciliation allowed the Church to harness the political power of the fascist government, and harness it they did. With the encouragement of the Vatican, the fascist government criminalized Pentecostal Christianity in 1935. This marked the height of the joint campaign of suppression, but it would continue through the end of the pontificate of Pius XI (1922–1939). It is in this context of both fear and suppression that makes sense of the polemical and physical violence of Catholic clerics against evangelical proselytes.

2 Tacchi Venturi's Tirade against "The Protestant Danger"

Among the most formidable clerics in fascist Italy was Jesuit priest Pietro Tacchi Venturi (1861–1956). When the Lateran Accords (1929) brought church and state in Italy into intimate union, after sixty years of mutual alienation and hostility, Tacchi Venturi would enjoy a particular rise in power. Christened by Italian contemporaries "Mussolini's Confessor" (and by a German newspaper "Mussolini's Rasputin"), Tacchi Venturi served as Il Duce's handpicked intermediary between his office and that of Pope Pius XI (r. 1922–1939). By the time Mussolini was deposed in 1943, Tacchi Venturi had had hundreds of meetings with Mussolini—this after surviving an attempt on his life (not, as the Jesuit tried to persuade the dubious police, because he was pro-fascist, but because an angry male lover very nearly murdered him with his own letter-opener). Yet he saw himself as no mere intermediary; nor, in fact, was he. Indeed, he has recently been described by one American historian as a "power broker extraordinaire."[14]

Tacchi Venturi became a Jesuit at age 17. A well-educated historian, he would become author of a massive history of the Order and editor of Matteo Ricci's letters. Eventually, he was appointed official historian of the Italian Jesuits and Secretary of the Society of Jesuits from 1914–1921. Since Włodzimierz Ledóchowski (r. 1915–1942), then-Superior General of the Jesuits, was considered Austro-Hungarian and thus an enemy combatant, he had to remain in Switzerland during much of the Great War. During that time, Tacchi Venturi

14 See Kertzer 2014, p. 12., especially Chapter 7, for an account of the attempted murder, Tacchi Venturi's evasions, and the suspicions of the police investigating the case.

was the de facto General of the Order. Having become friendly with Mussolini well before the latter came to power in 1922, Tacchi Venturi brought Vatican and the government into negotiations and played some, yet-to-be-written role in the substance of the Accords finally signed in 1929.

The leading anti-Protestant polemicist in the period ca. 1922–1929, Tacchi Venturi wrote an influential polemical tract, published under the pseudonym "Veritas," entitled *The Protestant Danger* (*Il Pericolo Protestante*). In the pamphlet, which may have been ghostwritten for him by an obscure governmental functionary,[15] Tacchi Venturi attacks the magisterial Reformers, as well as the destructive way in which they read the Bible. Tacchi Venturi was persuaded that the Protestants were dangerous, in part, because their founding ideas were plainly heretical and foolish. What good ideas could sprout from so contaminated a source? A presumptuous man, Calvin foolishly dared to try to reform the Catholic Church. He had an "extremely cruel spirit," which is of course why he "burnt everyone who did not think as he did!" (Needless to say, Tacchi Venturi here overlooks the unhappy history of the medieval Inquisition, or more pertinently, the Roman Inquisition, which burned many Italian Protestants in the early modern period.) Tacchi Venturi claims that the English Reformation had its origins in the King's predilection for polygamy. Risking a disingenuous compliment to Methodist piety, Tacchi Venturi comments that the immoral conduct and corruption of Henry VIII so disgusted John Wesley that he felt compelled to "reform the reform." Wesley loses all credit for reform, however, as he was the author, ultimately, of American Methodism, which Tacchi Venturi and most other Roman prelates agreed was the most sinister danger to Italian Catholicism. Luther was an apostate and schismatic crazed by a "mania," the imbecilic idea that each Christian could, without the authoritative guidance of the *magisterium*, interpret the scriptures according to his own lights (*a modo suo*) and for his own convenience. Moving to the modern day, heretical and apostate Protestantism had facilitated the development of "untold numbers of liberal, liberalistic, atheistic and agnostic philosophical theories"—like, for example, "humanitarianism—which had subverted the intellectual, moral, political and social order."[16]

Not surprisingly, much of the Catholic critique of the Protestant missionary effort centers on the Protestant view of revelation, the allegedly subjective and individualistic mode of reading the Bible by Protestant "sects" and the consequences of permitting, indeed encouraging the free interpretation

---

15 Surnamed Tinti, the ghostwriter submitted a long letter to Tacchi Venturi, which the latter edited and then published, with Tinti's agreement, under a pseudonym.

16 Tacchi Venturi 1927, p. 5 (ASV, ANI b. 49 fasc. 1, f. 6v).

(*libera interpretazione*) of the sacred text. These of course were issues at the core of the Protestant Reformation in the sixteenth century. Occasions of war in the early modern period, they remained points of theological and political conflict into the twentieth century. The result? Religious anarchy, as each Protestant sect, Tacchi Venturi observes contemptuously, now had its own savior and even its own form of Christianity, creating "a true intellectual, moral, religious, and social anarchy."[17]

Worst of all, though, were the dangerous, indeed heretical ideas, both theological and moral, to which biblical interpretation unencumbered by magisterial authority or interpretive limitation could lead—and had led. Lugubriously, Tacchi Venturi observes, "The throng of interpreters of the Bible unfailingly grows," with the result that Protestants had rejected many fundamental creedal propositions. Most troubling—almost monstrous—some Protestants no longer acknowledged the divinity of Christ, a heresy traceable back at least to Arius and the Arians in the early fourth century.[18] In Catholic eyes, this was simply to cut the heart out of traditional creedal, Chalecedonian Christianity, which had been established in antiquity (451 CE), had perdured through the centuries, was a tenet of belief for which many fought and some died, and without which, in the eyes of most, Catholicism would cease to be Christianity.[19] This was worse, even, than the Anglican episcopate suppression of the mention of Hell in the Creed.[20]

The chaos in Protestant biblical interpretation mirrored and was caused, Tacchi Venturi maintained, by the multitude of Protestant confessions, itself the result of liberal interpretation of the holy text of Christianity. Because of the free interpretation of the Bible, without the limiting restraints of the Catholic magisterium, there were "so many species of Protestantism: Anglicans, Methodists, Lutherans, Calvinists, Adventists, Presbyterians, Waldensians, Evangelicals," and so forth.[21] Though divided from one another theologically by

17 Tacchi Venturi 1927, p. 6 (ASV, ANI b. 49 fasc. 1, f. 6v).

18 See Hanson 1988 for an excellent study of Arianism.

19 For the Catholic Church, the definitive decree on the metaphysics of the incarnation was worked out at the Council of Chalcedon, to which indeed the pope, Leo the Great (440–461) made a critical linguistic contribution. See Denzinger 1854, p. 41 for the "Definition" in Greek and Latin. The Decree has always been authoritative for the Roman Catholic and Greek Orthodox Church, as well as other Orthodox churches. However, like many ancient creeds, it split churches it intended to unite, and those divisions have lasted to the present day. The Armenian, Coptic and Ethiopian churches—to name just three—are among those that never accepted the Chalcedonian Definition.

20 Tacchi Venturi, "Studio" (ARSI, Fondo TV, b. 22, fasc. 583, f. 6); Tacchi Venturi 1927, p. 6 (ASV, ANI b. 49 fasc. 1, f. 6v).

21 Tacchi Venturi 1927, p. 6 (ASV, ANI b. 49 fasc. 1, f. 6v).

profound and fundamental disagreements, only one malevolent motive united these disparate confessions: their "desire to battle Catholicism, Catholics, and all the governments of the Catholic nations."[22] Tacchi Venturi was only one of many Catholic polemicists impressed by the capacity of evangelical and other Protestant groups to suppress their differences in favor of a tactical unity concentrated against Rome and, especially, the papacy.

Later in *The Protestant Danger*, Tacchi Venturi gives his reasons for believing, additionally, the theory that Protestant success would lead inevitably to atheism. As always when construing such remarks, we must remember that for Tacchi Venturi, Protestantism was so insidious a danger because it was linked to and supported by socialism and communism, to which it inexorably led in the end: "Socialism," Tacchi Venturi declares, "is essentially atheistic and a fulfillment of materialism and of Judaism, which tends toward Communism."[23] Supporting this view, Tacchi Venturi observes that, insofar as it is essentially materialistic, Judaism is, in his words, a forerunner (*preludio*) to Communism. In the words of Tacchi Venturi, as Communism is "essentially atheistic," it "is a realization of the materialism of Judaism."[24] Every Protestant sect ("all these apostasies," in Tacchi Venturi's language) is propagated willingly by "Jewish-Masonic sectarianism, the most ruthless enemy of Catholicism." For that reason, Protestant confessions "quickly degenerate into atheism, or moral and religious agnosticism."[25]

This is one of countless instances in Tacchi Venturi's anti-Protestant writings which is fed by deeply-felt antisemitism.[26] One strain of Jesuit antisemitism, which pervaded the influential Jesuit journal CC in the nineteenth and early twentieth centuries, and then clerico-fascist writings in the mid-1930s, was

22 Tacchi Venturi, "Studio" (ARSI, Fondo TV, b. 22, fasc. 583, ff. 5–6); Tacchi Venturi, 1927, p. 6 (ASV, ANI, fasc. 49 b. 1, 6v). On this last point, some Catholic polemicists ridicule the American temperance movement. The *complete* prohibition, the tee*totalism*: this the Roman church could not accept or even comprehend. To practice or to preach complete abstinence was, after all, to deviate from the desirable Aristotelian mean. It was excessive, extreme. Taken to its logical conclusion, it even made consumption of Eucharistic wine illicit. What could be more absurdly *in*temperate? This was a theme popular among Catholic polemicists. In his pamphlet on the Protestant danger, Tacchi Venturi argued that there was a "dangerous Protestant tendency to religious and political extremism."

23 Tacchi Venturi, 1927, p. 10 (ASV, ANI b. 49, fasc. 1, f. 8v).

24 Tacchi Venturi, "Studio" (ARSI, Fondo Tacci-Venturi, b. 22, fasc. 583, f. 9).

25 Tacchi Venturi, "Studio" (ARSI, Fondo Tacci-Venturi, b. 22, fasc. 583, f. 5).

26 See Kertzer 2014, p. 123, where he discusses Tinti's *Zionism and Catholicism*, for a nice description of each man's anti-semitism.

that Judaism was not a religion, like Protestantism or Catholicism, but a race.[27] Emphatically *not* absent is the conviction that "Talmudic" Judaism was, at its core, materialistic and, in this sense, no different than atheistic Bolshevism (which was said, not accurately, to be dominated by Jews).[28] Indeed, according to this thinking, the essentially materialistic orientation of Jews explains why they were putatively allied with the plutocratic Anglo-Saxons.

Other anti-Protestant polemicists during the fascist period in Italy could argue, more bizarrely, that Judaism was in effect the originator and "instigator" (*fomentatore*) of Protestantism. Like Luther, Jews emphasized the plain rather than Christological sense of the Hebrew Bible. The Reformers' plea, particularly that of Calvin, to retrieve the texts of early Christianity, in practice, resulted in the implementation of Old Testament Law and "the spirit of Judaism." Like the Jews, Puritans "considered themselves the elect people." Lutheran Münster had (anachronistically) attempted, between 1524–1536, to establish a Bolshevik—that is to say, a Jewish—form of government. (The recent attempt (1919) in the wake of the Great War, by a German group dominated by Jews to establish a Soviet-style republic in Munich—in which Hitler held office—though quickly repressed, was surely fresh on clerical minds.) These two tiny religious communities, Jews and Protestants, together made up less than 1% of the Italian population. Yet they would both be targeted by the fascist government, and many clerico-facists, for suppression. It is little wonder their opponents found them not only conspiratorially but historically linked.

In summary, most of the problems with Protestantism detected by Tacchi Venturi were rooted in false and even heretical hermeneutics. Polemics was one way to resist; another was violence.

3 The Protestant Bible and Clerical Violence

The archives of the Vatican Nunziature to the State and of the Secretary of State contain several documents that suggest vendors of Protestant Bibles

27 See Kertzer 2007 throughout. An especially ugly example may be found on p. 123, where Kertzer quotes Giuseppe Oreglia, S.J. There Oreglia associates Catholicism, Protestantism—even paganism—as "religions," in contrast to Judaism, which is a "race" and a "people."

28 See Kertzer 2014, pp. 231–32. An article from *CC* 1932 claimed that the Russian Revolution had been led not by native Russians but "Jewish intruders." (Jesuits could use outsiderhood whenever their polemics called for it.) It went on to assert, though Jews constituted only about 5% of the population, roughly eighty percent of the highest 550 leaders of the Bolshevik regime were Jewish. This, as Kertzer points out, would become a pervasive theme in anti-Semitic literature in the 1930s and, then, a rationale for their extermination.

were vulnerable, if the Bibles were discovered to be Protestant, to crowd hostility and even violence. These were part of what Michael Ebner has called, aptly, "ordinary violence" in fascist Italy.[29] Indeed, in one case, mentioned below, a Jesuit priest, named Scorza, was brought before judicial authorities in Viterbo for assaulting a purveyor of Protestant Bibles in Soriano nel Cimino, a small town perhaps 10 miles east of Viterbo, within whose province it lay. The case is interesting, among other reasons, because the archival documents contain several different accounts, some Protestant, of the incident. Not surprisingly, the accounts do not agree; one of those authored by a Catholic narrator goes so far as to omit the fact that Scorza had been charged with assault against the itinerant seller of Protestant Bibles. The new Vatican nuncio to the Kingdom of Israel, Borgongini, by this point had taken over leadership of the Vatican anti-Protestant campaign from Tacchi Venturi. Borgongini attempted to argue that the Jesuit's violence was justified on the basis of the legislation touching on Protestant rights and restrictions; and that he recruited Buffarini, the powerful fascist official, in an attempt to exonerate the Jesuit and to tighten application of laws governing the sales of Bibles.

Two anonymous memoranda—one from a Jesuit community identifying itself as having been composed at the community of "Gesuiti degli Astalla/ Ostalla 6," another from an unnamed individual who must have been a Jesuit[30]—sets the context, though not an utterly unbiased one, for interpreting the incident. According to this report, several *americani* had recently committed a series of scams (collectively called *truffe all'Americana*), selling Protestant Bibles on the pretext that they were permitted and approved by the Catholic Church. During the previous June, a Book Fair was held at the Basilica of Maxentius in Rome. When it was discovered that some Catholics had been deceived into purchasing Protestant Bibles, indignant and sometimes violent reactions occurred. The anonymous Jesuit referred his reader to two newspaper articles in which the incident had been reported.[31] He also claims that, when confronted, Protestants sometimes claimed that the laws on permitted cults had been changed to allow the sale of non-Catholic books.[32] These were charges repeated in the Catholic sources, and were likely true, as Protestant protests tended to focus on harm done to a vendor of Protestant literature

---

29 See Ebner 2011.

30 "Pro Memoria Intorno al Lavoro che i Protestanti vanno compiendo in Italia" (ASV, ANI b. 49, fasc. 2, ff. 344–46 [n.d.]). The document is unsigned, but at the top of the first page, we find the acronym A.M.D.G: *Ad mairoem Dei gloriam* ("To the Greater Glory of God"), the motto of the Society of Jesus.

31 See ANI b. 49, fasc. 2, ff. 344.

32 "Pro-Memoria" (ASV, ANI fasc. 49, b. 2, f. 344).

rather than on the veracity of the charge of fraudulent sale. The incident described here fits neatly, in this respect, into this framework.

All documents—in this case, the anonymous memoranda, a letter from Borgongini to Director of Cults Montecchi, a letter from Buffarini to Borgongini, one newspaper article from a Catholic daily and one from the Baptist "Il Testimonio" and, finally, a letter from the Nuncio to Pacelli—agree on the following facts. A street vendor named Alfonso Maini, from Viareggio, boldly if brazenly claimed in 1934 to have been directed by Mussolini himself to sell Catholic Bibles and art. To the immense dismay of Borgongini, it was (again) not within the capacity of most ordinary Catholics, who were ordinarily poorly catechized, if at all, to distinguish Catholic from Protestant Bibles. Indeed, he acknowledges that many Catholics did not even know that the two had different contents. Undoubtedly traumatizing the Nuncio, Buffarini bluntly admitted that he had found himself in difficulty, as "the Bible is the Bible, and it is neither Protestant nor Catholic."[33] In this case, a thirteen-year old girl named Anna Sapori, evidently well-educated,[34] was the first to discover that the vendor Maini had "swindled" the crowd. At this point, one who had purchased the Bible asked that his money be restored. The vendor refused. Soon municipal guards arrived. After a brief interrogation, they discovered that the vendor was not sent by Mussolini but by the Società Biblica Brittanica. This Biblical Society was later said by Borgongini Duca to have been composed of "ex-priests and malefactors." Maini was selling books obviously not approved by the Catholic Church. The crowd, enraged at having been victims of fraud—and at the hands of a Protestant foreigner, no less—began to demand the wholesale restitution of their money. Soon, what began as a tiny protest against commercial fraud quickly turned into a "tumult," with the crowd supposedly chanting, "Viva Mussolini—Viva L'Italia—Vive Soriano Fedele a la Re, All'Italia, Al Papa!"[35] The transition from a small, commercial, apolitical protest to a raucous, dangerous, pro-fascist and -Catholic tumult apparently occurred quite rapidly. This was evidently a crowd composed of "good Catholics and good fascists." The second anonymous Jesuit memorandum concludes by suggesting the incident was begun because of "interference from foreigners."[36]

---

33 Reported in the first anonymous memorandum (ASV, ANI, b. 49, fasc. 2, f. 343 [n.d]); and in a letter from Borgongini-Duca to Pacelli on "Diffusione Bibbie protestanti" (ASV, ANI, b. 49 fasc. 2, f. 354 [10 March 1937]).

34 She was the niece of the local mayor. See the Jesuit memorandum (ANI, b. 49 fasc. 2, f. 344).

35 First Jesuit Memorandum (ASV, ANI, b. 49, fasc. 2, f. 343 [n.d]).

36 ASV, ANI, b. 49 fasc. 2, f. 346.

At this point, the moment at which Father Scorza enters the picture, accounts differ quite dramatically. According to the near-hagiographical account that appeared in the friendly Catholic newspaper "L'Avvenire d'Italia" (12 January 1934), and in both Jesuit memoranda, Father Scorza's main aim was to compose the crowd and restore calm among the defrauded Catholics. The author of the second Jesuit pro-memoria remarks of the danger: "Popular indignation was very great, as was the threat [to the vendor]." Generously, Father Scorza himself restored money to those who had lost it. The crowd, evidently not completely calmed by this gesture, then started a bonfire into which they threw the Protestant Bibles, along with (the Jesuit improbably claims), "pornographic books and journals," which, he need not have observed, were "prohibited by the Holy Church."[37]

We get a very different picture from the second account. Later, at a distance of months, the Società Biblica Brittanica took the case to the Procurator of Viterbo and charged Scorza with assault. Why? The Jesuit author of the anonymous memorandum had concluded, apparently in an effort to sanitize the record: "No violence was done" to the vendor. Indeed, Scorza had "saved him" from physical harm.[38] Yet neither the Jesuit nor the Catholic press revealed all. As the Baptist newspaper "Il Testimonio" accurately reported, Fr. Scorza, far from pacifying the crowd, violently attacked Maini and, if anything, intensified the furor. According to the newspaper account, the Jesuit priest stood accused of "violence and of commercial damage."

For this violent attack, Scorza was brought before the Penal Tribunal of Viterbo. At his trial, the lawyer for the Jesuit maintained that the vendor, with the sale of his books, was making Protestant propaganda. In his client's mind, this constituted a provocation and a violation of the law. He invoked the decree of 24 June 1929—the Law on Permitted Religions (*culti*), which gave permitted denominations rights, but with restrictions. He maintained that the sale of Protestant Bibles was tantamount to the "making of Protestant propaganda," which constituted a provocation against which it was lawful to respond. The Tribunal was not persuaded. It sentenced Father Scorza to fifteen days of *reclusione* (a sort of temporary clerical disbarment).[39] Here the law punished a Catholic offender.

Outraged, Borgongini leapt to the Jesuit's defense. He never denied that Scorza had committed the assault of which he was convicted. It was on other

37 First Jesuit Memorandum (ASV, ANI, b. 49 fasc. 2, f. 343 [n.d]); Second Jesuit Memorandum (ASV, ANI, b. 49 fasc. 2, f. 345 [n.d.]).

38 Second Jesuit Memorandum (ASV, ANI, b. 49 fasc. 2, f. 346 [n.d]).

39 From the December 1934 report of "Il Testimonio" (ASV, ANI, b. 49 fasc. 2, f. 279).

grounds that he defended the Jesuit and, in the process, used the case to escalate his campaign against Protestant propaganda and proselytism—and, tiresomely, for his interpretation of the law on permitted cults. As was typical for the determined Borgongoni, he wrote, involved, or conversed with Pacelli, two Directors General of the Affairs of Cults, Buffarini, the Minister for Press and Propaganda, and Pizzardo. In his mind, Scorza should have been acquitted, having been given legal protection by the Law, which was, he maintains, violated by Maini (and other Protestants). The Nuncio also complained about the dubious and biased source (thinking here of the account supplied by *Il Testimonio*) of the story, which he believed had convinced the Tribunal to convict the Jesuit.[40]

Borgongini began by writing, on 22 March 1935, to Pacelli. Surely unnecessarily, he reminded him that Mussolini had stated that to "injure the religious unity of the state was a crime against the nation." Borgongini then proceeds to argue that Scorza was convicted largely on the basis of an article that had appeared in a Baptist journal, which could not be expected to have reported objectively on the incident. He also insists that the laws on permitted cults distinguish clearly between freedom of religious speech and freedom of aggression against the Catholic faith, which is how he interpreted the sale of Protestant Bibles. He reports that the Director General of Cults was in full agreement with his theses, which he adds with his customary modestly, "are plainly in conformity with the law."[41] "In any case," the Nuncio proceeds, "it has been verified" (Borgongini does not say by whom) that the Tribunal's sentence was interpreted "in a contrary sense"—contrary, that is, to Borgongini's interpretation of the law.[42] According to the ever-troublesome law for permitted cults, Protestants were allowed *libertà di esercizio* (again reminding Pacelli of a law with which he was all too familiar) but not the freedom to proselytize; and the sale of Protestant Bibles clearly violated this restriction. Borgongini seems to imply that this violation excused, or perhaps justified, a violent attack on the Protestant vendor; in any case the only "aggression" he mentions is that experienced by "the Catholic religion." All the Protestants involved in the case were said to be apostates, malefactors, uneducated (*incolti*), and, of course,

40 ASV, ANI b. 49, fasc. 2, f. 343. At the same time, another, unnamed Jesuit from the Province of Napoli was, according to Borgongini, convicted on similar grounds by a Praetor (Pretore) in the Province of Naples. See Borgongini-Duca to Pacelli (ASV, ANI, b. 49, fasc. 2, f. 282 [22 March 1935]).

41 Borgongini-Duca to Pacelli (ASV, ANI, b. 49, fasc. 2, ff. 281–2 [22 March 1935]).

42 Ibid. f. 282.

foreigners; Borgongini suggests that their social status made them, and not the Jesuit, guilty of aggression.[43]

The nuncio then moved his campaign to the office of the Ministry of Cults. As late as February 1936, the Nuncio, still angry, wrote to the Mario Montecchi. "Allow me to bring to your enlightened attention," Borgongini wrote, "a case, which recurs often, of the diffusion of Protestant Bibles in the midst of our people, without any exterior sign that would allow one to avoid the deception of innocent Catholics." Protestant vendors sell their editions with the equivocal title of "Holy Bible." Borgongini continues (probably sarcastically, given Buffarini's ignorance): "It is known to Your Excellency that these Bibles differ from our Catholic editions." These Protestant editions vended on the street are either "mutilated or tendentiously translated to disseminate error and to combat the truth of the Catholic faith." Regrettably, "the greater part of Catholics is not capable of distinguishing the Protestant edition from the Catholic." These insincere methods (*metodi poco sinceri*) of propaganda have given rise to many regrettable incidents. He closes by asking the Minister to take his report into "sympathetic consideration."[44]

In response to the report of the trial of Father Scorza for violence against Pastor Maini, the Nuncio sent Pizzardo a transcription of the report in the Protestant periodical, "Il Testimonio." The article reviewed the laws on permitted cults. At the bottom of the attachment, the Nuncio left a handwritten note (for "the Minister"—that is, Buffarini) about his own response to the legal discussion in the article: "I ask you to read the attached opusculum, "Il proselitismo dei protestanti in Italia." He also sent Pacelli a copy of the pamphlet.[45] Over time, the case had morphed from a defense of Scorza to a defense of Borgongini's thinking on the law.

Shortly after a conversation with Buffarini, the Nuncio received a letter from the Undersecretary of State on 3 April 1936. He had met with the Minister for Publication and Propaganda regarding the diffusion of Bibles that carry no exterior sign that allow one to discern if the edition is Catholic or Protestant. He was pleased to report to the Nuncio that the Minister of Propaganda "was interested in examining the possibility of not allowing any longer the publication and dissemination in the Kingdom of any Bibles that are not clearly marked on

43 ASV, ANI, b. 49, fasc. 2, ff. 281–2.

44 Borgongini-Duca to Montecchi, (ASV, ANI b. 49, fasc. 2, f. 347 [25 February 1936]). The same correspondence is found in the archives of the Sacred Congregation of the Council, in a folder entitled "Circa la diffusione di bibbie protestanti in Italia" (ASV, SCC, SC, b. 1 fasc. 1936).

45 Borgongini-Duca to Pacelli, con allegato (AESI 795 fasc. 397, f. 4v., 8r [22 March 1935]).

the frontispiece by which church they are published."[46] Developments seemed to be going Borgongini's way.

The Nuncio's momentum was halted somewhat by a decree issued by the Prefect of Catania, a city on Sicily's East Coast, and one of the largest in all of Italy.[47] He had learned of Prefect Beer's decree from Pizzardo, who wrote to him on 28 February, with an attachment of Beer's 11 January 1937 circular.[48] Beer's decree started off promisingly enough: "The publication and diffusion in the Kingdom of Bibles without a frontispiece clearly indicating the Church or *curia* by which they have been published is not allowed." However, it then went on: "Exceptions are made for the Società Bibbie [*sic*] Brittanica," the organization that had sent the hated Maini, "which is authorized to publish Bibles with one of the following titles." (Borgongini would soon reveal why this exception had been allowed.) Beer then listed the versions he had authorized.[49] On the Prefect's decision to authorize the publication and diffusion of these two Protestant Bibles, Pizzardo simply says: "you will wish to consider judging if and how one can act."[50] This seems to invite Borgongini to quit.

Naturally, Borgongini acted, writing a letter on 10 March 1937 to Pacelli, a response to Beer's circular regarding the diffusion of Protestant Bibles. Borgongini kindly retailed for Pacelli the steps he had previously taken regarding the "grave abuse of the diffusion of Protestant Bibles, which threaten the good faith of Catholic readers." Regarding the remark by the Minister of Publishing and Propaganda, conveyed to him verbally by Buffarini, Borgongini now reveals that he was able to enlighten the Interior Minister to the differences, by describing "notable mutilations and deformations of the text" made by Protestants, as well as "heretical and tendentious prefaces and comments." He also insisted that the Società Biblica Brittanica, as an "interconfessional society," could not distribute a Bible that bore on its frontispiece the name of any single denomination. Having reviewed the facts of the case, the Nuncio goes on to insist that clergy ought to ensure that government norms not be ignored by Protestant Bible vendors, and remind their flocks not to accept the

46 Buffarini to Borgongini-Duca (ASV, ANI b. 49, fasc. 2, f. 349 [3 April 1936]).

47 Law N. 4917, dell 11. I. 1937.

48 Letter from Pizzardo to Borgongini-Duca, (ASV, ANI b. 49, fasc. 2, f. 351 [28 February1937]). The existence of the Beer decree was also reported to the Director of *OR* from the paper's local correspondent in Acireale (AESI pos. 795 fasc. 399, f. 17v [n.d]).

49 *La Sacra Bibbia*—translated by G. Diodati Lucchesi, Professor of Hebrew at the Academy of Calvin, published a cura della Società Biblica Brittanica; or La Sacra Bibbia—Revised Version in Original Text by Dr. Giovanni Luzzi, now Professor of the Waldensian Theological Faculty, Rome. Also published a cura della Soc. Bibl. Britt. See ASV, ANI b. 49, fasc. 2, f. 352 (1 November 1937).

50 Pizzardo to Borgongini-Duca, (ASV, ANI b. 49, fasc. 2, f. 351 [28 February 1937]).

Bibles of the various Protestant sects. Borgongini concludes his letter to Pacelli by suggesting that perhaps *CC* or *OR* could write an article along these lines.[51] In his letter acknowledging receipt of this letter, Pizzardo thanks the Nuncio for the steps he has taken and assures him that his suggestion regarding an article on the subject by the Vatican or Jesuits has been appreciated by Pope Pius XI.[52]

Sure enough, on 10 April 1937, *OR* published an article entitled "Honesty [*Sincerità*] in the Sale of Bibles." It begins by making many of the points already stressed by the Nuncio (who, indeed, may have written the article) and goes on to assert that Protestant propaganda occurs in Italy by the sale of Bibles. It then imagines a hypothetical scene of a street vendor attempting to put a Protestant Bible under a pair of unsuspecting Catholic eyes. In this imagined scene, the author puts the actual words of Buffarini into the mouth of the imaginary Protestant vendor: "The Bible is the Bible; it is neither Protestant nor Catholic." This, the article states, is the most common, deceitful and insidious mode of selling Bibles not approved by the Church. Recalling that at the Book Fair held in Rome in 1933, Bibles were sold that were said to be "accepted by all the churches." If challenged, a Protestant vendor would argue that different editions of *The Divine Comedy* were all by Dante. If challenged more vigorously, they would assert their legal right to "liberty of cult." This was a liberty, according to *OR*, that consisted primarily in "deceiving the people" and luring "Catholics with good faith to buy anti-Catholic books." Therefore, the article concludes, what is at issue is not a matter of civil or legal rights but of civil obligations, above all the obligation of honesty. The article concludes by alerting Catholics to editions of the Bible that Prefect Beer had exempted from the general rule. In short, the article reads as if written by Borgongini himself, whose own opinions undoubtedly reached the editors of *OR* through Pizzardo or Pacelli.[53]

In short, Borgongini, representing the Vatican, pins blame for the act of violence, not on the Jesuit priest who assaulted the colporteur, but on the deceit of the vendor and the just anger of the Jesuit and the Catholic mob. This was one of thousands of episodes of "ordinary violence" in Mussolini's Italy, this one accomplished and defended by two clerics. It was also rooted in ancient disagreement on the propriety of individual reading of scripture, a topic about which I learned so very much from my teacher Susan Schreiner, to whom I wish to conclude by attempting to express my inexpressible gratitude and admiration.

51 Borgongini-Duca to Pacelli (ASV, ANI b. 49, fasc. 2, ff. 353–55 [10 May 1937]).

52 Pizzardo to Borgongini-Duca (ASV, ANI b. 49, fasc. 2, f. 356 [20 March 1937]).

53 "Sincerità nella vendita delle Bibbie" (ASV, ANI b. 49, fasc. 2, f. 357).

Afterword: Pages on Life's Way

Elizabeth Palmer

Imagine a teacher who shares with her students her greatest secret: how to enter the world of an ancient text. She instructs them to number each line on the page and underline any words of significance. She teaches them to imagine what each of these words evoked in its context, to search for linguistic resonances that have been lost in translation, and to identify any polemical or political influences that lurk under the surface. In this way the students learn—line by line, word by word—the secret of inhabiting another person's thought world.

The students eagerly engage in this work because they admire the teacher. She dresses well; she wears high heels and stands tall, projecting the authority of one who is skilled at her craft. She weaves personal stories into her lectures: tales of the dog who ate her cheese bread, for instance, or of the police officer who stopped her for a traffic violation. The students believe that the cheese bread is a metaphor for temptation and that the police officer's chastisement demonstrates an Augustinian anthropology, although the real intent of the stories is to collapse the distance between instructor and student. Thus do the students view the teacher as fully human; thus are they encouraged that they too might learn to read texts as expertly as she does.

The teacher is a performer at heart. Like a stage actor who seduces the audience into empathy with a character, she inhabits the personas of the authors she teaches. "Your little wagonload of good works means *nothing* to God," she sneers in her Martin Luther voice, a deep fear of damnation thinly disguised as contempt for works-righteousness. "The human mind is a factory of idols," she says on another day, channeling the prophet Isaiah in one of his fiery moments, "and so we whittle away at our own little gods while the world is collapsing around us." Like a philosopher who uses pseudonyms to draw out his readers' subjectivity, she flits gracefully from one persona to another. She can embody the full range of early modern epistemic anxieties in a single lecture; so skilled is she that her students wonder if she has a background in theater studies.

The teacher uses humor to keep her students focused on difficult texts. "John Calvin took his theology straight up, no ice," she declares one day; and the next, "if we could save ourselves, then the crucifixion was a *massive overreaction* on God's part!" Her influence spills outside of the university's lecture halls, her reputation spreading so broadly that a local merchant becomes fascinated

 | DOI:10.1163/9789004527843_016

with her. As he wanders the dusty aisles of his theological bookshop, he imagines that he might someday marry her.

Year after year, the teacher cultivates in her students a passion for reading texts with curiosity, openness, and humility. She teaches not out of hope that her students would identify with thinkers of bygone eras; she has no desire to make of her classroom a factory that produces little Calvins. (*Nothing could be worse than hundreds of little Calvins roaming the halls of this divinity school,* she thinks, rolling her eyes.) She teaches, rather, so her students can know the simultaneous joy and struggle of entering the world of a thinker from another time and place—line by line, word by word.

Lucky the students who have such a teacher! Having tasted the sweetness of conversing with thinkers from another era, they grow into the kind of scholars who prefer the library to a meal at a fine restaurant. They delve into obscure texts with unending curiosity: Why do Jacob Fabricius and Jacob Stolterfoth disagree about the status of certain Protestant women's ecstatic visions? How does William Perkins find proof of God's existence in the "terrors of conscience which are stroken into the minds of the wicked after they have sinned"? What does Philip Melanchthon believe about the development of moral philosophy through the teaching of the liberal arts? These scholars think of the teacher often, and always with gratitude.

As they think fondly about their time with the teacher, the students characterize her in various ways. Some of them believe her to be a Professor Giovanni. (*They could be forgiven for thinking such a thing,* she says with a shrug, *especially if they've seen how many pairs of heels I keep in my office.*) Seeking to emulate the teacher, these students grow into scholars who are themselves charismatic and well-loved. Using the method of reading that they've learned from the teacher, they dip in and out of relationship with the most provocative texts they can find. (Leprosy metaphors in a Frenchman's systematic theology! A lion medallion in Lyon that cures kidney stones! A seventeenth-century girl who reads all of Calvin's *Institutes* by the age of 12! A Jesuit whose angry lover tries to stab him with his own letter-opener as he consorts with Mussolini!) These scholars gather large followings; they offer tantalizing glimpses of intimate textual encounters before adoring crowds at conferences.

Others regard the teacher as a pedagogical exemplar, noting that she teaches with the seriousness of a judge rendering verdicts or a newlywed delighting in the beloved. These students become the kind of scholars who are attentive to historiography; they always begin their investigations with honesty about their methodological concerns. They identify common themes in the teacher's approach to texts and seek to hand these useful hermeneutical principles down to their own students. Always identify the unarticulated assumptions behind the words on a page, from epistemic conundrums to theological beliefs—and thus you may become better at communicating with the people in your own life (*especially in the Midwest, where everyone pretends to be nice all the time*, the teacher says, narrowing her eyes). Always honor a text's strangeness and avoid the temptation to read your own concerns into it—and thus you may learn to grapple with similar temptations when they arise in your own life under various guises, from social media bubbles to single-issue voting to entire sermons that never once remember to mention Jesus.

And then there are those blessed few (*you must mean those cursed few*, she says with a chortle) who believe that the teacher embodies her own most provocative hermeneutical strategy, the collapse of time, whereby a piercing question—about certainty of knowledge, say, or the nature of authority—travels across the ages so adeptly that ancient writer and modern reader are united in the need to grapple with it. This grappling is a matter of salvation for some and a means of sanity for others.

These students find in the teacher's engagement with texts a mirror that reflects their own wrestling with God and the world. Committed disciples of the collapse of time, they believe that their struggles are the same as the struggles that plagued Luther and Eriugena and the author of Hebrews. They believe there's something in the human condition that transcends particularities: a brokenness, some might call it (*for God's sake*, she interrupts, *just call it what it is—sin!*), or a striving to move beyond our noetic failures even as we constantly brush up against the limitations of human reason, or perhaps just a knowledge deep in our bones that God created the world to be better than it currently is.

These blessed few are invisible to the multitude, for outwardly they appear no different from the Professor Giovannis and the pedagogical exemplars. They cannot even be certain whether they are among the blessed, and they wonder if their designation of the teacher as such is merely a projection. Nevertheless, they walk to the library with a spring in their step and a joyful tune on their lips because they believe, against all hope, that their labors will yield a life-changing insight.

Look, here is the insight. Where? There. Can you not see it? It appears more fleetingly than if angels were carrying it, its content ever shifting with the winds that buffet our fragile certainties. One day it's about the meaning of trust when all evidence seems to contradict God's promises; the next it's about the discernment of spirits in a world marred by the noetic effect of sin. Some may glimpse it in the internal kingdom of heaven that banishes fear, or in the power of a sacrament to smash our idols. It might appear in sixteenth-century devotional practices around Christ's Passion, or in the begrudging acceptance of an imperfect translation that the church regards as scripture. These insights are elusive. They skirt between the pages of dissertations; they lurk among the stacks in the dusty bookstore where the merchant dreams of marrying the teacher.

Thus do the teacher and her interlocutors stand upon the earth, producing page after page of new texts in conversation with old texts (which are themselves conversations with older texts). Word after word, line after line, these pages along life's way interact with one another, intermingling the questions and uncertainties and hopes that for millennia have driven scholars to the library and believers to prayer.

In the end, it may be impossible to know who the teacher really is. Is she a Professor Giovanni or a pedagogical exemplar or one of the blessed few? Perhaps it doesn't matter, for there is room enough in the pages of history (*pages that are still being written,* she reminds us) for all three.

Index

Adam 13, 15, 16
Agricola, Rudolph 80–82
anti-Catholicism 176, 182, 197–201, 227, 231–233, 235, 237, 239–240, 243 268
Antichrist 48
anti-Judaism 71, 122, 130, 194, 227, 231–234, 238–240, 300, 305–306
anti-Protestantism 299, 303–306, 308–309, 311
apostasy 61–62, 67, 68, 69, 70, 71, 72
Aquinas 144–147, 214, 222
Aristotle 85–86, 89
atheism 208–211, 305
Augustine 7–9, 11, 13–14, 140, 141, 185

Baker, Augustine 265–277
Beurlin, Jakob 109–110
Bible
  and classics 79
  authority of 60
  Catholic and Protestant 308, 310–313
  interlinear 23, 30
Bibliander, Theodor 35–38
biblical culture, Protestant 20
blasphemy 122
Borgongini-Duca, Francesco 297, 309–313
Brenz, Johannes 152–165
Bruno of Segni 143
Bucer, Martin 178, 180
Bugenhagen, Johannes 66–67, 70–71, 74, 152–165
Bullinger, Heinrich 29, 36, 37, 72, 75

Calvin, John 68, 175–202
Cary, Elizabeth Tanfield 265–269, 275
Cary, Lucy 273, 276–277
certainty. *See also* uncertainty vii–viii, 50–53, 58, 69, 76–77, 106–109, 115, 137, 148, 150, 153, 155, 164–166, 169, 174, 176, 180, 196, 247, 316
Christ
  king 236
  natures of 141, 151, 163
  priesthood 235
  suffering 228, 229, 238
Chrysostom, John 140, 141
compassion, divine 16, 146, 147, 158
confession 195, 197, 201
conscience 211, 222, 283, 289, 292, 294–295
Cruciger, Caspar 152–165
Cyril of Alexandria 140–141

demons 44, 47, 52
Denis the Carthusian 144–147
Dering, Edward 64–65, 69
d'Étaples, Jacques Lefèvre 148–154
Dietrich, Veit 224, 226–238, 242–243
doubt 139, 141, 142, 148, 151, 155, 157, 158, 161, 164

Erasmus 19, 21, 22, 28, 83–84, 148–152
Eriugena, John the Scot 3–18
ethics 89
  Aristotelian 85–88. *See also* Aristotle
Eucharist 112–135
exegesis 156
  Calvin, John 179–181, 188, 194, 195, 197, 199, 200, 201
  historical 3
  medieval 3, 140
  patristic 140, 185, 186
  Protestant 57, 58, 128, 137, 179

Fabricius, Jacob 247–264
faith 121–122, 145–146
  and divine agency 149, 150, 151
Ferrer, Vincent 46
Flaming, Darlene 178, 187–188
forgiveness 59, 66, 72, 154, 155, 198, 200, 228, 243
Friedeborn, Gottfried 255–256

Gerson, Jean 39–55
God
  existence 206, 207, 209, 210, 212, 213, 215
  immanence 12
  knowledge of 107, 204, 206, 208, 209, 216, 217, 221, 222
  transcendence 12
grace 59, 63, 282, 289

Gregory the Great 142, 176, 184–187
Guilliaud, Claude 167–174

hagiography 265, 268, 271, 274, 276
happiness 281, 283–287, 291, 292
healing 51
Hemmingsen, Niels 67–68, 71
hermeneutics
of conscience 279, 293–294, 296
of suspicion 42, 53
Hoffman, Melchior 73
Holy Spirit 88, 90, 101, 236
hope 52, 53, 238
humanism 82
humanities 80–81
human will 90, 100–101

interpretation, biblical 70, 304. *See also* exegesis
rigor in 60, 61, 62, 70, 73, 74
idolatry 42, 43, 45, 114, 115, 120, 123–126, 129, 132, 135

Jerome 19–38
Jones, William 65
justice 87, 90
justification 66

Karlstadt. *See* von Karlstadt
Kant, Immanuel 287–288
Kolne, Nicolaus 49–50

Lady Falkland. *See* Cary, Elizabeth Tanfield
law
divine 95, 96, 99
moral 98, 100
natural 96, 97
Leo the Great 142
leprosy 175–202
Ludolph of Saxony 144, 239
liberal arts 78–111
Luther, Martin 22, 26, 53, 54, 65–66, 70, 96, 113, 114, 115–120, 124–127, 129–135, 152–165, 224–243

magical practice 42
materiality 113, 114, 128
medicine
medieval 187–193
Melanchthon, Philipp 26, 78–111, 152–165, 180
mercy, divine 68, 121, 146, 165, 230, 234
More, Gertrude (Helen) 266, 269, 274, 276
Mornay, Philippe du Plessis 204, 206, 215–218, 220, 222
Münster, Sebastian 30–33

natura 7, 9, 10, 15
natural science 105–106
nature 9, 11, 15
Nicholas of Lyra 144–147
Novatian 60

Oecolampadius, Johannes 35, 64, 65, 72, 75, 132
Osiander, Andreas 26, 178–179
Osiander, Lucas the Elder 27–28, 62–63

Pacard, Georges 204, 206, 215, 217–218, 220, 222
Pacelli, Eugenio 297–298
Pellikan, Konrad 33–35
Perkins, William 203–222
Philipps, Dirk 70
philosophy 80, 109
moral 82, 83, 86, 92, 93, 94
and virtue 90
Pius XI 297
prophecy 30, 35, 36, 248, 249, 251, 252, 255, 257, 259, 262

realism in writing 269, 271, 273, 274–276
reason 86, 99, 116, 132, 283, 286–287
medieval 12
rebaptism 65
repentance 59, 61, 66, 73, 74

salvation 58, 60, 69, 116, 119, 124, 139, 162, 226, 237
and human agency 63
and self-reliance 66
anxiety over 229
loss of 71
Protestant view of 59
security 71, 76

Sarcerius, Erasmus 152–165
Schreiner, Susan vii–ix, 3, 18, 57, 76, 115, 136–137, 165–166, 176, 179–180, 185, 199, 226, 242, 248, 278, 298, 313, 314–317
selfhood 13
Servetus, Michael 178
sin 71, 89, 95, 229, 231, 233, 234
  and illness 182, 183, 184
  forgiveness of 118
  original 13
  post-baptismal 73, 75, 76
  unforgivable 67, 75
Spangenberg, Cyriacus 238–243
Steinmetz, David C. 175, 179–181
Stoicism 286
Stolterfoth, Jacob 258–260
suffering 230, 236, 237
superstition 41, 47, 48, 51, 52, 53
  and trust 43

Theophylact 142–143
Thomas the Apostle 136–174
trust in God 45, 46, 48, 53

uncertainty. *See also* certainty vii, 41, 44, 50, 53, 115, 196
Ursinus 206, 212–214

van Dorp, Martin 82–83
Venturi, Pietro Tacchi 297, 302–306
virtue 88, 91, 286
  and philosophy 90
visions 255–257
von Karlstadt, Andreas Bodenstein 114, 115, 120–127, 135
Vulgate
  and Lutherans 26–27
  and Reformation 21–22, 24, 25, 29, 38
  authorship of 31, 34, 38
  different versions 21
  in church life 29, 34, 36, 38
  reverence for 31

Warner, Johann 251–254
Wesley, John 278–297
Westphal, Joachim 178
works-righteousness 59, 124

Zwingli, Huldrych 28–30, 68, 72, 113, 114, 115, 127–135